Normative Spaces and Legal Dynamics in Africa

African legal realities reflect an intertwining of transnational, regional, and local normative frameworks, institutions, and practices that challenge the idea of the sovereign territorial state. This book analyzes the novel constellations of governance actors and conditions under which they interact and compete. The work follows a spatial approach as the emphasis on normative spaces opens avenues to better understand power relations, processes of institutionalization, and the production of legitimacy and normativities themselves.

Selected case studies from ten African countries deliver new empirical data and grounded insights from, and into, particular normative spaces. The individual chapters explore the interrelationships between various normative orders, diverse actors, and their influences. The encounters between different normative understandings and actors open up space and multiple forums for negotiating values. The authors analyze how different doctrines, institutions, and practices are constructed, contested, negotiated, and adapted in translation processes and thereby continuously reshape Africa's multidimensional normative spaces.

The volume delivers nuanced views of jurisprudence in Africa and presents an excellent resource for scholars and students of anthropology, legal geography, legal studies, sociology, political sciences, international relations, African studies, and anyone wishing to gain a better understanding of how legal constellations are shaped by unreflected assumptions about the state and the rule of law.

Katrin Seidel is a research fellow in the Law and Anthropology Department of the Max Planck Institute for Social Anthropology, Germany, a former post-doctoral fellow at Käte Hamburger Kolleg, Centre for Global Cooperation Research, and the Academic Coordinator of the 'RSF Hub' (Joint Network Rule of Law support) at Freie Universität Berlin, in collaboration with the German Federal Foreign Office. Based on her interdisciplinary background in law and African/Asian studies, her research is situated at the intersection of legal pluralism, heterogeneous statehood, and governance.

Hatem Elliesie is a Max Planck Group Leader in the Law and Anthropology Department of the Max Planck Institute for Social Anthropology as well as member of the Executive Committee of the African Law Association in Germany. He earned his PhD at the Freie University in Berlin, with a dissertation dealing with Ethiopia's and Eritrea's related legal history, and holds a Magister Legum Europae (MLE) degree from Malta University and the University of Hannover.

Law and Anthropology Series

Series Editor:

Marie-Claire Foblets, *Max Planck Institute for Social Anthropology, Germany*

The series is intended as a forum for the publication of outstanding scholarly contributions that strive systematically to involve legal practitioners in the research, thinking, and theorizing about the search for justice and the accommodation of diversity in contemporary pluralistic societies. It focuses on applied legal anthropology, giving equal weight both to an anthropologically informed understanding of diversity of normative orders (often existing side-by-side within a single state system) and to the practical, pragmatic experience and concerns of legal practitioners (judges, lawyers, legal services representatives, etc.) who, in their daily practice, confront the phenomenon of 'internormativity' – situations where different normative logics come into contact (and often conflict) with one another – and the resulting need for state legal systems to accommodate this diversity.

www.routledge.com/Law-and-Anthropology/book-series/LAWANTH

Normative Spaces and Legal Dynamics in Africa

Edited by Katrin Seidel
and Hatem Elliesie

Routledge
Taylor & Francis Group
LONDON AND NEW YORK

First published 2020
by Routledge
2 Park Square, Milton Park, Abingdon, Oxon OX14 4RN

and by Routledge
52 Vanderbilt Avenue, New York, NY 10017

Routledge is an imprint of the Taylor & Francis Group, an informa business

British Library Cataloguing-in-Publication Data
A catalogue record for this book is available from the British Library

Library of Congress Cataloging-in-Publication Data
Names: Seidel, Katrin, 1976– editor. | Elliesie, Hatem, editor.
Title: Normative spaces and legal dynamics in Africa / edited by Katrin Seidel and Hatem Elliesie.
Description: Abingdon, Oxon ; New York, NY : Routledge, 2020. | Includes bibliographical references and index.
Identifiers: LCCN 2019056940 (print) | LCCN 2019056941 (ebook) | ISBN 9780367859060 (hardback) | ISBN 9781003015734 (ebook)
Subjects: LCSH: Law—Africa, Sub-Saharan—Philosophy. | Legal polycentricity—Africa, Sub-Saharan. | Sociological jurisprudence—Africa, Sub-Saharan.
Classification: LCC KQC90 .N67 2020 (print) | LCC KQC90 (ebook) | DDC 340.1150967—dc23
LC record available at https://lccn.loc.gov/2019056940
LC ebook record available at https://lccn.loc.gov/2019056941

ISBN: 978-0-367-85906-0 (hbk)
ISBN: 978-1-003-01573-4 (ebk)

Typeset in Galliard
by Apex CoVantage, LLC

Contents

Acknowledgements

This book is the result of many years of research conducted at the Max Planck Institute for Social Anthropology in Halle/Saale (MPI) in Germany that culminated in a series of international cross-disciplinary exchanges in Halle in 2013. Most significantly, this included a workshop at the MPI in November 2013, entitled *Negotiating Normative Spaces: Insights from and into African Judicial Encounters.* The title of this volume, *Normative Spaces and Legal Dynamics in Africa* derives from the theme of two academic events; primarily, from a workshop at the MPI in November 2013, entitled *Negotiating Normative Spaces: Insights from and into African Judicial Encounters*, and from the *40th Anniversary Conference of the Gesellschaft für afrikanisches Recht* (African Law Association). Jointly organized by the MPI, the Martin-Luther University Halle-Wittenberg (MLU), the Justus-Liebig University Giessen, and the Tanzanian-German Centre for Eastern African Legal Studies at the University of Dar es Salaam School of Law (in cooperation with the University of Bayreuth), this conference was also held in Halle in the same year. Some contributions and conceptional lines of thoughts further stem from presentations made in 2017 at the Joint Institutes Colloquium, entitled *Space and Place* and from in-depth research and analysis of normative spaces in Africa.

We use a cross-disciplinary approach to bring anthropological and legal approaches into dialogue that are often considered antagonistic, if not irreconcilable. The idea is to identify, analyze, and present the diversity of regulatory mechanisms in African societies as well as to facilitate programmatic bridge building between the disciplinary traditions of law and anthropology. As a collective, we have chosen to do this by establishing novel analytical categories along the time and space continuum.

Although case studies on Africa's multidimensional plural legal arrangements have been widely researched in academic disciplines such as legal anthropology and sociology, they have only recently entered general legal discourse and are being currently discussed in comparative law, political science, and socio-legal studies. Our efforts in this volume highlight the epistemological and conceptual constraints of each academic discipline, while also illustrating the benefits of cultivating an openness towards a mutual understanding of the other discipline.

We would like to thank all those who supported us in bringing this volume to completion. We are particularly grateful to Marie-Claire Foblets, the

Director of the MPI, for extending her trust and support to us over the years, not only with respect to this book project but also our academic work in general. We would also like to express our profound gratitude to our colleagues at the MPI's Law and Anthropology Department, particularly to Bertram Turner, Keebet von Benda-Beckmann, and Brian Donahoe, whose words of advice at all stages of the project were of great value and helped us to improve the conceptual frame of the volume. Moreover, we would like to thank all those who shared their thoughts before, at and after the said workshop, the conference and colloquium.

It is with sadness that we mention the passing of someone who was invaluable to the conceptualization of this volume, as we were preparing it for publication: Gordon Roger Woodman (1937–2017), Emeritus Professor of Comparative Law at Birmingham Law School. Gordon was deeply involved in this project from the very beginning. We dedicate this volume to the memory of Gordon, who we wish would have seen the completion of the work. This volume has greatly benefitted from his outstanding academic work, particularly on law in legal plural settings and more generally in the field of law in Africa. As the founding member of the Commission on Legal Pluralism and an active member of the African Law Association, he continually advocated for a law-in-context approach over decades. His contributions are aptly summarized in the passage that follows:

> Gordon's long-time research and teaching in West Africa laid a rare foundation for the analytical and theoretical understanding of law and its social working in the region and beyond. His work combined knowledge of the tiniest detail of law – especially, but not only the law of Ghana – with a deep understanding of the fundamental dynamics of the interrelations and interactions within plural legal systems. [. . .] The main body of academic work is devoted to law in Africa. Indeed, he was one of the leading international scholars in African law.*

Gordon's vivid ideas on how to grasp plural legal interactions and realities in Africa have influenced several aspects of this volume.

We are grateful to Anne Griffiths, Emeritus Professor of Anthropology of Law at the School of Law at the University of Edinburgh, who accepted the challenging task of writing the Epilogue to this volume.

Last but surely not the least, we are indebted to all contributors of this volume for their commitment to the project, their patience, as well as the time and energy they were willing to invest to help complete what we were increasingly viewing as a giant jigsaw puzzle with their own meditations and explorations on this topic. All the jigsaw pieces have jointly contributed to the conceptual frame of *Normative Spaces and Legal Dynamics in Africa*.

We would like to express our immense appreciation to Gita Rajan for her thoughtful comments on earlier drafts of the volume and meticulous proofreading. Our special thanks also to Sina Nikolajew for her extraordinary commitment to the challenges of formatting the manuscript.

Likewise, we greatly benefitted from the professional guidance offered by Routledge, our publisher, and we extend our special thanks to Alison Kirk and Emily Summers of Routledge/Taylor & Francis Group. We also greatly benefitted from the expert feedback we received from our manuscript reviewers.

Note

* K von Benda-Beckmann and U Wanitzek, 'In Memoriam Professor Gordon Roger Woodman 1937–2017' (2017) *The Journal of Legal Pluralism and Unofficial Law* 1–4, 1f.

Contributors

Kelly Askew is an anthropologist and documentary filmmaker at the University of Michigan. Her publications include her monograph on *Performing the Nation: Swahili Music and Cultural Politics in Tanzania* (University of Chicago Press 2002), edited volumes and numerous articles. She has also made films, which include *Orkiteng Loorbaak: Rite of Elders* (37 min., 2017), *Poetry in Motion: 100 Years of Zanzibar's Nadi Ikhwan Safaa* (70 min., Buda Musique, 2016), and *The Chairman and the Lions* (46 min., Documentary Educational Resources, 2012). Her current projects focus on post-socialist poetics, pastoralism, rural energy access, African art, and land rights in Tanzania. She holds a PhD in Anthropology from Harvard University (e-mail: kaskew@umich.edu).

Shakira Bedoya Sánchez is currently serving as an appointed ISO delegate within the Technical Committee ISO/TC 292 *Security and Resilience* at the International Organization for Standardization. She is a member of the ISO IWA – 31 for Enterprise Risk Management. She is currently also an advisor for NGOs and for the private sector on topics of security, disaster risk management, business continuity, and organizational resilience. Previously, she was affiliated with the Max Planck Institute for Social Anthropology and the Max Planck Institute for Foreign and International Criminal Law and was a visiting scholar at the University of Cambridge. She was a post-doctoral fellow in Berlin at the Rechtskulturen programme, where she worked on international criminal justice, science and technology, and humanitarian forensics (e-mail: shakira.bedoya@gmail.com).

Jonas Bens is an anthropologist/lawyer and post-doctoral research fellow at the Collaborative Research Center Affective Societies, Freie Universität Berlin. He specializes in legal and political anthropology with a research focus on indigeneity, transitional justice, democracy, and the politics of affect and emotion. His publications include *The Indigenous Paradox: Rights, Sovereignty, and Culture in the Americas* (University of Pennsylvania Press, 2020). He is currently finishing a monograph titled *The Sentimental Court: The Affective Life of International Criminal Justice*. (e-mail: jonas.bens@fu-berlin.de).

Stefanie Bognitz is a faculty member and lecturer at the Institute for Social and Cultural Anthropology at the University of Halle. She is also a fellow at the Research Network on Law, Organization, Science and Technology (LOST) and associate at the Max Planck Institute for Social Anthropology. Her doctoral dissertation on *Promising of Access to Justice: The Everyday of Legal Aid and Mediation in Rwanda* analyzes ordinary people's regimes of engagement in and with legal institutions. Her recent publications include 'Mistrusting as Mode of Engagement in Mediation: Insights from a Socio-Legal Practice in Rwanda' in F Mühlfried (ed), *Mistrust: Ethnographic Approximations* (Bielefeld: transcript 2017) 147–168 (e-mail: bognitz@eth.mpg.de).

Hatem Elliesie is a Max Planck Group Leader in the Law and Anthropology Department of the Max Planck Institute for Social Anthropology in Germany and member of the Executive Committee of the *Gesellschaft für afrikanisches Recht*. Elliesie took on a deputy professorship on Islamic Law at the University of Münster (2017). Prior to that he was a research fellow and coordinator of the project *Horn of Africa* at the Freie University Berlin, as well as a lecturer for the courses *Islamic Law* and *Law and Society in the Horn of Africa* at the Humboldt University in Berlin, and a visiting lecturer at the Addis Ababa University Center for Human Rights. In 2012 he was also a research fellow within the Collaborative Research Center (SFB) 700 *Governance in Areas of Limited Statehood* at the Rule of Law Center of the Berlin Social Science Center (e-mail: elliesie@eth.mpg.de).

Daniel Behailu Gebreamanuel is an Associate Professor of Law at Hawassa University, School of Law, Ethiopia. He completed his LL.B. at Addis Ababa University, and earned his masters degree in comparative law at Delhi University, India, in 2006, and his doctor of law at the Justus Liebig University, Germany, in 2014. He has lectured and researched in the areas of land law and governance, investment law, indigenous society rights and land, international environmental law, law and governance, human rights, and international law (e-mail: danielbehailu@yahoo.com).

Anne Griffiths is Emeritus Professor, Anthropology of Law, at the School of Law Edinburgh University. She has held visiting positions at a number of academic institutions over the years including Humboldt University, Max Planck Institute for Social Anthropology, the University of Texas at Austin, University of Toronto, University of Botswana, University of Witwatersrand, University of Zimbabwe (Southern and Eastern African Regional Centre for Women's Law), and the International Institute for the Sociology of Law, Oñati–Gipuzkoa. Her research projects on gender and land in southern Africa have been funded by the E.S.R.C., the British Academy, the South African Human Sciences Research Council, the Commonwealth Foundation, the Ford Foundation (USA), the Wenner-Gren Foundation for Anthropological Research (USA), and the Leverhulme Trust (UK). Her most recent research on *Transformations on the Ground: Space and the Power of Land in Botswana* was published by Indiana University Press in 2019 as part of their series on Framing the Global (e-mail: Anne.Griffiths@ed.ac.uk).

Lisa Heemann studied law and African studies in Berlin and Dar es Salaam. For her PhD in law, she did research on the recognition of traditional institutions in the constitutions of South Africa, Ghana, and Uganda as well as the relevant human rights law. In 2012, she joined the University of Giessen as research fellow to study the constitutional review mechanisms in francophone West Africa. Since 2016, she has been serving as Secretary-General of the UN Association of Germany (Deutsche Gesellschaft für die Vereinten Nationen e. V.) where she continues to work on questions of international and human rights law (e-mail: heemann@dgvn.de).

Markus Virgil Hoehne is a lecturer at the Institute of Social Anthropology at the University of Leipzig. He works on conflict, identity, state formation, borderlands, transitional justice, and forensic anthropology in Somalia and the Horn of Africa. His most recent publications include the books *The State and the Paradox of Customary Law in Africa*, co-edited with Olaf Zenker (Routledge 2018) and *Between Somaliland and Puntland: Marginalization, Militarization and Conflicting Political Visions* (Rift Valley Institute, 2015) (e-mail: markus.hoehne@uni-leipzig.de).

Julia Kriesel (maiden name: Schaarschmidt) is a lawyer at Petersen Hardraht Pruggmayer PartmbB in Leipzig, Germany. With an interdisciplinary background in law and European/American studies she was a former research assistant and doctoral student with Professor Dr Christian Tietje at Martin-Luther-University Halle-Wittenberg (topic of PhD thesis: *Peoples' Rights: Group Rights in Public International Law: Theory and Practice of Collective Human Rights in Africa, America and Europe)*. Her PhD thesis has been published recently at Mohr Siebeck (e-mail: j.kriesel@phplaw.de).

Felix-Anselm van Lier is a public law expert focusing on constitution-making processes. Felix is a postdoctoral research fellow at the Max Planck Institute for Social Anthropology, where he researches the role of technology in constitution-making. He holds degrees in law and anthropology from the universities of Bremen, Turin, and the London School of Economics. He completed his doctorate at the University of Oxford in 2018. Amongst others, he has worked as a consultant for the Bingham Centre for the Rule of Law, Democracy Reporting International, the Berghof Foundation, and Lawyers for Justice in Libya (e-mail: vanlier@eth.mpg.de).

Prosper S Maguchu is a lawyer and activist with a special interest in transitional justice, financial crimes, large-scale conspiracies/serious crimes, sanctions and odious debts, and a penchant for an African customary law approach. He has a decade of experience working as a human rights lawyer with national, regional, and international organizations. He naturally combines an academic-practitioner approach in his teachings and publications.

Prosper is an assistant professor at Vrije University Amsterdam. (e-mail: p.s.maguchu@vu.nl).

Tillmann Schneider is an independent consultant for rule of law reforms, human rights and organizational development. He is a law school graduate of Humboldt University in Berlin. From 2007 until 2009 he was a fellow of the multi-disciplinary research training group 'Multilevel Constitutionalism' at Humboldt University in Berlin, writing a PhD thesis on legal pluralism and customary law in Ghana. Questions of access to justice, the role of the judiciary as well as the relationship between state institutions and traditional authorities were central parts of this research. He managed for the German *Gesellschaft für Internationale Zusammenarbeit* (GIZ) a project on justice sector reforms in Sierra Leone, and worked as an advisor on human rights (e-mail: till.schneider@zoho.com).

Katrin Seidel is a former postdoctoral research fellow at the Law and Anthropology Department of the Max Planck Institute for Social Anthropology (2012-2019) and currently an associate of the Institute. She was also a fellow at Käte Hamburger Kolleg/Centre for Global Cooperation Research (2015-16) and was the Academic Coordinator of the Joint Network Rule of Law Support at Freie Universität Berlin, in collaboration with the German Federal Foreign Office (2017). With an interdisciplinary background in law and African/Asian studies, her research is situated at the intersection of legal pluralism, heterogeneous statehood, and governance. Seidel's research is focused on interdependent relationships between plural normative and judicial orders at different levels of regulations, and on the intertwinings of respective social actors involved. Her current research is a comparative analysis of post-conflict constitution-making in South Sudan and Somaliland (e-mail: kseidel@eth.mpg.de).

Hannah Wanderi is a lecturer at the Jomo Kenyatta University of Agriculture and technology in the School of Law, Nairobi, Kenya. Her teaching interests are in environmental law, information, communication, and technology law, and in subjects related to criminal justice. She is a PhD candidate at the Center for Advanced Studies in Environmental Law and Policy based in University of Nairobi, Kenya. She is also a member of Center for Justice Governance and Environmental Action, a non-governmental organization whose main activity is to push for environmental justice for vulnerable communities (e-mail: wamuyuhanna@gmail.com).

Hakeem O. Yusuf is Professor of Law and Global Studies at Derby Law School, University of Derby. He was a reader in global legal studies at the Birmingham Law School. He has researched extensively in transitional justice, economic and social rights, and comparative judicial constitutionalism. In 2011, he served on a truth and reconciliation commission in Osun State, Southwest Nigeria. His book *Transitional Justice, Judicial Accountability and the Rule of Law* (Routledge 2010) was shortlisted for the 2010 Kevin Boyle Prize. His second book *Colonial and Post-Colonial Constitutionalism in the Commonwealth Peace, Order and Good Government* (Routledge 2014) was awarded the John T Saywell Prize for Canadian Constitutional Legal History 2015 (e-mail: h.yusuf@bham.ac.uk).

Olaf Zenker is Professor of Social and Cultural Anthropology at the Martin Luther University Halle-Wittenberg, Germany. Focusing on South Africa, Northern Ireland, and Germany, his research has dealt with political and legal issues such as statehood, the rule of law, plural normative orders, modernity, justice, conflict and identity formations, as well as sociolinguistics and anthropological epistemologies. His recent book publications include *The State and the Paradox of Customary Law in Africa* (Routledge 2018), *South African Homelands as Frontiers: Apartheid's Loose Ends in the Postcolonial Era* (Routledge 2017) and *Transition and Justice: Negotiating the Terms of New Beginnings in Africa* (Wiley-Blackwell 2015) (e-mail: olaf.zenker@ethnologie.uni-halle.de).

Prologue
Normative spaces in Africa: constructing, contesting, renegotiating, and adapting dynamics[1]

Introduction

Normative spaces, as we conceptualize this plural term in our volume, allows for a deeper exploration of *lawscapes*[2] in Africa. It refers to legal pluralities – the intertwining of (trans)national, regional, and local normative frameworks, institutions, and practices – that are constantly being (re)produced, shifted, and reinterpreted in different spatio-temporal arrangements. Signifying statehood and rule of law, they function as governance frameworks and represent actor constellations. One of the unique features of the African socio-political configurations that distinguish them from the US-European experiences is that in the case of Africa, 'external' political and legal interventions have been central to how law has been inscribed into space. This has happened, first and foremost, with the concept of the 'territorial (modern) state' and its rule-of-law approaches, so that, generally speaking, multiple authorities, including international agencies, have been involved in co-authoring the script for governance in Africa. In parallel, the African continent continues to rely on diverse concepts of statehood and rule of law that are disregarded in the conceptualization of rule of law on different territories. Revealing those multiplicities of concepts in this volume is a rich array of localized studies that take a closer look at novel constellations of governance actors, processes of institutionalization, and institutional configurations that arise in multifarious instances and take on multiple forms. They become visible, for instance, in new legal and judicial designs and practices at different scales, as well as in constitution-making processes, transitional justice mechanisms, and efforts to implement *the* rule of law (RoL). In our view, the encounters or the interplay between different normative orders, and the constant negotiations among shifting constellations of actors, remain underinvestigated.

The volume at hand aims to bridge this research gap. It conveys how *rule of law* is being currently understood in different parts of Africa and what must be considered an indispensable point of departure and reference in conceiving, propagating, and implementing a broader notion of rule of law. The studies in this volume offer new empirical data and well-substantiated insights from and into dynamic legal realities in Africa. Here, the wide spectrum of normative regulatory mechanisms and how they are practised in the legislative, executive, and judicial arenas has inspired this spatial framework of analysis we put forth in this volume. Our emphasis on *normative spaces* also opens up avenues for better understanding power relations, processes of institutionalization, as well as different modalities of legitimacy in novel plural constellations of governance actors and the conditions under which they interact and compete. Highlighting several unique features of the socio-political configurations in Africa, our analysis of *normative spaces* within an African context aims to enrich the debate on rule of law from an African perspective.

African lawscapes are comprised of interactions and interrelations between a multitude of normative frameworks and social actors that are (trans)national, regional and local. They continuously reshape and transform not only structures and processes of governance but also the nature of sovereignty and power relations. These socio-legal dynamics move along 'historically specific collection of practices' and 'techniques of administration',[3] deriving from but also adapting to histories and their reinterpretations. The past decades have seen a shift in the modes of analysis adopted to study the numerous transformations and fluctuations in the configuration of governance actors, especially owing to the global conditions under which they coexist:

> So, the sheer number of actors involved, their character, as well as the global networks they are each involved in, are of a different scale than previous constellations of plural governance. Moreover, the normativity that shapes their relations has been transformed through international law, transnational legal norms and international conventions. These are all contested in their interpretation and application.[4]

These new complexities have given rise to the question of how to address and analytically grasp the nature of these changing configurations of spatial governance as they risk being overlooked. Different chapters in the volume engage with the question of how African legal plural configurations are being shaped and negotiated. In so doing, they offer multiple, empirically based insights into emergent plural legal dynamics and how they are to be apprehended both in and as space. The authors address how to grasp the dynamics of contemporary governance in different countries under study, both concretely and analytically, and how to then explore the interrelations between normative orders, actors, and their spheres of influence in Africa. Taken as a whole, this volume also provides a comprehensive overview of the *changes* in plural configuration of governance actors and the conditions under which they compete or cooperate on the continent, whereby the spatial dynamics of law in African countries is paramount here.

Plural state-space-law interconnectivities in African lawscapes

As histories – both shared and separate – have shaped the socio-political and legal configurations on the African continent, studies analyzing the numerous political and legal interventions from overseas on the African continent show how law has been inscribed into African *spaces*, particularly with the concept of the 'territorial (modern) state' and its rule-of-law approaches. It has been rightly claimed that *rule of law* has become 'the dominant paradigm for state governance in the international arena',[5] structuring the politico-legal discourse as well as the 'use of concepts like people, self-government, citizen, rights, equality, nation, and popular sovereignty'.[6] Connecting most rule-of-law narratives is the belief that rule of law has universal qualities that makes it stand apart 'as a non-ideological, even technical solution'. International rule-of-law promotions that shape and reshape African lawscapes go on to define what strategies of action are appropriate for realizing the shared belief in rule of law. Enormous normative transfers[7] – of constitutions and institutions with state-making technologies and techniques[8] – are involved in its promotion and implementation.

However, contradicting the still prevailing (neo-)evolutionary narrative, 'which has the global south tracking behind the curve of Universal History, always in deficit, always playing catch-up',[9] is a range of rule of law and statehood understandings and configurations on the African continent. In a sense, African settings do not (perhaps even seek to) fulfil the 'promise of territorial or systemic integrity, since they [the communities of states] are made through the spatiality of flow, juxtaposition, porosity and relational connectivity'.[10]

In this volume, we present a 'multiplicity of stories'[11] along prevalent geopolitical lines – on configurations of statehood and/or of rule of law. In shining the spotlight on the interconnectedness of an African state-space-law, we shift the focus from the US-European domination of knowledge production towards a possible 'provincialization' of the respective hegemonic categories of US-European intellectual traditions.[12] This is intended as a critical reflection specifically on positions and perspectives from which stories are told, some of which feature Europe as the protagonist.[13] As Jean and John Comaroff[14] argue, it is time to move 'beyond the northern-southern binary', in order to 'lay bare the larger dialectic processes that have produced and sustain it [i.e. the binary]'. It is important, therefore, to subvert 'the epistemic scaffolding on which it is erected'. This volume reflects on those ongoing processes in Africa to demonstrate the interconnectedness of different sets of normative orders and the relevant actors. Addressing 'the problem of knowledge',[15] the contributions in the volume underscore the responsibility of actors to inquire into diverse understandings of normative orders in Africa beyond the overly simplistic dichotomies of formal law versus informal law or state law versus traditional law. If anything, this would offer rich insights into how law is already being understood, interpreted and implemented. The studies in this volume interrogate the binary of 'African customary law' and 'state law' and reveal the legal diversity of countries and voices represented in it, as they interweave the manifold rule-of-law narratives at the local, regional, and global levels.

Statehood and the idea of a territorial (modern) state in Africa

African states were created by the colonial powers on the assumption that the 'modern territorial state' was the paramount framework for organizing polities,[16] although, for many centuries, not land or resources but people and manpower were considered the scarce resource in most African political orders:[17] '[B]efore colonization, the attachment to the territory and to the land was entirely "relative" '.[18] And, this 'relativity' is the crux of the matter: Historically speaking, African states differ from the transposed European concept of a nation-state that privileges a one-nation-one-state ideology. A European nation, according to this imagining, was more or less a homogeneous entity with a shared culture, ethnicity, language, and historical experience; the people were conceived as sovereigns (owners) of their state, which represented the natural expression of something that existed *a priori*. This fiction became popular in a way that the division of humanity into 'nations' eventually came to seem as 'natural' as the division of species.[19] However, the construction as well as the maintenance of this fiction has led to massive violence, involuntary inclusion, forced exclusion, and technologies of homogenization, including genocide and ethnic cleansing. Specific moments in history and in the present, such as colonialism and post-colonial liberation movements, throw light on this inversion of 'state' and 'nation'.[20]

Since the fiction of the 'nation' can no longer be used as a stable point of departure, the studies in this volume gravitate towards an analysis that Achille Mbemebe offers:

> Over the past two centuries the visible, material, and symbolic boundaries of Africa have constantly expanded and contracted. . . . New forms of territoriality and unexpected forms of locality have appeared. Their limits do not necessarily intersect with the official limits, norms, or language of states. New internal and external actors, organized into networks and nuclei, claim rights over these territories, often by force.[21]

However, the notions of territoriality (borders), internal and external 'sovereignty', and the state as a body of administrative institutions prevail, even though 'the territorial state' is imbued with different meanings and exists in contestation with other forms of authority and social organization.[22] The idea that 'a plurality of non-state actors [from overseas] has become involved in what until recently was considered the sole domain of state agencies'[23] has been gaining momentum over the past decades. Since the legal realities in Africa have paved the way for rather heterogeneous statehood constellations and a plurality of normative ordering – which do not necessarily intersect with conventional understandings of the territorial (nation) state – '[t]here is always something for international actors to fix, always a plan that the international community should contribute something to, and always something that goes wrong and needs fixing through further intervention and programs'.[24]

This 'fixing' is steered through '[g]lobal discourses on development, democratization, human rights, peace' and on rule of law, which 'have become the code for institutionalized international interventions'.[25]

Rule-of-law promotion in Africa

African countries continue to be plagued by neo-modern perceptions of them as lacking the *rule of law*, which has become a catch-all concept[26] and the locus of numerous, diverse, and sometimes incompatible claims.[27] How *rule of law* is perceived and conceived in divergent contexts, and by a variety of actors, gives rise to competing ideological concepts. Intergovernmental institutions, supported by public and private donors, have urged various African countries to introduce institutional and legal reforms as a way to establish the *rule of law*. These efforts are accompanied by the hope of creating, maintaining, or at least improving, legal and political institutions of the state.[28] For instance, rule-of-law promotion is ingrained in the so-called 'state-building missions', as described in this volume by Felix-Anselm van Lier for Libya. Constitution-making and state-building in war-torn contexts now represent common normative tools of rule-of-law promotion that set the 'rules of the game' within the meaning of the territorial state. Moreover, one can identify manifold ways in which state actors – hand in hand with international actors – seek to maintain and strengthen their position by engaging with and embedding themselves in the legal-plural conditions 'on the ground', since, very often, they are not the predominant regulative governance actors.[29] *Rule of law* highlights the demarcation between 'state actors' and 'non-state actors' as well as 'state law' and 'non-state law', for instance, the processes of state and constitutional recognition of the so-called 'customary law' and religious law in Africa's lawscapes. In particular, one can identify the diverse ways in which state actors navigate legal plurality, such as in situations of multiple jurisdictions offering a more comprehensive choice of forum(s). These approaches range from jurisdiction over certain claims, 'ethnicity-' or community-based jurisdiction, consent-based jurisdiction to *ad hoc* jurisdiction and tribunals.[30] By going beyond the binary of 'customary law' and 'state law', the contextual specificities of these different judicial variations will be analyzed in the volume by Lisa Heemann, Prosper S Maguchu, Tillmann Schneider, and Olaf Zenker.

Travelling normative ideas in translation

As we reconsider the topic of rule-of-law promotion, we would like to stress that all these efforts are embedded in multi-layered interactive processes. This means that '[m]obile policies [such as policy approaches to *rule of law*] rarely travel as complete "packages", they move in bits and pieces – as selective discourses, inchoate ideas, and synthesized models – and therefore "arrive" not as replicas but as policies already-in-transformation'.[31] Thus, *rule of law* is constantly in *translation* as much as it is also constantly reconstituted.[32] According to Richard Rottenburg,[33] 'the key form of knowledge diffusion is *translation* in the sense that without translation an idea loses its meaning on its travels from one conceptual scheme to the other and is essentially lost'. When, for instance, legal norms or legal institutions travel from one legal setting to another through modes of appropriation and vernacularization,[34] each translation becomes part of a 'translation chain'.[35] Not only are they translated into other legal codes, their distinctive logical ordering enters other institutional frameworks, legal procedures, and administrative practices. Ideas about rule of law are translated into new contexts and framed in culturally specific ways. But they retain their core emphasis on specific legal notions embedded in the legal codes of the origin, of the international law system.[36] Notably, those translation dynamics are heavily embedded in asymmetric power relations. For instance, even though legal realities in African settings are complex, fluid, uncertain, and evolve through interactions of a multiplicity of normative ideas, actors, and normative frames (which Rottenburg calls meta-codes, which refers to 'a reality construction that is necessary among parties with divergent positions to agree that things are . . . for communication to be meant to lead to co-operation in order to get things done').[37] In that sense, *rule of law*, as a meta-code, endorses the participation of international governance actors based on the idea that 'one reality can be grasped, represented, and used a second time for verification'.[38] In a similar vein, Rottenburg argues that without such distortion via translation and transfer, 'the development discourse distinguishes between the one meta-code [rule of law] and many cultural codes [local rule of law understandings]'. At the same time, 'different cultural codes can only be "wrong" since they design different realities while it is assumed that there is only one'.[39]

International and transnational actors rely on such frames or meta-codes as they exercise what is considered an undeniably dominant influence, especially through agenda-setting, designing, and implementation of *rule of law* or of transitional justice programmes and projects, as demonstrated in this volume by Jonas Bens, Stefanie Bognitz, Markus Virgil Hoehne/Shakira Bedoya Sánchez, and Julia Kriesel.

Legal pluralism as a point of departure

One of the main conceptual challenges here is of grasping the heterogeneity of the notions of statehood and of *rule of law* in African socio-political and socio-legal settings, where the dynamic interactions between various framework conditions occur within a plural universe of co-existing normative orders that are generated and used by complex actor constellations and, as Benda-Beckmann have argued, with different sites of authorization.[40] In order to grasp the empirical question of 'how', *legal pluralism* offers a general framework for paying special attention to

> *how* – the ways in which, the practices by which, and the technical means by which – authority is exercised. . . . These include the practices of authorisation and assertion themselves, or the ways in which authority is claimed. It also includes the idioms of law, the forms through which things are organised and the way relations are shaped or instituted in terrains that are usually uneven, already full of other people's claims of belonging, ownership, authority and law.[41]

It offers insights into the multifaceted ways in which contemporary law is made and arranged, as it has been argued, because 'pluralism had always sought to identify hybrid legal spaces, where multiple normative systems occupied the same social field'.[42] Benda-Beckmann et al. argue that '[t]he notion of legal pluralism is a sensitizing concept that draws attention to the possibility of law of various kinds, with different foundations of legitimacy, validity, power and authority, and with different degree of institutionalization and formalization, can coexist in the same social space, often at different scales'.[43] Scales refer to the coexistence of different hierarchies of authorities, as Mariana Valverde emphasizes: 'highly local ("local" not just in the sense of quantitatively small) scales of governance persist alongside, and are intertwined with, national and international scales of governance'.[44] Therefore, legal pluralism is taken here as a general point of departure for developing analytical categories for distinguishing variations within empirical legal plural complexities.

Following up on this idea, the thirteen central chapters of this volume attempt to capture glimpses of the African legal pluralities as they zoom into settings as diverse as Ethiopia, Ghana, Kenya, Libya, Nigeria, Rwanda, Somaliland, South Africa, Tanzania, and Uganda. All contributors reflect on the manifold intertwinings of various authority claims, legal doctrines, institutions, and practices. The various case studies on Africa show inherent tensions and conflicts in light of the existence of multiple competing and partly overlapping normative orders, legal doctrines, institutions, and practices. That means that the encounters of different normative ideas create inherent inconsistencies, which lead to adaptations, inventions, and reinventions. The constant interactions, and especially the encounters of different legal ideas, specific governance-actor constellations and their practices, jointly create, navigate, and shape what we call *normative spaces* in the conceptual design of the volume.[45]

Normative spaces as an analytical framework

Our neologism, *normative spaces*, analytically grasps the dynamics of spatial plurality. We partly contest the still prevailing perception in legal theory that space is 'the dead, the fixed, the undialectical, the immobile':[46] As 'spaces tend to serve as passive containers, symbols, or geographical coordinates for political theories, ideologies, and histories'[47] in academic and popular discourses, and spaces are to that extent still widely perceived as the fixed backdrop against which, for instance, legal ideas and norms are implemented or as either 'naturally' given or created by actions of free-acting human agents. It is in that sense that Sarah Keenan argues that 'law tends to operate with an implicit understanding that space is something pre-existing, inert and singular in meaning. . . . Legal judgements, executive powers, legislation and legal commentaries tend to treat space as something planned over, built on, cultivated, bought, sold and/or protected'.[48] Legal analyses may have had little to say about space as a dynamic entity. Perhaps they may not have reflected adequately on the impact of law on society, or on society as a transforming and transformative space. It was neither necessary for legal theory to reflect on space in considering how legal norms, doctrines, and institutions are created,[49] nor was it acknowledged that 'law constructs itself . . . in a social net of spaces'.[50] However, in light of the increasing significance of the spatial turn since the 1990s, various works by legal scholars and social scientists have integrated the notion of 'spatialization of social theory' into their analyses and paid greater attention to examining the relationship between law and space.[51] Particularly the pioneering works within the interdisciplinary academic branch of geography and law merit a mention here.[52] Literature in this area provides meaningful insights into 'space-in-law' and 'law-in-space',[53] even though this conjunction of law and geography was long criticized for being self-imprisoned in the conceptual dualism of 'law' and 'space'. It is important to emphasize the interconnectivity between law and spatiality and the reciprocal construction of law and space as a way to overcome the binary categories of 'law' and 'space'.[54] To that end, the concepts of 'nomicity' and nomosphere introduced by David Delaney – a prominent representative of the aforementioned academic branch – are vital to this study. According to Delany, nomicity is a 'dimension of social order and ordering implicated by normatively inflected world constituting rules'.[55] Nomosphere, as he defines it, as 'the cultural-material environs that are constituted by the reciprocal materialization of "the legal", and the legal signification of the socio-spatial, and the practical, the performative engagements through which such constitutive moments happen and unfold'[56] emphasizes the co-constitutive nature of the social, the spatial and the legal. These different normativities would thus not necessarily be identical to 'the legal'. 'Normative', for the purposes of this volume, needs to be understood in the broader sense and includes diverse 'normativities, such as etiquette, customs, and ethics, religious rules, familial rules, and rules of professional associations, and the like'.[57]

Spatio-temporal arrangements

Moreover, we propose that 'space' – the other constituent element of the conceptual approach – be understood in a relational and not in a Euclidean sense in awareness of its physical, symbolic, and lived multidimensionality. Spaces are 'products' of interrelations and embedded practices, and, therefore, in the sense of a sphere of multiple possibilities which are inherently accompanied by a certain instability and unpredictability. Space might be understood as an assemblage of relations and networks that 'make' social action and, consequently, as something that is dynamic, 'a way of approaching alterity, diversity, and multiplicity'.[58] Following David Harvey's understanding of space as 'a reference system by means of which we locate ourselves with respect to the world',[59] space must be viewed as a 'dynamic heterogeneous simultaneity'.[60] Emphasis needs to be placed on the frame of reference of connections, which are 'constantly being (re)produced in no fixed direction'.[61] We embrace the uncertainty that comes with this understanding of space as being unfixed and dynamic. That means also that 'space can operate simultaneously on conceptual, social and physical levels to the extent that it blurs the three'.[62] Different spaces might temporarily evolve different (material) spatial formations. '[T]hrough their design and transformation, spaces site, articulate, and produce a sense of self in the world, relationships with others, and forms of control and influence'.[63] Since 'social relationships are set into time',[64] '"time" and "space" are not taken as separate dimensions to be considered one after the other'.[65] One might examine social practices under plural legal conditions and by asking how actors operate within the various temporalities shaped by asymmetric power relations.[66]

Seeing space as spheres of possibilities for the co-existence of a multiplicity, always under construction, dynamic, simultaneous, and heterogeneous,[67] we examine how spatial and temporal dimensions of normativity and governance affect each other and how distinct spaces are specifically (re)shaped in processes of multiple relations and connections that intersect.

African normative spaces in motion

Normative spaces and legal dynamics in Africa are constituted through practices of social actors and these practices might be simultaneous and overlapping.[68] They might be viewed as moments or preliminary products of those interactions. They are continuously transformed through negotiations and regulations in different *nomospheres. Normative spaces* are therefore highly dynamic, or 'non-linear, non-measurable, non-calculable . . . a way in which the law both fulfils [sic!] and transcends itself'.[69] We also pay attention to temporalities of – and within – normative spaces,[70] since 'law is not simple there; it begins and ends, comes and go, is anticipated and lingers on'.[71]

> Law connects the present with the past and future either implicitly or explicitly in an array of ways, for instance, in basic legal concepts, in specific regulations, and in claims to concrete property objects. Legal orders also define the temporal and spatial validity of regulations, decisions or institutions in normative terms. This does not mean that these time frames are actually followed and that people always abide by these limitations.[72]

By temporalities of law we mean 'the temporal validity of law, temporal aspects of legislation, decision-making, and of evidence and causation'.[73] Conflict and disputes of different scales connect the past, present, and the future, as contributors to this volume demonstrate. For instance, transitional justice efforts in African settings are connected by 'remembering the past' in judicial criminal trials, as Jonas Bens goes on to show, through evidence construction (Markus Virgil Hoehne/Shakira Bedoya Sánchez) as well as through specific reconciliation efforts (Stefanie Bognitz). They also become visible in processes of legislation (Felix-Anselm van Lier) or quasi-legislation of judicial actors (Hakeem O Yusuf). The same applies to conflicts and disputes in contexts of ecological resources management. Kelly Askew, Hannah W Wanderi, and Daniel Behailu Gebreamanuel illustrate the impact of actors and the role of the judicial sphere.

Hence, the multi-perspectives generated by way of *normative spaces* and legal dynamics allow us to illustrate processes, structures (iterations of actual actions), and relations that constitute normativity for whose description conceptual tools of jurisprudence are generally not well suited.[74] In order to grasp various forms of normativities within spaces beyond the conceptual tools provided by jurisprudence methods and methodologies, this volume draws attention to the manifold possibilities in which normative orders and institutions exist and compete, especially within the same social space. By focusing on the engagement or differentiations of the space 'in which authority takes shape and is set in motion we will be able to better understand the manner and mode of authorization of social relations, and the technical forms, idioms, and institutions'[75] through which something resembling the (rules of) law is jointly produced.

Thus, normative spaces and legal dynamics comprise multiple competing and partly overlapping individual and collective actors, evoking in different ways, as Keebet von Benda-Beckmann reminds us, 'concepts, regulations, and rights and obligations', and thereby constituting 'social and legal hierarchies'.[76] All individual and collective actors involved give these structures meaning through processes in which they articulate identities and position themselves.[77] They produce normative spaces where conflict and fragmentation are inherent and manifested in diverse practices, representations, and (symbolic) imaginations.[78]

Particularly due to the existence of multiple competing and partly overlapping normative orders, legal doctrines, institutions, and practices, conflicts are inherent. The intermingling of different normative understandings opens up spaces and forums for negotiating values through which space itself is reshaped.[79] These negotiations bring to light the diversity of legal practices for dealing with coexisting individual and collective belongings and identity constructions. The contributors analyze a multitude of constellations that arise in encounters between different normative orders, whereby doctrines, institutions, and practices are re-produced in select settings and shaped by complex translation processes in Africa's multidimensional ***normative spaces***. The objective is to highlight the conflicting constructions of space that force actors to continuously redefine the 'imagined' boundaries of their respective normative spaces. Thus, for instance, the aforementioned problem of garnering state recognition for non-state legal orders in African settings is a very diffuse, heterogeneous, spatial process, in that 'it invokes a wide range of social processes, structures and networks that give force to relations and belonging'.[80] At the same time, uncertainty and the inherent inconsistencies become driving forces for continuous adaptations and (re-)inventions. This requires revisiting processes of re-vitalization and re-invention of religious and 'traditional' law, whereby it is possible to track the emergence of a neo-traditional form of authority. The plural legal situation creates hybrid forums and authority constellations with divergent doctrines, institutions, and practices, as specifically characterized by Stefanie Bognitz, Lisa Heemann, Tillmann Schneider, and Olaf Zenker. Consequently, the emphasis on normative spaces opens up analytical avenues to shed more light on existing and changing power relations, processes of institutionalization, and the construction of legitimacy and normativities, as well as to vividly demonstrate the plurality of lawscapes in Africa along with their inherent tensions and conflicts.

Constructing, contesting, negotiating, and adapting dynamics

In order to unravel and explain the multiplicity of normative spaces, 'we need to take a place, enter at a specific moment in time',[81] and, thus, we must construct specific frames of references as our points of departure. As space formations are continuously (re)constituted in African legal settings, we have limited the range of variables examined here in order to be able to offer more in terms of analysis. Given that the specific spatio-temporal constellations can be viewed as a product of interrelations, embedded practices and representations, the constructed frames allow us to extract dimensions and to determine spatial and temporal scales. This seems to be crucial since 'without a specific, situated social/political issue whose practical implications can be examined, debates about scale can only be battles of abstractions'.[82]

The dimensions we have chosen allow a deeper understanding of the processes within a certain time-space continuum. In order to lay bare some key dynamics, we have identified four major dimensions to a discussion of normative spaces in Africa, which represent the four parts of this volume: (I) constructing, (II) contesting, (III) (re-)negotiating, and (IV) adapting. Those chosen analytical categories should not be seen as space containers for holding legal ideas and norms, for, as already indicated, these categories are dynamic, with inherent fluid overlaps, and in constant move.

As notions of fluidity and uncertainty are vital to these four chosen dimensions, the contributions in Part I and Part II highlight aspects of constructing and contesting regulation mechanisms in different normative spaces. Since '[l]egal construction of space is used as an instrument to control people and resources',[83] the contributors will focus on the legislative, administrative, and coercive measures to 'order' space and regulate conduct at different scales. We show how those regulative mechanisms and arrangements are challenged and resisted with our focus on constructing and contesting dynamics shining the spotlight on the pull and push factors of social normativity. Such interplays of spaces challenge the actors involved to continuously redefine the boundaries of their respective normative space. Since negotiation processes of 'boundaries' are embedded in power imbalances, they may reinforce tensions and conflict of normative values, and often challenge involved actors' willingness to make concessions. One may ask, what is 'inside' and 'outside' of the space of ordering. The normative structure of 'order' is one of 'inclusive-exclusion' in which the boundary markers characterize demarcations between the periphery and the centre, insiders and outsiders, public and private sphere, or civil and criminal matters. They are constructed and resisted or do not exist, or, such binaries are dissolved in complexities etc. The 'outside' and different relations of (non)belonging are created in the contestability of the 'orderly borders', as demonstrated by Jonas Bens, Markus Virgil Hoehne/Shakira Bedoya Sánchez, Felix-Anselm van Lier, Julia Kriesel, Prosper S Maguchu, and Hakeem O Yusuf.

The other two dimensions in Part III and Part IV emphasize the motions, the continuous (re-)negotiations, and adaptation dynamics when divergent authorities and jurisdictions converge as modes of political engagements. The focus is on ongoing encounters that represent important links that generate heterogeneity. Specific actor constellations engage in complex negotiation processes and thereby create connections. Those connections might be viewed as 'interstitial spaces, where conflicts and their management are subject to dynamic adaptations, negotiations and contestations',[84] the transfer of different normative ideas becomes visible.[85] In these intersections, the contributors analyze the complex array of social actors' constellations and their interactions and how they jointly re-negotiate and adapt the normative spaces, as demonstrated by Kelly Askew, Stefanie Bognitz, Daniel Behailu Gebreamanuel, Lisa Heemann, Tillmann Schneider, Hannah W Wanderi, and Olaf Zenker.

All four dimensions – exemplified by the contributors' case studies in this volume – go on to demonstrate how the manifold intertwinements of different normative frames, institutions, and practices constantly reproduce and re-innovate Africa's multidimensional normative spaces. Moreover, they show that ***normative spaces*** and legal dynamics are navigated and patterned by specific actors and practices, thereby continuously transformed through negotiations and regulations. The specific plural constellations and dynamics improve our understanding of the ways in which space is constructed in different normative orders through spatial claims for validity. Moreover, the multiple legal constructions of space and spatial constructions of law open up new arenas through which to engage with notions of political authority and localization of rights and obligations.[86]

Katrin Seidel and Hatem Elliesie

Notes

1 We would like to express our gratitude to our colleagues Bertram Turner and Keebet von Benda-Beckmann for their thoughtful advice, comments, and suggestions on earlier drafts of the Prologue.

2 The term lawscape is borrowed from Philippopoulos-Mihalopoulos to emphasize the co-constituting connection between normativity and space and the inherent yet tortuous way in which law and space come together. See A Philippopoulos-Mihalopoulos, *Spatial Justice: Body, Lawscape, Atmosphere* (Routledge 2015) 2.

3 S Pahuja, 'Laws of Encounter: A Jurisdictional Account of International Law' (2013) 1 *London Review of International Law* 63–98, 70.

4 F von Benda-Beckmann, K von Benda Beckmann, and J Eckert (eds), 'Rules of Law and Laws of Ruling: Law and Governance Between Past and Future' in *Rules of Law and Laws of Ruling: On the Governance of Law* (Ashgate Publishing 2009) 1–30, 3.

5 L Grenfell, *Promoting the Rule of Law in Post-Conflict States* (Cambridge University Press 2013).

6 DB Maldonado, *Towards a Constitutionalism of the Global South: The Activist Tribunals of India, South Africa, and Colombia* (Cambridge University Press 2012) 1; T Carothers, 'The Rule of Law Revival' (1998) 77 *Foreign Affairs* 95–106, 99; see also B Rajagopal, 'Invoking Rule of Law in Post-Conflict Rebuilding: A Critical Examination' (2008) 49 *William and Mary Law Review* 1347–1376.

7 See Rajagopal (n 6) 1347f; S Kendall, 'Constitutional Technicity: Displacing Politics through Expert Knowledge' (2013) *Law, Culture and the Humanities* 1–15, 9f.

8 See comprehensively K Seidel, 'The Promotion of Rule of Law in Translation: Technologies of Normative Knowledge Transfer in South Sudan's Constitution Making' in T Berger and A Esguerra (eds), *World Politics in Translation: Power, Relationality and Difference in Global Cooperation* (Routledge 2018) 76–92.

9 J Comaroffs, *Theory from the South: Or How Euro-American Evolving Toward Africa* (Paradigm Publishers 2012) 12.

10 A Amin, 'Regions Unbound: Towards a New Politics of Place' (2004) 86 (1) *Geografiska Annaler: Series B, Human Geography* 33–44, 34.

11 S Keenan, *Subversive Property: Law and the Production of Spaces of Belonging* (Routledge 2015) 47.

12 We are borrowing the term 'provincializing' from D Chakrabarty, *Provincializing Europe: Post-colonial Thought and Historical Difference* (Princeton University Press 2000) 5.

13 Keenan (n 11) 47.

14 Comaroff (n 9) 1f.

15 T Carothers (ed), 'The Problem of Knowledge' in *Promoting the Rule of Law Abroad: In Search of Knowledge* (Carnegie 2006) 15–30.

16 VY Mudimbe, *The Invention of Africa: Gnosis, Philosophy, and the Order of Knowledge* (Indiana University Press 1988).

17 Comprehensively J Iliffe, *Africans: The History of a Continent* (Cambridge University Press 1995).

18 A Mbembe, 'At the Edge of the World: Boundaries, Territoriality, and Sovereignty in Africa' (2000) 12 (1) *Public Culture* 259–284, 263. In some cases, political entities were not delimited by an imbrication of multiple spaces constantly joined, disjoined, and recombined through wars, conquests, and the mobility of goods and persons, see I Kopytoff (ed), *The African Frontier: The Reproduction of Traditional African Societies* (Indiana University Press 1987).

19 See comprehensively, K Seidel, T Sureau, and R Rottenburg, 'Assembling the South Sudanese State' (unpublished paper 2015) 6.

20 Seidel, Sureau, and Rottenburg (n 19) 6.

21 Mbembe (n 18) 261.

22 K Schlichte, 'Staatlichkeit als Ideologie: Zur politischen Soziologie der Weltgesellschaft' in K-G Giesen (ed), *Ideologien in der Weltpolitik* (Leske + Budrich 2004) 149–166, 150–151; see also A Hobart and B Kapferer (eds), *Contesting the State: The Dynamics of Resistance and Control* (Sean Kingston Publishing 2012); T Hagmann and D Péclard (eds), 'Negotiating Statehood: Dynamics of Power and Domination in Africa' (2011) 41 (4) *Development and Change* 539–562.

23 Benda-Beckmann, Benda Beckmann, and Eckert (n 4) 1, 5ff.

24 JS Migdal and K Schlichte, 'Rethinking the State' in K Schlichte (ed), *The Dynamics of States: The Formation and Crises of State Domination* (Ashgate 2005) 1–40, 33.

25 Migdal and Schlichte (n 24) 33.

26 Constitutional theorist, Richard Fallon, comments on RoL as 'a much celebrated, historical ideal, the precise meaning of which may be less clear today than ever before' (R Fallon, '"The Rule of Law" as a Concept in Constitutional Discourse' (1997) 97 (1) *Columbia Law Review* 1–56, 1). The RoL concept is very attractive since it allows each of us to project his or her own sense of the ideal government onto the phrase.

27 For more information, cf. the RoL working paper series M Koetter and GF Schuppert (eds), *Understandings of the Rule of Law in Various Legal Orders of the World*, which presents different understandings of the *rule of law* and their specific normative implications in various normative spheres of the world on <http://wikis.fu-berlin.de/display/SBprojectrol/Home> accessed 18 August 2018.

28 See comprehensively, Seidel (n8) 80–82, 'State Formation Through Constitution Making in Emerging South Sudan: Unveiling the Technicity of the Rule of Law' (2015) 18 (1) *Recht in Afrika* 3–16, 5–8; RZ Sannerholm, *Rule of Law After War and Crisis: Ideologies, Norms and Methods* (Intersentia 2012); S Humphreys, *Theatre of the Rule of Law: Transnational Legal Interventions on Theory and Practice* (Cambridge University Press 2010).

29 See comprehensively, O Zenker and MV Hoehne (eds), *The State and the Paradox of Customary Law in Africa* (Routledge 2018).

30 D Pimentel, 'Rule of Law Reform Without Cultural Imperialism? Reinforcing Customary Justice Through Collateral Review in Southern Sudan' (2010) 2 (1) *Hague Journal on the Rule of Law* 1–28.

31 J Peck and N Theodore, 'Mobilizing Policy: Models, Models, Methods and Mutations' (2010) 41 *Geoforum* 169–174, 170.

32 Translation emphasizes the navigation of perceptions, values, norms, practices, procedures, institutional frameworks, and interpretations between contexts (see R Rottenburg, *Far Fetched Facts: A Parable of Development Aid* (MIT Press 2009); SE Merry, 'Legal Transplants and Cultural Translation: Making Human Rights in a Vernacular' in M Goodale (ed), *Human Rights: An Anthropological Reader* (Wiley-Blackwell 2009) 265–302; S Shimada, 'Cultural Differences and the Problem of Translation' in R Rottenburg et al. (eds), *The Making and Unmaking of Differences: Anthropological, Sociological and Philosophical Perspectives* (Transcript 2006) 83–95; D Bachmann-Medick, 'Menschenrechte als Übersetzungsproblem' (2012) 38 *Geschichte und Gesellschaft* 331–359; A Behrends, SJ Park and R Rottenburg, *Travelling Models in African Conflict Resolution* (Brill 2014); T Berger and A Esguerra, *World Politics in Translation: Power, Relationality and Difference in Global Cooperation* (Routledge 2018).

33 R Rottenburg, 'On Juridico-Political Foundations of Meta-Codes' in J Renn (ed), *The Globalization of Knowledge in History: Based on the 97th Dahlem Workshop* (Ed. Open Access 2012) 483–500, 483; Rottenburg (n 32).

34 SE Merry, 'Transnational Human Rights and Local Activism: Mapping the Middle' (2006) 108 (1) *American Anthropologist* 38–51.

35 Rottenburg (n 32).

36 Behrends, Park, and Rottenburg (n 32).

37 Rottenburg (n 32) 489.

38 Rottenburg (n 32) 489.

39 Rottenburg (n 32) 489.

40 Benda-Beckmann, Benda Beckmann, and Eckert (n 4).

41 Pahuja (n 3) 70.

42 P Schiff Berman, 'From Legal Pluralism to Global Legal Pluralism' in R Nobles and D Schiff (eds), *Law, Society and Community: Socio-Legal Essays in Honour of Roger Cotterrell* (Ashgate 2014) 255–271, 256f.

43 F von Benda-Beckmann, K von Benda Beckmann, and J Eckert (eds), 'Trust and the Temporalities of Law' Special Issue (2014) 46 (1) *The Journal of Legal Pluralism and Unofficial Law* 34.

44 M Valverde, 'Jurisdiction and Scale: Legal "Technicalities" as Resources for Theory' (2009) 18 (2) *Social & Legal Studies* 139–157, 143. See also F von Benda-Beckmann, K von Benda-Beckmann, and A Griffiths (eds), 'Space and Legal

Pluralism: An Introduction' in *Spatializing Law: An Anthropological Geography of Law in Society* (Ashgate 2009) 1–29, 15–18.

45 'Space' understood as social products embodying social relationships emphasizes the sphere of multiple possibilities (see DB Massey, *For Space* (Sage 2008); H Lefebvre, *The Production of Space* (Blackwell 1991).

46 M Foucault, 'Question on Geography' in C Gordon (ed), *Power/Knowledge: Selected Interviews on Other Writings 1972–1977* (Pantheon Books 1980) 63–77, 70.

47 DDB Wendel, 'Introduction: Toward a Spatial Epistemology of Politics' in DDB Wendel and FS Aidoo (eds), *Spatializing Politics: Essays on Power and Place* (Harvard Graduate School of Design 2016) 10.

48 Keenan (n 11) 21.

49 Y Blank and I Rosen-Zvi (eds), 'The Spatial Turn in Legal Theory' (2010) 10 (1) *Hagar Studies in Culture, Polity and Identities* 37–60, 37f; Benda-Beckmann, Benda Beckmann, and Eckert (n 4) 2 f.

50 A Philippopoulos-Mihalopoulos, 'Law, Space, Bodies: The Emergence of Spatial Justice' (2011) *University of Westminster School of Law Legal Studies Research Paper Series* (2015).

51 J Holder and C Harrison (eds), 'Connecting Law and Geography' in *Law and Geography* (Oxford University Press 2006) 3–16, 3 f; F von Benda-Beckmann, K von Benda-Beckmann, and A Griffiths (eds), *Spatializing Law: An Anthropological Geography in Society* (Ashgate 2009); Blank and Rosen-Zvi (n 49) 39.

52 N Blomley, *Law, Space and the Geographies of Power* (Guilford Press 1994); N Blomley, D Delaney, and R Ford (eds), *The Legal Geography Reader* (Blackwell 2001); Holder and Harrison (n 51); Benda-Beckmann, Benda-Beckmann, and Griffiths (n 51); D Delaney, 'Tracing Displacements: Or Evictions in the Nomosphere' (2004) 22 *Environment and Planning D: Society and Space* 847–860; D Delaney, *The Spatial, the Legal, and the Pragmatics of World-Making: Nomospheric Investigations* (Routledge 2010).

53 See D Delaney, 'Beyond the Word: Law as a Thing of this World' in J Holder and C Harrison (eds), *Law and Geography* (Oxford University Press 2006) 67–84, 68f.

54 I Braverman et al. (eds), *The Expanding Spaces of Law: A Timely Legal Geography* (Stanford University Press 2014) 1.

55 Delaney (n 52) 27.

56 Delaney (n 52) 25.

57 M Ramstedt, 'Anthropological Perspectives on the Normative and Institutional Recognition of Religion by the Law of the State' in S Ferrari et al. (eds), *Religious Rules, State Law, and Normative Pluralism: A Comparative Overview* (Springer 2016) 45–60, 54.

58 Braverman (n 54).

59 D Harvey, *Justice, Nature and the Geography of Difference* (Blackwell 1996) 207.

60 Massey (n 45).

61 Keenan (n 11) 6, 11.

62 Keenan (n 11) 11.

63 Wendel (n 47) 11.

64 F von Benda-Beckmann, *Property in Social Continuity: Continuity and Change in the Maintenance of Property Relationships through Time in Minangkabau, West Sumatra* (Martinus Nijhoff 1979) 48.

65 M Valverde, *Chronotopes of Law: Jurisdiction, Scale and Governance* (Routledge 2015) 10.

66 See Rottenburg (n 32) 12.

67 See Keenan (n 11) 48 f.

68 S Müller-Mall, *Legal Spaces: Towards a Topological Thinking of Law* (Springer 2013) 84, 89, 79.
69 Cf. Philippopoulos-Mihalopoulos, 'Law's Spatial Turn: Geography, Justice and a Certain Fear of Space' (2010) XX (X) *Law, Culture and the Humanities* 1–16, 10–11; Massey (n 45) 11–12.
70 See comprehensively, CJ Greenhouse, *A Moment's Notice: Time Politics Across Culture* (Corn-well University Press 1996); Rottenburg (n 32).
71 See Rottenburg (n 32) 46.
72 Rottenburg (n 32) 5.
73 Rottenburg (n 32) 3.
74 Müller-Mall (n 68) 3, 62.
75 Pahuja (n 3) 69.
76 Rottenburg (n 32) 4.
77 G Schlee and EE Watson, *Changing Identifications and Alliances in North-East Africa: Vol. I: Ethiopia and Kenya* (Berghahn Books 2009) 2.
78 See Lefebvre (n 45).
79 Philippopoulos-Mihalopoulos (n 50) 9.
80 Keenan (n 11) 7.
81 Müller-Mall (n 68) 79.
82 Valverde (n 44) 146.
83 Benda-Beckmann, Benda Beckmann, and Eckert (n 43) 9.
84 Behrends, Park, and Rottenburg (n 32) 25.
85 Behrends, Park, and Rottenburg (n 32) 14.
86 Benda-Beckmann, Benda Beckmann, and Eckert (n 4) 3f; Rottenburg (n 32).

Part I

Constructing normative spaces

1 'Forensic Fetishism' and human rights after violent conflict

Uncovering Somaliland's troubled past

Markus Virgil Hoehne and Shakira Bedoya Sánchez

> [T]he dead body is valuable insofar as it is a 'body of evidence', or, more specifically, the 'evidence of crime' – corpus delicti – bearing the marks of a person's experiences before death (tortures) and the kind of death (homicide) he or she endured, and insofar as it can be used for political purposes or is the object of mourning through which a community is consolidated and reborn.[1]

Introduction

Somaliland, in Northwestern Somalia, unilaterally declared its independence from Somalia in 1991 after a decade of massive human rights violations and civil war in the region. First reports on the crackdown of government forces on local civilians, particularly in the late 1980s, estimated the number of civilians killed at between 5,000[2] and 50,000.[3] More recently, Somaliland human rights activists have claimed that up to 250,000 people were killed in the war the Somali government waged against its own people in the northwest.[4] Similar numbers, ranging between 100,000 and 200,000, have also been cited by Somaliland officials in their reports about this matter.[5] Scholars have also recently claimed that 'as many as 100,000 people' had been killed, however, citing oral sources that are vague.[6] Many of the dead are buried in mass graves (sometimes anonymously), or are still considered missing. Somaliland has existed for over 25 years and succeeded in becoming largely stable, peaceful, and democratic. It functions as a 'de facto' state,[7] which, however, does not enjoy international recognition. Officially, the country is subsumed under the name of 'Somalia', which many Somalilanders perceive as an insult. Globally, Somalia stands for 'state collapse' and ongoing war (including terrorism and counter-terrorism). Locally, it also stands for the history of the past abuses, from which Somaliland supporters wish to distance themselves; some demand accountability for past atrocities. The first systematic investigations into past crimes committed by Somali government officials began around 2000, when the Centre for Justice and Accountability (CJA) in San Francisco assisted a group of Somali plaintiffs who had fled Somalia and become

American citizens to open proceedings against General Maxamed Cali Samatar, the former Somali minister of defence and subsequently the prime minister.[8] General Samatar found refuge in the US in the 1990s. The Somali plaintiffs, supported by CJA, accused him of having ordered the attack in 1988 of the Somali army against civilians in Hargeysa and Burco, the two largest cities in Northwestern Somalia. During the course of the legal proceedings, which dragged on for more than a decade, contact was established between Somali plaintiffs and forensic experts from Peru, who began forensic investigations in Somaliland in 2012. The idea of CJA was that these investigations could produce evidence that could be used in future court cases against former Somali officials in the US. As of 2020, forensic experts continue to hold international field schools on an annual basis, advertised under the title 'Uncovering Somaliland's troubled past', to exhume mass graves and analyze human remains, and these efforts are supported by the Somaliland government. Yet, our ongoing ethnographic research shows that these forensic operations are highly challenging owing to the lack of proper equipment, facilities (laboratories etc.), and local expertise needed for forensic work. Added to that, the local population often has little information and understanding about the work of the foreign forensic experts, and misunderstandings lead to tensions between locals, forensic experts, and government officials. We argue that the forensic endeavours in Somaliland shed light on the contemporary role of forensic anthropology in general, but in particular on the phenomenon of forensic fetishism (discussed below). They show the contested nature of 'truth' across a spectrum of normative spaces within which forensic interventions take place and which are variously intertwined (e.g. ranging from Somaliland and the US to other locales on the globe where forensic experts come from and/or practice).

War crimes and human rights investigations have made a shift from the traditional approach reserved for the testimony of human witnesses to an approach that privileges forensic science. What was previously written, filmed, recorded, and exhibited in verbal or photographic testimony (the dominant form of testimony, e.g. during the Nuremberg trials) has now been replaced by the attribution 'of an inherent power and a certain agency to inanimate objects or technologies'.[9] The logic behind this is that

> unlike the testimony of victims, scientific evidence pronounced by expert witnesses is more difficult to contest; that bullets and missile casings, ruins, medical and autopsy reports and tissues showing the burn mark of white phosphorus presumably cannot be undermined by any suspect political subjectivity. . . [because] an evidentiary truth seems to linger, fossilized in the object, ready to be unpacked by science.[10]

The process by which 'bodies' are constructed as forensic evidence is twofold: According to Renshaw,[11] it entails a moment of 'disembodiment', as the human body 'loses its integrity and becomes a sum of materials and tissues upon which are recorded the marks of certain acts such as injury and disease, which can be decoded to reconstruct an individual's death'. At the same time, it implies a process of 'hyperembodiment where any personhood and socially meaningful identity is removed from the discursive space occupied by the body, leaving space only for physical characteristics to be enumerated'.[12]

> When the complete grave is exposed and the total number of bodies are visible, the episode of killing is seen in its totality and the bodies are viewed as collective, forming a tableau that communicates the scope of the event to the observers. This simultaneously materialises both the scale and the particularity of the event.[13]

Forensic fetishism does not reside, as Weizman writes,[14] in the Marxist notion of the mystification of objects but rather in our contemporary 'attraction to the objects of violence'. In this sense it is akin to (sexual) fetishism that is related to the belief in the inherent value or power of an object. Weizman understands 'forensic fetishism as the return to the object, to the non-human in human rights work'.[15] The origins of this fascination with objectification and the human body can be traced back to the beginnings of physical anthropology as a discipline. Around 1900, some anthropologists such as Rudolf Virchow and Felix von Luschan in Germany insisted on the scientific power of bodily objects, bones, and particularly skulls that were collected in the colonies and sent to them by military officers. In their eyes, measuring and classifying these human remains was a superior scientific method that could help to understand human history, evolution, and contemporary race relations.[16]

Contrary to the seemingly objective character ascribed to bones by physical and forensic anthropologists, we wish to emphasize in line with much of the critical literature generated on this matter by social scientists and historians that mass grave exhumations resulting from episodes of violence constitute a highly political endeavour. In addressing the political side of exhumations, it is impossible overlook the fact that forensic science involves a process of re-association of the disarticulated mortal remains of victims that takes into account not only the original acts of killings, but also the *ongoing* treatment of victims – by the perpetrators and in humanitarian responses.[17] This cross-temporal aspect opens up and creates a number of new forums and (normative) spaces that can reach far beyond the local or 'ethno-cultural' setting.[18] In (post-)conflict settings, as those in Rwanda, the Congo, Uruguay, Peru, Cambodia, and of course Somaliland, the bodies in the graves are not just 'dead'. Although death is officially conceived as a point in time (and frequently as a kind of 'end point'), 'historical and ethnographic studies give plenty of examples of how death can be imagined as something with a duration, something which partakes in life'.[19] Exhumations change the temporality of death. Renshaw found that 'buried bodies have a power to effect change if they are "gathered" through an act of exhumation'.[20] In this way they are 'revived' and attributed with new social and political lives.[21] Moreover, even if dead bodies are absent, because they are (still) unexhumed or missing, they possess a huge potential to fire the imagination of the living. The general issue of interpreting dead bodies and questions of (partial) truth is outlined by Ferrándiz, who argues that

> [s]tate institutions often become involved in the exhumations in one way or another – sometimes in order to prevent them. On other occasions the work is done by international or grassroots organizations. The regime responsible for the dead bodies becomes the subject of heated social debates challenging hegemonic versions of an uncomfortable past and provoking disputes about the politics of victimhood.[22]

Somewhat in contrast to this critical perspective on dead bodies as 'subject of debate', some – particularly forensic anthropologists – argue that 'forensic analysis is today the most effective ritual procedure to allow things to *speak for themselves* [emphasis added]',[23] as, for instance, the famous forensic expert Clyde Snow would have it when he told judges during a trial in Argentina in 1985 that 'in many ways the skeleton is its own best witness'.[24] This belief in the 'objectivity' or 'agency' of the dead bodies plays a key role in the production of facts and fetishes. In relation to that, 'the dead seem to have become inexhaustible batteries for political power'.[25]

The problem lies in the assumption that fundamental truths are written on the body as if 'bones never lie'. This assumption begs the questions: '[W]hat can it [the body] tell us about the social context in which we find it? What can it obscure?'[26] Fetishizing bodies can 'ultimately deflect attention from the social condition in which bodies are shaped'.[27] The point is to understand the substance of bodies, their parts, and composition by focusing on the very properties, processes, and techniques through which they are 'constantly constituted and negotiated as persons or things, subjects or objects, meanings or matter'.[28] Weiss, referring to the DNA testing of bodies of the babies of Yemenite Jews who immigrated to Israel around 1950, argues that 'it is ultimately not genetic testing that identifies us, but social interests that provide an impetus and a text for our identity/ies'.[29] In the process of exhumations, the body – and other material traces – is produced and constructed as a meaningful object. It has no 'voice' of its own but is made to talk.[30] Crossland adds that this shows that 'bodies are created as objects within society'.[31] This is where ethnographic research on forensic work has to begin.

This is also where our focus on forensic fetishism relates to considerations about (normative) spaces. The social space is, after all, a site of entanglement of non-human materialities and human subjectivities in a complex topology.[32] To that extent, the *object value of something* is not naturally given but has political underpinnings. In considering the key subject of this chapter – the exhumation of mass graves in Somaliland – one can argue that if value is a political construct then it is not politics that

> give meaning to bones; rather it is bones that support or animate processes of mourning and historicization, individualization and othering,

> marginalization and silence, subversion and reassertion. It is bones that affirm kinship relations and memory.[33]

This quote points to the dialectical relationship between bones as the material imbued with a certain 'ontological' force and the need to construct their relevance in particular normative spaces. These theoretical considerations provide the framework for our case study in Somaliland on the forensic work, which also includes a field school organized by the Peruvian NGO *Equipo Peruano de Antropología Forense* (EPAF).

Dealing with the violent past in Somaliland

Every state, possibly every political community, is based on a dominant narrative about itself, its emergence and its role in people's lives (of course, these narratives may be contested and/or changed over time). A key part of the currently dominant political narrative of Somaliland concerns the suffering of the local population in Northwestern Somalia at the hands of the military regime under Maxamed Siyaad Barre (1969–1991). In the 1980s, Somalia descended into clan antagonism and clan-based civil war.[34] President Barre, who belonged to the Darood/Marrexaan clan by patrilineal descent, assembled many relatives from different clans to form his government. At one point, he relied on the so-called M.O.D.-alliance. The 'M' stood for his own clan, the 'O' for his mother's clan called Ogadeen, and the 'D' for 'Dhulbahante', a clan to which one of his sons-in-law belonged. Members of these clans held important positions in the military and security apparatus.[35]

Particularly members of the Isaaq clan-family, who resided predominantly in Northwestern Somalia, increasingly fell under the suspicion of the dictatorship. Many Isaaq were traders and some were wealthy business-people. Additionally, Isaaq military elites were unhappy that the Darood officers were being promoted while they were being side-lined. In 1981, they formed the Somali National Movement (SNM) supported by the Isaaq in the diaspora and established military bases in Ethiopia, back then considered the 'archenemy' of Somalia. Both countries had engaged in the so-called Ogadeen-War (1977–1978) over territories in eastern Ethiopia that were Somali-inhabited but according to the government in Mogadishu, belonged to Somalia; Somalia had lost the war. Yet according to the government in Mogadishu, Somalia had lost the war. The aim of the SNM was to overthrow the dictatorship in Mogadishu.[36] From 1982 onwards, the SNM began its armed struggle against the Somali government. In reaction, Northwestern Somalia came under military administration. Gersony, a close observer of the situation at the time, stressed:

> The Somali Armed Forces conducted what appears to be a systematic pattern of attacks against unarmed, civilian Issak [sic!] villages, watering points and grazing areas of northern Somalia, killing many of their residents and forcing the survivors to flee for safety to remote areas within Somalia or to other countries.[37]

Lewis, who visited Northwestern Somalia in 1985, confirmed that the region 'began to look and feel like a colony under a foreign military tyranny'.[38] The government's oppressive campaigns culminated in 1988 in the area bombardments of Hargeysa and Burco, the two major towns in the northwest. Thousands of civilians, mainly Isaaq, were killed and hundreds of thousands had to flee their homes. Compagnon found that state violence 'created a deep rift between the Isaaq and other Somalis'.[39] Bradbury argued that '[t]he targeted nature of the repression gave rise to accusations that the government had embarked on a genocidal campaign against Isaaq'.[40]

The remainder of this chapter looks at a series of endeavours to come to terms with this part of Somaliland's violent past. In dealing with the past in the region, it is possible to conceptually distinguish four phases: silencing the past, containing the past, legal proceedings, and forensic proceedings. Our analysis focuses on the motives of various actors involved (mainly ordinary Somalis, diaspora actors, international human rights activists and forensic experts) and the role played by 'facts' pertaining to the current political situation of Somaliland as established by forensic anthropologists. This also points to different normative spaces within which the past is negotiated and forensic anthropology is situated. These spaces are constructed by various local and (trans-)national practices and politics that are partly intertwined.

Basic peace building and silencing the past

The rule of Maxamed Siyaad Barre finally crumbled in early 1991, when he was ousted from Mogadishu by guerrillas of the United Somali Congress (USC), which was a Hawiye-based force that had entered into alliance with the SNM. Simultaneously, the SNM took over much of the northwest. Already for some years, the SNM had cooperated with traditional authorities belonging to various Isaaq clans. In the peripheral regions of northern Somalia, elders and other traditional authorities had functioned as important governance actors, mediating between patrilineal descent groups and taking decisions at clan or lineage meetings (Somali: *shir*).[41] From the end of 1990 on, they presided over a long series of inter-clan meetings throughout the region to discuss the grievances of the local groups involved in the civil war. Somali 'customary law' (*xeer*) was used to settle conflicts. The problem was that during the war of the Issaq-based SNM against the Somali government, most non-Isaaq in the northwest had sided with the government. Consequently, Gadabuursi and Ciise (in today's western Somaliland) and Dhulbahante and Warsangeli (in today's eastern Somaliland) formed militias supported by the government and fought against the SNM. The civil war disrupted the close-knit social and economic relations of the exogamous descent groups in the region, who were accustomed to sharing water and grazing[42]

The main issues on the agendas of the various peace meetings related to restitution of property, particularly livestock, vehicles, houses, and gardens. Due to the great number of dead people on all sides, it was agreed *not* to compensate for killings.[43] According to *xeer*, normally 'blood money' (Somali: *mag*; Arabic: *dīya*) would have to be paid by the killer's group to the victim's group. It is noteworthy that *xeer* usually establishes collective responsibility for any crime committed by a person.[44] In this way, however, killing becomes relatively 'cheap' for the killer who pays only a small part of the blood compensation (the total compensation is usually 100 camels for a man and half of it for a woman). While the normative matrix of *šarīʿa* also recognizes compensation (*dīya*), it generally establishes individual responsibility. *Šarīʿa* even allows for the execution of the killer by the closest relative of the victim. In contrast, Somali custom allows generalized revenge killings, meaning that even distant relatives of the victim could be expected to attempt to kill a member of the extended family of the perpetrator(s).[45]

A decisive innovation of the new *xeer* agreements introduced in many parts of Somaliland in the early 1990s was that the elders deliberately decreed harsh punishments according to *šarīʿa* to deter future violators of the peace. This was important against the backdrop of the general lawlessness that followed the Somali state collapse in 1991. A number of the former SNM fighters in Somaliland, particularly those who had joined the movement in the last years as youngsters, had turned from guerrillas to ordinary criminals engaged in drugs, rape, and looting. Farah and Lewis observed that

> [t]o dissuade armed militias from seizing herds of opposing groups, the elders decreed that the responsibility of paying damages inflicted by armed groups should be shouldered by the immediate families of the perpetual offenders (the family of the offender, his father, his brothers and uncles). This presumably unprecedented ruling that placed the responsibility for acts of violence upon the family and the immediate kin of the villain, undoubtedly discouraged the practice of blatant and opportunistic raiding of property.[46]

The authors also added that 'the introduction of capital punishment appears to be gaining currency in northern Somalia as an effective instrument to curtail homicide'.[47]

Another measure to create peace after war in Somaliland was amnesty. At a major clan conference in Burco in May 1991, where representatives of all clans residing in the Northwestern Somalia came together, an unconditional amnesty was granted to those who were from the region and had committed war crimes and crimes against humanity between 1981 and 1991.[48] This is also where Somaliland's independence was declared. Basic peacebuilding therefore included *reconciliation*, property *restitution*, *amnesty* and provisions to *prevent* future violence. These are key components of what has come to be known in the contemporary debate on dealing with violent pasts as 'transitional justice'.[49] It is noteworthy that these measures were taken in Somaliland in the early 1990s based on 'Somali traditions', and they were driven by the local people and were not the result of an external intervention. The decisive normative space constructed here for dealing with the recent violent past was local and did not (yet) extend beyond northern Somalia.

This transitional phase in Somaliland in the early 1990s involved many political compromises and deliberate silences. Clearly, individual perpetrators involved in killings were not held accountable. Sexual violence was not accounted for. On the one hand, men interviewed by Hoehne during various phases of field research stressed that, according to the 'traditional' conduct of war among Somalis, women had to be spared.[50] On the other hand, some ex-guerrillas and others indicated that during the civil war in the north the parties involved did not always follow these norms. Women did not talk about this sensitive matter, which entailed the threat of 'social death' for the victim.[51] Finally, the larger issue of systematic state repression and gross human rights violations was not on the agenda of the peace meetings in Somaliland in the early 1990s. The main reason for these gaps was that, initially, the situation in Somaliland was extremely volatile. Everybody was armed and ready to defend particular clan interests. The 'civilian' authority was wielded solely by the elders, who themselves represented a clan-based order.

As a rule, the views about the past and what had been right or wrong differed according to patrilineal descent. For most members of the larger Darood (Dhulbahante and Warsangeli) and Dir (Gadabursi and Ciise) clans in the region, the collapse of Somalia and the secession of Somaliland soon became the dominant traumatic experience. Field research since 2002 has made it clear to Hoehne that many remembered Somalia as a 'great' state and Maxamed Siyaad Barre as a 'strong' ruler. The present was viewed as a time of collapse or breakdown (Somali: *burbur*). Particularly members of Darood clans felt subordinate to the Isaaq in Somaliland, whereas in Somalia (before 1991) they had been the most powerful group. Among members of the Isaaq clan-family, however, the pre-1991 atrocities had caused a lasting shock for which they held the Darood-led government responsible. What happened after 1991 was largely seen as a difficult but steady 'way up' to peace, democracy, and economic development in some sectors, e.g. telecommunication. The basic peacebuilding process in the early 1990s had thus provided the starting point for many positive developments for the majority of the Isaaq, whereas many others, particularly Dhulbahante and Warsangeli, perceived peace as the only achievement of Somaliland, and otherwise complained about stagnation and the lack of 'real' Somali (meaning: Mogadishu-based) governance.

Containing the past

In 1997, when heavy rains uncovered mass graves in the city of Hargeysa, there was a sense of foreboding in the local population in nascent Somaliland that the past had yet to be revealed and reconciled. The discovery of the graves immediately led an upset local population to voice the need to establish a war-crimes tribunal. Upon the request of the Somaliland government under President Maxamed Xaaji Ibraahim Cigaal (1993–2002), the United Nations (UN) sent an explorative forensic mission. The mission reported:

> The nature of the graves, evidence of perimortem injury, and the occurrence of bodies bound together by ligature, in combination with the haphazard placement of the bodies in the graves . . . leads the forensic team to conclude

> that the deaths of these individuals are suspicious and constitute a violation of human rights. In addition, the forensic team has verified that features described by witnesses as mass graves are indeed mass graves.[52]

However, there was no follow-up on the visit of the experts, and no tribunal was set up. While some blamed the lack of interest on the side of the international community, others accused Maxamed Xaaji Ibraahim Cigaal of not having pursued the issue.[53] In our reading, the president sensed that pursuing the matter would threaten the still fragile peace in the country. When interviewed by Integrated Regional Information Networks (IRIN), a UN-information service, in 2001 and asked about local perpetrators, President Cigaal answered thus:

> One of the first resolutions they passed [at the clan conference in Burco in 1991] was that everything is forgiven and forgotten. And it was the right thing to do, because at that time there were fingers being pointed at certain clans. If that had continued, the unity of Somaliland would have been completely undermined. So one of the first resolutions was that we were starting on a clean page, we are all brothers. But there are some troublemakers. For example, when these graves were discovered [in Hargeysa in 1997] – when very, very heavy rains revealed shallow graves–I went there. The whole of Hargeysa went there to look. I made a speech there. Some politicians – some of the former colonels of the SNM and all that – made capital of that and said: 'What is going to be done about this? How are we going to avenge these people?' And for a moment the atmosphere was very tense. I took the microphone and said to them: 'So whom are you going to wreak vengeance on? The people who informed upon them? The people who are standing here and sold them for a bundle of qat [catha edulis, a mildly narcotic shrub]? Or the people who pulled the trigger? Who is the guilty one?' There was a hullabaloo. . . . But I think among the people here in Somaliland there is a conspicuous lack of bitterness. Once the thing is established and it is recognised that we have been wronged, I don't think anybody will look for revenge.[54]

Maxamed Xaaji Ibraahim Cigaal de-escalated the situation by decreeing the establishment of the War Crimes Investigation Commission (WCIC) (Somali: *Xafiiska Badhitaanka Xasuuqa*). During visits to the commission in 2002, 2004, and 2009, Hoehne learned that the commission had compiled many testimonies of survivors. But, at the same time, the reports remained 'strictly confidential', as one official stressed. The commission was also severely underfunded. In this way, the government could show the public that it was doing something about the problem of the past atrocities. But it made sure that the initiative of the commission was not disturbing the informal 'pact of silence' on which the fragile status quo in the country was built between those who liked to see themselves as 'victims' of past atrocities and the others who feared being blamed as 'perpetrators'.[55]

The leading staff members of the commission stated: '[M]any of the perpetrators are still alive and powerful; some of the killers live in Hargeysa; some in the south'.[56] During interviews with Hoehne in 2002, the members of the commission expressed their hope that the materials gathered would provide the basis for an international investigation into the matter. But several years later, nothing decisive had happened. In 2009, Xuseen Caydiid, then chairman of the commission, was frustrated. He mentioned that there was a general lack of funding and interest in their work on the side of the Somaliland government.[57] Adam argued that the ignorance towards the victims of the conflict (in the northwest in the 1980s) was one of the most important pitfalls of Somaliland's reconciliation process in the 1990s.[58] 'Great importance has been given to achieve peace and stability, but victims' fundamental . . . human rights have been marginalized'.[59] This is one example of the politicization of dealing with the past in general: whether past violations of human rights are taken on or not depends on overarching political interests of the ruling elites. While a realistic perspective had certainly been voiced by President Cigaal (see above), who stressed that, in order to save the unity of Somaliland in 1991, one had to start 'on a clean page' – as 'brothers' – the perspective of victims would probably have been different.

For many years, peace and stability (Somali: *nabad iyo degenaansho*) was, in fact, the first priority, particularly in view of the escalating violence in southern Somalia, where the civil war only started in 1991 and is still ongoing as of 2020. But the longer the people in Somaliland enjoyed peace and stability, the more they questioned the 'let's-forgive-and-keep-silent-attitude' that had informed the first transition from war to peace in their region. Still, the government was not yet ready to 're-open the books', as the actions of the late President Maxamed Xaaji Ibraahim Cigaal indicated. From around 2000 onwards, his government focused on democratization, and on creating a new constitution that provided for the introduction of a multi-party system.[60] The hope many related to this was that a peaceful and democratic Somaliland would gain international support and recognition. The victims of the past dictatorship did not yet feature as part of this project.

Legal proceedings against general Maxamed Cali Samatar

The first legal steps to hold individual perpetrators of past human rights violations in Northwestern Somalia accountable were taken abroad by Somali diaspora actors in the US. According to Kathy Roberts, then a staff attorney with the Centre for Justice and Accountability (CJA) in San Francisco that supported the Somali plaintiffs in that case, the investigations against General Maxamed Cali Samatar had already begun around 1999. General Samatar was minister of defence and the first vice-president of Somalia between 1980 and 1986. From 1987 to 1990 he was Somali prime minister and a close ally of President Barre. After the fall of the Somali government, Maxamed Siyaad Barre fled to Nigeria, where he died in exile in 1995. Maxamed Cali Samatar, his second-in-command at the end, first fled to Italy and then, in 1997, to the US. Many Somalilanders held him personally accountable for the harsh military campaigns in Northwestern

Somalia throughout the 1980s. In an interview that General Samatar gave to the BBC Somali Service in London in 1989 (which had to be reconstructed in a complicated process supported by the CJA for it to be submitted to the court as evidence around two decades later), he mentioned that he had ordered the Somali army stationed in the north to crack down on the 'terrorists' in the cities of Hargeysa and Burco in June 1988.[61] The investigations were triggered by Baashe Yusuf, a US citizen of Somali origin, who had personally experienced torture at the hands of Somali soldiers and, after conviction in 'a sham trial of belonging to an anti-government organization', was held for seven years in solitary confinement, until he was released upon pressure by international human rights activists in 1989.[62] The CJA prepared the case. A scholar working with the CJA conducted online research, contacted human rights NGOs in Somaliland, and finally, in 2004, visited Somaliland to collect information. The CJA also cooperated with the War Crimes Investigation Commission in Hargeysa.[63]

By the time General Samatar's case was opened before a district court in Virginia, USA, in 2004, the number of plaintiffs who had been tortured, imprisoned, and injured by Somali soldiers in the north had risen to four. The case followed civil proceedings. Its legal basis was the Torture Victim Protection Act and the Alien Tort Claims Act.[64] There was no legal basis for a criminal prosecution in the US.[65] In 2007, General Samatar successfully moved to dismiss the case on immunity grounds under the Foreign Sovereign Immunities Act. This decision was appealed, and finally, in June 2010, the US Supreme Court affirmed that individual foreign government officials did not fall within the scope of the immunity granted under this Act. The case proceeded, and after the last motion to stay the proceedings had failed, General Samatar filed for bankruptcy on 19 February 2012. On 23 February, General Samatar 'appeared in court to enter his default, conceding both liability and damages', thereby admitting responsibility for the military actions against civilians in Northwestern Somalia in the 1980s.[66] Nonetheless, when speaking to the BBC Somali service after the trial, Maxamed Cali Samatar insisted that he personally had not committed any crime. But the CJA simultaneously released an enthusiastic statement:

> On February 23, 2012, after aggressively defending the case for more than seven years, litigating it to the U.S. Supreme Court and back, General [Samatar] appeared in a federal court in Virginia and did something that no high ranking person from the former military dictatorship of Siad [sic!] Barre has ever done – he accepted liability for torture, extrajudicial killing, crimes against humanity, war crimes, and other human rights abuses committed against the civilian population of Somalia during the 1980s. This is the first time that anyone has been held to account anywhere in the world for atrocities committed by General Samatar and the military dictatorship that ruled Somalia for over 20 years.[67]

During fieldwork in Eastlight, Nairobi, and Somaliland in February and March 2012, Hoehne could get some reactions to the decision in the case that was widely broadcasted in Somali media. Most Somalis interviewed in Eastlight were from southern Somalia. They found that the case against Maxamed Cali Samatar divided Somalis at a time when political unity was needed to cope with the manifold problems of (southern) Somalia, including militant Islamism, piracy, and humanitarian catastrophe. They accused the plaintiffs (all of whom were Isaaq) of moving against General Samatar, who belonged to a so-called minority group called Tumaal, on account of his 'inferior' origin. They argued that members of all Somali clans had committed atrocities in the past and that one should forgive and forget.

The reactions Hoehne subsequently gathered in Somaliland were more diverse. Some argued that Maxamed Cali Samatar was responsible for the human rights violations in the north in the 1980s. Maxamed Hadraawi, a famous poet who had personally opposed the Barre regime and had been imprisoned for many years, emphasized the need for General Samatar 'to be brought before court. He should be brought to justice and punished, if one can find something against him; . . . he was in fact in charge of what happened here [in north-western Somalia]'.[68] Others were more nuanced in their appraisal of the Samatar case. Prof Cabdisalaam Yasiin Maxamed, who had been one of the founders of the SNM and an active SNM fighter throughout the 1980s, stressed that 'if one can prove a case [like the one against General Samatar] it is good. But otherwise, one should just leave the issue [past crimes] be, and concentrate on something more productive, such as bringing about development for the ordinary people [in Somaliland]'.[69] This means that it was the right step to bring General Samatar before court. But instead of spending much time and resources on pursuing the perpetrators of the past, one should, according to Prof Cabdisalaam Yasiin Maxamed, rather focus on the problems of the present, including poverty and high unemployment, in order to safeguard the future of Somaliland. An Isaaq businessman from Ceerigaabo mentioned: 'It is not good to just bring Maxamed Cali Samatar before court. All the [former] criminals have to be persecuted'.[70] Finally, a woman, who had experienced the bombardment of Burco in 1988 as a young mother and had fled the town with her small children, argued:

> It was not only Maxamed Cali Samatar. There was also General Morgan, who was much worse than General Samatar.[71] . . . Samatar is an old man, he is sick, he is from a small group [minority group]. Even so he committed horrible crimes against people here I would like to forgive him.[72]

Particularly in the last statement, the interlocutor indicated that it was good for Muslims to forgive and have mercy.[73] Her feeling that it was 'unfair' to prosecute a sick old man from a minority group was in fact shared by a great number of Somalis, who voiced their opinion about the Samatar case in various online forums right after the sentence was issued in 2012. This debate shows the contested nature of any attempt to deal with the past human rights violations in Somali territories. It also shows the potential for politicization of the matter along clan lines or other forms of sub-national identities. In the statements previously mentioned, the contours of competing normative spaces become visible. While the Somali refugees in Nairobi prioritized peace over justice, the inhabitants of a stable Somaliland exhibited more complex thoughts about justice, between forgiving and systematic legal persecution. The diasporic actors and their aides driving the case against General Samatar operated in a normative space constituted largely by 'Western' ideas of justice. All of these spaces overlapped to some degree, given a shared history of violence and partly shared cultural traits (including Islamic normativity).

Exhumation of mass graves and the issue of 'Genocide'

The Samatar-case played a role in bringing forensic experts to Somaliland. The contact between *Equipo Peruano de Antropología Forense* (EPAF), a Peruvian NGO specialist in forensic anthropology, and officials in Somaliland was made through a diasporic Somali from Somaliland, Cabdiasiis Maxamed Ciid, who resided in the US. Cabdiasiis belonged to a well-known family from Hargeysa, and several of his family members had been disappeared or executed by the Somali army in the 1980s. He was one of the plaintiffs in the Samatar case representing his sister who could not come to the US. In 2010, he was present at a ceremony in San Francisco when Jose Pablo Baraybar, the (then) leading forensic expert of EPAF was awarded a price by the CJA for his work achievements.[74] Subsequently, Cabdiasiis facilitated a first visit of the Peruvian forensic anthropologist to Hargeysa.

In early 2012, EPAF signed a memorandum of understanding with several Somaliland ministries, among them the Ministry of Justice, the Ministry for Religious Affairs and the Ministry of the Interior. The War Crimes Investigation Commission in Hargeysa was also part of the agreement. It was tasked with facilitating the work of EPAF on the ground. Additionally, its staff was supposed to receive training from the EPAF specialists and eventually be able to carry out exhumations in the future. The agreement between EPAF and various partners in Somaliland included a series of exhumations over a period of five years. The remains found in the mass graves should be documented and – if possible – the living relatives of the victims should be identified to 'reconnect' with their loved ones before the bones were to be reburied according to Islamic provisions. The latter point was stressed by the minister for religious affairs, who referred to a passage in the Qur'an and a ḥadīṯ, according to which it was allowed to exhume and rebury bodies if it was clear that they had not been properly buried.[75]

EPAF choose the format of a 'field school' that was open to participants around the globe who were interested in gaining practical experience in exhumation and were also interested in the Somaliland case. The participants had to pay a considerable course fee (around US $4,000, not including travel costs). The CJA played a sponsoring role. At least from 2015 onwards, the Somaliland government has been supporting the field school on opening mass graves with reduced room prices in a government-owned hotel in Hargeysa, where the forensic team was accommodated. Before that, EPAF tried to finance everything based on participants' fees, which did not prove successful. Also, local transport and security arrangements were made by the authorities. Besides international students, some staff of the War Crimes Investigation Commission and local students from the University of Hargeysa attended the training.

The first field course took place in September and October 2012. CJA opened an internet blog accompanying the 'international forensic training program'. The course was presented as fact-finding and forensic investigation of human rights violations in Somaliland that would allow access to truth and justice for the families of the victims.[76] During this first course, when two mass graves in Hargeysa were opened, 49 skeletal remains were recovered, and the bones were stored with the government.[77] EPAF was highly pleased with this initial work.[78] The second course, after several postponements, took place in February 2014, and its task was to undertake further documentation of the bones and, if possible, the identification of the exhumed bodies.

The reactions to the initiative inside Somaliland were mixed, according to interviews Hoehne conducted in 2012 and 2013. As mentioned earlier, peace in Somaliland was forged in the 1990s without accounting for massacres or atrocities and without dealing with the massive human rights violations against civilians in Northwestern Somalia in the hands of the government. This 'chosen amnesia'[79] facilitated the cooperation of the non-Isaaq groups in the region in rebuilding peace and political order. The opening of the mass graves via EPAF was about to change this 'pact of silence'. Dr Aaden Aboqor, an Isaaq intellectual and prominent medical doctor, who had been arrested by the Somali government for 'anti-regime' activities and held in solitary confinement for many years in the 1980s, mentioned that it worried him that the EPAF initiative had not been properly discussed or at least announced to the public in Somaliland in 2012. The media had not covered the issue in any depth and the government had refrained from presenting a public plan of dealing with the past. The initiative of EPAF looked to Dr Aaden Aboqor almost like a 'private project' of Cabdiasiis Maxamed Ciid who had brought the Peruvian NGO into the country. Dr Aaden Aboqor also mentioned that he had spoken to friends of non-Isaaq clans and they had reacted quite sensitively to the project of opening the mass graves. They asked themselves what the 'real' agenda behind the initiative was. In the doctor's view, the initiative had the potential of disturbing peace in Somaliland.[80]

Maxamuud Cismaciil Xiis, who had fought with the SNM throughout the 1980s, confirmed that the EPAF initiative might cause problems in eastern and western Somaliland, where non-Isaaq descent groups resided. Maxamuud mentioned several massacres conducted in the Sanaag region in eastern Somaliland and argued that

> if one starts opening the mass graves in Hargeysa and surroundings, one has to open all graves in the country. This will cause tensions, since such an operation will lead to the question: 'Who was responsible for this and that massacre?' Those responsible are partly still alive and reside in Somaliland. It also will cause others to voice their grievances louder.[81]

He added that most people were not ready to open the graves. In his view, the EPAF initiative was not driven from within the country but from the outside, and it was potentially destructive: 'If one wants to destroy Somaliland then one needs only to start opening the mass graves'.[82]

Members of the government, such as the Minister of Justice (who had served as chairman of the War Crimes Investigation Commission before) or the Minister for Religious Affairs represented a different perspective. This perspective reflected to some degree the 'official' Somaliland position on the matter, but was also influenced by personal convictions of the interlocutors. Xuseen Caydiid, the then Minister of Justice (until 2015), argued that it was appropriate to open the mass graves and to return the dignity to those who have been killed in an undignified way. The bones needed to be buried in a proper Islamic way, after they had been – if possible – identified. A DNA analysis would be good, but – in the case of Somaliland – this was too expensive, as the minister stressed.[83] The minister assured that the mass graves needed to be investigated everywhere in the country, and not just in Hargeysa and its surroundings. The purpose of the project, according to Xuseen Caydiid, was not to cause problems for ordinary individuals from non-Isaaq groups, e.g. the Dhulbahante or the Gadabuursi, but to bring to justice the main perpetrators who had served in higher government positions.[84] The then Minister for Religious Affairs, Khalil Cabdilaahi Axmed, stressed that it was in accordance with Islamic rules to open a grave and rebury the remnants if the original burial was not conducted in a proper Islamic way.[85]

Khadar Axmed, the current chairman of the War Crimes Investigation Office stressed that most people in Hargeysa appreciated the EPAF initiative. He added that the data collected through forensic investigations should inform court cases in Somaliland or abroad against the perpetrators.[86] In general, those welcoming the EAPF initiative stressed that it would establish 'facts' and a clear memory that would help to, first, not repeat past violations of basic human rights and, second, support Somaliland's claim to international recognition.

The issue of recognition – connected to the issue of 'genocide' – featured directly and prominently in an interview of the then foreign minister of Somaliland, Maxamed Bixi Yoonis, with CNN in February 2014, which carried the heading '[o]n recognition, terrorism and the 1980's genocide'.[87] In this interview, the minister rehearsed the well-established arguments as to why Somaliland deserved recognition, stressing the goals of peacebuilding, and democratization. In this context, 'genocide' was used as a very important but rather recent addition:

CNN: Why it is that you feel it's so important for Somaliland to be recognized as sovereignty state? What exactly will this do for the people of Somaliland?

MR BIXI: . . . We have done all the requirement that is needed to become a democratic state and I think it is important for the world to recognize Somaliland because we could contribute a lot in terms of issues related to security, to piracy to terrorisms and Somaliland has done well over the years and proofed to be worthwhile nation that can contribute to the development of the continent and that of the region.

After a question related to piracy, the reporter asked about 'genocide'. The minister had just come from a meeting with representatives of the current Somali government in Istanbul, in a dialogue between Mogadishu and Hargeysa facilitated by Turkey, which, however, had not gone beyond mutual assurances that one needed 'to talk':

CNN: I do want to ask you about the reports of genocide in Somaliland from back in the 80s, and the claims that some 200,000 people were massacred in clan based attacks at the behest of the former dictator. What's been done to try to uncover the truth and to try to punish those responsible, I imagine that many of the people responsible are still walking free?

MR BIXI: The first time we had the talks now a months ago in Istanbul, the Somalia government has acknowledged and accepted the fact that there were atrocity and genocide against the people of Somaliland and they have accepted in writing during the talks of last month that the regime of Siyaad Barre has committed crimes against humanity, there was genocide and we do hope one of these days those who have committed those crimes will be brought to justice.

The normative space within which the violent Somali past was negotiated had widened again. It now not only involved local and diasporic actors but also international forensic specialists, lawyers, and a potentially global audience provided by media outlets such as CNN.

Conclusion

The debate about the past violence in Northwestern Somalia, today's Somaliland, has proceeded in various steps from basic peace to containment, to (transnational) transitional justice. Particularly the latter aspect illustrates what has been mentioned in the introduction, namely that normative spaces for dealing with the past reach far beyond local and 'ethno-cultural' settings. At least for some actors, these proceedings entailed a development from silencing to voicing. As was to be expected, voicing involved gaining the power to interpret the past. While this is typical for societies coming out of 'dictatorship' or civil war, the particularity of the Somaliland case is that the debate about human rights and past atrocities is related to the question of political recognition. In this way, the debate about how to deal with the past touches on personal and national matters at the same time. Those who have been harmed personally or whose relatives and/or loved ones have been killed or are missing may have made their 'peace' with the past, often in accordance with Islamic provisions about forgiving and/or leaving the final judgement to Allah. Many ordinary people in Somaliland are more concerned about daily survival than about legal proceedings against members of the former Somali regime. Influential human rights activists like Cabdiasiis Maxamed Ciid, on the other hand, frequently have a background in the diaspora, are well off and internationally connected. They recently began to change the discourse about

Somaliland's violent past, and the scope of engagement with it by introducing a legal element, which became evident in the proceedings against General Samatar. This engagement also created the opportunity to connect with forensic experts from abroad, in this case, from Peru, and to invite them to introduce their technologies of approaching the 'truth' about past crimes and human rights violations in Somaliland. The assumed power of 'scientific proof' by forensic experts connects the exhumations of mass graves and the analysis of the human remains to the still pending political recognition of Somaliland. The political elites of the de facto state, and many Somaliland supporters hoped that peace and democratization, which have been achieved since the early 1990s, would bring about recognition. Since this has not been the case, it seems that politicians of Somaliland saw a chance related to the forensic interventions in Somaliland to forge a moral argument about 1980s 'genocide' in Northwestern Somalia. This line of argument has found the support among human rights activists and some international lawyers.[88] Indeed, at least in legal theory, massive human rights violations would add weight to a group's claim for independence from a 'parent'-state that violated their rights. Schoiswohl found that the deprivation of internal self-determination and violations of fundamental human rights could constitute a justification for secession – particularly in the case of genocide.[89] EPAF's work in Somaliland is vital in this regard.

The instrumentality of forensic work is not only related to the definition, recollection, and production of a legitimate institutional knowledge about the violent past of a 'nation' but, furthermore, to the establishment of the 'parameters of reference' that would indicate what is made relevant for future readings and understanding of *what happened*.[90] Investigative or war crimes commissions reinterpret the past based on a pre-established interpretative matrix that guides the investigations, which includes data obtained through forensic interpretations and methodologies. The violent past is then re-enacted and actualized from a realm of memory and subjectivity – in the accounts of victims – to the realm of history and objectivity – as for example established in forensic reports.[91] Currently, this is exactly what is happening in Somaliland.

Given the history of past violence in Somaliland, accounts of what happened and who was responsible are contested. Therefore, the recent endeavours to investigate legally and scientifically into the past (in the case against General Samatar in the US and in the context of EPAF's forensic intervention in the country) has led to controversial debates. One can observe the intermixing of opposing political positions based on different political identities, including different interpretations of the past, which is frequently connected to clan chauvinism and what Liban has called 'clannish nationalism'.[92] This concept refers to the loyalty many people have 'to a clan's idealized view of a Somali polity. . . . Clannish nationalism is [an] exclusionary, *victimhood-based* [emphasis added] response to challenges to revive the Somali nation-state'.[93] This connects with what Ferrándiz calls 'the politics of victimhood', that are related to forensic investigations in general.[94] It also connects with the notion of forensic fetishism in the sense that different sides involved in (re-)interpreting the past lay claim to an 'objective' truth produced using the tools of scientific analysis on human remains. In the case of Somaliland, the political elite and some (transnational) human rights activists seek preferential access to the technologies of 'truth' to advance the case of the country's political recognition. EPAF, of course, is interested in opening up new fields of work and in popularizing its approach to forensic anthropology (in 'southern' countries), and this can be done in Somaliland, given its peace and stability and the support of the government, all of which facilitates running an international 'field school' there (whose participants' fees partly finance EPAF's work elsewhere). Such a welcoming attitude of the government towards forensic work is quite rare; in most other post-conflict settings, governments view forensic interventions with suspicion or only accord very limited space to them.

These different engagements with past atrocities in northern Somalia happen within different but increasingly overlapping normative spaces populated by local and international actors and their various orientations. What interested us, particularly in this chapter, and with regard to the most recent phase of these engagements involving the intervention by forensic experts, was how seemingly neutral scientific technologies, expressed by the concept of forensic fetishism, are embedded in a contested political field. Bones are administered, interpreted and mediated by scientific and semantic 'translations' in a way that is not just about how the dead are presented as factual evidence, for it also concerns the modalities through which they serve as evidence both of and for something.[95] Relating these insights to the ongoing EPAF initiative in Somaliland, one realizes that there is not just one past, but, rather, that many 'troubled pasts' are yet to be uncovered.

Notes

1 E Domanska, 'Toward the Archaeontology of the Dead Body' (2005) 9 (4) *Rethinking History* 389–413, 403.
2 R Gersony, 'Why Somalis Flee: A Synthesis of Conflict Experience in Northern Somalia by Somali Refugees, Displaced Persons, and Others' (1990) 2 (4) *International Journal of Refugee Law* 4–55.
3 Africa Watch, *Somalia: A Government at War with Its Own People. Testimonies About Killings and the Conflict in the North* (New York Africa Watch 1990).
4 Cabdiasis Maxamed Ciid (2014), in an EPAF video available at <www.youtube.com/watch?v=Xb7k6FfqjaI> (minute 1:22–1:24) accessed 16 November 2018.
5 CNN, '17 February 2014: Interview with Mohamed Yonis Bihi, Somaliland's Foreign Minister' available at <www.youtube.com/watch?v=fgIwZv-Jyuw> (minute 3:02–3:47) accessed 16 November 2018; Diplomat Tv, '25 May 2017: Interview with Somaliland Foreign Minister Sa'ad Ali Shire: Why Somaliland Broke from Somalia, Its State Building and Struggle for Recognition' available at <www.youtube.com/watch?v=5C50SCU-jAA> (minute 3:49–3:59) accessed 16 November 2018.
6 MH Ingiriis, 'We Swallowed the State, and the State Swallowed Us: The Genesis, Genealogies, and Geographies of Genocides in Somalia' (2016) 9 (3) *African Security* 237–258, 247.
7 S Pegg, *International Society and the De Facto State* (Aldershot Ashgate 1998).
8 Somali special terms, place and personal names in this text follow the Somali orthography (with the exception of 'Mogadishu' [Somali: Muqdisho], which is

so well established in English orthography) and names of Somali authors who themselves use an English transliteration. In Somali, the Latin 'c' stands for a sound close to the Arabic 'ع' (ayn); 'x' denotes 'ح' (ḥa), as in, e.g. Laascaanood or in Faarax.

9 E Weizman, *The Least of All Possible Evils: Humanitarian Violence from Arendt to Gaza* (London Verso 2011) 128.
10 Weizman (n 9) 104.
11 L Renshaw, *Exhuming Loss: Memory, Materiality and Mass Graves of the Spanish Civil War* (Walnut Creek Left Coast Press 2011) 126.
12 Renshaw (n 11) 126.
13 Renshaw (n 11) 151.
14 Weizman (n 9) 128.
15 Weizman (n 9) 128.
16 M Bunzl and GH Penny, 'Introduction: Rethinking German Anthropology, Colonialism and Race' in HG Penny and M Bunzl (eds), *Worldly Provincialism: German Anthropology in the Age of Empire* (Ann Arbor The University of Michigan Press 2003) 1–30; A Zimmermann, 'Adventures in the Skin Trade: German Anthropology and Colonial Corporeality' in GH Penny and M Bunzl (eds), *Wordly Provincialism: German Anthropology in the Age of Empire* (Ann Arbor University of Michigan Press 2003) 156–178.
17 S Sheikh, 'Forensic Theatre: Grupa Spomenik's Pythagorean Lecture: Mathemes of Re-Association' in E Weizman (ed), *Forensis: The Architecture of Public Truth* (Berlin Sternberg 2014) 166–188, 167.
18 Sheikh (n 17) 170 f.
19 F Stepputat, 'Elevating Bodies: The Management of Death Between War and Peace' unpublished manuscript, n. p.; see also R Hertz, *Death and the Right Hand* (London Routledge 2004 [1960]) for a 'classic' perspective on the temporal and transitory aspects of death and death-related rituals.
20 Renshaw (n 11) 145.
21 K Verdery, *The Political Lives of Dead Bodies* (New York Columbia University Press 1999).
22 F Ferrándiz, 'The Return of Civil War Ghosts: The Ethnography of Exhumations in Contemporary Spain' (2006) 22 (3) *Anthropology Today* 7–12, 7.
23 G Pereira, 'Dead Commodities' (2011) 43 *Cabinet: A Quarterly of Art and Culture* 90–94, 94.
24 Cited in C Joyce and E Stover, *Witness from the Grave: The Science of Identifying Human Remains* (London Bloomsbury 1991) 268.
25 Pereira (n 23) 94.
26 E Klinenberg, 'Bodies That Don't Matter: Death and Dereliction in Chicago' (2001) 7 (2–3) *Body and Society* 121–136, 122.
27 Klinenberg (n 26) 132.
28 C Krmpotich, J Fontein, and J Harries, 'The Substance of Bones: The Emotive Materiality and Affective Presence of Human Remains' (2010) 15 (4) *Journal of Material Culture* 371–384, 372.
29 M Weiss, 'The Immigrating Body and the Body Politic: The "Yemenite Children Affair" and Body Commodification in Israel' in N Scheper-Huges and L Wacquant (eds), *Commodifying Bodies* (London Sage 2002) 93–110, 95.
30 I Paperno, 'Exhuming the Bodies of Soviet Terror' (2001) 75 (1) *Representations* 89–118, 105.
31 Z Crossland, 'Buried Lives' (2000) 7 (2) *Archaeological Dialogues* 146–159, 156.
32 K Hetherington, 'In the Place of Geometry: The Materiality of Place' in K Hetherington and R Munro (eds), *Ideas of Difference: Social Spaces and the Labour of Division* (Oxford Blackwell 1997) 183–199, 187.

33 Krmpotich, Fontein, and Harries (n 28) 375.
34 See MH Ingiriis 'Many Somalia[s], Multiple Memories: Remembrances as Present Politics, Past Politics as Remembrances in War-Torn Somali Discourses' (2016) 14 (4) *African Identities* 348–369, on the multiplicity of competing memories and narratives of suffering going back to the more recent history of violence in Somalia.
35 IM Lewis, *Blood and Bone: The Call of Kinship in Somali Society* (Lawrenceville Red Sea Press 1994) 165; H Elliesie, 'Statehood and Constitution-Building in Somalia: Islamic Responses to a Failed State' in R Grote and TJ Röder (eds), *Constitutionalism in Islamic Countries Between Upheaval and Continuity* (Oxford Oxford University Press 2012) 553–581, 558.
36 Lewis (n 35) 184–198; Elliesie (n 35) 563.
37 Gersony (n 2) 49.
38 IM Lewis, 'The Ogaden and the Fragility of Somali Segmentary Nationalism' (1990) XIII (1–2) *Horn of Africa* 55–61, 58.
39 D Compagnon, 'The Somali Opposition Fronts: Some Comments and Questions' (1990) 13 (1–2) *Horn of Africa* 29–54, 33.
40 M Bradbury, *Becoming Somaliland* (Oxford James Currey 2008) 60.
41 MV Hoehne, *Traditional Authorities in Northern Somalia: Transformation of Powers and Positions. Working Paper Nr 82* (Halle Saale Max Planck Institute for Social Anthropology 2006).
42 Interviews in Hargeysa, Ceerigaabo, and Laascaanood (September 2003 to November 2004).
43 AY Farah and IM Lewis, *Somalia: The Roots of Reconciliation. Peace Making Endeavors of Contemporary Lineage Elders. A Survey of Grassroots Peace Conferences in 'Somaliland'* (London Action Aid 1993).
44 IM Lewis, *A Pastoral Democracy: A Study of Pastoralism and Politics Among the Northern Somali of the Horn of Africa* (Oxford Oxford University Press 1961) 167.
45 MV Hoehne, *Political Orientations and Repertoires of Identification: State and Identity Formation in Northern Somalia* (PhD Dissertation, Martin-Luther Universität Halle-Wittenberg 2011) 100 f; G Schlee, 'Customary Law and the Joys of Statelessness: Idealized Traditions versus Somali Realities' (2013) 7 (2) *Journal of Eastern African Studies* 258–271; G Schlee and B Turner, 'Einleitung: Wirkungskontexte des Vergeltungsprinzips in der Konfliktregulierung' in G Schlee and B Turner (eds), *Vergeltung: Eine interdisziplinäre Betrachtung der Rechtfertigung und Regulation von Gewalt* (Frankfurt am Main Campus) 7–47.
46 Farah and Lewis (n 43) 57 f.
47 Farah and Lewis (n 43) 58. The harsh rulings according to *shari'a* were temporarily limited. During Hoehne's field research (2002–2018) he came across many cases of homicide and other matters in which the traditional compensation payments were negotiated. Also revenge killings were not uncommon – without endangering the regional peace as a whole.
48 Adam Haji Ali Ahmed, 'Politics of Transitional Justice Mechanisms from Below: The Case of Somaliland' (2010) *Peace & Conflict Monitor* available at <www.monitor.upeace.org/innerpg.cfm?id_article=732> accessed 16 November 2018.
49 RG Teitel, 'Transitional Justice Genealogy' (2003) 16 *Harvard Human Rights Journal* 69–94; UN, *The Rule of Law and Transitional Justice in Conflict and Post-Conflict Societies: Report of the Secretary General* (UN/S/2004/616).
50 See also ICRC, *Spared from the Spear: Traditional Somali Behaviour in Warfare* (Nairobi ICRC 1998).
51 MH Ingiriis and MV Hoehne, 'The Impact of Civil War and State Collapse on the Roles of Somali Women: A Blessing in Disguise' (2013) 7 (2) *Journal of Eastern African Studies* 314–333.

52 Report of a mission to conduct an on-site assessment of alleged mass graves in the vicinity of Hargeysa, Somalia (1997).
53 Adam (n 48).
54 IRIN, 'Interview with Muhammad Ibrahim Egal, President of Somaliland' (2001) available at <www.irinnews.org/q-and/2001/05/28/irin-interview-muhammad-ibrahim-egal-president-somaliland> accessed 19 November 2018.
55 In Spain, after General Franco's death in 1975, left- and right-wing parties agreed on the pact of forgetting (Spanish: *el pacto del olvido*) to avoid dealing with the legacy of Francoism. In Somaliland, we argue, it was not about 'forgetting' (which hardly can be agreed upon) but about remaining silent (which is based on a conscious decision and includes remembering).
56 Interview with Khadar and Xuseen Caydiid, Hargeysa (18 August 2002).
57 Interview with Xuseen Caydiid, Hargeysa (17 February 2009).
58 Adam (n 48).
59 Adam (n 48).
60 K Seidel, 'Involvement and Impact of External Actors on Constitution Making in South Sudan and Somaliland: A Comparative Study' (2017) 18 *Käte Hamburger Kolleg/Centre for Global Cooperation Research: Global Cooperation Research Papers* 26–29.
61 'General Ali Samatar Admits War Crime in Hargeisa City in 1991 in Interview with BBC' *YouTube* available at <www.youtube.com/watch?v=bBEMpooEVJw> accessed 19 November 2018.
62 CJA, 'Somalia: Siad Barre Regime' (2018) available at <https://cja.org/wp-content/uploads/2018/05/CJA-20th_anniversary-FINAL-1.pdf> accessed 19 November 2018.
63 Interview Kathy Roberts, Halle (2013).
64 CJA (n 62).
65 Interview Kathy Roberts, Halle (2013).
66 K Roberts, 'Yousuf v. Samantar: The Long Road to Justice' (2013) 53 (Spring) *Journal of the Anglo-Somali Society* 23–30, 27.
67 <https://law.stanford.edu/event/yousuf-v-samantar-defending-human-rights-through-extraterritorial-litigation-room-90> accessed 19 November 2018. See also the summary of the case by Pamela Merchant, former Executive Director of CJA, in *The WorldPost* (a part of Huffington Post) available at <www.huffingtonpost.com/pamela-merchant/general-samantar-trial_b_1305733.html> accessed 19 November 2018.
68 Interview with Maxamed Ibraahim Warsaame Hadraawi, Burco (21 March 2012).
69 Interview with Cabdisalaam Yasiin Maxamed, Hargeysa (15 March 2012) [italics added].
70 Interview with Jaamac Cabdi Shire, Ceerigaabo (26 March 2012).
71 General Maxamed Siciid Xirsi Morgan is Majeerteen/Cabdiraxiin. He was military commander over the northwest in the mid-1980s and was given the nickname 'butcher of Hargeysa' by locals after 1988.
72 Interview with Faarax Axmed Daahir, Burco (22 March 2011).
73 Cf., among others, Qur'ān Sura 21 (al-Anbiyā'), Verse 107: وَمَا أَرْسَلْنَاكَ إِلَّا رَحْمَةً لِّلْعَالَمِينَ.
74 Interview Kathy Roberts, Halle (2013).
75 Interview with Khalil Cabdilaahi Axmed, Hargeysa (9 March 2013).
76 See the online presentation of CJA about their Somaliland engagement <https://cja.org/what-we-do/transitional-justice-initiatives/somaliland/?list=type&type=512> accessed 19 November 2018.
77 Interview with Xuseen Caydiid, Minister of Justice of Somaliland, Hargeysa (17 December 2012).

78 Skype interview of Shakira Bedoya with EPAF staff (13 January 2013).
79 S Buckley-Zistel, 'Remembering to Forget: Chosen Amnesia as a Strategy for Local Coexistence in Post-Genocide Rwanda' (2006) 76 (2) *Africa* 131–150.
80 Interview with Dr Aaden Aboqor, Hargeysa (15 December 2012).
81 Interview with Maxamuud Cismaciil Xiis, Ceerigaabo (2 March 2013).
82 Interview with Maxamuud Cismaciil Xiis, Ceerigaabo (2 March 2013).
83 EPAF specialist told Hoehne during an interview in Hargeysa in March 2018 that the DNA test of a bone sample costs between US $500 and 1,200, depending on how many samples are to be tested (price per sample decreases as the number samples increases). Additionally, saliva of possible relatives has to be collected in the field and tested in the laboratory to create a 'reference sample' to which the bone samples can be compared. The saliva testing costs between US $75 and 250 (again, more samples lower the price per sample). This means that a complete DNA test costs between US $575 and 1,450 per body, or in average around US $ 1,000.
84 Interview with Xuseen Caydiid, Hargeysa (17 December 2012).
85 Interview with Khalil Cabdilaahi Axmed, Hargeysa (9 March 2013).
86 Interview with Khadar Axmed, Hargeysa (9 March 2013).
87 CNN, '17 February 2014: Interview with Mohamed Yonis Bihi, Somaliland's Foreign Minister' available at <www.youtube.com/watch?v=fgIwZv-Jyuw> accessed 19 November 2018.
88 Besides CJA and EPAF, a group called 'Combat Genocide' has shown an interest in the case of Somaliland; see <http://combatgenocide.org/?page_id=150> accessed 19 November 2018.
89 M Schoiswohl, *Status and (Human Rights) Obligations of Non-Recognized De Facto Regimes in International Law: The Case of Somaliland* (Leiden, Boston Martinus Nijhoff 2004) 74.
90 AC Cuéllar, 'La Globalización Del Testimonio: Historia, Silencio Endémico Y Los Usos de La Palabra' (2007) 4 *Antípoda: Revista de Antropología Y Arqueología* 77 f.
91 AC Cuéllar, 'The Domestication of Testimony: Truth, Endemic Silence, and the Articulations of a Violent Past. Working Paper 4.2012 E' (2012) *Recht im Kontext Working Paper Series* 12.
92 Liban Ahmed, 'Clannish Nationalism in Somali Politics' available at <www.somalilandsun.com/somaliland-clannish-nationalism-in-somali-politics> accessed 19 November 2018.
93 Ahmed (n 92).
94 Ferrándiz (n 22) 7.
95 M Engelke, 'The Objects of Evidence' in M Engelke (ed), *The Objects of Evidence: Anthropological Approaches to the Production of Knowledge* (Princeton Wiley-Blackwell 2009) 1–20, 2.

2 Transitional justice atmospheres

The role of space and affect in the International Criminal Court's outreach efforts in Northern Uganda

Jonas Bens[1]

Introduction

On 6 December 2016, I travelled from Gulu, a small urban centre of Northern Uganda where I was staying, to Abok, a village about 90 minutes away from there. From the late 1990s until a little over ten years ago, Abok had been the location of a camp for internally displaced persons (IDPs). In the early 2000s, during the height of the war in Northern Uganda, about 1.5 million people, nearly 90% of Northern Uganda's population, were forced to live in such IDP camps, where the living conditions were highly precarious. The camps were poorly defended by the Ugandan army and regularly looted by the Lord's Resistance Army (LRA). The LRA rebels under the leadership of Joseph Kony fought a twenty-year guerrilla war against the Ugandan Army in an attempt to overthrow the government under President Yoweri Kaguta Museveni, who came to power in 1986.[2] The war ended about ten years ago, and, since 2007, the LRA has not been able to operate on Ugandan soil.[3]

During the height of the war, on 8 June 2004, the LRA raided the IDP-camp in Abok and massacred dozens of civilians. The fate of the man who commanded the LRA troops on that day, a former brigade commander named Dominic Ongwen, is now in the hands of the International Criminal Court (ICC) in The Hague. Over ten years ago, the Court had put out a warrant for his arrest accusing him of war crimes and crimes against humanity. Ongwen avoided arrest until the end of 2014 when he was captured under somewhat unclear circumstances by Séléka rebels[4] in the Central African Republic.[5] He was finally delivered to the ICC in the beginning of 2015. In January 2016, I attended the confirmation of charges hearing against Ongwen in The Hague to conduct courtroom ethnography.[6] Afterwards I went to Northern Uganda to conduct ethnographic fieldwork specifically at those massacre sites relevant to the case. My goal was to come to terms with how people there understand these proceedings and how they assess their legitimacy.[7]

On that day in Abok, the International Criminal Court's outreach unit had planned a large two-day event to communicate to the villagers the opening of the trail against Dominic Ongwen. I had also heard that the Registrar, a high-ranking ICC official responsible for the administration of the Court, was planning to attend the Abok screening. Media representatives were also expected.

Shortly after I had arrived together with two colleagues from Northern Uganda, we could see two very large tents that had been recently put up around the administrative building, a small structure in the middle of an open field. Trucks had brought plastic chairs for about 2,500 to 3,000 visitors. People started to arrive in large numbers and after a while it became clear that the number of visitors far exceeded the seating capacity. Only two very small television screens had been installed in both tents, and we already suspected that it would be difficult for all to see what was going to be displayed on these screens. As people gathered, the mood of the place changed. It seemed to us that something was 'hanging in the air', there was a sense of excitement and anticipation.

Already these first impressions, only a few minutes after our arrival, point to the topics I explore in this chapter. Conducting an outreach event means, first and foremost, to create a spatial arrangement. To do that, humans (villagers and ICC employees, for instance) and non-humans (things such as television sets and plastic chairs, for instance) have to be assembled at one place. The way in which this spatial arrangement is engineered has consequences for the mood that enfolds in the event and for the general atmosphere. It is exactly this role of space and affect in conducting transitional justice events that I flesh out in this chapter. I claim that the ICC's outreach efforts strive to create what I call *transitional justice atmospheres* which are supposed to influence people's sense of justice in relation to the past violence and their demands for a just future.

The International Criminal Court and transitional justice in Northern Uganda

The International Criminal Court tries individuals for committing mass scale atrocities in military conflicts. Such international criminal trials are practically always embedded in larger transitional justice projects.[8] Transitional justice describes the processes and practices that facilitate a coming to terms with past mass violence in a society, usually following regime change. Transitional justice measures often include not only criminal prosecution of those individual actors most responsible for the mass violence, but also truth and reconciliation commissions, institutional reforms – be that relating to the security sector or the administrative and political branches of government – and other non-judicial measures.[9]

A major focus of the literature on transitional justice is on the question of effective measures for facilitating a democratic transition and bringing about justice after mass violence.[10] Anthropological approaches to transitional justice have more specifically sought 'to explore the local justice dynamic by considering what justice means and how it is negotiated in different localities where transitional justice efforts are under way (or related rhetorics and processes are in play) after genocide and mass atrocity'.[11] I situate the ethnographic study on which this chapter is based within an anthropology of transitional justice.

In the last years, the International Criminal Court's legal interventions in Africa have caused significant controversy. At the heart of this controversy is the ICC's 'Africa problem',[12] namely that the Court has so far only managed to prosecute Africans for international crimes.[13] African politicians and academics alike have painted the Court as a neo-colonial institution, a discussion that has been openly led at the forum of the African Union. Although most Member States of the African Union had been in favour of the establishment of the International Criminal Court initially, winds shifted when the ICC put out an arrest warrant for ʿUmar Ḥasan Aḥmad al-Bašīr, the sitting president of Sudan.[14] Since then the African Union has criticized the indictment practice of the ICC in several decisions and resolutions,[15] and has started a process to establish an international criminal chamber with the African Court of Justice and Human rights.[16]

The ICC's engagement in Northern Uganda has proven similarly controversial, although not always along the lines of the macro-discourse on neo-colonialism. Some have celebrated the Court's intervention as an important transitional justice measure,[17] others have criticized the ICC's criminal justice approach as counterproductive.[18] Especially in the beginning, the ICC was seen by many observers in Northern Uganda and elsewhere as a possible impediment for a peace process. Along the lines of a broader 'peace v. justice'-debate,[19] it was feared that ICC's intervention would prove to be a disincentive to the LRA leaders to enter into a peace agreement for the fear of criminal prosecution in The Hague 1 afterwards.[20] Many thought then (and still do now) that an African solution tailored to the specific challenges in Northern Uganda was needed to address the violence, instead of an internationalized one-fits-all approach of international criminal justice.[21] Even now, ten years after the conflict, at a time when most people in Northern Uganda are not afraid that the LRA violence could be reignited immediately, much scepticism of the ICC largely remains. The ongoing case against Dominik Ongwen, a former commander of the Lord's Resistance Army in Northern Uganda is no exception.[22]

Not least to strengthen its perceived legitimacy in light of these controversies, the Court conducts outreach activities in the so-called situation countries, including Northern Uganda. These efforts include organized public screenings of the trial proceedings in the regions where the violence has taken place. The ICC sees such outreach activities as part of their transitional justice mandate. That includes, in a narrow sense, allowing the victims to participate in the trial,[23] as a way to contribute to the larger goal of coming to terms with past violence and facilitating a transition from the violent past into democracy, accountability, and justice.[24] The specific temporality of international criminal law is crucial here. International criminal proceedings are slow and, typically, the proceedings take place long after the atrocities have been committed.[25] In this context, one function of the international trials at the ICC is to provide a historical record of the past abuses,[26] and outreach events play an important role in that.

Translating International Criminal Law in Northern Uganda

The International Criminal Court is an institution that works within an international criminal law framework based on the *Rome Statue of the International Criminal Court* of 1998, a multilateral international treaty. International law is, by its own description, independent of spatial demarcations.[27] Anthropologists have argued, however, that space indeed does matter in the analysis of international legal regimes, because these regimes crystalize in all kinds of localities.[28] Such places include, for example, courtrooms in The Hague, UN conference rooms in New York City, activist meetings all over the world and, in our case, trial screenings in rural Northern Uganda. These localities matter for how international law, although global in its outlet, comes into being, is maintained, challenged, and transformed.

In reference to international criminal law, Gerhard Anders has elaborated on this global-local dialectic in his ethnographic work on the Special Court for Sierra Leone.[29] He has shown that although international criminal law claims to be a universal and remote mode of justice-making independent of local concerns, it has to be instantiated in specific places at specific times and is shaped by them to a large degree. These places have a particular history and are embedded in particular power relations. In-depth ethnography is essential to clarifying the complex interplay of the inner workings of international criminal law and the (political) influences of the diverse localities in which it becomes manifest.[30]

How the local sneaks into international criminal legal law can also be observed in the ICC's intervention in Northern Uganda. In his recent article on the Dominic Ongwen case, Branch indicates a number of local political matters in Uganda that have a significant influence on the international legal proceeding.[31] It was Uganda's president Yoweri Museveni, one party to the conflict, who invited the ICC to investigate LRA crimes in December 2003.[32] Since then, the Court has been perceived by many in Northern Uganda as an instrument of the government in their conflict with the rebel forces.[33] And Branch highlights how much the Office of the Prosecutor (OTP) still depend on the Ugandan government's cooperation to make their case and secure access to evidence and witnesses.

The remoteness of the trial in The Hague has provoked some controversy in Northern Uganda regarding the appropriate location of the proceedings. Thus, one example of a broader discussion in transitional justice circles concerns the question of whether transitional justice should not be conducted in a much more localized fashion.[34] Such issues were communicated to me in numerous instances during my fieldwork in Northern Uganda.[35]

Mainly based on the work of Sally Engle Merry, anthropologists have understood the interplay of global international law and its entanglement with the local as a matter of legal translation.[36] Merry's terminology in this regard is borrowed from the realm of language. She speaks of the *vernacularization* of human rights[37] and describes the role of those intermediaries who facilitate the transposition of global international law such as human rights into local contexts (and the other way around) as the role of *translators*.[38] Merry and others have highlighted that when international law manifests in different places, it must be *translated* into the local context and that in this translation it is also, to a certain degree shaped and transformed.[39]

This also happens in Northern Uganda. The ICC Outreach team and their collaborators from local NGOs do the work of translators to make the workings of international criminal law understandable to local audiences. And indeed, many members of local massacre survivors' associations I talked to framed their claims for recognition and reparation in terms of international law and human rights. As such, the anthropological literature on legal translation provides an important entry point to understanding ICC's outreach efforts.

Successfully translating international criminal law into local contexts is crucial for the ICC, because the plural legal Northern Uganda's transitional justice landscape also provides alternative normative systems to address the atrocities of the past.[40] The ICC, as the main actor of international criminal law,[41] competes with other transitional justice forums.[42] The most relevant contenders are the Acholi legal system, which is dominated by traditional leaders and a strong system of religious moralities of forgiveness dominated by the local religious leaders. Both these normative orders claim, not unlike international criminal law, to provide an adequate normative frame for assessing justice and injustice, and for coming to terms with the past violence in a productive way. The ICC engages in legal translation work to compete against other normative alternatives, mainly using outreach events like the one I attended in Abok. In addition, the church and the traditional leaders also organize public gatherings.[43] The numerous traditional Acholi rituals and the many public prayers structuring everyday life for many people in Northern Uganda are spatialized events and similar to the ICC outreach events I describe here.

In this chapter I would therefore like to go beyond the linguistic metaphorics of translation to focus more directly on the role of space and place in a more literal sense for bringing international law into local context. In this perspective, 'the local' appears not only as an abstract space that is culturally constructed in relation to the global,[44] but also as a set of very concrete places in which not only linguistic utterances and discourses, but also the co-presence of material and immaterial bodies have an impact on how things work out. To be equipped for such an analysis, it is important to connect to a strand of scholarship that combines perspectives on law, space, and affect. The challenge is to better understand how the transnational normative spaces of an international criminal proceeding are engineered through legal micro-practices in their concrete spatial technicality and affectivity.

The spatial and affective micro-workings of legal translation

Andreas Reckwitz has argued that social scientific thinking is generally characterized by a double blind spot that is both anti-technical and anti-aesthetic.[45] In his view, 'the anti-aesthetic outlook . . . has hindered the observer . . . to grasp the full extent of the affective structuration of the social; the anti-technological perspective has blocked a full grasp of its necessary spatial structuration'.[46] Consequently, Reckwitz proposes following both the 'affective turn'[47] as well as the 'spatial turn'[48] in the study of social phenomena. I believe this approach to be fruitful also for the analysis of socio-legal phenomena.

Andreas Philippopoulos-Mihalopoulos proposes combining an analysis of space and affect by introducing the concepts of *lawscape* and *atmosphere* into the analysis of legal phenomena.[49] Philippopoulos-Mihalopoulos claims that law is always spatial. He makes a plea for thinking about the law not as something abstract that manifests in specific places, but as something that is always-already spatialized and made abstract by operations of the mind. Philippopoulos-Mihalopoulos uses the term 'lawscape' to signify this tautology of law and space. I use this framework to understand the outreach event I started describing at the beginning of this chapter.

Philippopoulos-Mihalopoulos goes on to describe the micro-workings of the lawscape using the term *atmosphere*. By that, he refers to the affective tonality, the mood that enfolds in a place.[50] ICC outreach events, the topic of this text, can also be seen as creating a specific atmosphere.

This idea is well explored in the anthropological investigation of ritual and collective emotion. Emile Durkheim has described how the gathering of people at a place generates an emotional arousal he calls *collective effervescence*.[51] Victor Turner has referred to this phenomenon by introducing his concept of *communitas*, by which he describes the emergence of an enhanced sense of community in collective rituals.[52] Because of this affective and emotional dimension, public gatherings are seen as a prime device in creating group ties and social cohesion as they can provide a space in which values can be generated and group symbols be reified by a common affective experience.

More recently, authors such as Birgitt Röttger-Rössler[53] and Christian von Scheve[54] have pointed out that these classical accounts of the emotional workings of collective gatherings lack a theoretical approach to the micro-workings of how exactly people are emotionally affected and collective emotions are elicited. While they connect to more recent insights from social scientific emotion research and the neurosciences, I argue with Philippopoulos-Mihalopoulos that it is similarly fruitful to explore in more detail how the atmosphere created in the public gatherings of the ICC outreach events result from the co-presence of bodies in space.

Of specific interest in this context is affect theory, a strand of thinking that emerged in philosophy and cultural studies in the 1990s[55] and has recently gained some prominence in anthropology.[56] Anthropologists who refer to affect theory, usually do not mobilize established approaches of the anthropology of emotion[57] (for some regrettably)[58] but connect to a philosophical strand based on Baruch de Spinoza's philosophy[59] – particularly in the way it has been read by Gilles Deleuze.[60] The anthropology of affect explores the realms of sensing and feeling as it emerges relationally between bodies. *Bodies* in this sense are not only physical or biological bodies, but also all kinds of entities, such as things and other non-humans.[61] Affect, according to the basic idea of affect theory, as it is felt and sensed by humans, emerges relationally in the co-presence of bodies as a 'multi-directional flow, at the same time in and exceeding one's body that affects other bodies'.[62] This means that in the co-presence of several bodies in space, affect is always experienced not only as an inner feeling, but as an affective atmosphere.[63]

In this sense, transitional justice events have an 'atmosphere'. Their organizers try to engineer the event in a way that creates specific atmospheres to influence the processes of collective emotion and feeling that take place there. As I will argue in the course of this chapter, the ICC aims to create a specific *transitional justice atmosphere* to further their project of justice-making. The organizers influence the atmosphere by designing a spatial arrangement in which different (human and non-human) bodies are placed and moved around. From this perspective, collective gatherings, such as the ICC outreach events described here, are analyzed along the lines of what Slaby et al. have described as *affective arrangement*:

> In our understanding, affective arrangements are heterogeneous ensembles of diverse materials forming a local layout that operates as a dynamic formation, comprising persons, things, artefacts, spaces, discourses, behaviors, and expressions in a characteristic mode of composition and dynamic relatedness. Our approach facilitates microanalyses of affective relationality as it furthers both an understanding of the entities that coalesce locally to engender relational affect, and also the overall 'feel', affective tonality or atmosphere that prevails in such a locale.[64]

The prevailing atmosphere can be brought to life by describing the affective arrangement of human and non-human bodies positioned, or moving around within a given space and by analysing both its discursive and non-discursive components.[65]

The potential of collective gatherings to transform atmospheres and collective emotion is key here. In their normative dimension, such outreach events aim at the participant's *sense of justice*. Generally speaking, the sense of justice is 'a general moral competence that consists of a bundle of affective and cognitive capacities'.[66] The sense of justice develops as a moral sentiment; a feeling of what is just is not only felt at an individual level but also shared collectively with others.[67] The sense of justice can be investigated empirically by focusing on how people make assessments of the legitimacy and justice of specific phenomena and how they justify these assessments.[68] In this sense, outreach events are designed to influence how people perceive justice and injustice with regard to the past violence by tapping into the affective and emotional dimensions of collective gatherings.

Philippopoulos-Mihalopoulos has highlighted that for any atmosphere to remain stable the fact that it is engineered must be rendered invisible.[69] An atmosphere would be 'functioning' as long as it seems natural to the participants, as intended by those who engineer it. Participants must be able to immerse themselves in the event. As I describe next, the ICC personnel are not always able to create the atmosphere they seek, mainly because they are not able to arrange the bodies in a way that best suits their aims.

Based on these theoretical ideas, I make three points in this chapter: First, I describe the International Criminal Court's outreach efforts in northern Uganda as the project of setting up affective arrangements in order to highlight the importance of the atmospheres that emerge during these events. Second, I argue that the aim of the international criminal proceedings is to produce 'transitional justice atmospheres' and I list some strategies that are adopted towards achieving this purpose. Third, I show that, sometimes, these transitional justice atmospheres 'fail', because the affective arrangement created is not sufficiently able to render invisible how intensely it is trying to engineer the atmosphere.

The ICC outreach-event as an affective arrangement

On the day we came to Abok, and also on the following day, the ICC was in session in The Hague. The Court conducted the opening of the trial against Dominic Ongwen. During these two days, the Office of the Prosecutor, the Representatives of the Victims and the Defence team gave their opening presentations. However, the second day was strikingly different from the first one: both with regard to the affective arrangement and the resulting atmosphere.

About an hour after our arrival, at least two thousand people had gathered. There was no specific introduction by the organizers and the two small televisions had just been switched on. People began to converse loudly, and this continued even after the broadcast started. Apparently, the official ICC delegation had not yet arrived. We had expected a live feed from the courtroom in The Hague, but instead the televisions showed NTV, the Ugandan news channel. The proceedings were broadcast nationwide with intermittent interruptions of the newscast. While people watched the images being shown, a clear majority of the visitors did not understand sufficient English to be able to follow the proceedings as technical as this one. The local language in Abok is *leb lango*, a Western Nilotic language of the Luo group, which is quite similar to the neighbouring Acholi – the language of Dominic Ongwen and the LRA. Only those with several years of schooling speak fluent English, the national language in Uganda.

Shortly after the proceedings had been opened in The Hague, the 70 counts of crimes against the accused Dominic Ongwen were read out aloud by the court clerk in the courtroom. People seemed to realize that something important was going on, but by the looks on their faces and the frequent discussions among the viewers, it seemed that they could not fully follow what was happening. Instead of sitting quietly and following the proceedings attentively, people frequently engaged in conversations, and often moved around in the tents for that purpose. The excitement in the air before the television screens had been switched on seemed to have vanished. Instead people behaved as they would while passively waiting for something. The crowd seemed to be characterized by the same mixture of boredom an unease, one can observe at a bus station. People attended the event voluntarily, but not to engage in some kind of action beyond waiting.

While the charges were being read to Dominic Ongwen in The Hague, the Registrar of the Court arrived in a motorcade of several white SUVs – accompanied by some ICC personnel and embedded journalists. Barring me, the very few whites who attended this event had been brought there in one of the SUVs. Shortly after their arrival, speeches were made by the local councillor (one of the leading figures in the village) and the Registrar. The Registrar declared that in his fifteen years working for the ICC he had never seen this magnitude of community engagement in court proceedings. People clapped as his remarks were being translated. Subsequently the ICC official took a few questions from the audience.

During the Registrar's appearance Dominic Ongwen made his statement in the courtroom in The Hague. Although he spoke Acholi, NTV only broadcasted the English translation. Just a few people were following. The LRA had committed heinous crimes, Ongwen conceded, but referring to his abduction as a child in the 1990s, he said: 'I am not the LRA'.[70] Only a minority of community members was able to follow this important moment in the proceeding.

During this encounter, people followed the speeches and the question and answer session quite eagerly. They remained in their seats and listened carefully. Even as the noise died down once people became less engaged in conversations, their attention was directed to the Registrar of the ICC and what he said, not so much to the proceedings being broadcast simultaneously on the television screens.

After the Registrar left, NTV did not screen much more of the proceeding, and people became bored staring at always the same image of a Prosecutor presenting evidence. Many started loud conversations, left their seats and gathered in groups inside and outside the tents. Long before the end of the court day in The Hague, it became clear that NTV would not broadcast the trial any longer. People began to leave in the hundreds and some men began loading hundreds of white plastic chairs onto a truck. We also decided to leave and to return the next day to watch the continuation of the trials.

When we arrived in Abok the next day, we were in for a surprise. The tents in front of the administrative buildings had vanished and, at first glance, nobody was to be seen. We approached an official who worked in the building that had been the centre of the huge constructed space with tents and screens only the previous day. He directed us to a small community centre down the road, where the second day of the trial opening would be screened. Upon arrival, we realized that the place was a small courtyard with benches with 40 people already seated and watching NTV. A telenovela from Latin America was on – dubbed in English (about an enchanting white woman trying to seduce a dashing white businessman into participating in her evil plots, but in vain).

No ICC official was to be seen. On the second day, only local organizers from the village were present and I was the only white person attending the second day of the televised proceedings. NTV screened more of the trial opening than the day before. With a one-hour delay, the submission by the Office of the Prosecutor was broadcast only in part. Instead of using NTV's English audio feed, the organizers had tuned into MegaFM, the Acholi-speaking radio station that transmitted the Acholi translation of the proceedings. They were getting the feed directly from The Hague – the trial was being translated into Acholi for Dominic Ongwen.

The smaller room was now equipped with photocopied 'Case Information Sheets' translated into Acholi. These one-page documents contained basic information about the case and the participants and were also available in The Hague in English and French. Obviously, the ICC personnel had left them there the day before the Registrar visited Abok. Many people helped themselves to one of these leaflets before taking a seat. By the time the proceedings began, the hall had filled up to about 250 people – only 10% of the visitor numbers from the previous day. No ICC officials came to Abok to view the remainder of the proceedings on the second day.

The arrangement felt different not only to us but, apparently, also to the villagers. People behaved calmly and remained serious; the mood was tense. If people talked at all, they did so quietly and did not gather in larger groups. Mostly people kept to their seats and seemed to follow the screened proceedings attentively, and most seemed to understand what was going on. When the prosecution described Dominic Ongwen's crimes, one could see the reactions on people's faces. At one point, Benjamin Gumpert, the senior trial lawyer for the prosecution described in detail how Dominic Ongwen had ordered his men to rape an underage girl the LRA had abducted after she had refused to have sex with him. A number of older women shook their heads and looked away from the screen. That seemed to hit a raw nerve. Their sense of justice seemed to have been triggered one way or another.

The production and maintenance of transitional justice atmospheres

The second day of the event in Abok was very different from the first day in terms of the prevailing atmosphere. The first day was characterized by the hectic industriousness by the ICC staff, paired with the boredom and confusion of many of the local participants. On the second day, the atmosphere was calmer and more focused. Both days of the event differed in two respects: the presence of vernacular discourse and the degree to which they were structured and organized by foreign ICC staff. I claim that analysing these two features through the lens of affect theory sheds light on how they contribute to the production of different atmospheres.

The language in which the proceedings were being screened was a crucial component of the affective arrangement. Englund has pointed to the salient empirical problems that occur when the language of international law is translated into African vernaculars.[71] In this case, people obviously were not able to follow the legal process in a language they did not understand. But apart from this problem of translation, in a narrow sense, this fact severely influenced the affective setup of the event. Sara Ahmed has highlighted the role of language for the production of affect.[72] In her analysis inspired by affect theory, words can be circulated in what she calls 'affective economies'.[73] Such an affective economy can stick words to bodies, which not only marks and names them in the linguistic sense, but also shapes peoples' experiences in the co-presence of bodies in space.[74]

The atmosphere of confusion, boredom and indifference at the outreach event on the first day is a good indicator that words, which are of central relevance in court proceedings, did not 'stick' to the bodies in attendance in Ahmed's sense. The opposite was true for the second day of the event. Both the audio feed of the proceedings and the case information sheets (one example of the role of non-human bodies in the affective arrangement) were in Acholi language. What was being said during the proceedings could be incorporated in an affective economy into the bodies present at the event. The story of the young rape survivor was circulated in a way that it stuck with people. As to whether it actually had the same impact on everybody is doubtful, however. The affective arrangement cannot programme how linguistic and discursive utterances are experienced, but it can be set up in such a way at least some kind of affective economy emerges.

A second difference between the two days concerned the presence or absence of 'white bodies'. Berg and Ramos-Zayas have recently argued that the manner in which affect is experienced by individual bodies and collectives, is deeply racialized.[75] The deep history of racism and colonialism in Africa is not only a macro-discourse against the background of concrete events, but inscribes itself into the micro-politics of affect that is manifest in spatialized events such as the one I describe here. The discourse on the International Criminal Court as a neo-colonial institution I alluded to in the beginning exemplifies how much the current politics of international criminal justice is enmeshed in the racialized colonial history that connects Africa and Europe.

Within the framework of her 'phenomenology of whiteness', Sara Ahmed has highlighted the racialized ordering of how bodies are able to move in space.[76] While the white body is free to move, the non-white body is obstructed. In her view, 'whiteness' is not an essential or substantial 'thing in the world', but more of a structuring principle for bodies in space. The movement of white bodies in expensive SUVs, while most black bodies remained seated on a cheap plastic chair, can be read as a metaphor from Ahmed's theoretical writings. The presence of white bodies in an African village shapes the atmosphere of the events taking place in such a way that the arrangement of bodies is determined, at least to some degree, according to racialized orderings: white bodies (the Registrar) talk, black bodies (the villagers) listen; white bodies move (in SUVs), black bodies are stationary (on plastic chairs) etc.

During my fieldwork in Northern Uganda, I realized in my conversations with the ICC outreach officers that they were very conscious of the fact that the presence of a *muno* (the *luo* word for white foreigner) disturbed the atmosphere of an outreach event. All members of the ICC outreach team highlighted to me the importance of recruiting local NGOs and civil society members to organize the events. These efforts of 'localizing' transitional justice measures are on the one hand the result of a lack of funding for the ICC outreach unit so that, in fact, there is no availability of foreign personnel to do the work. On the other hand, the members of the ICC outreach team understand that local mediators are more readily accepted by the local population and confer legitimacy upon the outreach work. One can also read this reliance on local translators as an attempt to render invisible the fact that the atmosphere of touching the sense of justice in these events is the product of a purposeful production process. If the events appear engineered by foreign personnel, the intended atmosphere will not emerge.

Philippopoulos-Mihalopoulos, invoked in the beginning, has argued that for an atmosphere of any kind to be stabilized, the fact that the atmosphere is engineered must remain invisible.[77] As Rainer Mühlhoff has argued most convincingly, the ability to immerse people into an affective arrangement is in itself a form of power.[78] An atmosphere must appear to be just occurring without the appearance of organizers trying a little too hard. On the first day, the attentiveness of the ICC's staff, their visible engineering of the affective arrangement, rendered the atmosphere rather ambiguous. People were not fully immersed in the event. The ICC brought many different bodies together, very importantly, they included foreign journalists and the Registrar of the ICC in the event, which filled the arrangement with bodies that were unfamiliar to the villagers. It was visible to the participants that the ICC Outreach Unit had put up a show for the Registrar and the international press and this seemed to have disrupted the transitional justice atmosphere for other bodies (the villagers).[79]

Following the idea that an affective arrangement must be able to conceal the fact that it is a product of careful crafting, the role of the failing audio-visual infrastructure must be described in its affective dimension. In the affective arrangement of the outreach event, the strategic positioning of non-human bodies such as television screens, radios, and sound systems plays an integral role. It is a truism that such infrastructural arrangements determine to a large degree the atmospheres of any kind of event.[80] In the case of this outreach event, on the first day, the ICC did not manage to sufficiently organize this technical infrastructure, another important aspect as to why the event had produced such a hectic and at the same time boring atmosphere on the first day. For example, the sound system at a Christian service in one of the numerous Pentecostal Churches in Northern Uganda never fails. There is no traditional function, no matter the ritual, without enough food for all. Actors in these affective arrangements are highly sensitive to the arrangement of bodies in the right way to engineer the right atmospheres and are able to wheel in their 'immersive power'[81] effectively in order to address people's sense of justice. On the first day, it seems, the ICC had problems arranging the bodies in a way as to create an immersive atmosphere of transitional justice.

Conclusion: the spatial and affective micro-politics of transitional justice

I have argued in this chapter that it is insightful to describe the International Criminal Court's outreach efforts in northern Uganda as an affective arrangement, in order to shift the focus on the kinds of atmospheres that are produced at these events. I have further argued that the ICC, same as any transitional justice actor in Northern Uganda, aims to engineer a transitional justice atmosphere that affects people's sense of justice. Finally, I have tried to indicate that the production of such transitional justice atmospheres can fail when the affective arrangement of bodies is not able to produce an atmosphere that enables people to immerse themselves in the event. I claim that such a perspective opens up the perspective to better understand the process of different transitional justice concepts competing in Northern Uganda.

In the literature on transitional justice, many have tried to come to terms with the question of why and how transitional justice fails, because the models of transitional justice formats (especially criminal trials) do not fit into the local context. In anthropology, there are basically three ways in which this mismatch of (global) transitional justice and the (local) reality on the ground is conceptualized.

A culturalist and postcolonial conceptualization of the mismatch articulates the idea that those people in Africa who are the 'targets' of transitional justice measures have conceptions of legality, justice, and responsibility etc. that are different from those inherent in transitional justice. The imposition of these Euro-American legal ideas is conceptualized by actors on the ground as a neo-colonial imposition.[82]

A political-economy analysis sees the mismatch on the level of what transitional justice should actually be about. Although African violence is based on political-economic structures of inequality, and is thus a political matter, the law is mobilized to deal with it and individualizes a complex problem to guilt or innocence of individual persons. Terms such as 'judicialization of politics'[83] and 'legal encapsulation'[84] are mobilized to shed a critical light on such processes.

A third line of analysis refers, not unlike a broader critique of humanitarianism,[85] to the temporal bias of transitional justice processes. Transitional justice implies a crisis, a short-term moment in which transition must be facilitated. The mismatch occurs when people on the ground experience the problems not as transitory but as permanent – a phenomenon transitional justice measures cannot address and tend to make invisible.[86]

Such contributions on mismatches between global expectations and local perceptions have provided many insights into the workings and failings of transitional justice on the ground. But what they all have in common is that they refer to mismatch as cognitive, purportedly rational, and conscious views people hold. People are able to clearly articulate the mismatches between their expectations and what transitional justice offers. They say: 'That is not our culture that is your culture'. 'It is not about law, it is about money, power, and politics'. 'You speak of exceptionality and crisis, but this is my everyday life'. I have tried to show in this chapter that this might not be the whole story.

Deploying an analysis based on space and affect refers to the myriad of unconscious, emotional, and affective dynamics that emerge between co-present bodies in space relating to people's sense of justice. Perceptions of justice are not only produced on the level of translations of abstract norms into local understandings of justice. There is also a materiality and affectivity to the production of justice. The material and affective micro-workings of these processes of justice-making shape to a large degree what people feel is right and just – not only on the level of abstract concepts but in the everyday structure of materiality and affect. Purportedly petty questions about how bodies are arranged in concrete events can have an impact that is as important to large-scale discourses of justice.

In this chapter, I have argued that it is beneficial to investigate how the law is translated and shaped in the interplay of global and local by paying close attention to how these translation processes are carried out in concrete spatial and affective arrangements. The ethnographic endeavour is the prime methodology to provide such in-depth analyses.

Notes

1 The field research on which this chapter is based was funded by the German Research Foundation Affective Societies Research Centre at Freie Universität Berlin (DFG-SFB 1117). During my field research, I worked together with Lioba Lenhart whose advice on how to find my way in Northern Uganda was invaluable and with whom we had long discussions about the ICC outreach activities. Arthur Owor and Julius Omony accompanied me to Abok on 6 December 2017 and we discussed many ideas represented in this text. My colleagues in Berlin were a huge help in developing my arguments, most importantly Olaf Zenker, Leonie Benker, Kerstin Schankweiler, Katrin Seidel, and Victoria Kumala Sakti who commented extensively on a previous version of this text as well as the members and participants of the Political and Legal Anthropology Seminar Series where a previous version of this chapter was discussed.

2 On the history of the LRA conflict, see T Allen and K Vlassenroot (eds), *The Lord's Resistance Army: Myth and Reality* (Zed Books 2010); S Finnström, *Living with Bad Surroundings: War, History, and Everyday Moments in Northern Uganda* (Duke University Press 2008) 63–98; T Allen, *Trial Justice: The International Criminal Court and the Lord's Resistance Army* (Zed Books 2006); C Dolan, *Social Torture: The Case of Northern Uganda, 1986–2006* (Berghahn 2009) 39–71; H Behrend, *Alice Lakwena and the Holy Spirits: War in Northern Uganda 1986–97* (Currey 1999); L Lenhart, 'Der Krieg im Norden Ugandas: Konfliktdimensionen und Friedenspotenziale' (2006) 12 (3) *Journal für Entwicklungspolitik* 84–113.

3 In 2006, the LRA entered into peace talks with the Museveni government, which were carried out in the capital of South Sudan. The 'Juba Peace Talks' eventually failed to bring an accord, because the rebel leader Joseph Kony eventually decided not to sign the negotiated settlement, see M Schomerus, *Even Eating You Can Bite Your Tongue: Dynamics and Challenges of the Juba Peace Talks with the Lord's Resistance Army* (PhD Thesis, London School of Economics 2012). Since that time the LRA has not been able to operate in Northern Uganda. The group still exists, though reduced in size, and carries out attacks mainly in the Democratic Republic of Congo, and the Central African Republic. A webpage called 'LRA Crisis Tracker' still documents all LRA activities in the region, available at <www.lracrisistracker.com> accessed 26 February 2018.

4 Séléka (Sango for alliance) is a coalition of several Muslim rebel groups in the Central African Republic, see I Käihkö and M Utas, 'The Crisis in CAR: Navigating Myths and Interests' (2014) 49 (1) *Africa Spectrum* 69–77.

5 BBC, 'LRA Rebel Dominic Ongwen Surrenders to US Forces in CAR' (7 January 2015) available at <www.bbc.com/news/world-africa-30705649> accessed 23 February 2018.

6 I have elaborated elsewhere on some methodological questions of how to conduct ethnographic investigation in courtrooms based on my fieldwork in The Hague, J Bens, 'The Courtroom as an Affective Arrangement: Analysing Atmospheres in Courtroom Ethnography' (2019) 50 (3) *Journal of Legal Pluralism and Unofficial Law* 336–355.

7 J Bens, 'Gerechtigkeitsgefühle und die Legitimität des Internationalen Strafgerichtshofs in Norduganda' in J Bens and O Zenker (eds), *Gerechtigkeitsgefühle: Zur affektiven und emotionalen Legitimität von Normen* (Transcript 2017) 215–241.

8 OC Okafor and U Ngwaba, 'The International Criminal Court as a "Transitional Justice" Mechanism in Africa: Some Critical Reflections' (2014) 9 (1) *International Journal of Transitional Justice* 90–108.

9 RG Teitel, *Transitional Justice* (Oxford University Press 2000).

10 One important point of contention in these debates is on the question of whether criminal justice measures should be at the heart of transitional justice, see Teitel (n 9), or if an all-too strong focus on legal measures hinders a coming to terms with a violent past, see M Kieran, 'Beyond Legalism: Towards a Thicker Understanding of Transitional Justice' (2007) 34 (4) *Journal of Law and Society* 411–440.

11 AL Hinton, 'Introduction: Toward an Anthropology of Transitional Justice' in *Transitional Justice: Global Mechanisms and Local Realities After Genocide and Mass Violence* (Rutgers University Press 2010) 1–22, 2.

12 SA Dersso, 'The ICC's Africa Problem: A Spotlight on the Politics and Limits of International Criminal Justice' in KM Clarke, AS Knotterus, and E de Volder (eds), *Africa and the ICC: Perceptions of Justice* (Cambridge University Press 2016) 61–77.

13 Since its inception in 2002, the ICC has tried 25 cases, all against perpetrators from Africa, available at <www.icc-cpi.int/Pages/cases.aspx> accessed 23 February 2018. Ten situations are under investigation by the office of the Prosecutor, all but one (Georgia) concerning situations in African countries, available at <www.icc-cpi.int/pages/situation.aspx> accessed 23 February 2018.

14 RJV Cole, 'Africa's Relationship with the International Criminal Court: More Political Than Legal' (2013) 14 (2) *Melbourne Journal of International Law* 1–29; CC Jalloh, D Akande, and M du Plessis, 'Assessing the African Union Concerns About Article 16 of the Rome Statute of the International Criminal Court' (2011) 4 *African Journal of Legal Studies* 5–50.

15 Assembly/AU/Dec.296 (XV), Assembly/AU/Dec.221 (XII), Assembly/AU/Dec.245 (XIII), Assembly/AU/Dec.366 (XVII), Assembly/AU/Dc.482 (XXI).

16 M Matasi and J Bröhmer, 'The Proposed International Criminal Chamber Section of the African Court of Justice and Human Rights: A Legal Analysis' (2012) 37 (1) *South African Yearbook of International Law* 248–268.

17 Allen (n 2).

18 A Branch, *Displacing Human Rights: War and Intervention in Northern Uganda* (Cambridge University Press 2011) 179–215.

19 On the 'peace v. justice debate' there are basically three positions. Some argue that criminal justice measures negatively impact peace negotiations and that the international community should refrain from imposing them not to endanger peace talks, see e.g. Anonymous, 'Human Rights in Peace Negotiations' (1996) 18 (2) *Human Rights Quarterly* 249–258. Some have argued against this view by stating that an ICC involvement does not negatively impact peace negotiations, but can even promote them, see e.g. P Akhavan, 'Are International Criminal Tribunals a

Disincentive to Peace? Reconciling Judicial Romanticism with Political Realism' (2009) 31 (3) *Human Rights Quarterly* 624–654; LE Gissel, 'Justice Tides: How and When Levels of ICC Involvement Affect Peace Processes' (2015) 9 *International Journal of Transitional Justice* 428–448. Others have argued again that international justice measures should be taken even if they negatively impact peace negotiations not to sacrifice accountability for peace, see MC Bassiouni, 'Justice and Peace: The Importance of Choosing Accountability Over Realpolitik' (2003) 35 (2) *Case Western Reserve Law Journal* 191–204.

20 A Branch, "Dominic Ongwen on Trial: The ICC's African Dilemmas" (2017) International Journal of Transitional Justice 11 (1): 30–49.

21 KM Clarke, *Fictions of Justice: The International Criminal Court and the Challenge of Legal Pluralism in Sub-Sahara Africa* (Cambridge University Press 2009) 117–150.

22 A Branch, 'Dominic Ongwen on Trial: The ICC's African Dilemmas' (2017) *International Journal of Transitional Justice* 1–20.

23 G Carayon and J O'Donohue, 'The International Criminal Court's Strategies in Relation to Victims' (2017) 15 (3) *Journal of International Criminal Justice* 567–591.

24 G Anders and O Zenker (eds), *Transition and Justice: Negotiating the Terms of New Beginnings in Africa* (Wiley-Blackwell 2014).

25 K von Benda-Beckmann, 'Trust and the Temporalities of Law' (2014) 46 (1) *The Journal of Legal Pluralism and Unofficial Law* 1–17, 7.

26 RA Wilson, *Writing History in International Criminal Trials* (Cambridge University Press 2011).

27 F von Benda-Beckmann, K von Benda-Beckmann, and A Griffiths, 'Space and Legal Pluralism: An Introduction' in F von Benda-Beckmann, K von Benda-Beckmann, and A Griffiths (eds), *Spatializing Law: An Anthropological Geography of Law in Society* (Routledge 2009) 1–29, 5.

28 SE Merry, 'Anthropology and International Law' (2006) 35 *Annual Review of Anthropology* 99–116.

29 G Anders, 'The New Global Legal Order as Local Phenomenon: The Special Court for Sierra Leone' in F von Benda-Beckmann, K von Benda-Beckmann, and A Griffiths (eds), *Spatializing Law: An Anthropological Geography of Law in Society* (Routledge 2009) 137–156.

30 Anders (n 29) 154. Much of the transitional justice debate is structured by an analysis that sees the legal and political aspects of transitional justice add odds with each other, see L Vinjamuri and J Snyder, 'Law and Politics in Transitional Justice' (2015) 18 *Annual Review of Political Science* 303–327.

31 Branch (n 22).

32 V Freeland, 'Rebranding the State: Uganda's Strategic Use of the International Criminal Court' (2015) 46 (2) *Development and Change* 293–319.

33 Allen (n 2) 84; Branch (n 22) 191.

34 R Shaw, L Waldorf, and P Hazan (eds), *Localizing Transitional Justice: Interventions and Priorities After Mass Violence* (Stanford University Press 2010). For a criticism of an international criminal justice approach to Northern Uganda that neglects local demands see A Branch, 'International Justice, Local Injustice' (2004) *Dissent* 22–26. A number of scholars question if local transitional justice alternatives are fairer or more effective than its international counterparts, see e.g. S Thomson, 'The Darker Side of Transitional Justice: The Power Dynamics Behind Rwanda's Gacaca Courts' (2011) 81 (3) *Africa* 373–390; P McAuliffe, 'Romanticization Versus Integration: Indigenous Justice in Rule of Law Reconstruction and Transitional Justice Discourse' (2013) 5 (1) *Goettingen Journal of International Law* 41–86.

35 For Northern Uganda some have proposed that localized non-state forms of transitional justice are preferable to international criminal justice, see EK Baines, 'Spirits and Social Reconstruction After Mass Violence: Rethinking Transitional Justice' (2010) 109 *African Affairs* 409–430, B Meier, '"Death Does Not Rot": Transitional Justice and Local "Truths" in the Aftermath of the War in Northern Uganda' (2013) 48 (2) *Africa Spectrum* 25–50. Others are skeptical about resorting to such local and traditional transitional justice measures, see A Branch, 'The Violence of Peace: Ethnojustice in Northern Uganda' (2014) 45 (3) *Development and Change* 608–630; T Allen, 'The International Criminal Court and the Invention of Traditional Justice in Northern Uganda' (2007) (107) *Politique Africaine* 147–166.

36 SE Merry, *Human Rights and Gender Violence: Translating International Law into Local Justice* (University of Chicago Press 2006).

37 P Levitt and SE Merry, 'Vernacularization on the Ground: Local Uses of Global Women's Rights in Peru, China, India and the United States' (2009) 9 (4) *Global Networks* 441–461.

38 SE Merry, 'Transnational Human Rights and Local Activism: Mapping the Middle' (2006) 108 *American Anthropologist* 38–51.

39 Harri Englund has criticized that Merry understands the local translation of human rights too unidirectional from the global to the local. He suggests also investigating how global human rights ideas create tensions with local concepts and how local actors bring normative ideas beyond those enshrined in human rights into the debate, H Englund, 'Human Rights and Village Headmen in Malawi: Translation Beyond Vernaculatization' in JM Eckert et al. (eds), *Law Against the State: Ethnographic Forays into Law's Transformations* (Cambridge University Press 2012) 70–93. Similar: M Goodale and KM Clarke, 'Introduction: Understanding the Multiplicity of Justice' in KM Clarke and M Goodale (eds), *Mirrors of Justice: Law and Power in the Post-Cold War Era* (Cambridge University Press 2010) 1–27.

40 J Griffiths, 'What Is Legal Pluralism?' (1986) 24 *Journal of Legal Pluralism and Unofficial Law* 1–55; F von Benda-Beckmann, 'Who's Afraid of Legal Pluralism?' (2002) 47 (1) *The Journal of Legal Pluralism and Unofficial Law* 37–82. Specifically, on the normative pluralism of Northern Uganda's transitional justice landscape see Bens (n 22).

41 There exists an International Crimes Division (ICD) at the High Court of Uganda. This special chamber of the High Court was created as a result of the Juba Peace Talks. Because of the Amnesty Act of 2000 and the warrants of the 'top 5' commanders by the ICC, the scope of the ICD is quite narrow. Until now the ICD has only tried one case, which is still ongoing: against former LRA commander Thomas Kwoyelo, see A Macdonald and H Porter, 'The Trial of Thomas Kwoyelo: Opportunity or Spectre? Reflections from the Ground on the First Lra Prosecution' (2016) 86 (4) *Africa* 698–722; K McNamara, 'Seeking Justice in Ugandan Courts: Amnesty and the Case of Thomas Kwoyelo' (2013) 12 (3) *Washington University Global Studies Law Review* 653–671.

42 On competing dispute resolution forums, see K von Benda-Beckmann, 'Forum Shopping and Shopping Forums: Dispute Settlement in a Minangkabau Village in West Sumatra' (1981) 13 (1) *Journal of Legal Pluralism* 117–159.

43 For analytic purposes I have separated Acholi law and religious ethics of forgiveness in this text. In practice, these two normative systems frequently interact. Traditional leaders employ religious rhetoric and religious leaders talk about Acholi tradition. Both systems have grown to become discursively more and more compatible, see K Ward, '"The Armies of the Lord": Christianity, Rebels, and the State in Northern Uganda' (2001) 31 (2) *Journal of Religion in Africa* 187–221.

44 See e.g. A Appadurai, 'Disjuncture and Difference in the Global Cultural Economy' (1990) *Theory, Culture & Society* 295–310.
45 A Reckwitz, 'Affective Spaces: A Praxeological Outlook' (2012) 16 (2) *Rethinking History* 241–258.
46 Reckwitz (n 45) 242.
47 PT Clough and J Halley (eds), *The Affective Turn: Theorizing the Social* (Duke University Press 2007).
48 B Warf and S Arias (eds), *The Spatial Turn: Interdisciplinary Perspectives* (Routledge 2008).
49 A Philippopoulos-Mihalopoulos, *Spatial Justice: Body, Lawscape, Atmosphere* (Routledge 2015).
50 The idea that objects and places create affective dynamics has been explored recently in other disciplines, such as sociology, see e.g. M Löw, 'The Constitution of Space: The Structuration of Spaces Through the Simultaneity of Effect and Perception' (2008) 11 *European Journal of Social Theory* 25–49, anthropology; Y Navaro-Yashin, 'Affective Spaces, Melancholic Objects: Ruination and the Production of Anthropological Knowledge' (2009) 15 (1) *Journal of the Royal Anthropological Institute* 1–18, and human geography NJ Thrift, *Non-Representational Theory: Space, Politics, Affect* (Routledge 2008).
51 E Durkheim, *The Elementary Forms of Religious Life* (George Allen & Unwin 1915).
52 V Turner, 'Liminal to Liminoid, in Play, Flow, Ritual: An Essay in Comparative Symbology' in *From Ritual to Theatre: The Human Seriousness of Play* (PAJ Publications 1982).
53 B Röttger-Rössler, 'The Emotional Meaning of Ritual' in A Michaels and C Wulf (eds), *Emotions in Rituals and Performances* (Routledge 2012) 41–54.
54 C von Scheve, 'Collective Emotions in Rituals: Elicitation, Transmission and a "Matthew Effect"' in G Sullivan (ed), *Emotions of Collective Pride and Group Identity: New Directions in Theory and Practice* (Routledge forthcoming) 55–77.
55 M Gregg and GJ Seigworth (eds), *The Affect Theory Reader* (Duke University Press 2010); Clough and Halley (n 47).
56 For a recent review article on the anthropology of affect, see D Rutherford, 'Affect Theory and the Empirical' (2016) 45 (1) *Annual Review of Anthropology* 285–300. Anthropologists who have explicitly referred to affect theory in their ethnographic works include Y Navaro-Yashin, *The Make-Believe Space: Affective Geography in a Postwar Polity* (Duke University Press 2012); K Stewart, *Ordinary Affects* (Duke University Press 2007).
57 Reviews of the anthropology of emotions include C Lutz and GM White, 'The Anthropology of Emotions' (1986) 15 (1) *Annual Review of Anthropology* 405–436; A Beatty, 'Current Emotion Research in Anthropology: Reporting the Field' (2013) 5 (4) *Emotion Review* 414–422. Classical texts in the field include JL Briggs, *Never in Anger: Portrait of an Eskimo Family* (Harvard University Press 1970); MZ Rosaldo, 'Toward and Anthropology of Self and Feeling' in RA Shweder and RA LeVine (eds), *Culture Theory: Essays on Mind, Self, and Emotion* (Cambridge University Press 1984) 137–149; C Lutz, *Unnatural Emotions: Everyday Sentiments on a Micronesian Atoll and Their Challenge to Western Theory* (University of Chicago Press 1988); L Abu-Lughod and CA Lutz (eds), *Language and the Politics of Emotion* (Cambridge University Press 1990). For a more recent line of the anthropological research on emotion, see the works of the Berlin school of psychological anthropology, such as B Röttger-Rössler, *Die kulturelle Modellierung des Gefühls: Ein Beitrag zur Theorie und Methodik ethnologischer Emotionsforschung anhand indonesischer Fallstudien* (Lit 2004); T Stodulka, *Coming of Age on the Streets of Java: Coping with Marginality, Stigma and*

Illness (Transcript 2016); G Scheidecker, *Kindheit, Kultur und moralische Emotionen: Zur Sozialisation von Furcht und Wut im ländlichen Madagaskar* (Transcript 2017); A-M Reynaud, *Emotions, Remembering and Feeling Better: Dealing with the Indian Residential Schools Settlement Agreement in Canada* (Transcript 2017); VK Sakti, 'Im/Mobile Subjects: Identity, Conflict and Emotion Work Among East Timorese Meto Diaspora' (2017) *Social Identities* 1–16.

58 C Lutz, 'What Matters' (2017) 32 (2) *Cultural Anthropology* 181–191.

59 B de Spinoza, *Ethica, ordine geometrico demonstrata* (1677).

60 G Deleuze, *Spinoza et le problème de l'expression* (Les Editions de Minuit 1968); G Deleuze, *Spinoza: Philosophie practique* (Presses Universitaires de France 1970).

61 L Blackman, *Immaterial Bodies: Affect, Embodiment, Mediation* (Sage 2012); C Papoulias and F Callard, 'Biology's Gift: Interrogating the Turn to Affect' (2010) 16 (1) *Body & Society* 29–56.

62 Philippopoulos-Mihalopoulos (n 49) 120.

63 B Anderson, 'Affective Atmospheres' (2009) 2 (2) *Emotion, Space and Society* 77–81; T Griffero, 'Atmospheres and Lived Space' (2014) 14 *Studia Phenomenologica* 29–51.

64 J Slaby, R Mühlhoff and P Wüschner, 'Affective Arrangements' (2017) 11 (1) *Emotion Review* 3–12.

65 I have elaborated elsewhere on this ethnographic approach being an aspect of an ethnography of discourse practice: J Bens, 'The Ethnography of Affect in Discourse Practices: Performing Sentiment in the Time Machine' in A Kahl (ed), *Analyzing Affective Societies: Methods and Methodologies* (Routledge 2019) 199–213.

66 Together with Olaf Zenker, I have made some general theoretical remarks on the concept of sentiment elsewhere, J Bens and O Zenker, 'Sentiment' in J Slaby and C von Scheve (eds), *Affective Societies: Key Concepts* (Routledge 2019) 96–106.

67 I have made some general theoretical remarks on the concept of sentiment elsewhere, O Zenker and J Bens, 'Sentiment' in J Slaby and C von Scheve (eds), *Affective Socieities: Key Concepts* (Routledge forthcoming).

68 J Bens and O Zenker, 'Gerechtigkeitsgefühle: Eine Einführung' in J Bens and O Zenker (eds), *Gerechtigkeitsgefühle: Zur affektiven und emotionalen Legitimität von Normen* (Transcript 2017) 11–36.

69 Philippopoulos-Mihalopoulos (n 49) 144.

70 Dominic Ongwen was himself abducted as a child by the LRA in the early 1990s, a biographical fact that in the analysis of Erin Baines makes him into a 'complex political perpetrator': EK Baines, 'Complex Political Perpetrators: Reflections on Dominic Ongwen' (2009) 47 (2) *Journal of Modern African Studies* 163–191.

71 H Englund, *Prisoners of Freedom: Human Rights and the African Poor* (University of California Press 2006) 47–69.

72 S Ahmed, *The Cultural Politics of Emotion* (Edinburgh University Press 2004).

73 S Ahmed, 'Affective Economies' (2004) 22 (2) *Social Text* 117–139.

74 I have argued elsewhere that affect and emotion in courtroom rhetoric have an important role in creating meaning and plausibility. Crucial here is the interface between language and affect. J Bens, 'Sentimentalizing Persons and Things: Creating Normative Arrangements of Bodies Through Courtroom Talk' (2018) 2 (1) *Journal of Legal Anthropology* 72–91.

75 UD Berg and AY Ramos-Zayas, 'Racializing Affect' (2015) 56 (5) *Current Anthropology* 654–677.

76 S Ahmed, 'A Phenomenolgy of Whiteness' (2007) 8 (2) *Feminist Theory* 149–168, 161.

77 Philippopoulos-Mihalopoulos (n 49) 144.

78 R Mühlhoff, *Immersive Macht: Affekttheorie nach Foucault und Spinoza* (Campus 2018) 355–373.

79 One important further aspect in this event was the multiple publics that the ICC Outreach Unit was trying to address in this event: The local population, the international media audience, their direct superiors in the Court hierarchy, to name a few. I have elaborated on this aspect elsewhere, see J Bens and O Zenker, 'Affective Transference and the Problem of Multiple Publics: What Is the Audience for Transitional Justice?' *Public Emotions: Affective Collectivity in Audiences.* International Conference, Berlin.

80 Infrastructure itself can be the object of ethnographic research, see SL Star, 'The Ethnogrpahy of Infrastructure' (1999) 43 (3) *American Behavioral Scientiest* 377–391; B Larkin, 'The Politics and Poetics of Infrastructure' (2013) 42 (1) *Annual Review of Anthropology* 327–343.

81 Mühlhoff (n 78).

82 Such analyses can be found, for instance, with Clarke (n 21) and Meier (n 35).

83 J Comaroff and J Comaroff, 'Law and Disorder in the Postcolony' (2007) 15 *Social Anthropology* 133–152.

84 KM Clarke, Affective Justice: The International Criminal Court and the Pan-Africanist Pushback (Duke University Press 2019).

85 D Fassin, *Humanitarian Reason: A Moral History of the Present* (University of California Press 2012); M Ticktin, 'Transnational Humanitarianism' (2014) 43 (1) *Annual Review of Anthropology* 273–289.

86 G Anders and O Zenker, 'Transition and Justice: An Introduction' (2014) 45 (3) *Development and Change* 395–414, particularly for Northern Uganda, see A Macdonald, 'Justice in Transition? Transitional Justice and Political Economies of Survival in Post-Conflict Northern Uganda' (2017) 48 (2) *Development & Change* 286–311.

3 The Libyan constitution-making process

A tool for state-building in a divided socio-normative space?

Felix-Anselm van Lier

Introduction

It is often claimed that '[w]e live in an era of constitution-making'.[1] Since the end of the Cold War, constitution-making has become a key element of post-conflict reconstruction and development programmes and a 'central aspect of democratic transitions, peacebuilding and state-building'.[2] Be it in Somalia, Yemen, Iraq, South Sudan, or Afghanistan, constitutions, and the constitution-making process itself, are deemed to be part of the solution for ending 'violent conflict, or to contribute to reconciliation and consensus in otherwise deeply divided societies'.[3] Post-2011 Libya represents such a deeply divided society. In 2011, Libya's new political leaders and international policy makers were confronted with a country that largely lacked formal structures of governance. Some saw this as a chance to start with a 'clean slate'. Soon first steps were initiated to 'rebuild the state from scratch'. Echoing current policy approaches, a constitutional declaration set out a 'roadmap' for the transition of the country to democracy via a constitution-making process in the hope that democratic legal procedures would channel the diverse visions for a future Libyan state into a process of national unification.

However, as the transitional process showed, such a perspective underestimated the ongoing practical importance of the fragmented informal institutional and normative structures, which framed politics under Muʿammar al-Qaḏḏāfī's rule (1969–2011). Soon after the upheaval in 2011, a multitude of new actors with subnational and national ideologies and interests emerged onto the political scene, struggling for access to resources and political power. Some of these actors strategically influenced legislative processes to lock in certain contested world views, policy preferences or institutional structures – often by relying on the violent leverage of allied armed groups consisting of an uncontrolled number of town-, 'tribe'-, and military-based networks. Hopes that Libya's fragmented socio-political scene could be united through the rapid establishment of a constitution-making process were in vain.

Current constitution-making practice

Both in academia and in practice, a widely held belief is that constitution-making processes 'can play an important role in peaceful political transitions and post-conflict peace consolidation'.[4] It is held that constitution-making has the potential to contribute to both the short-term goal of conflict-resolution and peace-making and the long-term goal of peace- and state-building by creating 'a common vision of the future of the state and a road map on how to get there'.[5]

In fact, the making of a constitution is *itself* governed by 'road maps'. Constitution-making is informed by standards and good practice guidelines, which are authored and disseminated by inter-governmental organizations or international non-governmental organizations. For example, the United Nations Development Programme's (UNDP) *Guidance Note on Constitution-Making Support* is considered to be one such good practice guideline. It consolidates some of the principles that emerged from experience in constitution-making and seeks to offer a 'stronger knowledge platform to guide UNDP country offices [and other intergovernmental and international non-governmental organizations] on good-practice constitutional assistance approaches'.[6] International IDEA serves as an example for an international non-governmental organization that has drawn on the experience of its staff and constitution-making experts to draft constitution-making guidelines.[7]

Academia contributes to such practice guidelines by identifying and refining constitution-making standards and principles. For example, the Comparative Constitutions Project (CCP), an initiative originally launched at the University of Illinois in 2005, was born out of the experience of constitution-making processes, such as in 'Iraq and Afghanistan, which indicated that political scientists and legal scholars are not adequately equipped to advise constitutional assemblies about how to craft documents that solve important problems of governance'.[8] To remedy this gap, CCP researchers assembled 'a cross-national historical dataset of written constitutions, to service . . . the design of constitutions in developing and transitioning democracies'.[9] Another example is the Centre for Constitutional Transitions at the University of Berkeley, California, which is dedicated to the generation and mobilization of 'knowledge in support of constitutional building'.[10]

Such constitution-making standards and principles – e.g. a commitment to human rights, democracy, and the rule of law, as well as procedural standards, such as inclusivity, participation, representation, and transparency – may influence domestic constitution-making processes in various ways and for manifold reasons. They are actively promoted by international actors, such as intergovernmental agencies, international non-governmental organizations, academics and research centres, and 'global *pro bono* law firms'.[11] External actors typically influence domestic constitution-making processes in the form of 'technical assistance' to the drafters of the constitution. As noted earlier, the work that foreign actors carry out in the service of constitution-making often falls under broader organizational mandates comprised of terms such as 'democracy promotion', 'rule of law promotion', and 'peacebuilding' during a time when constitution drafting is regarded as a necessary response to post-conflict reconstruction. However, constitution-making standards and practices do not necessarily need to be the outcome of direct international interference. Scholars have illuminated some of the complex ways in which constitutional norms might be diffused and translated.[12] Moreover, constitution-making is generally subject to comparative influence in that constitution drafters explore procedures used for the enactment of new constitutions in other countries as well as substantive normative content of foreign constitutions to address issues of constitutional design.[13] Adding more empirical detail, Goderis and Versteeg claim that the motivation for adopting a comparative approach may derive from coercion, e.g. when former colonizers and donors push for the adoption of specific constitutional arrangements; from competition, when states strategically imitate foreign constitutional provisions to attract investment; from learning, when states share pre-existing constitutional similarities; or from acculturation, when states emulate foreign rules because they are believed to foster international acceptance and legitimacy.[14]

Irrespective of the way in which constitutional norms are diffused, the elaboration of models and standards for constitution-making and the embeddedness of constitution-making in peace- and state-building processes create a normative framework for constitutional reform which has contributed to the increasing 'legalization' or 'positivization' of such processes.[15] As Lollini and Palermo note, constitutions are generally not seen as the outcome of a 'single act of political will, but a more complex series of constitutional facts and acts, including political, judicial and international conditionality, and in the end it becomes a legally driven process and procedure'.[16] They use the term 'procedure' to describe a trend to legally define 'mere' processes by more (and increasingly sophisticated) legal rules and guarantees. In the light of these scholarly accounts, 'making constitutions appears as a process that follows certain rules (and) or rites which have been progressively established'.[17]

This trend to legalize, formalize, and rationalize constitution-making processes through normative standards and 'best practices' can be referred to as *legal-procedural approach to constitution-making.*

A legal-procedural framework for the Libyan constitution-making process

Initially, the leaders of Libya's post-Qaḏḏāfī state-building efforts followed this trend of *legal-procedural constitution-making*. The *Mağlis al-Waṭanī al-Intiqālī*/المجلس الوطني الانتقالي (*National Transitional Council*, NTC) was established very soon after first protests erupted in Benghazi in February 2011 and consisted of a group of lawyers, academics, former government officials, and defected diplomats. In a 'Founding Statement' issued only days after the eruption of first protests, the council declared itself as the 'sole representative of all Libya with its different social and political strata and all its geographical sections',[18] seeking to steer Libya into a post-Qaḏḏāfī era. In this initial phase of the revolution, the NTC heavily depended on the support of the international community to achieve its goal of ending Qaḏḏāfī's rule. Defected high-ranking diplomats played a decisive role in convincing the international community to support their cause.[19] The NTC also issued various statements, which were 'clearly written for [the NTC's] external audience' and 'designed to project as favourable an image as possible to the outside world'.[20] For example, the NTC presented its 'Vision of a Democratic Libya' at the first formal international conference in London on the 29 March 2011. The document comprised an eight-point plan for the transformation of country into a 'free and democratic society'. In the first point of this plan, the NTC declared that it recognized

> without reservation [its] obligation to: 1. Draft a national constitution that clearly defines its nature, essence and purpose and establishes legal, political, civil, legislative, executive and judicial institutions. The constitution will also clarify the rights and obligations of citizens in a transparent manner, thus separating and balancing the three branches of legislative, executive and judicial powers.[21]

Indeed, the constitution-making process was seen by many national and international actors as the key process of Libya's transition.[22] It was hoped that the constitution-making process, and finally, the constitution, would establish a legal framework within which the construction and reconstruction of the Libyan state would be peacefully negotiated.

Notwithstanding the NTC representatives' clout, their bold statements glossed over various problems, such as the revolutionary movement's fragmented nature or the NTC's actual lack of control over myriads of armed groups that had formed erratically during the revolution on a local or regional level, united only by the aim to topple Qaḏḏāfī. Soon significant division started to simmer over *how* a new Libyan state should be built.

First tensions surfaced within the NTC during the debates over the Constitutional Declaration, which was supposed to govern the country's transitional phase. Debates about how to approach the transitional phase divided the NTC into two camps: some NTC politicians, such as Maḥmūd Ǧibrīl, felt that Libyans had too little democratic experience to rush into elections and preferred the NTC to oversee the transitional process until a new constitution was drafted. Islamist-leaning members opposed the idea of prolonging the NTC's tenure, arguing that the self-appointed NTC had no democratic legitimacy and thus pushed for the election of a legislature immediately after the end of the revolution.[23] Behind these arguments lay a more concrete political interest. Ǧibrīl was aware that Islamists were far better organized than the scattered liberal camp and was concerned that they could potentially secure a large number of votes during early elections. Islamist factions, on the other hand, wanted to prevent liberal-leaning NTC leaders, such as Ǧibrīl and Muṣṭafā Muḥammad ʿAbd al-Ǧalīl, from using a prolonged NTC-tenure to consolidate their political power.[24]

After fierce internal debates, the Islamist camp prevailed. The final version of the Constitutional Declaration contained the roadmap for the election of a parliament, the establishment of a government, and for the launch of a constitution-making process.[25] The Constitutional Declaration entrusted the newly elected parliament, the *al-Muʾtamar al-Waṭanī al-ʿāmm* /المؤتمر الوطني العام

(General National Congress, GNC), with the task of selecting the members of the الهيئة التأسيسية لصياغة الدستور الليبي/*al-hai'a at-ta'sīsīya li-ṣiyāġat ad-Dustūr al-Lībīy* (Constitution-Drafting Assembly, CDA). According to the timeframe set out in the Constitutional Declaration, the transition period should have ended with the adoption of a new constitution in December 2013.

The controversy about how to govern Libya's transition was indicative of a change of trajectory of Libya's legal discourse. With the impending defeat of the Qaḏḏāfī regime, Libya was less dependent on international support and political debates became more embedded in Libya's internal discourse. While the Constitutional Declaration, officially issued on 3 August 2011 after Qaḏḏāfī's death, largely maintained the liberal undertone of the NTC's earlier 'Vision for Democracy', gradually, religious norms, regional, tribal and local power structures and preferences started to be voiced.[26] Internal power struggles came to the fore in the wrangle over Article 30 of the Constitutional Declaration, which set out the procedural and institutional arrangements for the transitional phase. These were early signs that a national vision for re-building the state may be more difficult to achieve than initially hoped.

Legal politics before the election of the CDA

The federalist challenge

Originally, Article 30 of the Constitution Declaration did not specify the composition of the constitutional assembly. It merely stated that an elected parliament, the GNC, would 'opt for a Constitutional Power in order to formulate the constitutional draft for the State'. Federalist leaders in the eastern region of Cyrenaica (Arab. Barqa) were dissatisfied with the proposed proportional system of seat allocation, as they feared that the parliament was dominated by Libya's more populous West. Such fears were rooted in the region's historical experience of marginalization under Qaḏḏāfī, who had systematically neglected Cyrenaica.[27] Protests erupted in March 2012 and a group of an estimated 3000 tribal leaders, military commanders, and political figures convened in Benghazi to declare the eastern region of Cyrenaica semi-autonomous.[28] NTC politicians harshly condemned these movements, warning federalists that 'national unity would be defended by force, if needed'.[29] At this very early post-revolutionary stage, revolutionary euphoria was still running high in the country and thus the politicians' call for national unity was supported by nationwide anti-federalist protests, proclaiming 'Libya is one'.[30]

The initiative for self-administration and the Federalist's protests did exercise enough political pressure on the NTC to make it feel compelled to react.[31] In a first of a series of amendments to Article 30, Amendment No. 1 of 2012 clarified that the CDA would be structured 'along the lines of the sixty-member commission that was formed to prepare the constitution of the independence of Libya in the year 1951'.[32] The GNC was now required to select (outside of its own members) a body consisting of sixty delegates, with 20 representatives from each of the three major regions in Libya, namely Tripolitania (Arab. Ṭarābulus), Fezzan (Arab. Fizzān), and Cyrenaica.[33]

Cyrenaican Federalists were still not satisfied with these adjustments. They were aware that the GNC's composition would also impact the set-up of the CDA, as the Constitutional Declaration still entrusted the GNC with the task of selecting the members of the so-called 'Committee of the 60'.[34] In the run-up to the first parliamentary elections in 42 years, Federalist leaders called on Libyans to boycott the elections to the new Parliament, engaged in partly violent protests, and forced oil sites to shut down.[35] Facing a boycott of the parliamentary elections in the east and the threat of a rupture of Libya's economic lifeline, the NTC took the controversial decision of amending Article 30 again two days before the elections, ruling that the CDA should be directly elected by the people rather than selected by the GNC.[36]

Political exclusion

Despite these early political tensions, there was still widespread enthusiasm for the forthcoming elections of the new parliament and, more generally, for rebuilding the country. However, the GNC elections in July 2012 brought about a highly fragmented and heterogeneous legislature that was divided along ideological, regional, and local lines. The manifold fault lines that ran through the parliament's parties and wings led to highly unstable and short-lived political alliances within the GNC, which often coalesced around a particular policy issue and ceased to exist as soon as the short-term goals had been realized.[37] This caused prolonged and protracted debates and negotiations and severely delayed the timeframe of the roadmap, including the election of the CDA.

Minorities

The CDA's electoral law presented a direct opportunity of influencing the CDA set-up. The drafting of the law largely took place behind closed doors. This left very little room for different interest groups to voice their opinion during the process. After the law was adopted by the GNC in July 2013, fervent criticism was voiced by minority groups, in particular by the Tubu and the Amazigh. These groups had suffered under the previous regime's ideology of 'Arab nationalism', epitomized by his slogan كلنا ليبيين / *kulunā lībīyīn* [*we are all Libyans*]. Minorities were either integrated into this vision, assimilated, or marginalized.[38] Hence, these minority groups had a vital interest in securing language and cultural rights, as well as citizenship rights, and in having a say on the national symbols of the Libyan state, such as its name and its flag.

According to the Electoral Law, Libya's three main minority groups, Amazigh, Tubu, and Tuareg, were each allocated two seats, despite considerable differences in their population size.[39] Minorities claimed that the Law did not allow for an adequate representation and meaningful participation in the proceedings of the assembly and started demanding guarantees in the voting procedure within the CDA. They insisted that issues of particular importance to minority groups should be decided by consensus rather than by the 2/3 + 1 majority, as provided for in the Constitutional Declaration.[40] Amazigh minority groups went even further in demanding certain rights to be guaranteed before the negotiations within the Assembly had started. In August 2013, a group of Amazigh activists 'forced their way into the Parliament building in Tripoli, . . . smashing windows and destroying furniture', demanding guarantees that their language, *Tamazight*, would be officially recognized in the constitution.[41] Since the demands remained unanswered, the Amazigh minority boycotted the elections from the beginning – as did the Tubu and Tuareg minority in the days leading up to the CDA election. While the Tubu and the Tuareg eventually participated in the constitution-drafting process, the Amazigh remained unrepresented in the CDA throughout the entire process.

The marginalization of minorities, especially Tubu and Tuareg, was problematic for the question of state-building. Given the transnationality and the trans-border connectivity of these minorities, particularly in the southern region of the Fezzan, much of the Libyan southern borders remain under their control. Thus, the minorities' boycott of the constitution-making process presented a potential threat for the stability of Libyan southern borders.

The effect of a fragmented political environment on the CDA

Meanwhile, many Libyans had become increasingly disillusioned with the political process and had lost trust in their political institutions.[42] In their eyes, the GNC had failed to manage the transitional process effectively due to the parliament's increasing factionalization and political infighting.[43] Many Libyans shared the view that the GNC's activities had 'come to be characterized by patronage rather than political decision making on issues of national importance'.[44]

Additionally, competing interests between a plethora of militia groups led to a rapid deterioration of the security situation.[45] Against the backdrop of an increasingly volatile security situation, a failing parliament, and emerging ideological conflicts, some Libyans felt that the country was experiencing the gradual deterioration of the national idea:

> We were all one, you know. I was here in Tripoli, I didn't move during the revolution. I witnessed everything here. And when I was watching TV, I was crying for Benghazi, I was crying for Misrata. I felt that this is my country, these are my people. I wasn't talking about different cities, I was talking about my country. We were one at that time. But now I don't think we are.[46]

Towards the end of 2013, the country was being steered into a governance crisis. The CDA was not yet elected and the parliament's mandate was about to end in early 2014 with no plan in place for the time after the end of its tenure.

CDA elections

To prevent a looming institutional vacuum, preparations for the election of the CDA were sped up. After new delays, elections were hastily organized for February 2014. However, the emerging 'democracy fatigue' among Libyan citizens and the lack of trust in formal institutions that had built up during the transition had an impact on the CDA election. The net participation of eligible voters for the CDA is believed to have been below 14%, in effect, less than 10% of the total population.[47]

Despite the low voter turnout, some Libyan politicians and activists remained carefully optimistic that a constitution-making process could reignite a sense of national belonging. Ahmed Gebreel, a Libyan diplomat and subsequently adviser to the CDA, argued that the low voter turnout merely showed how 'frustrated the people are. But it does not really affect [the CDA's] work that much'. He continued to explain that Libya needed

> a constitution more than any time before at this stage. We need something to hold us together, something to determine everyone's responsibilities and rights at this very critical stage. Because now every group, every region in the country, every city is trying to say that they have more rights than others because of their contribution to the revolution or because they have been suffering during Gaddafi's time, or that they are really suppressed. We need the constitution to show everyone's rights and responsibilities to end these discussions.[48]

Similarly, Elhām Saʿūdī, founder and director of the non-governmental organization, Lawyers for Justice in Libya, expressed her hopes that the constitution-drafting process may 'result in some kind of national dialogue in its own right that might resolve some of our concerns'.[49] Indeed, the issues tatlie at the core of the conflict, name the decentralisation of the country, the re-organisation of the security apparatus, finding an effective government system, and the fair distribution of resources, are fundamentally constitutional issues. On a broader level, the constitution should also address questions of national unity and identity.

Civil war and split of governments

Shortly after the CDA was inaugurated, in April 2014, new divisions emerged. Ḫalīfa Bilqāsim Ḥaftar, an ex-Qaḏḏāfī general who defected in 1990 and returned to Libya during the 2011 revolution, formed an alliance with eastern military units and tribal or regional-based armed groups codenamed *maʿrakat al-karāma* / معركة الكرامة 'Operation Dignity' and launched an attack against Islamist forces in Banġāzī in early May 2014. Two days later, the operation spread to Tripoli, when the Ḥaftar-loyal militias from the city of az-Zintān stormed into the parliament building in Tripoli and declared the GNC suspended, claiming that the body would no longer represent the Libyan people and had lost its legitimacy.[50] The GNC was forced to organize new parliamentary elections, *mağlis an-Nūwāb* /مجلس النواب (House of Representatives, HoR). Elections for the HoR in June 2014 resulted in a landslide electoral defeat of Islamist factions. Consequently, Islamist politicians, supported by militias from the town of Miṣurāta, launched a military campaign countering Ḥaftar's Operation dignity, dubbed 'Libya Dawn'. The country slipped into civil war, and former GNC members re-established the GNC in Tripoli in the course of the conflict. The country was now divided between two parliaments: a rump of the elected HoR convened in the eastern town of Ṭubruq and remnants of the GNC in Tripoli. With Operation Dawn countering Operation Dignity and the split of the parliaments, the two dominant sides in Libya's current civil war were largely set.[51]

CDA continues work in isolation from national politics

After the split of the institutions, the CDA remained the only elected and undivided institution of Libya's political transition. Despite having been elected by a margin of the population, the CDA still enjoyed widespread public support and was seen by many as a 'last glimpse of hope'.[52] This has partly to do with the composition of the body. Members of the GNC, of the interim government, or of official security or military authorities were not permitted to stand as candidates.[53] The CDA was a 'fresh' institution whose members had been largely uninvolved in the political turmoil of the other institutions. Also, since its inauguration, this body has worked in near total isolation in the city of al-Baiḍāʾ in eastern Libya. The remoteness of the town allowed the CDA to deliberate largely unstirred from the influence of the political factions and armed militias. Furthermore, the CDA took the decision to abstain from any direct involvement in the political process. Thus, for the most part, the body has maintained its political independence, and for a while remained the only largely uncontested and elected institution in the country.

However, the CDA's isolation had its downsides. For one, the CDA struggled to include wider segments of the Libyan people in the constitution-making process. The process became less accessible to Libyan civil society and was largely disconnected from the Libyan citizens. An outreach tour conducted in summer 2014 was described by one observer as more of a 'carnivalesque performance' rather than a substantive contribution to the process.[54] Eventually, Libyan civil society activists, including women's groups and youth groups, started to criticize the CDA's lack of communication and expressed concerns that their comments and demands were not seriously considered.[55] Against the backdrop of a failing transition and a civil war, which threatened to tear the country apart, some Libyans started to dismiss the CDA as irrelevant to their everyday concerns.[56] The extremely slow progress of the constitution-drafting process fuelled scepticism about the viability of the proceedings.

A second challenge was that the CDA had isolated itself from the UN-led Political Dialogue, which had been kicked off with a meeting in Ġadāmis in September 2014 with the goal of solving the institutional crisis at a national level by forming a unity government and reaching an agreement between rival factions on confidence-building measures, and a comprehensive ceasefire.[57] CDA Chairman, ʿAlī ʿAbd as-Salām at-Tarhūnī, and other members of the assembly, repeatedly stressed that the CDA would only be successful if it continued to 'distance itself from the political conflict in the country'.[58] While the decision to detach constitution-making from the UN-led Political Dialogue may have secured the political independence of the CDA, the uncoordinated operation of the two processes entailed risks. Some mediators warned that if the CDA produces a constitution that reaches very different conclusions with respect to the dialogue process or, indeed, 'does not address or aggravates the issues . . . which are at the heart of the ongoing conflict, the constitution risks reigniting fighting'.[59]

Thirdly, the ongoing civil war had created two (albeit three after the UN's successful conclusion of a peace agreement in December 2015) governments with very limited authority. Real authority continued to be exercised by local power holders. The Constitutional declaration provided that the constitution had to be approved via popular vote before coming into force.[60] With no effective central government to rely on, even a successful constitution-drafting process would probably not have solved Libya's problems, as the constitution's implementation was at the mercy of local power holders, who were likely to block a referendum on a constitution that did not reflect their interests.

Controversies and fragmentation of the CDA

After issuing a first patchworked draft constitution in December 2014 (i.e. the CDA did not present a consolidated draft, but merely published individual drafts of the CDA's different working groups), the CDA approached complete silence for nearly a year. Despite the Chairman's assertions that neither he, nor the members of the assembly were paying 'attention to the political pressure', old and new societal rifts of Libya's fragmented social and political landscape started to be reflected in the assembly's proceedings.[61] A CDA member noted in 2015: 'The conflict has a very serious effect on the negotiations in the assembly. Everyone is somehow affected by the conflict. As a result, political positions have hardened and it has become very difficult to overcome the divisions'.[62] Among other divisive issues, questions of how to deal with minorities, the question of federalism, and the CDA's role in the current transitional framework, brought the constitution-making proceedings to a standstill.

Minorities' boycott of the proceedings

Despite initial participation, by August 2015, representatives of the two remaining minorities, the Tubu and the Tuareg, boycotted the negotiations, after what they perceived as being a 'violation of the constitutional declaration and the democratic principles for a multicultural state'.[63] The CDA's minorities felt that the Arab majority of CDA members had not been responsive to their demands throughout the process. Since the boycott, the minorities have not re-joined the proceedings at the assembly.

Members of the Tubu community subsequently warned the CDA of adopting 'a non-comprehensive, non-concord constitution', noting that if the CDA's Arab majority continued to pursue their policy of 'Arab nationalism' there would be no constitution.[64] Some added that there was still the 'option of the secession of the south from the rest of the cities of Libya' given the 'legitimate right of self-determination of oppressed minorities in countries which exclude and marginalize their people'.[65] Similar secessionist tendencies have also been voiced by some members of the Tuareg.[66] While secessionist movements have not yet gained momentum and many minority members still primarily identify as Libyans, such comments underlined the fragility of Libyan statehood.[67]

The divisive question of federalism

Soon after, the CDA was confronted with another question relating to the question of national unity. In January 2016, shortly before the adoption of a second draft constitution, an additional eleven CDA members, primarily from the western part of Libya, started boycotting the proceedings. Previously, conflict had broken out within the assembly over the question of how to politically organize Libya's fragmented *body politic*. The draft constitution sought to appease the hardline federalist CDA members, some of whom had 'no problem if Libya would be divided', by decentralizing government power through the establishment of three government centres in Tripoli, Banġāzī, and Sabhā.[68] The boycotters refused this proposal, noting that such an approach would render effective governance impossible.[69]

Notwithstanding the protest, Chairman ʿAlī ʿAbd as-Salām at-Tarhūnī presented the contested draft to the public on the 3 February 2016. While the CDA had not officially adopted the draft, at-Tarhūnī's push for the adoption of the contested draft fuelled lingering resentment among CDA members about the assembly's leadership, who claimed that at-Tarhūnī was trying to force a finalization of the constitution for his own political gain. Seeking to impeach at-Tarhūnī, the boycotting members filed a claim at the local administrative Court in Al-Baiḍāʾ, which dismissed at-Tarhūnī as the CDA's Chairman in mid-February 2016.[70]

Controversial international involvement and the stalling of the proceedings

Fearing a collapse of the constitution-making process, the United Nations Support Mission in Libya (UNSMIL) started an attempt to speed up the constitution-drafting process. UNSMIL-mediators had previously managed to forge a fragile peace agreement between moderate factions of the two rivalling parliaments in December 2015. While the agreement was made largely without participation of the CDA, it still hinged on the CDA proceedings.[71] UNSMIL mediators were concerned that the constitution-making process might jeopardize the already fragile peace agreement.

In March 2015, the UN arranged and oversaw a meeting in Ṣalāla, Oman. In late April 2016, the CDA presented a slightly amended third constitutional draft. UNSMIL Head Martin Kobler praised the draft as a

> basis moving Libya beyond the transition period, and building a new modern Libyan state, anchored in the principles of democracy and separation of powers, rule of law, and respect for human rights, including equality for all, and guaranteeing the rights of women and all components of the Libyan national identity.[72]

Other than Kobler's optimistic comment suggested, the draft was highly contested among CDA members and UNSMIL's initiative had brought further division into the Assembly. Only 33 of the originally 58 CDA members had been present at the negotiations in Ṣalāla. In addition to boycotting minorities and anti-federalists, more CDA members now abstained from the proceedings, claiming that constitution-writing was a matter of national sovereignty and should take place on Libyan soil, without international involvement.[73]

Crucially, the adoption of the draft had only been made possible after the contested amendment of CDA's rules of procedure, which lowered the required 2/3 + 1 majority threshold for the adoption of the draft. Boycotting members, such as Mohamed al-Tumi, condemned the amendment as 'legal piracy' and subsequently filed another claim at al-Beyda's administrative court, arguing that the draft was invalid due to the procedural flaws of the adoption process.[74] The fact that the claim was supported by boycotting Tripolitanian CDA members suggests that the rejection of the draft was due to a more complex mix of reasons, including that the draft proposed the decentralization of government, parliament, and the judiciary into the three provinces.[75] In December 2016, the administrative appeals court in al-Beyda issued its final verdict and annulled the constitutional draft.[76]

A final draft with an uncertain future

After the annulment of the April 2016 draft, the boycotting members joined the CDA again, and new attempts were made to finalize a constitution – this time without the involvement of the UN. After approximately another year of deliberation amidst an ongoing chaotic and divided political scene, the CDA adopted a final draft constitution in June 2017. Emblematically, for the entire process, the vote took place under dramatic circumstances: the final adoption procedures were interrupted by violent protests, during which protesters broke into the assembly, beating, and threatening some CDA members and demanding to postpone the voting. CDA members refused to interrupt the procedure and adopted the draft constitution with a majority of 43 of 44 remaining CDA members after the situation was brought back under control by local security forces on Saturday, 29 July 2017.[77]

Whether the constitution will actually enter into force any time soon, however, is very much up in the air.

First, the constitution-making process took place in near complete isolation and remained largely uncoordinated with major political forces. Some politicians have already voiced their dismay with the draft and it remains uncertain whether the parliament, the HoR, will be able to agree on organizing a referendum soon.[78] Also, even if the HoR agrees on holding a referendum, it is neither sure whether the plethora of militia groups who hold the *de facto* power in Libya will support the implementation of a referendum, nor whether the Libyan people will actually approve of the draft.

Second, the draft was adopted without the inclusion of Libya's main minorities – the Tubu, Tuareg, and the Amazigh. Tubu and Amazigh immediately rejected the draft.[79] A website, ostensibly run by Amazigh, reported that the Amazigh were preparing to file another claim on the basis that the CDA had adopted the constitution without achieving consensus on minority issues, which is required both by law and the Rules of Procedure.[80] They also vowed to write their own Berber constitution.[81]

Finally, the new UN Head Ghassan Salamé has announced that he seeks resolve potential discrepancies and roadblocks in the course of a National Dialogue to be held in mid-2018.[82] However, CDA members who voted in favour of the July 2017 draft consider the text to be the final version and are unwilling to re-enter negotiations – not least due to the experience of the violent circumstances within which the final draft was adopted. Taken together, the future of the constitution and the question of whether it will positively contribute to the challenge of building a new Libyan state remains deeply uncertain.

Conclusion

Rather than starting with a 'clean slate', the Libyan constitution-making process remained deeply embedded in the complex political, social, and historical aspects of Libya's transitional phase. The Libyan constitution-making process, and the transitional process in general, underlined the state institution's vulnerability *vis-a-vis* local power holders and exhibited the fragmentation of the Libyan political landscape and the fragility of Libyan state- and nationhood.

Hopes of achieving a peaceful transition via legal procedures set out by the Constitutional Declaration, and of devising a constitutional architecture for a new state, remained unfulfilled. Rather than discouraging violent political discourse, legal procedures became yet another battleground for warring political entities, who sought to lock in certain contested worldviews, policy preferences, institutional structures, before and during the constitution-making process. This increased political division as partisan political interests became 'entrenched' as a normative perspective of the state at the expense of other, less powerful actors. The outbreak of the civil war in mid-2014 fuelled existing division and created new ones. The CDA was not able to isolate itself from this conflict. The rifts of Libya's socio-political landscape soon emerged within the Assembly and finally brought the constitution-making process to a halt.

The Libyan example emphasizes that when societal conflict is high and the political landscape is deeply divided, conflicts are unlikely to be solved through a redistribution of power or resources or the elaboration of a unitary vision for a state in a constitution. As demonstrated, the disagreements that the constitution seeks to solve often lie at the core of the political conflict. Since the idea of a constitution is to entrench the law at a higher legal level, constitution-making risks becoming a high-stakes arena of political conflict. Given the importance placed on the constitution for the future distribution of power of the country, constitution-making might enflame the political conflict rather than bridging different positions. Alternatively, if constitution-making is isolated from the political process and seen as a purely legal endeavour, thus disregarding the political process through which allegiance is forged, it risks becoming irrelevant in the eyes of political actors, and decisions about the future of the state are going to be taken elsewhere.

The collapse of the Libyan constitution-making process underlines the contingent, indeterminate, and haphazard aspects of post-conflict normative ordering. Once the open, provisional, and dynamic dimensions of constitutional ordering is acknowledged, it becomes more pertinent to read comparable situations as long-term processes of state-*formation* rather than as short-term state-*building* projects. Such a reading may encourage policy makers to rethink current policy approaches and to put more thought into options that go beyond the *legal-procedural approach* in a complex normative space.

Notes

1 V Hart, *Democratic Constitution Making* (United States Institute of Peace 2003) 1.
2 United Nations Development Programme, *UNDP Guidance Note on Constitution-Making Support* (United Nations Development Programme 2014).
3 M Brandt and Others, *Constitution-Making and Reform: Options for the Process* (Interpeace 2011) 2.
4 J Benomar, *Constitution-Making and Peace Building: Lessons Learned from the Constitution-Making Processes of Post-Conflict Countries* (United Nations Development Programme 2003) 3.
5 K Samuels, 'Post-Conflict Peace-Building and Constitution-Making' (2006) 6 (3) *Chicago Journal of International Law* 663.
6 Programme 3 et seq (n 2).
7 M Böckenförde, N Hedling, and W Wahiu, *A Practical Guide to Constitution Building* (International IDEA 2011) or constitutionnet.org, 'About Constitutions' (International IDEA 2014) available at <www.constitutionnet.org/about#c1332> accessed 14 October 2015.
8 T Ginsburg, Zachary Elkins, and James Melton, 'About Comparative Constitutions Project' (Comparative Constitutions Project 2015) available at <http://comparativeconstitutionsproject.org/about-ccp> accessed 15 October 2015.
9 Ginsburg, Elkins, and Melton (n 8).

10 Centre for Constitutional Transitions, 'Research' (Centre for Constitutional Transitions 2015) available at <http://constitutionaltransitions.org/research> accessed 19 October 2015.

11 C Daase, 'Making the Client's Peace: "Privatizing" Peace? Global Law Firms Offering Pro Bono Services in Post-Conflict Settings' (2014) 21 *Indiana Journal of Global Legal Studies.*

12 See e.g. K Seidel, 'The Promotion of the Rule of Law in Translation' in T Berger and A Esguerra (eds), *World Politics in Translation* (Routledge 2018).

13 A Lollini and F Palermo, 'Facets and Practices of State-Building' in J Raue and P Sutter (eds), *Facets and Practices of State-Building* (Martinus Nijhoff 2009).

14 B Goderis and M Versteeg, *The Transnational Origins of Constitutions: An Empirical Investigation* (2013) 1, CentER Discussion Paper, Vol. 2013-010 (Tilburg: Economics)

15 P Al-Ali Zaid Dann, 'The Internationalized "Pouvoir Constituant": Constitution-Making Under External Influence in Iraq, Sudan, and East Timor' (2006) 10 *Max Planck Yearbook of United Nations Law* 423, 427.

16 Lollini and Palermo (n 13).

17 C Klein and A Sajó, 'Constitution-Making: Process and Substance' in M Rosenfeld and A Sajó (eds), *The Oxford Handbook of Comparative Constitutional Law* (Oxford University Press 2012) 421.

18 National Transitional Council, *Founding Statement of the Interim Transnational National Council* (5 March 2011).

19 See e.g. P Bartu, 'The Corridor of Uncertainty: The National Transitional Council's Battle for Legitimacy and Recognition' in B McQuinn and P Cole (eds), *The Libyan Revolution and Its Aftermath* (Oxford University Press 2015).

20 Bartu (n 19).

21 National Transitional Council, *A Vision for a Democratic Libya* (29 March 2011).

22 See e.g. United Nations Security Council, *UNSC Res 2009 (2011)* (16 September 2011); E Labott, 'As Libyan Plans Unfold, NTC Chairman Offers Thanks' (2 September 2011) *CNN News* available at <http://edition.cnn.com/2011/WORLD/africa/09/01/libya.paris.meeting> accessed 7 March 2015; B al-Baker, 'Mahmoud Jibril: Libya's Touted Statesman' in *Al-Akhbar* available at <http://english.al-akhbar.com/node/528> accessed 7 March 2015.

23 P Bartu, *Libya's Political Transition: The Challenges of Mediation* (International Peace Institute, December 2014) 9. Note that the categorization of 'liberal' and 'Islamist' actors is a reductive account of a much more complex political landscape. The term 'liberal' in the egalitarian, individualist, and market-oriented sense of the word, only applies to a limited number political actors. Equally, 'Islamist groups' are not a monolithic bloc. Different strands of Islamists exist in Libya, ranging from moderate factions, such as the *al-ʾIḫwān al-Muslimūn* / الإخوان المسلمون (Muslim Brotherhood), to more radical Salafist and jihadist ideologies, such as *Dāʿiš* / داعش ; aka *ad-Daula al-Islāmiyya fīl-ʿIrāq wa-š-Šām*, the Islamic State of Iraq and the Levant. Here the term refers to the moderate strand of Islamist factions. See e.g. W Lacher, 'Was Libya's Collapse Predictable?' (2017) 59 *Survival* 139 f and *Fault Lines of the Revolution: Political Actors, Camps and Conflicts in the New Libya* (SWP Research Paper 2013) 10.

24 Bartu (n 19) 52.

25 National Transitional Council, *Constitutional Declaration* (2011) Article 30.

26 For example, references to Islam became more prominent after the revolution was won. When Muṣṭafā Muḥammad ʿAbd al-Ǧalīl declared Libya's 'liberation', he also made sure to stress that Libya was 'an Islamic country. . . . We take the Islamic religion as the core of our new government. The constitution will be based on our Islamic religion'. A Nossiter and F Kareem, 'Revolution Won: Top Libyan Official

Vows a New and More Pious State' (23 October 2011) *The New York Times* available at <www.nytimes.com/2011/10/24/world/africa/revolution-won-top-libyan-official-vows-a-new-and-more-pious-state.html> accessed 13 November 2015. He further announced that Islamic *šarīʿa* would be 'the main source of legislation, and so any law which contradicts Islamic principles is void'. Mohamed Madi, 'Libya Looks Set to Chart Moderate Course on Islam' (4 November 2011) *BBC News* available at <www.bbc.co.uk/news/world-africa-15500682> accessed 20 January 2011. This commitment to Islamic law was cemented in Article 1 of the Constitutional Declaration, which defined *šarīʿa* as the principal source of legislation. The commitment to *šarīʿa* subsequently permeated several subsequent legislative acts of the NTC, such as the abolishment of Qaḏḏāfī's ban on polygamy was abolished; or the established *dār al-Iftāʾ* / دار الإفتاء, an independent religious body tasked with giving religious advice and opinions in the form of *fatāwā*.

27 Federalists further based their claims on Cyrenaica's particular history and identity. Eastern tribes had been brought together under the leadership of the Sanūsīya family in the 19th century; they had fought against Italian Fascist rule under the leadership of the Libyan national hero ʿcent al-Muḫtār; Qaḏḏāfī's coup was a direct overthrow of eastern, Sanūsīya power; and the 2011 revolution had started in Benghazi, see S Kane, 'Barqa Reborn? Eastern Regionalism and Libya's Political Transition' in P Cole and B McQuinn (eds), *The Libyan Revolution and Its Aftermath* (Hurst 2015). At a later stage of the transition, new Federal movements emerged that were more economically driven. They were about the control of Libya's oil resources, which are predominantly to be found in Cyrenaica, see M Galtier, 'Rebel Leader Ibrahim Jedran Seeks Separate Government for Eastern Libya' (23 December 2013) *The Washington Times* available at <www.washingtontimes.com/news/2013/dec/23/rebel-leader-ibrahim-jedran-seeks-separate-governm> accessed 8 August 2014.

28 Kane (n 27) 217.

29 AFP, 'Libyan National Unity Will Be Defended "with Force if Needed"' (7 March 2012) *The Telegraph* available at <www.telegraph.co.uk/news/worldnews/africaandindianocean/libya/9128278/Libyan-national-unity-will-be-defended-with-force-if-needed.html> accessed 11 February 2015.

30 J Gluck, *Debating Federalism in Libya* (US Institute of Peace 2012) available at <www.usip.org/publications/debating-federalism-in-libya> accessed 23 April 2019.

31 In a first attempt to calm federalist's tensions in eastern Libya, Prime Minister ʿAbd ar-Raḥīm al-Kīb announced that the NTC would open offices in Banġāzī and Sabhā and that a law on administrative decentralization would be prepared to 'avert the policy of federalism to run the state's affairs', see Financial Times Agency, 'Libya to Open Government Offices in Benghazi, Sabha "to Avert" Federalism' (14 March 2012) as cited by Kane (n 27) 219.

32 The reference to the 1951 Committee of Sixty as the CDA's historical predecessor had an important symbolic significance as the 1951 constitution had become a central unifying narrative during the revolution, see e.g. L Updike Toler, 'Back to the Future in Libya' (1 August 2014) *Foreign Policy* available at <http://foreignpolicy.com/2014/08/01/back-to-the-future-in-libya> accessed 20 March 2015.

33 National Transitional Council, *Amendment No. 1 to the Constitutional Declaration* (13 March 2012).

34 Given the lower population in the east, federalist groups feared the domination of the selection process of CDA members by the deputies from the more populous west.

35 Sapa-AFP, 'Armed Forces Shut Down East Libya Oil Production' (6 July 2012) *Times Live* available at <www.timeslive.co.za/africa/2012/07/06/

armed-forces-shut-down-east-libya-oil-production> accessed 13 January 2015. See also K Mezran and D Pickard, *Negotiating Libya's Constitution* (Atlantic Council-Rafik Hariri Center for the Middle East, January 2014) 6.

36 National Transitional Council, *Amendment No. 3 to the Constitutional Declaration* (5 July 2012).

37 See Lacher (n 23); F Gaub, 'A Libyan Recipe for Disaster' (2014) 56 *Survival* 101, 103.

38 The relationship between these minorities and the Qaḏḏāfī regime was complex and needs to be analyzed separately. Tuareg tribes, who inhabit vast Saharan areas stretching from southwestern Libya to southern Algeria, Niger, Mali, and Burkina Faso, were glorified as 'Arabs of the South' and were gradually integrated into the regime's structures. The Amazigh were officially seen as a 'colonial invention' and were denied cultural and language rights. The Tubu, who are dispersed among four states (Chad, Libya, Niger, and Sudan), were neglected and often denied Libyan citizenship because they could not prove that they descended from grandparents who had lived within the 1951 borders of Libya. See I Kohl, 'Libya's 'Major Minorities': Berber, Tuareg, and Tebu: Multiple Narratives of Citizenship, Language, and Border Control' (2014) 23 *Middle East Critique* 423.

39 The Amazigh minority population is about twenty times the size of the Tubu, for example.

40 National Transitional Council (n 33).

41 Reuters, 'Libya: Berbers Protest in Assembly' (14 August 2013) *New York Times* available at <www.nytimes.com/2013/08/14/world/africa/libya-berbers-protest-in-assembly.html?_r=0> accessed 20 January 2015.

42 K Mezran, 'The Political Process in Libya' (22 April 2014) *Middle East Institute* available at <www.mei.edu/content/political-process-libya> accessed 20 January 2015.

43 CS Chivvis and J Martini, *Libya After Qaddafi Lessons and Implications for the Future* (RAND Corporation 2014) 41 ff.

44 Carter Center, *The 2014 Constitutional Drafting Assembly Elections in Libya* (Final Report 2014) 5.

45 See W Lacher and P Cole, *Politics by Other Means: Conflicting Interests in Libya's Security Sector* (Small Arms Survey Working Paper 20, 2014).

46 Interview with Amira Aribe (16 April 2014).

47 M Eljarh, 'Democracy Fatigue in Libya' (26 Februrary 2014) *Foreign Policy* available at <http://foreignpolicy.com/2014/02/26/democracy-fatigue-in-libya> accessed 18 January 2015.

48 Interview with A Gebreel (15 April 2014).

49 C House, *Libya's Long Road Ahead: Constitution, National Dialogue and the Security Challenge* (Middle East and North Africa Programme 2014).

50 G Mezzofiore, 'Libya Military Coup Fears: General Khalifa Haftar Calls for Suspension of Parliament' (14 February 2014) *International Business Times* availableat<www.ibtimes.co.uk/libya-military-coup-fears-general-khalifa-haftar-calls-suspension-parliament-1436410> accessed 14 March 2015.

51 This said, it is important to keep in mind that beneath this 'meta-narrative of Islamists versus liberals or Miṣurāta *versus* az-Zintān, the Dawn-Dignity fighting reflected long-standing feuds between rival towns, clans, and patronage networks'. In the course of the conflict Libya's many powerful 'city-states' and tribes were starting to create loose and ever-shifting ties of allegiance with one or the other. F Wehrey, *Ending Libya's Civil War: Reconciling Politics, Rebuilding Security* (Carnegie Endowment for International Peace, 24 September 2014) 23.

52 M Eljarh, 'Libya's Last Glimpse of Hope' (1 December 2014) *Foreign Policy* available at <http://foreignpolicy.com/2014/12/01/libyas-last-glimpse-of-hope>

accessed 4 April 2015; M Eljarh, 'Libya's Assembly Faces Major Challenges' (2014) *Middle East Eye* available at <www.middleeasteye.net/fr/node/579> accessed 15 March 2015.

53 *Law No. 17 of 2013 on the Election of the Constituent Assembly in Charge of Drafting the Constitution* (2013) Article 9.

54 Interview with O Hammady (16 June 2014).

55 Democracy Reporting International, *Civil Society's Sober Assessment of the Libyan Constitution-Making Process* (Briefing Paper 71, 2016).

56 O Hammady and M Meyer-Reisende, 'These 56 People Have a Chance to Save Libya' (21 April 2015) *Foreign Policy* available at <http://foreignpolicy.com/2015/04/21/these-56-people-have-a-chance-to-save-libya> accessed 4 June 2015. CDA members returning from visits in their constituencies said that they were perceived as being 'from a different planet', Jamal al-Ghazal (15 August 2015).

57 UNSC Res 2174 (2014).

58 The Libya Observer, 'Facebook Post' (5 December 2014) available at <www.facebook.com/lyobserver/posts/622877161150701> accessed 16 December 2014.

59 Interview with C Thornton (22 December 2016).

60 National Transitional Council (n 25) Article 30.

61 B Daragahi, 'Battle to Write Constitution for a Libya at War with Itself' (28 May 2015) *Financial Times* available at <www.ft.com/cms/s/0/7fff922e-022c-11e5-92ce-00144feabdc0.html#axzz3d4aUlQMd> accessed 3 June 2015.

62 Interview with Abdulsalam al-Jilani (14 August 2015).

63 M Khalifa, 'Libya: Tebus and Tuareg Members Walk Out of Constitution Drafting Assembly' (20 August 2015) *Marsad Libya* available at <www.marsad.ly/en/2015/08/20/tebus-and-tuareg-members-walk-out-of-constitution-drafting-assembly> accessed 24 August 2015.

64 Libyan Express, 'Libya's Tabu Tribes Reject Oman-Based CDA Outcomes' (7 April 2016) *Libyan Express* available at <www.libyanexpress.com/libyas-tabu-tribes-reject-oman-based-cda-outcomes> accessed 7 March 2017.

65 Notably, this Tubu speaks of 'cities of Libya' rather than the 'state of Libya', Khaled Wahli (2016) <www.facebook.com/photo.php?fbid=10200920225924833&set=a.1238466738727.28584.1741040802&type=3> accessed 17 March 2017.

66 T Chelali, *On the Casual Calls for Secession: Part IV Libya* (Working Paper 2016).

67 I Kohl notes that 'national and ethnic and tribal affiliations are not mutually exclusive categories', Kohl (n 38) 424.

68 Interview with anonymous CDA member (18 August 2015); see Libyan Constitution Drafting Assembly, *Draft Constitution (Not Adopted)* (2 February 2016) Article 3.

69 An underlying issue of these debates is the question of the fair distribution of Libya's oil revenues, as 80 % of the oil reserves are located in Libya's east.

70 The Libya Observer, 'Al-Tarhouni Dismissed from CDA Membership' (14 April 2016) *The Libya Observer* available at <www.libyaobserver.ly/news/al-tarhouni-dismissed-cda-membership> accessed 7 February 2017. Notably, the basis of the claim was not the substance of the constitutional draft, but the fact that at-Tarhūnī had dual citizenship. The way in which at-Tarhūnī was dismissed again shows how Libyan actors strategically used legal tools for their own interests.

71 The newly created *Government of National Accord* (GNA) was meant to lead the country until the adoption of the *Constitution, Libyan Political Agreement (LPA)* (2015) Preamble.

72 UNSMIL, *Kobler Welcomes Significant Progress Made in Latest Draft Constitution Agreed on by CDA Members* (Working Paper 2016).

73 K Hanly, ‘Libyan Constitutional Drafting Assembly Holds Meetings in Oman’ (20 March 2016) *Digital Journal* available at <www.digitaljournal.com/news/world/op-ed-libyan-constitutional-drafting-assembly-holds-meetings-in-oman/article/460678> accessed 7 March 2017; A Assad, ‘CDA Boycotting Members Consider Oman and Al-Bayda Meetings Illegal’ (19 April 2016) *The Libya Observer* available at <www.libyaobserver.ly/news/cda-boycotting-members-consider-oman-and-al-bayda-meetings-illegal> accessed 7 March 2017.

74 Libyan Express, ‘CDA Boycotting Member, Al-Tumi: Some Members Are Missing with CDA Domestic Codes’ (11 April 2016) *Libyan Express* available at <www.libyanexpress.com/cda-boycotting-member-al-tumi-some-members-are-missing-with-cda-domestic-codes> accessed 14 April 2016.

75 Libyan Constitution Drafting Assembly, *Draft Constitution (Adopted)* (4 April 2016) Art. 108, 101, 147.

76 Libya Observer, ‘News Roundup-Wed, Dec 07, 2016’ (9 December 2016) *Libya Observer* available at <www.libyaobserver.ly/inbrief/news-roundup-wed-dec-07-2016> accessed 9 December 2016.

77 Libyan Express, ‘Libya’s Constitution Drafting Assembly Attack: What Happened?’ (30 July 2017) *Libyan Express* available at <www.libyanexpress.com/libyas-constitution-drafting-assembly-attack-what-happened> accessed 2 August 2017.

78 M Toaldo, ‘A Constitutional Panacea for Libya?’ (22 August 2017) *Carnegie Endowment for International Peace* available at <http://carnegieendowment.org/sada/72878> and A Elumami and A Lewis, Libya’s Supreme Court Blocks Legal Challenges to Draft Constitution (15 February 2018), *Reuters* available at <https://www.reuters.com/article/us-libya-security-constitution/libyas-supreme-court-blocks-legal-challenges-to-draft-constitution-idUSKCN1FY2CB>.

79 Al Wasat, ‘‘ممثلا التبو بـ «تأسيسية الدستور» يرفضان مخرجات الهيئة’’ *Al Wasat* (30 July 2017).

80 Temehu.com, ‘Constitutions’ (2017) available at <www.temehu.com/constitutions.htm> accessed 6 February 2018; see also Constitution Drafting Assembly, *Decree 1/2014 Regarding the Rules of Procedures* (2014) Article 60.

81 Temehu.com (n 80).

82 UNSMIL, *Remarks of SRSG Salamé at the High-Level Event on Libya* (Working Paper 2017).

Part II

Contesting normative spaces

4 Challenges, limits, and prospects of 'Judicial Governance' in Nigeria's political translation (1999–2014)

Hakeem O Yusuf

Introduction

The judiciary has become a strategic institution in Nigeria's post-authoritarian transition. Following the country's unnegotiated transition from almost three decades of military rule to civil rule, when the military left power without consulting with diverse relevant stakeholders,[1] the political elite has found considerable motivation to judicialize political conflict on a number of issues that ought to be resolved through political processes. These range from important fiscal policy issues like revenue allocation and public accountability to management of local-level governance. In the Nigerian context, such matters of critical political importance had long been suppressed by a legacy of authoritarian military regimes that followed closely on the heels of colonial rule; ordinarily, they should have been resolved through political processes. Analysts of political processes have noted that political elites, especially in divided societies, sometimes adopt consociation as a political mechanism for resolving power contestations,[2] with a core feature of consociation being the privileging of depoliticized approaches over majoritarian ones.[3] This approach to governance, particularly with reference to intergovernmental contestations, has led to an unprecedented level of judicialization of politics or governance in the country, especially in the first decade of the transition. But this continues to varying extents even today.

The judiciary has been the focus of both national and international attention as a forum that ostensibly offers the opportunity for resolving ongoing disputes and contestations in the country's troubled political transition. It is thus relevant to consider whether or how the judiciary has been instrumental in furthering the transition to proclaimed democratic rule and in fostering the necessary respect for human rights and the need to uphold the rule of law. What has been the nature of judicial intervention in ongoing tensions that emerge from the interplay of a largely fused federal system in a heterogeneous, resource-rich but increasingly impoverished polity? These issues (and similar ones) have repeatedly been framed and pursued not merely as political, but, rather, as constitutional matters and as fundamental rights claims. Such framing brings to the fore the critical nature of the role of the judiciary in times of political change. The theoretical parameters for evaluating such a role have been commendably set out by Ruti Teitel, whose work provides some of the theoretical foundations for the analysis that follows.[4] In the main, as Teitel has explained, in a polity undergoing political change from authoritarian rule, the lack of a sustained institutional experience and practice of constitutional democracy may result in the society being saddled with a fragile political branch.[5] In the Nigerian experience, the fragile state of the political branch has facilitated considerable engagement with and contribution of the judiciary to policy-determination, economic development, and political stabilization of the society.

Setting out the context of the discussion, the first part highlights the historical, political, and constitutional background of the Nigerian society, the nature, and role of the judicial institution in it, not only generally, but also particularly in reference to the focus of this chapter. The next part considers several experiences of the judicialization of politics in the post-authoritarian political transition. Politicization of the judiciary sometimes results from the widespread incidence of a judicialization of politics. This has arguably played out in the Nigerian experience, albeit with serious consequences for the institutional integrity of the judiciary, an analysis of which is presented in the third part of this chapter. All through, the discussion is structured in a style that attempts to engage in reflections on the implications of judicial governance in the Nigerian experience in its post-authoritarian period, and demonstrates that in light of its institutional legacy the significant judicial role in governance has been as strategic as it has been problematic during the period.

Context: historical, political, and constitutional background

Historical and political context

Nigeria is a federation with a central (federal) government and 36 subnational units (states). It gained independence from Britain in 1960.[6] Colonial rule, with its culture of violence and subjugation,[7] set the stage for military rule, which was introduced barely six years after Nigeria gained independence from the United Kingdom. For some, Nigeria 'epitomises the military in government'.[8] During that period, the country's economic and social fortunes took a nosedive as the military acted on many occasions like an army of occupation ruling over captured territory. By the time the military handed over power to a civilian government in 1999, it had substantially weakened all state and civil society institutions in a bid to maintain its hold on power. The unedifying experience of the country under various military juntas over the course of almost three decades with two brief spells of democratic government is documented both in the legal and political science literature.[9]

All institutions of civil governance suffered as the military ruled with authoritarian legislation that undermined the Constitution. The military head of state, usually with an inner cabal of loyalists, formed a ruling council and made decrees under powers for 'the peace, order and good government' of the country.[10] The decrees were declared by the military to be superior to the Constitution. The common feature of military legislation was to either oust or limit the jurisdiction of the courts to question military fiats, which in more than a few instances, abrogated or violated national, regional, and international human rights provisions and standards. The first military legislation, Decree No. 1 of 1966, illegally abolished the Parliament.[11] Section 3 of the Decree provided that the Federal Military Government shall have the power to make laws for the peace, order, and good government of Nigeria or any part on any matter.[12]

Following decades of military rule, the dynamics of democratic transition in Nigeria already presage state and society disputes in addition to the intergovernmental disputes. Both levels of contestations, to varying extents, are key to this discourse. The military left a legacy of institutional distortions and dysfunctions, as a result of which the country now faces a series of ongoing and formidable challenges. The distortions and dysfunctions extend beyond the economic, social, and political sectors to the constitutional and legal order. This is due in part to the nature of military rule with its legendary disregard for the rule of law, constitutionalism, and due process. The Nigerian experience is complicated by the predilection of military rulers for a unified command-structure approach to governance in a heterogeneous society. To take an important example, successive military regimes were notably strong in their rhetoric about the pivotal status of federalism in the polity. However, in practice, the command-structured governance that characterized military rule saddled it with a caricature federation. The military legacy, not surprisingly, led to considerable tension between the federal (central) government and the states, thus setting the issue of federalism at the core of most intergovernmental disputations, which were rife in the first decade of the post-authoritarian period and remain significant to date.

Constitutional context and judicial review

Irrespective of its authoritarian context, judicial review has always been an important part of the post-independent constitutional arrangements in Nigeria, as testified to by the fact that the courts still exercised powers of judicial review during the period of military rule. The military, it must be noted, were typically interested in rule-of-law rhetoric. The country has neither had a constitutional court of that nature in some European countries like Hungary (Magyarország Alkotmánybírósága), France (Conseil Constitutionnel), Belgium (Cour constitutionelle/Grondwettelijk Hof), Germany (Bundesverfassungsgericht), or even African ones like South Africa (Constitutional Court of South Africa) and Egypt (Supreme Constitutional Court of Egypt/al-Maḥkama ad-Dustūrīya al-ʿUlyā, المحكمة الدستورية العليا) nor such a unique innovative concept as in Ethiopia (House of Federation/Yä-Federešən Məkər Bet, የፌዴሬሽን ምክር ቤት). Each of these institutions has a central, purpose-designed role in resolving fundamental constitutional issues in those countries. Nonetheless, Nigeria's judicial system features a diffusion of the power of judicial review virtually through and across its hierarchical federal/state structure. Principally, courts of superior records, the Federal and

State High Courts, the Court of Appeal, and the Supreme Court of Nigeria (the Supreme Court, the Court) have general constitutional powers of judicial review, augmented by statutory provisions and procedural rules of court. In that respect, the operation of judicial review within the legal system in Nigeria resembles the American system.[13] Nigerian courts exercise concrete powers of judicial review with a rigorous test for standing to institute action. The position has been that the standing to file a lawsuit is only available to individuals or groups that can establish a real stake in the outcome of the case.[14]

While the Nigerian judiciary has been noted for a restrictive judicial leaning on *locus standi*, or the right or capacity to institute an action in court, it is arguable that a careful reading of relevant constitutional provisions, especially sections 6 and 46 of the 1999 Constitution, and reflection on the judicial practice suggests that the Nigerian legal system accommodates both *ex ante* and *ex post* facto judicial review. Equally relevant is the fact that section 315 (3) of the 1999 Constitution vests wide powers of judicial review in the court with regard to any form of legislation. Consequently, at least in theory, the courts can declare legislation or a part of it void for inconsistency with the Constitution.

The role of the Supreme Court in judicial review is quite prominent, and this is not just because it is the apex judicial institution in the country, but also as a result of its 'exclusive original jurisdiction'. This is significant, as will become clear in relation to the discussion of federal and subnational jurisdictional disputes. By virtue of section 232 of the Constitution, the Supreme Court is conferred with exclusive original jurisdiction over any dispute between the central and subnational units where there is a dispute on any question (whether of law or fact) on which the existence or extent of a legal right depends. This provision is important, because it is the reason why the Supreme Court became a focal judicial venue for the resolution of intergovernmental disputes among the central and sub-national units on the numerous occasions where political measures appeared not to have served the interests of the political elite in the post-authoritarian era.

The judiciary as a strategic actor in political transition

The insight that Teitel provides on the role of law and the judicial function in transitional contexts is germane to the analysis in this chapter. In her evaluation of the contexts in various regions that have distanced themselves from authoritarian pasts in the 'contemporary wave of political change' across (Eastern) Latin America, Europe, and Africa, she identifies the judiciary as a critical institution for social transformation. However, she argues that despite its important position, the judiciary faces immense institutional challenges in the task of mediating ensuing transitional tensions. This, Teitel notes, is due to the peculiar nature of law and justice in transitional societies. On this account, not only is law an agent of change, but changing circumstances also remould the law. In other words, the exigencies of the transition context require a reconceptualization of law and justice, making law, at the same time, 'transformative . . . extraordinary and constructivist'.[15]

It is fair to argue that in Nigeria's post-authoritarian era, the political branch actively created a predisposing environment for the judicialization of politics. Judicialization of politics, as defined by Alec Sweet, refers to the 'process by which triadic lawmaking progressively shapes the strategic behaviour of political actors engaged in interactions with one another'.[16] Ran Hirschl defines it as 'the ever accelerating reliance on courts and judicial means for addressing core moral predicaments, public policy questions and political controversies'.[17] Javier Cuoso further points out that the judicialization of politics extends, beyond visible judicial control of policy, to the internalization of formal procedures and language of courts by non-judicial decision-making forums.[18]

As a result of the predisposing environment created by the political branches, the judiciary has since become a very strategic actor in the country's political space, following its transition to civil rule in 1999. The question is: What factors drive recourse to the constitutionalization of political space in Africa's potentially largest democracy, considering the rather limited liberal democratic credentials of the country? With the benefit of hindsight, we can identify a number of interrelated factors responsible for this over the last one and a half decades of civil rule in the country. Indeed the courts have become critical in governance and seek to hold the country together through their active involvement in mediating diverse political issues, especially in spaces where power relations are contested.

Such contested spaces have direct implications for socio-economic arrangements, fiscal policy, and economic control, making them the staple of conflict among political elite. As forums for the exercise and expression of power, either at the domestic or international level, political and economic spaces, like geographic spaces, are also highly contested. Analyses of contested spaces are mostly focused on physical territory like colonial territories, urban spaces and sites of physical violence like war.[19] However, it is possible to extend the analysis of contested spaces to sites of political conflict over key public policy issues (like taxation, revenue allocation, and public accountability), intergovernmental claims of jurisdiction as well as individual claims of rights.[20] The relevance of such an extension can be located in the fact that as forums of contestation both geographic and political spaces have to do with claims of authority, ownership, and/or identity bounded up in real or assumed historical experience with direct implications for residents of the contested spaces.[21] Political conflict of this nature and rights claims are commonplace and topical in societies emerging from authoritarianism.

Litigating political conflict, the judicialization of political questions has been an important feature in the Nigerian experience of contested political space in the country's post-authoritarian transition. There are two separate dimensions to the Nigerian experience of the judicialization of politics – one localized, the other globalized. The global dimension is an external dimension that can be located in the worldwide experience of a general rise in judicial power across the world. This tends to be acute in (but by no means limited to) countries experiencing political transition. It is manifested in a notable – though controversial – increase in the involvement of the judiciary in governance. As courts take on 'first-order questions'[22] on governance, unlike any other time in contemporary history, in the last two and a half decades, judicial involvement in policy or political decision-making has gained in significance. Even authoritarian polities have not been left out. Despite variations in local experiences, the main issue remains the same: The power of courts is indubitably on the rise in many societies in Africa, Asia, Latin America, North America as well as in Europe (notably in countries where the revolutions of 1989 transpired).[23] Thus, from a comparative perspective, an explanation can be found in a globalized experience of what is also known as the constitutionalization of politics.[24]

The local or internal dimension of the judicialization of politics in the Nigerian experience can be attributed to four factors. One, it can be attributed to the incongruous and lopsided federal arrangement handed down by the military to the civilian regime. This is one of the legacies of an unnegotiated political transition where diverse and relevant stakeholders – civil society groups, economic actors, traditional authorities, workers' unions, women groups, youth formations, and so on – were not afforded the opportunity of contributing to the shape of the political transitions by the military government that managed the political transition. Another is the rather ironical institutional pedigree of the courts in comparison with the political branches of the state. While the role of the executive and legislative arms had long been fused and assumed by the military, the courts remained separate at all times, even if arguably somewhat marginalized. Thirdly, the combination of a chequered experience of democratic governance, coupled with the assumption of power by a former military ruler with a messianic self-imagining as head of state and government (as president), contributed substantially to the ascension of the judicialization of politics in the country, especially between 1999 and 2007. This phenomenon is well captured by Prempeh as the 'imperial presidency'.[25] Finally, Nigeria's ruling political elite have typically had 'suspect democratic credentials', dominated as they are by former military rulers, their protégés, cronies or associates.[26] Due partly to this fact, electoral processes have been largely manipulated. Recourse to judicialization to legitimize the exercise of power has proved to be an attractive option for the political class.

As a result of the earlier dynamics, 'the judiciary has been faced with the difficult task of maintaining the normative balance between pure politics and law in its interpretive institutional role'.[27] It is now relevant to consider a number of cases that bears out the judicialization of politics claim and the opportunity that has afforded the possibility of judicial governance. Critical analyses of some indicative cases also signpost the challenges of that approach to governance, especially in the context of a post-authoritarian experience.

Formalism and justice in transitions

Rights and truth-seeking

Soon after the inception of the political transition, the courts were inexorably drawn into adjudicating on issues that concerned recovering justice in the context of change from the repressive past. The case, *Justice Chukwudifu Oputa (Rtd.)*

and Human Rights Violations Investigation Commission and Gani Fawehinmi v General Ibrahim Babangida, Brigadier Halilu Akilu and Brigadier Kunle Togun (the *Oputa Panel Case*)[28] is of outmost significance in this regard. It had resounding impact on the truth process, which was the basic transitional justice mechanism adopted by the country to address gross violations of human rights after almost three decades of authoritarian rule.

At the dawn of its transition to civil rule, the Nigerian government attempted to engage with this past. The main mechanism for this purpose was to establish the Human Rights Violations Investigations Commission (Oputa Panel)[29] under the Tribunal of Inquiries Act (TIA).[30] The public hearings of the Oputa Panel included the murder by letter bomb (the first in the country's history) of Dele Giwa, a prominent investigative journalist and editor of the country's leading newsmagazine in 1986. It was widely believed that the office of the military head of state at the time, General Ibrahim Babangida, was implicated in the murder. The late journalist's solicitor, Gani Fawehinmi, petitioned the Oputa Panel, and at the public hearing, he successfully applied to summon General Babangida and his predecessor, General Muhammadu Buhari, as well as the former's security chiefs ('the Generals') as witnesses. The generals insisted they would not attend in person but would rather be represented by a legal team at the public hearing, a move strongly opposed by the petitioner. There was contention about whether the Oputa Panel had the power to issue and serve summons to them and, having objected to appear, the question remained as to whether the generals could give and cross-examine evidence by proxy. The Oputa Panel took the view that the proceedings before such a truth-seeking commission did not constitute adversarial proceedings and the personal attendance of the summoned generals was required for the fulfilment of its mandate.

The generals, however, resisted, and filed an action in the Federal High Court against the summons. Their main argument was that the TIA, under which the Oputa Panel was established, was not an existing law within the meaning of section 315 of the 1999 Constitution of the Federal Republic of Nigeria, which provides for the preservation and modification of existing laws in the country. They sought to have the summons issued under the compulsive powers of the Oputa Panel under the TIA set aside for being in breach of their fundamental rights guaranteed by sections 35 and 36 of the 1999 Constitution. Section 35 of the Constitution provides for the right to liberty, while section 36 guarantees the right to fair hearing.

A consensual reference of the constitutional issues arising from the case was made to the Court of Appeal. Precisely ten days to the close of the Oputa Panel public hearings (31 October 2001), the Court of Appeal ruled in favour of the Generals and their security chiefs. Further appeals by both sides to the Supreme Court facilitated the completion of the Oputa Panel in the meantime.

The Supreme Court held that the Tribunal of Inquiry Act was valid under section 315 of the 1999 Constitution. However, the Constitution does not confer powers on the National Assembly to enact a general law on the tribunals of inquiry for the whole country, which means that the president had exceeded his jurisdiction in establishing the Oputa Panel. Such a body could not be established to carry out a national inquiry into the violations of human rights in all parts of the country. This was a matter within the exclusive jurisdiction of the states, and federal powers of inquiry of such a nature were restricted to the federal capital territory.

Upon reflection, two features of the legal and statutory framework of governance in Nigeria's political transition, among a number of others that are important and disconcerting, can be discerned in the Oputa Panel Case. First is the continued extensive reliance of all branches of government on autocratic legislation deriving from the colonial past and authoritarian military regimes. It is relevant that there is greater awareness now about the undesirability of the situation, but positive action to displace it nonetheless has been marginal at best. Owing to that, an elected transition government chose to rely on the TIA, a pre-republican legislation, to set up a truth commission by executive fiat at a time when it had become standard practice to do so elsewhere under purpose-specific legislation. The Oputa Panel was aware of this problem and requested that the anomaly be rectified. But to date, every other truth process that has been initiated in the country (principally at the state level, like in Rivers and Osun States) has continued to rely on the (state equivalent) same legislation.

Secondly, there is conventional, uncritical judicial adherence (more acutely in a transition context) to precedents based on principles of common law that were imported into the country during colonial rule. This naturally formed the basis of decisions during that period and shortly thereafter. Such uncritical adherence accounts for why the Supreme Court relied extensively on the case of *Sir Abubakar Tafawa Balewa & Others v Doherty & Others* (*Balewa v Doherty*)[31] in the Oputa Panel Case. In *Balewa v Doherty*, the Federal Supreme Court as well as the Privy Council (the latter in its capacity as the final judicial forum for Nigeria in its post-independent but pre-republican period) upheld objections to the compulsive powers and the jurisdictional reach of the Commissions of Enquiry Act, 1961, which had similar provisions to the TIA. Judicial precedent, a core feature of the common law system, has value. However, the point is that the post-republican Nigerian Supreme Court is neither bound in fact, nor by law, by the decisions of both authorities. In light of this, an argument could be made with the imperatives of the transitional justice specifically in mind that there was simply no compelling basis in law for the Supreme Court to rely on *Balewa v Doherty*. The adoption of a plain-fact approach by the court, to which it was no doubt accustomed, hit at the root of the transitional context and, at least implicitly, undermined the rule of law.

What it is to die (or not): rights in a more 'political' context

Within the context of transition, the engagement of state institutions would be required for the desired social transformation. In view of the foregoing discussion on the Oputa Panel Case, it is interesting to find that, given a more 'political' context, the Supreme Court could even contemplate, let alone deliver a radical, purposive decision in a transition context even if without direct acknowledgement of it. This is precisely what the majority decision of the Supreme Court had done in an earlier case, *Peoples Democratic Party (PDP) and 1 Or. v Independent National Electoral and 4 Ors* (PDP Case).[32]

The case concerns litigation on elections that ushered in civil rule into the country in 1999. Atiku Abubakar, the governor-elect (in Adamawa State), was nominated to run as vice presidential candidate and, accordingly, he was no longer available to be sworn in as governor. The electoral body, the Independent National Electoral Commission (INEC), moved to conduct fresh elections for the office of governor as well as deputy governor of the concerned state on the premise that Abubakar's nomination as vice-presidential candidate rendered the position of governor-elect vacant. In a letter on the issue, INEC stated that since he had not been sworn-in, his deputy, having run on a joint ticket as constitutionally required, could not automatically take over the position. However, Deputy Governor-Elect Bonnie Haruna challenged the move in court, arguing that he ought to be sworn in as governor.

The main issue in the contention was the interpretation of the provisions of section 37 (1) of the State Government (Basic Constitutional and Transitional Provisions) Decree 3 of 1998, according to which, '[i]f a person duly elected as governor dies before taking and subscribing to the oath of allegiance and oath of office, the person elected with him as deputy shall be sworn in as Governor'. The critical point of the case was the absence of a direct provision in the electoral laws on the situation that arose in the context of an important political transitional process.

The Supreme Court held that in order to enable the judiciary to play its constitutional role 'effectively and satisfactorily', Courts had to be 'purposive' in their construction of constitutional provisions. Accordingly, the judges had an obligation to ensure that a narrow interpretation of constitutional provisions did not deny citizens of the rights intended to benefit them by the framers of the Constitution.[33] The Court held that the intention of the framers of the constitutional provisions was to make provisions for circumstances where, as a result of a condition or circumstance (the ultimate being death), the deputy governor should step into the office of the governor if the latter is no longer available to take up the position.[34] In a split decision (4–3), the bare majority premised the decision on legislative intent, a radical departure from its customary plain-fact approach to judicial interpretation.

In the lead judgment, Chief Justice Uwais held that the word 'die' in section 37 (1) was not sacrosanct. Rather, a liberal construction that was to be preferred under the circumstances accommodated a situation, as had arisen on the facts of the case, where the elected candidate was 'unavailable' to be sworn in. A narrow or literal construction failed to advance 'the intention, spirit, objects, and purposes of the Constitution'.[35] In light of the fact that Abubakar was barred from reclaiming the position of governor-elect, which he had relinquished (due to his new position), his action could be likened to 'permanent incapacity or even death',[36] and thus would be within the contemplation of the law. To reach its decision, the Court further relied heavily on section 45 (1) of the same law, which provided that the deputy governor was to hold the office of governor once the latter becomes vacant by reason of death, permanent incapacity, or removal for any reason.

The three dissenting justices strongly criticized the majority decision as a form of lawmaking, and as having usurped the function of the legislature.[37] For Justice Ogundare, it represented a 'policy' decision above and beyond the duties of the court. According to him, the business of the court was only to interpret what the legislators actually said rather than discover legislative intention.[38] There was no gap to be filled in the relevant legislation, and even if there was, it was the role of the legislature alone to fill such gaps.[39] He was supported on this point by Justice Mohammed, who declared that 'policy, expediency, political exigency and convenience' ought to be excluded from constitutional interpretation.[40] Despite conceding the value of a liberal interpretational approach to deal with 'eventualities due to changing times, different social environments . . . not fully contemplated or overlooked at the time the constitution was drawn up', Justice Uwaifo also expressly dismissed the majority's preference for a 'purposive approach' in the case.[41]

It is interesting to note (as conceded by the Court) that the provisions of section 45, unlike section 37 (1), only applied after the governor and the deputy governor had assumed office and to that extent, should be deemed inapplicable on the specific facts of the case. However, the majority took the view that because the legislation in issue was of a constitutional nature, the document had to be 'read together as a whole'. They stated that the rationale for the provisions, taken as a whole, was to avoid a vacancy in the important office of Governor and ensure a 'smooth succession' where required.[42]

A fundamental consideration, as far as the Court was concerned, was the rights of Bonnie Haruna. Whereas INEC argued that the law in question, though of a constitutional nature, was only intended to set the framework for governance of the country in the transition period and not to create individual rights, the Court rejected this argument. The majority held that, although both candidates were elected on a joint ticket, in the event that the governor-elect abandoned or relinquished his mandate, the deputy governor-elect would not thereby lose his right to the latter position. Each had acquired individualized rights[43] of a public nature, which could not accrue to the benefit of an individual who was not elected, and to hold to the contrary was not simply 'fallacious but dangerous to the democratic process'.[44] It is logical to share this view.

Conflicting constitutional values?

Federalism v corruption

The foregoing purposive approach to judicial interpretation was also adopted by the Supreme Court in another important case in the transition period, namely in *Attorney General of Ondo State v Attorney General of the Federation & 35 Ors* (the ICPC case).[45] In this case, the Supreme Court was required to determine the propriety of federal legislation, the Independent Corrupt Practices Commission Act, which sought to establish a federal agency, the Independent Corrupt Practices Commission, for combating corruption in the country. The context was that the country had been declared one of the most corrupt in Transparency International's Corruption Index. The incoming president Olusegun Obasanjo, who took office after the end of the military rule, had, in his inaugural address, affirmed the determination of his government to deal with the menace of corruption, which had become 'a full-blown cancer' and 'the greatest single bane' of the country.[46]

It is relevant that, like many federal systems, there is an allocation of legislative powers between the two tiers of government in the Constitution. The 'Exclusive Legislative List' itemizes the exclusive jurisdiction of the federal (central) government while the 'Concurrent Legislative List' specifies the shared sphere of legislative powers between the two tiers. There is an unwritten Residual Legislative List that is constitutionally deemed the exclusive province of respective state governments on unlisted matters. Under the residuary rule, all matters that can be subject of legislation but not stated in any of the two lists are deemed to form a part of the unwritten Residual Legislative List by virtue of section 4 (7) (a) of the Constitution.[47] Notwithstanding the ostensible merits of a central agency for checking corruption in the country, it is important to point out that there are no specific provisions in the itemized list of legislative competencies in the Constitution conferring power on the National Assembly to enact law and establish such a body. As *amicus curiae* rightly noted, the court was faced with a difficult task in the case as the establishment of the ICPC 'impinges on the cardinal principles of Nigeria's federal system'.[48]

In an exceptional unanimous judgment, the Court upheld the validity of the ICPC Act mainly by virtue of section 4 (2) of the Constitution, which provides that the National Assembly has the power to make laws for the peace, order, and good government of the federation with respect to any matter included in the Exclusive Legislative List. This was despite the fact that each of the states had similar powers in respect of their territories and there was no provision under the legislative list for the federal government to make laws criminalizing corruption of state (as against federal) officials. Justifying the position of the court, Chief Justice Uwais stated that if corruption was to be 'eradicated effectively, the solution to it must be pervasive to cover every segment of the society'.[49]

In contrast, the Court upheld the federalism principle over another claimed anti-corruption measure in a dispute between the states and the federal government in *Attorney General of Abia State and 2 Ors v Attorney General of the Federation and 33 Ors* (Revenue Monitoring case),[50] which was decided four years after ICPC. The gravamen of the case was the constitutionality of the Monitoring of Revenue Allocation (MRA) to Local Governments Act, 2005, and was passed by the National Assembly. This law purported to enable the federal government to directly disburse and monitor the revenue-share of local governments, the third arm of government, rather than through the states, as was the practice. The ostensible objective of the MRA was to ensure that allocations from the Federation Account – the joint national purse – were properly distributed to the local governments, since there was strong evidence of widespread practice of deductions from such allocations made through the federal states. The states raised an objection to this on the premise that it was an unconstitutional interference with their jurisdictional powers for the administration of local governments under section 7 of the Constitution.[51]

The Court gave judgment for the states, stressing that no matter how salutary the objective, legislation had to conform to the principle of constitutionality.[52] The Court emphasized the significance of the supremacy clause, which requires all actions of the three arms of government to be in conformity with the provisions of the Constitution. The Court recognized there was some tension in this judgment with its decision in the ICPC case, but restated its support for the anti-corruption policy, insisting, however, that it be executed in line with the Constitution.[53] Interestingly, unlike the ICPC case, two justices dissented based on the unanimous decision in the ICPC case, maintaining (with good reason) that the shared objective of checking inappropriate fiscal practices and corruption commended following the precedent set in the earlier decision.

The question, of course, concerns what seems to be a reversal, given its publicly expressed commitment to the anti-corruption policy of the federal government. The answer may lie in the changing context. The ICPC case was delivered against the background of overwhelming national clamour and international support for action against corruption. Following an initial progressive focus on stemming grand corruption, the federal government then proceeded on a policy course that severely tested and undermined the federal political arrangement of the country, leading to a series of cases instituted by aggrieved states, all of which were taken to the Supreme Court as the only constitutionally prescribed judicial forum for such disputes. In effect, if nothing else, the Court was conscious of its rising docket – particularly from cases filed against the federal authorities by states led by opposition parties.[54] The Court must have become concerned about the implicit abuse of its liberal construction of the powers of the centre in the ICPC case and hence opted for a more restrictive view of the federal principle. This change is consistent with what Teitel has called the 'ambivalent directionality of law'[55] in transitional constitutionalism.

Of political quiescence

Floundering politics, strong judges

The quiescence, or even complete deference, of the executive and legislative branches to the judicialization of politics is sometimes related to the aspiration of the political branch to secure 'regime legitimization'.[56] This is a particularly attractive strategy for the political branch in the context of democratizing polities, which face the challenge of the (re)institution of the rule of law as a principal issue, especially in the context of the demands of the dominating liberal capitalist approach to political transition programming. Equally so is the desire to obtain legitimacy in times of crisis where there is a legitimacy-deficit, deriving from any of a number of dynamics (not least sham elections) of the political branches of government. This legitimacy-deficit has been particularly important in the Nigerian context as a catalyst element in the judicialization of politics. From the inception of the new civil rule era (the fourth republic) to date, there has been a constant and predictable flow of so many pre- and post-elections cases at virtually all levels, but especially at the state gubernatorial and presidential elections, reflecting in part the literal 'winner-takes-all' psyche of the political elite. It has since become a veritable feature of the political landscape for the political elite to secure power and public office or legitimize their hold on it through well-oiled litigation in the face of unresolved political differences. *Rt. Hon. Rotimi Chibuike Amaechi v Independent National Electoral Commission (INEC) & 2 Ors* (*Amaechi v INEC*)[57] aptly demonstrates how the political elite have adopted this strategic preference for securing power through the grace of the courts.

The remarkable political intrigues in *Amaechi v INEC* led to what can be considered an unprecedented level of judicial intervention in the political process in the country's post-authoritarian period. *Amaechi v INEC* relates to political dissension that arose within the ranks of the Peoples' Democratic Party (PDP) in the lead up to the gubernatorial elections in 2007, which was, at the time, an integral part of the milestone civil-civil-transition elections in the country. Rotimi Amaechi, the plaintiff, had won an overwhelming victory at the party primaries, polling 6,527 of the 6,575 delegates' votes in Rivers State. To his consternation, despite having initially submitted his name to INEC (the electoral body), it had been substituted with that of the 2nd Defendant, Celestine Omehia, who did not participate in the primaries. The PDP did this despite a pre-emptive suit filed a week earlier by Amaechi, to stop it from such action.[58] INEC had accepted the substitution on the premise that it was obligated to uphold the PDP's choice of candidate, which the latter had the right to determine. INEC further argued that the substitution was justified by a governmental 'White Paper', which indicted Amaechi for corruption (at the time Speaker of the State House of Assembly). It was argued for Omehia that the sponsorship of a candidate for elective office by a party was 'not a guaranteed right of any member' in which case Amaechi (or for that matter, any other individual) had no statutory or constitutional right to be sponsored by a party as its candidate for an election.[59]

While the case was progressing through trials and appeals (and cross-appeals), the general election proceeded in defiance of court injunctions to stop it from being held, with Omehia declared the winner. The case ended up at the Supreme Court, which deplored the party's breach of its own Constitution, which required the participation of the candidates in the primaries, and, as a result, there was no room for a candidate who did not contest the primaries to emerge as the party's candidate in the general elections. Of greater interest is the holding of the Court that, as a result of the illegal substitution, it was Amaechi who had been elected Governor in the elections. This was despite the fact that his participation in the electoral process had been aborted after the party primaries. This, of course, is curious, but the Court was faced with a context in which the Constitution did not have a place for independent candidature; all candidates are required to be sponsored by a political party. The Court justified its position on the premise that, under the circumstances, it was the party; the PDP that had been voted in by the electorate, and not the candidate. As Justice Aderemi put it, the fact that 'a good or bad candidate may enhance or diminish the prospect of his party in winning' does not detract from the fact that the electoral contest is 'between parties' and 'at the end of the day, it is the party that wins or loses an election'.[60]

In this way, the decision transformed the case from a purely 'intra-party dispute'[61] or contestation in an electoral process. This disregard for the impact of the standing of the candidate on the outcome of an election one way or the other, raises the fundamental question of the propriety of relocating the fundamental majoritarian dimension of elections even in a democratizing polity. It is relevant in this regard that about half a million of the electorate in Rivers State voted in an election in which 19 political parties other than the PDP had participated. In the leading judgment, Justice Oguntade stated that 'the one unchanging feature is that PDP was the sponsoring party' and 'even if Omehia had lost the election', the Court 'would still be entitled to declare' Amaechi as PDP's candidate in the election.[62] While declaring Amaechi the winner of an election he had not participated in, the Court argued that the intention was to avoid 'a dangerous precedent'[63] that would require that fresh elections be ordered whenever an improperly nominated candidate was presented to the electorate in an election, irrespective of whether he or she was going on to eventually win. The Court reasoned that a sure way out of the quagmire was to disregard the result of the ensuing election.

Invoking the imperative of due process, it stated that '[i]n the eyes of the law', Amaechi's nomination earlier forwarded to INEC remained intact,[64] which meant that the candidate that wins in court 'simply steps into the shoes of his invalidly nominated opponent, whether as loser or winner'.[65] But this decision remains problematic for, while it is logical to resolve the nomination issue in Amaechi's favour on the basis of conditions that persisted prior to the election, declaring him winner of a general interparty election in which he had not participated is quite another matter. The latter decision is arguably as inacceptable – if not downright reprehensible – as the action of the PDP and INEC of imposing Omehia illegally as they did.

Like *Amaechi v INEC, Action Congress (AC) and Alhaji Atiku Abubakar v Independent National Electoral Commission* (*AC v INEC*)[66] is a poster child for how prominent political actors enlist the judiciary to settle the ground rules on participation and exclusion in the political space. In 2006, contemporaneous with *Amaechi v INEC*, the presidency was also experiencing high politics resulting from the resistance to the attempt by then incumbent President Obasanjo to extend his tenure, a common practice among African incumbent Heads of State.[67] The constitutional amendment proposed for the move fell through on 16 May 2006.[68] Importantly, the resistance was not only from the opposition parties, but also from important and high-ranking members of his party, the PDP.

Significantly, the latter group was led by Obasanjo's deputy, Vice-President Atiku Abubakar, who by all accounts had a firmer hold of the political machinery of the PDP at the time.

Aspects of the reprisal measures set in motion by President Obasanjo against his Vice-President foregrounded *AC v INEC*. Indeed, the case was the only one in a series of over a dozen instituted by Abubakar alone, or in conjunction with others (including notably, the Action Congress, a new political party he joined), to ward off the multipronged attempts by Obasanjo, not only to neutralize the former's political influence but, more importantly, to prevent him from participating in the 2007 presidential elections. One such measure was a failed bid by Obasanjo to have Abubakar impeached from the office of Vice-President. He was also investigated by the Economic and Financial Crimes Commission (EFCC) in his position as chair of the Petroleum Development Fund. Based on that investigation, Abubakar was indicted for abuse of office by an Administrative Panel of Inquiry (Panel) set up by the federal government. On the strength of this indictment, INEC disqualified him from the presidential poll as the candidate of his new party, the Action Congress (AC).[69] Abubakar and AC challenged this exclusion in a suit filed at the Federal High Court. The Court found in their favour, declaring the exclusion was illegal. INEC appealed and the Court of Appeal allowed the appeal, leading the plaintiffs to also appeal to the Supreme Court.

In a unanimous decision allowing the appeal, the Court declared that INEC had acted illegally, as it lacked the constitutional or statutory powers to disqualify any candidate in the elections and only a conviction by a court of law was sufficient to bar the eligibility to contest for public office.[70] As the court noted, this decision of the parliament derived in part from the experience of abuse of the power (as previously provided in legislation) by the electoral commissions. As the Court stated, in the past, candidates had been disqualified on the day of the elections, owing to which the legislators, wary of previous experience, excluded the power from electoral law and the Constitution.[71] Thus, disillusionment with the exercise of an otherwise political power informed the decision to cede it to the judiciary with the expectation that it would be neutrally and judiciously exercised. The previous position had been that judicial mediation of the process of nomination and selection of candidates would involve the judiciary in strictly domestic affairs of political parties, which, from a majoritarian perspective, was outside its purview.[72]

Courts play a critical role in confronting the designs of incumbents in power to circumvent democratic competition through artful control of electoral bodies like INEC.[73] In this regard, it is germane that the Supreme Court's decision in this case was central to opening up the deliberate constriction of the democratic space by an incumbent intent on subversion of the rule of law and the democratic process.

A good number of cases illustrate the claim of the judicialization of politics in the context of the democratic transition. Apart from those considered previously, some other notable ones include *Attorney General of the Federation v Attorney General of Abia and 35 Ors*,[74] which concerns a disagreement between the federal authorities and the littoral states for oil resources, stemming from the continental shelf of the country. *Attorney General of the Federation v Attorney General of Abia & 35 Ors* (No. 2)[75] and *Attorney General of Ogun State v Attorney General of the Federation*[76] both relate to disputes on fiscal matters (control of revenue and withholding of statutory allocations by the federal government). The Lagos State Government challenged the inherited military legislation, which conferred wide-ranging and ultimate physical planning powers on the Federal Government in *Attorney General of Lagos State v Attorney General of the Federation*.[77]

Politicization of the judiciary

There are numerous instances where the foregoing account of active judicial mediation of politics has been replicated. This experience mainly accounts for the Supreme Court of Nigeria being nominated for two consecutive years (2007 and 2008) as 'Man of the Year',[78] no doubt in recognition of the critical judicial role in 'shaping pathologies of stabilization in a floundering political transition, upholding constitutionalism, rule of law and ultimately, staving-off customary excuses for military incursions in the governance of the country'.[79] It even received commendation from unusual quarters both home and abroad, including the London-based weekly magazine *The Economist* and the United States Congress, for demonstrating independence and for swaying the country's democratization process, and for upholding human rights.[80] From an internal perspective, the words of a renowned social critic and law professor, who argues that the Court has assumed the role of 'sentinel . . . guard for democracy and good governance'[81] are a testament to how especially the image of the Supreme Court (and, by extension, that of the judicial branch as a whole) had become writ large like never before. However, this is not the whole story. Indeed, inasmuch as it implicitly presents the image of a model and reformed judiciary, this would be inaccurate.

Politicization of the judiciary is a possible consequence of the judicialization of politics. On a general note, with the concession of its power in the political space, as alluded to earlier, the political branch had stooped low to conquer, since the political branch can be expected to maintain an interest in recovering such space at some point.

The institutional legacy of not only a decidedly plain-fact jurisprudence but also corruption has made the strategic role of the judiciary in governance in the post-authoritarian period even more problematic. The legacy has had noticeable impact on the institutional relevance of the judiciary. As an example, Rotimi Amaechi, a state governor, who was embroiled in a political power tussle with then president, Goodluck Jonathan, for reasons which included alleged attempts at influencing who succeeds the former, was accused of influencing the acting Chief Judge of the State (Rivers) to transfer 'political cases' away from 'four incorruptible' judges. This implies, among others, that only four of thirty-five judges in the state were 'upright'.[82] While the judiciary itself has declared its support for the anti-corruption campaign, it has continued to face the challenge of securing or maintaining an institutional moral high ground. A number of scandals have seriously threatened, if not considerably diminished, the status of the judiciary in a very challenging transitional context, arguably leaving the country in a precarious position in terms of the efficacy of the admittedly problematic concept of the rule of law. Some judges have been indicted for corruption in high profile – mainly political – cases, especially concerning election petition matters. Corruption in the lower courts has remained a problem in the perception of many. Worse still, the appellate courts have also been seriously enmeshed in questionable conduct, which are essentially carryovers of the authoritarian period.

The constant and widespread recourse to election tribunals for resolving election disputes has made the courts into 'Kingmakers' in a winner-takes-all political system. This has raised the stakes and created considerable pressure on judges, right to the top of the judicial hierarchy. Quite commonly, judges have been accused of, and in some cases, proven to have received very handsome bribes in deciding gubernatorial and presidential election petitions. Some judges have been investigated by and removed on the recommendation of the National Judicial Council (NJC), a Federal Executive Body created by virtue of section 153 of the 1999 Constitution.

The rationale for the creation of the NJC, which is vested with enormous powers is to 'insulate the Judiciary from the whims and caprices of the Executive; hence guarantee the independence of this Arm of Government, which is a sine qua non for any democratic Government'.[83] Thus the NJC is responsible for advising on the appointment, promotion, and disciplining of judges as well as on the training and development of the judiciary. There is much to be said for the positive role the NJC has played in sanitizing the judiciary since its establishment fourteen years ago. However, critics have pointed out that the NJC has sometimes been accused of lack of transparency, as well as a reactive rather than proactive approach to its work, among a number others. Suffice it to say that the NJC has, within its ranks, too, been faced with challenges to its integrity. The 'Salami saga' illustrates a particularly disturbing instance of how the NJC itself has been affected by the general malaise of corruption and lack of principled institutional direction, which the judiciary has struggled with over the years.

Justice Ayo Salami was the President of the Court of Appeal (PCA), the second highest court in Nigeria's court hierarchy.[84] He had been involved in a long drawn controversy with then Chief Justice of Nigeria (CJN) and head of the judiciary, Chief Justice Aloysius Katsina-Alu. Justice Salami, who had been promoted to the Supreme Court, turned down his promotion, claiming that it was a ruse to get him out of the Court of Appeal because he had rejected a directive of Chief Justice Katsina-Alu to pervert the cause of justice by influencing the decision of a panel of Justices of Appeal sitting as the final court for the resolution of gubernatorial election petitions for a part of the country. The NJC subsequently became divided on the issue. The chair of the NJC, Chief Justice Katsina-Alu, was directly implicated in the allegation raised by Justice Salami. Yet the chief justice headed a meeting that suspended Justice Salami. This was followed by litigation from various parties: Justice Salami, politicians from the President's party who were aggrieved because they had lost out in election petition tribunals set up by Justice Salami in his function as PCA, and some members of the public.

Disturbingly, the issue remained unresolved despite the succession of two other chief justices (both of whom found Justice Salami not guilty) after the retirement of Chief Justice Katsina-Alu. This is because former President Goodluck Jonathan complicated matters by refusing to reinstate Justice Salami contrary to the advice of the NJC following various investigations and meetings on the issue. In the end, Justice Salami retired in October 2013, after almost two years of what many perceived to be a political persecution for demonstrating judicial firmness against the electoral malpractices of the president's party, which controlled the government at the centre. The Salami saga can rightly be considered the lowest point in the dwindling institutional integrity and *auctoritas* of the Nigerian judiciary. As one respected commentator put it, it is clearly 'one of the ugliest episodes in Nigeria's judicial history'.[85]

In 2014, the series of self-inflicted or externally generated politicization of the judiciary took a more sinister dimension with direct physical attacks on judges with the complicity of highly placed government officials, including the law enforcement agencies. In Rivers State (whose governor is at logger-heads with the president), a state high court was the site of a shooting episode while a judge was sitting over a contested political case. In Ekiti State, two state high court judges were beaten up by hired thugs and supporters of one of the parties in Ekiti State while sitting over a petition on a controversial gubernatorial election. The petition involved an incumbent state governor who is a member of the country's main opposition party that had lost the election, and the newly elected, albeit yet to be sworn-in governor-elect from the national ruling party at the time. After a ruling by one of the judges assuming jurisdiction over the matter, one of the judges was virtually stripped naked, while thugs tore up court records. In each instance, the courts and the judges were under the watch of law enforcement agents (police and state security services) controlled by the national authorities, who did nothing to secure the safety of the judges.[86] While the NJC promptly condemned the incidents and urged investigation and action on the part of the appropriate agencies,[87] the leadership of the police and respective security agencies as well as the national authorities were ominously silent on it. This was despite widespread media reports indicating that the newly elected governorship candidate from the national ruling party had instigated the beating up of one of the judges, allegedly for a 'dubious ruling' aimed at depriving him of his electoral victory. The candidate was eventually sworn-in as governor with the national government deploying a massive contingent of soldiers to the state. In this regard, it is important to note that disruption of judicial proceedings by members of the public was virtually unheard of in the heydays of military rule. It is also not on record that judges were physically assaulted during the period. The apparent complicity of the federal government in the physical attacks on judges perceived to be against its political interests further undermines the authority of the judiciary and the prospects for deepening the culture of rule of law in the country.

Conclusion

In view of its potential to promote economic development and rule of law, judicial reformation is a key aspiration in a democratizing polity. This is particularly important where the political branches have a democratic legitimacy-deficit. The Nigerian courts, most notably, the apex court, have adopted both constitutional and extra-constitutional principles in mediating intergovernmental contestations and human rights challenges in the turbulent transition in the country. The judiciary has been actively involved in the democratization process and also occupied a central role in the process of political accountability. This forms a critical part of the project of social transformation that underwrites the important process of transition from years of authoritarian military rule. However, the judicialization of politics can result in the politicization of the judiciary, which would severely affect its decisional independence and, ultimately, have serious implications for the rule of law.[88]

Courts easily run into difficulties when they are tasked with overseeing political processes.[89] The Nigerian experience of an unaccountable judiciary, with the privilege of participation in governance in a post-authoritarian transition, persuasively demonstrates some of the challenges. The judiciary has a questionable record of accountability and has been accused of complicity in the country's experience of authoritarian military rule. Like dancing on ice, getting a judiciary that has not been accountable for its role in past authoritarian regimes to perform the function of stabilizing the polity and to resolve major political disputes was never going to be easy. The institutional accountability-gap of the Nigerian judiciary resonates in the close involvement of the courts in post-authoritarian challenges of governance in the country, suggesting that only a transformed judiciary can effectively play this critical role in such transitioning and liberal democratic societies as Nigeria.[90]

Notes

1 'Civil rule' or 'civil governance' seems to be an appropriate description of what the transition has achieved as against the aspirational 'democratic rule'.

2 HO Yusuf, *Colonial and Post-Colonial Constitutionalism in the Commonwealth: Peace, Order and Good Government* (Abingdon Routledge 2014) 128.

3 RB Andeweg, 'Consociational Democracy' (2000) 3 *Annual Review of Political Science* 509–536, 511.

4 RG Teitel, 'Transitional Jurisprudence: The Role of Law in Political Transformation' (1997) 106 *Yale Law Journal* 2009.

5 Teitel (n 4) 2230.

6 British colonial rule in Nigeria commenced with the cession of Lagos to the British monarch in 1861 though the British had for some time previous to that been interfering in local politics of the people of the territory. See IA Ayua and DJ Dakas, 'Federal Republic of Nigeria' in J Kincaid and GA Tarr (eds), *Constitutional Origins, Structure and Change in Federal Countries* (Montreal and Kingston McGill University Press 2005) 241. A narrative of how the cession came about is provided in Attorney General of Southern Nigeria v. John Holt and Company (Liverpool) Limited and Others [1915] A.C. 1, 4–7.

7 T Falola, *Colonialism and Violence in Nigeria* (Bloomington Indiana University Press 2009).

8 J Hatchard, M Ndulo, and P Slinn, *Comparative Constitutionalism and Good Governance in the Commonwealth: An Eastern and Southern African Perspective* (Cambridge University Press Cambridge 2009) 242.

9 The country was under civil democratic rule from 1 October 1960 to 15 January 1966 and from 1 October 1979 to 31 December 1983. See, for example, B Owasanoye and C Nwankwo, *Suppressed Rights: Constitutional Rights Violations in Military Decrees 1984 to 1999* (Constitutional Rights Project Lagos 1999); BO Nwabueze, *Military Rule and Constitutionalism in Nigeria* (Lagos Spectrum Books 1992); HO Yusuf, 'Travails of Truth: Achieving Justice for Victims of Impunity in Nigeria' (2007) 1 (2) *International Journal of Transitional Justice* 268; O Oyediran (ed), *Nigerian Government and Politics under Military Rule, 1966–79* (New York St. Martin's Press 1980); E Osaghae, *The Crippled Giant: Nigeria Since Independence* (Bloomington, IN Indiana University Press 1998).

10 I Elaigwu, 'Federalism Under Civilian and Military Regimes' (1988) 18 (1) *Publius* 173, 183; Yusuf (n 2) 133–140.

11 The military named federal and state legislation Decree and Edict respectively.

12 See also section 2 (1) of the Constitution (Suspension and Modification) Decree No. 1 of 1984.

13 L Epstein, J Knight, and O Shvetsova, 'The Role of Constitutional Courts in the Establishment and Maintenance of Democratic Systems of Government' (2001) 35 (1) *Law & Society Review* 117–164, 117; Ayua and Dakas (n 6) 258.

14 The restrictive approach to locus standi is mainly an instance of judge-made law. As it is not a matter of legislation, ironically, it was formulated by the Supreme Court during the country's four year-interlude of civilian-led government. See Abraham Adesanya v. President of the Federal Republic of Nigeria & Anor (1981) 2 *Nigeria Constitutional Law Reports* 358.

15 Teitel (n 4) 2014.

16 A Stone Sweet, 'Judicialisation and the Construction of Governance' (1999) 32 (2) *Comparative Political Studies* 147, 164.

17 R Hirschl, 'The New Constitutionalism and the Judicialization of Pure Politics Worldwide' (2006) 75 (2) *Fordham Law Review* 721.

18 JA Cuoso, 'The Judicialization of Chilean Politics: The Rights Revolution that Never Was' in R Sieder, L Schjolden, and A Angell (eds), *The Judicialization of Politics in Latin America* (New York Palgrave Macmillan 2005) 105–130, 106.

19 See comprehensively, for instance, L Purbrick, J Aulich, and G Dawson (eds), *Contested Spaces Sites, Representations and Histories of Conflict* (Palgrave Macmillan 2007); W Fahmi and K Sutton, 'Greater Cairo's Housing Crisis: Contested Spaces from Inner City Areas to New Communities' (2008) 25 (5) *Cities* 277; J Barr and E Countryman, *Contested Spaces of Early America* (University of Pennsylvania Press 2014); R Desai and R Sanyal (eds), *Urbanizing Citizenship: Contested Spaces in Indian Cities* (London Sage 2012).

20 See, for instance, the contributions in J Unger (ed), *Associations and the Chinese State: Contested Spaces* (New York ME Sharpe Inc. 2008), examining the impact of the exponential growth of associations of various types in China on state and societal action in the country.

21 See the contributions in F von Benda-Beckmann, K von Benda-Beckmann, and A Griffiths (eds), *Spatializing Law: An Anthropological Geography of Law in Society* (Farnham Ashgate 2009), exploring, among others, how legal rules may map on to social and physical spaces or conceptions of them for organizing social, political and legal activities in different societies.

22 S Issacharoff, 'Democracy and Collective Decision Making' (2008) 6 (2) *International Journal of Constitutional Law* 231.
23 See, for instance, A Bâli, 'Courts and Constitutional Transition: Lessons from the Turkish Case' (2013) 11 (3) *International Journal of Constitutional Law* 666–701, 666; RH Bork, *Coercing Virtue: The Worldwide Rule of Judges* (Vintage 2010); J Klaaren and T Roux, 'The Nicholson Judgment: An Exercise in Law and Politics' (2010) 54 (1) *Journal of African Law* 143; S Balme, 'The Judicialisation of Politics and the Politicisation of the Judiciary in China 1978–2005' (2006) 5 (1) *Global Jurist Frontiers*; RH Pildes, 'The Supreme Court 2003 Term Foreword: The Constitutionalization of Democratic Politics' (2004) 118 (29) *Harvard Law Review* 28; R Hirschl, 'The Judicialization of Mega-Politics and the Rise of Political Courts' (2008) 11 *Annual Review of Political Science* 93; T Moustafa, *The Struggle for Constitutional Power: Law, Politics and Economic Development in Egypt* (Cambridge, MA Cambridge University Press 2007); W Sadurski, *Rights Before Courts: A Study of Constitutional Courts in Postcommunist States of Central and Eastern Europe* (Dordrecht Springer 2005); T Moustafa, 'Law Versus the State: The Judicialisation of Politics in Egypt' (2003) 28 (4) *Law and Social Inquiry* 883; A Stone Sweet, *Governing with Judges: Constitutional Politics in Europe* (Oxford Oxford University Press 2004); T Ginsburg, *Judicial Review in New Democracies* (Cambridge Cambridge University Press 2003); J Priban, *Dissidents of Law* (Dartmouth Hampshire Ashgate 2002); T Ginsburg, 'Constitutional Courts in New Democracies: Understanding Variations in East Asia' (2002) 2 (1) *Global Jurist* 1; J Ferejohn, 'Judicializing Politics, Politicizing Law' (2002) 65 *Law and Contemporary Problems* 41; T Ginsburg and G Ganzorig, 'When Courts and Politics Collide: Mongolia's Constitutional Crisis' (2000–2001) 14 (2) *Columbia Journal of Asian Law* 309; H Klug, *Constituting Democracy: Law, Globalism and South Africa's Political Reconstruction* (Cambridge Cambridge University Press 2000); S Issacharoff, 'Constitutionalizing Democracy in Fractured Societies' (2004) 82 *Texas Law Review* 1861; NC Tate and T Vallinder, *The Global Expansion of Judicial Power* (New York New York University Press 1995); A Stone Sweet, *The Birth of Judicial Power in France: The Constitutional Council in Comparative Perspective* (New York Oxford University Press 1997); R Teitel, 'Post-Communist Constitutionalism: A Transitional Perspective' (1995) 26 (1) *Columbia Human Rights Law Review* 167.
24 Hirschl (n 23).
25 H Kwasi Prempeh, 'Presidential Power in Comparative Perspective: The Puzzling Persistence of Imperial Presidency in Post-Authoritarian Africa' (2008) 35 *Hastings Constitutional Law Quarterly* 761.
26 T Oyekola, 'Ex-Military Officers Are Doing Well in Politics: Gowon' *Nigerian Tribune* Online Edition (Lagos Tuesday 4 September 2007); HO Yusuf, 'Colonialism and Dilemmas of Transitional Justice in Nigeria' (2018) 12 (2) *International Journal of Transitional Justice* 257–276, 273–274; R Joseph, 'Africa: States in Crisis' (2003) 14 (3) *Journal of Democracy* 159–170, 159, 163.
27 HO Yusuf, 'The Judiciary and Political Change in Africa: Developing Transitional Jurisprudence in Nigeria' (2009) 7 (4) *International Journal of Constitutional Law* 654, 656.
28 MJSC [2003] 63.
29 Named after its chairman, Justice Chukwudifu Oputa, Justice em., Supreme Court of Nigeria. For a discussion of the Oputa Panel see HO Yusuf, 'Human Rights Violations Investigations Panel (Oputa Panel)' in L Stan and N Nedelsky (eds), *Encyclopedia of Transitional Justice* 3 (New York Cambridge University Press 2013) 160–165; see also for wider issues of transitional justice in the country, HO

Yusuf, 'Country Studies: Nigeria' in L Stan and N Nedelsky (eds), *Encyclopedia of Transitional Justice* 2 (New York Cambridge University Press 2013) 333–339.
30 Cap. No. 447, Vol. XXIII, Laws of the Federation of Nigeria 1990.
31 (1963) 1 Weekly Law Reports 949.
32 (1999) 7 S.C. Part II 35.
33 PDP Case (n 32) 47 f. Emphasis mine.
34 PDP Case (n 32) 71 f.
35 PDP Case (n 32) 71 f.
36 PDP Case (n 32) 61.
37 The dissent was so extensive it doubled the length of the lead judgment and the concurring decisions of the majority put together.
38 PDP Case (n 32) 91.
39 PDP Case (n 32) 85–99.
40 PDP Case (n 32) 111.
41 PDP Case (n 32) 123.
42 PDP Case (n 32) 72 f.
43 PDP Case (n 32) 50.
44 PDP Case (n 32) 148 per Justice Ayoola. Emphasis mine.
45 (2002) 6 S.C. Part I 1.
46 Nigeria World, 'Inaugural Speech by His Excellency, President Olusegun Obasanjo Following His Swearing-in as President of the Federal Republic of Nigeria on May 29, 1999' available at <http://nigeriaworld.com/feature/speech/inaugural.html> accessed 31 October 2013.
47 Attorney-General, Ogun State v. Aberuagba (2002) 22 (52) *WRN* 77.
48 ICPC Case (n 45) 17.
49 ICPC Case (n 45) 28.
50 (2006) 7 NILR 71 1.
51 (2006) 7 NILR 71 4 f.
52 (2006) 7 NILR 71 24.
53 (2006) 7 NILR 71 19.
54 See e.g. Attorney General of Abia & 2 Ors v. Attorney General of the Federation & 33 Ors (2006) 7 NILR 71; Attorney General of the Federation v. Attorney General of Abia & 35 Ors (No. 2) (2002) NWLR 542 S.C.
55 Teitel (n 4) 2033.
56 P Domingo, 'Judicialization of Politics: The Changing Political Role of the Judiciary in Mexico' in R Sieder, L Schjolden, and A Angell (eds), *The Judicialization of Politics in Latin America* (New York Palgrave Macmillan 2005) 21–46, 22; Issacharoff (n 22).
57 (2008) 1 S.C. Pt. I, 36.
58 Ibid., 54–56.
59 Amaechi v. INEC (n 57) 57.
60 Ibid., 110.
61 This is the characterization of the case by the Court. See lead judgment per Oguntade JSC, Amaechi v. INEC (n 57) 111.
62 Amaechi v. INEC (n 57) 111 f, emphasis mine.
63 Ibid., 112.
64 Ibid., 111, emphasis mine.
65 Ibid., 112.
66 (2007) 6 S.C. Pt. II 212.
67 This was known as the 'Third Term Project'. See, for instance, SJ Omotola, 'Political Globalisation and Citizenship: New Sources of Security Threats in Africa' (2008) 52 (2) *Journal of African Law* 263–268, 268; S Adejumobi (ed), *Governance and Politics in Post-Military Nigeria: Changes and Challenges* (Palgrave

Macmillan 2010) 173–206; A Isumonah, 'Imperial Presidency and Democratic Consolidation in Nigeria' (2012) 59 (1) *Africa Today* 43.

68 Isumonah (n 67) 57; DK Posner and DJ Young, 'The Institutionalization of Political Power in Africa' (2007) 18 (3) *Journal of Democracy* 126–127.

69 Omotola (n 67) 278.

70 AC v. INEC (n 69) 230, emphasis mine.

71 Ibid., 265.

72 See, for instance, Dalhatu v. Turaki (2003) 15 NWLR Pt. 843, 300 and Onuoha v. R.B.K Okafor (1983) 2 SCNLR 244.

73 Issacharoff (n 23) 264.

74 (2002) 4 S.C. Pt I, 1.

75 (2002) NWLR 542.

76 (2002) 12 SC Pt II, 1.

77 (2003) 6 SC Pt I, 24.

78 O Omenuwa, '2007: The Year of the Supreme Court' (Lagos Thursday 27 December 2007) *The Daily Independent* Online Edition available at <www.independentngonline.com/?c=129&a=7908> (20 February 2008).

79 HO Yusuf, 'Robes on Tights Ropes: The Judicialisation of Politics in Nigeria' (2008) 8 (2) *Global Jurist* 1, 29.

80 See 'Belgore, Oputa, Sagay, Others Hail Supreme Court' (Lagos Sunday 24 June 2007) *The Guardian* Online Edition available at <www.nigerians-abroad.com/news/headlines/belgoreoputa-sagay-others-hail-supreme-court> accessed 18 February 2008; C Ikokwu, 'Nigerian Judiciary Strong, Independent, Says US Congress' (Abuja Thursday 19 July 2007) *This Day* Online Edition and 'Nigeria-Democracy by Court Order' (London Thursday 24 January 2008) *The Economist* available at <www.economist.com/displaystory.cfm?story_id=10567560&fsrc=RSS> accessed 21 October 2013. But cf. Mo Ibrahim Foundation, 'Ibrahim Index of African Governance 2007' available at <www.moibrahimfoundation.org/nigeria> accessed 12 October 2013 in which the country ranked a dismally in a continental survey of 48 countries on issues of rule of law, judicial independence, human rights, etc.

81 C Adingupu, 'Obi's Judgement Is Warning to Political Gangsters' (Lagos Sunday 24 June 2007) *The Guardian* Online Edition.

82 'Amaechi Does Not Teleguide Judges, Boms Insists' (21 October 2013) *Daily Independent* Online available at <http://dailyindependentnig.com/2013/10/amaechi-doesnt-teleguide-judges-boms-insists> accessed 21 October 2013.

83 Nigeria National Judicial Council, 'About the Council' available at <http://njc.gov.ng> accessed 27 October 2013.

84 He retired on 12 October 2013 after attaining the mandatory retirement age of 70.

85 See, for instance, T Dare, 'Salami: An Epic Injustice' (13 August 2013) *The Nation* available at <http://thenationonlineng.net/new/salami-an-epic-injustice> accessed 12 October 2013; see also A Adedeji, 'NJC, CJN and Justice Ayo Salami Saga' (November 2013) *The Daily Independent* available at <http://dailyindependentnig.com/2012/11/njc-cjn-and-justice-ayo-salami-saga> accessed 31 October 2013; Ihuoma, 'No Regrets Over Clash with Former CJN: Justice Salami' *The Punch* available at <www.punchng.com/news/no-regrets-over-clash-with-former-cjn-justice-salami> accessed 31 October 2013.

86 G Ariyibi and D Akinrefon, 'Judiciary Attacked: Thugs Beat up Ekiti Judge, Tear his Suit' (26 September 2014) *Vanguard* available at <www.vanguardngr.com/2014/09/judiciary-attacked-thugs-beat-ekiti-judge-tear-suit/#sthash.WKXUxncV.dpuf> accessed 5 November 2014; 'Ekiti Election Tribunal Adjourned as Thugs Beat Up Judge' available at <www.informationng.com/2014/10/

fayose-led-thugs-to-beat-judges-ekiti-state-chief-judge-tells-njc.html> accessed 11 September 2018.

87 'NJC Begins Probe of Attacks on Ekiti Judges' (3 October 2014) *This Day* available at <www.thisdaylive.com/articles/njc-begins-probe-of-attacks-on-ekiti-judges/190454> accessed 5 October 2014.

88 Domingo (n 56) 28.

89 Issacharoff (n 22) 261.

90 Further references are to be found in AS Mohammed, 'The Masquerade Unmasked: Obasanjo and the Third Term Debacle' in S Adejumobi (ed), *Governance and Politics in Post-Military Nigeria: Changes and Challenges* (Palgrave Macmillan 2010) 173–206; *Attorney-General, Ogun State v. Aberuagba* (2002) (22) WRN 52.

5 Contesting normative spaces

The status of African traditional courts under international human rights law

Prosper Simbarashe Maguchu

Introduction

The advent of colonialism resulted in legal pluralism. That is to say that the settler's legal systems were applied alongside indigenous customary laws.[1] This necessitated the continuation of African traditional courts as arbiters for customary law in many African states. Today, African traditional courts continue to play a significant role in the lives of large segments of the population, partly because the limited subject matter they govern, such as family law, property law, and traditional authority, are those that greatly affect the daily lives of many Africans. Moreover, in modern times, access to courts is recognized as a fundamental human right in a number of human rights instruments. Yet, for the indigen and the illiterate, the right of access to the courts will remain illusory due to the exorbitant legal costs, as well as the confusing and rigid procedures associated with the formal courts.[2] Efforts to smooth this situation have entailed resorting to traditional courts.

Despite their enormous popularity, African traditional courts are persistently criticized for violating international human rights norms in the administration of justice, particularly with regard to gender justice.[3] It is against this background that this chapter seeks to critically analyze the normative space within which African traditional courts operate in the context of the normative frameworks of international and regional human rights law that guarantee the right to equality and fair trial before courts and tribunals.

Definition and discussion of terms

At this juncture, some key terms useful for the purposes of this chapter need to be defined. First, the term 'customary law' will be used throughout this chapter to refer to

> an established system of immemorial rules . . . evolved from the way of life and natural wants of the people, the general context of which was a matter of common knowledge, coupled with precedents applying to special cases, which were retained in the memories of the chief and his councillors, their

> sons and their sons' sons until forgotten, or until they became part of the immemorial rules.[4]

Second, 'pluralism', as defined here, refers at the very least to the following:

> (1) the way the state acknowledges and relates to different social fields within society and represents itself ideologically and organisationally; (2) the internal diversity of state administration, the multiple directions in which its official subparts struggle and compete for legal authority; (3) the ways in which the state itself competes globally with other states in larger arenas, (in the African context with the African Union (AU), for instance and other global organisations); (4) the way in which the state is interdigitated (internally and externally) with non-governmental, semi-autonomous social fields which generate their own (non-legal) obligatory norms, with regard to which they can induce or coerce compliance; (5) the ways in which law may depend on the collaboration of non-state social fields for its implementation and so on.[5]

Third, the term, African traditional court, as used here, is to be understood in both the simplest and the most complicated forms. In its simplest form, it is defined as 'a body, based in and serving a particular locality. It is recognized as having the power to resolve disputes in accordance with the local customs, cultural or ethnic values, religious norms or tradition'.[6] In its more complex form, it can be understood to mean those judicial administrative bodies that resolve disputes among ethnic groups on the basis of the concept of group rights, and they existed in different countries prior to colonization, albeit under different names.

Some characteristics of African traditional courts

Before proceeding to examine the tension between African traditional courts and the international human rights norms, it is important to note that customs vary from place to place, and from one ethnic group to another; concomitantly characteristics of traditional courts also vary between places and ethnic groups. What this suggests is that there is no homogeneous body of customary law, rather only different systems for different tribes. As Mahmood Mamdani points out: '[T]here was not a single customary law to govern all tribes defined as one racialized group-natives. Instead, each tribe was ruled under a separate set of laws, called customary laws'.[7] This notwithstanding, some common salient features discussed next distinguish African traditional courts from regular courts.

Conceptual basis

The basic concept of African traditional courts has been the subject of much analysis by scholars studying African jurisprudence. According to Owor, the African traditional court system operates within an interconnected web of kinship, law, religion, and culture, which is based on the African philosophy of humanism called *Ubuntu*.[8] The author further explained that the concept of *Ubuntu* is expressed in the rule of reconciliation that seeks to restore harmony in society through principles derived from the concepts of group rights and natural justice.[9] She also mentioned that the entire clan took part in the administration of justice through a communitarian notion of human rights.[10]

What is more, this is not the only evidence that supports this hypothesis. In another major study, Matavire, remarks that under the African principle of personhood,

> it is the community which defines an individual as a person, and the same community defines traditional values and ethics that are to be upheld by the members of the customary community. Any violation of these ethical values is an offence to the whole community and is punishable.[11]

Matavire generally views matters as concerning the whole community or group, a perspective that also represents the conceptual basis of African traditional courts in seeking truth, reconciliation, compensation, and retribution. Premised mainly on a strong communitarian character, conceptually, it presents a stark contrast to procedural justice, retribution, incarceration, and revenge, all of which form the basis of the European justice administration system.[12] This was necessary and was influenced by the natives' need for continued close social and economic cooperation for their survival.[13]

Consequently, African traditional courts are characterized by a high degree of public participation insofar as every adult member of the community is free to participate in its proceedings, such as in the cross-examination of the accused or witnesses.[14] The process is voluntary and the decision is based on consensus. The *Ibo* village assembly in eastern Nigeria, the Eritrean village assembly *bayto*, the Təgrəñña-speaking areas of Eritrea and Təgray (Northern Ethiopia), the *gadaa* (age-set) system of the Oromo societies of Ethiopia and partially also Kenya, as well as the *kiama* (council of elders) of the Kikuyu in Kenya, are among the popular examples of spaces where decisions are made in a consensual manner before clan courts.[15]

Composition

African customary courts are commonly headed by the traditional leader, normally the chief or the headman, who is also an arbitrator appointed from within the community, and this appointment is based on status or lineage.[16] In traditional patriarchal societies, women could not succeed to chieftainship and were unable to preside over traditional courts; however, some evidence suggests that this practice is now changing owing to a paradigm shift. For instance, in South Africa, Zimbabwe, Ghana, Uganda, and Namibia, women can be appointed as tribal chief or headman. In urban or peri-urban areas, where there are no traditional chiefs or headmen, it is possible to establish community courts through a committee of elected members by the residents of a particular village or urban locality with the mandate to adjudicate over disputes.[17]

The presiding chief or headman is customarily accompanied by a group of councillors or advisors who are appointed mainly on the basis of seniority. In part, however, factors such as intelligence, knowledge of the customs, and eloquence of speech, as well as personal credentials, such as integrity and good sense of judgement, could also play an important role.[18] The final judgment rests exclusively with the head of the community who also holds executive and legislative power.[19] Even if all members of the community are allowed to participate in the process, the terms of participation are not always equal.[20] In many communities, adults are categorized along various levels in the hierarchy, whereby some categories of persons may not be permitted to speak in public. This applies differently in different traditions. In some traditions, such as that of the Shona tribes in Zimbabwe, a young man may not speak in the presence of his father, and in others, adult women may not be allowed to speak at public gatherings. All that is changing, and sometimes gender representation at the traditional courts is guaranteed.

Powers

In general, the traditional courts have limited mandate with respect to personal jurisdiction, subject matter, the law or other relevant normative regulations, and the type of remedies they can award. These issues will be discussed seriatim in the next section.

During colonialism, the personal jurisdiction of traditional courts was premised on ethnicity, and this meant that traditional courts could only exercise their jurisdiction on issues where the parties were indigenous people. Today, race and colour no longer form the basis for determining the personal jurisdiction of African traditional courts; only such factors as residence, proximity, nature of transaction or subject matter, and the applicable law will apply. For instance, in South Africa, if the nature of the case is such that it falls under customary law, whereas other facts favour jurisdiction, then the matter shall be addressed by the traditional court regardless of the parties.[21]

With regard to the subject-matter jurisdiction of African traditional courts, in many countries it is limited as well when it comes to specific issues, including that of the status of women or youths. By way of example, Zimbabwe excludes traditional courts from adjudicating matters where women are likely to be prejudiced in male-dominated traditional courts, particularly on issues such as maintenance, custody, and guardianship of minor children, on dissolution of marriage or the interpretation, validity, and effect of wills.[22]

Similarly, in most countries, traditional courts do not have the mandate to deal with criminal issues (Zimbabwe[23] and Uganda),[24] and in other states, they deal with minor crimes (Botswana[25] and Swaziland).[26] In some countries, they have jurisdiction over offences that are known to customary law (Namibia).[27] Having said that, the distinction between civil and criminal matters is irrelevant under customary law, 'since customary law does not distinguish between civil matters and penal matters, the latter being the prerogative of the individuals who submit them to customary courts as well as the tribal chief'.[28]

Finally, another key fact to remember is that, in terms of jurisdiction, African traditional courts normally order the losing party to pay only towards the compensation or restitution. They do not have the mandate that common law courts would to order retribution, or award deterrent damages.[29] In other words, their aim is to restore the relationship between the parties and not to punish the offender.

Effectiveness

The effectiveness of the African traditional courts can be attributed to a series of factors, for instance, its simplicity and informality, as Koyana has observed:

> [T]he simplicity of the procedure they follow, the absence of interpretation, the absence of anything like 'a trial within a trial', and the facts that postponements are surprisingly infrequent as compared to magistrates courts, are all factors which contribute to these courts being preferred by many in the rural areas.[30] Moreover, many litigants approach these courts because they are familiar to customary law and the proceedings are conducted in local dialects. Further, traditional courts are almost free of charge thus making them affordable and accessible. In South Sudan, for instance, one source found that African traditional courts provide the only practicable and affordable method of resolving conflicts amongst the rural population located far away from the modern court systems.[31]

This view is supported by a study of the Institute for Security Studies (ISS) in three African states, which reveals that people prefer greater access, speed, and familiarity with law on the one hand, and processes that are rooted in their own culture and traditions on the other.[32] It corroborates Fremont's findings insofar as many African populations, especially rural populations, remain under the direct influence of their traditions on a day-to-day basis and resist the rules and approaches of modern law.[33]

Although the enforcement of the decisions of the traditional courts varies from state to state, in general, their decisions are enforced through sanctions against parties. Despite the absence of prisons or police force, and even though fines may have been rare, the force of public opinion could be overwhelming. If an entire community ostracized an individual member, life on a day-to-day basis would become impossible. As one author noted, customary law does not need a strong individual or institution for its enforcement; rather, it is respected because each individual recognizes the benefits of abiding by law, so that only laws that are made by the minority and applied from the top down need strong enforcement mechanisms.[34] Public consensus is key to the effectiveness of African traditional courts, especially in their ability to facilitate enforcement of decisions secured through social pressure, because disobeying a final ruling is tantamount to disobeying the entire community and may result in social isolation.[35]

Normative framework of the right to equality before courts and tribunals and to a fair trial

The normative framework for the right to equality before the courts and tribunals and to a fair trial is crystallized in many international human rights law instruments. The key legal text on fair trial is Article 14 of the International Covenant on Civil and Political Rights (ICCPR).[36] According to the UN Human Rights Committee (HRC), General Comment No. 32, Article 14 on the Right to Equality before the Courts and Tribunals and to a Fair Trial is of a particularly complex nature, combining various guarantees with different scopes of application.[37] More importantly, the HRC 'recognises the existence of legal plurality' insofar as it holds that Article 14 of the ICCPR, which protects the right to fair trial applies 'where a State, in its legal order, recognises courts based on customary law, or religious courts to carry out or entrust them with judicial tasks'.[38] The HRC further highlights certain significant standards and requirements, which should be observed by traditional courts before their judgments can be considered binding by the state, as follows:

i proceedings before such courts are limited to minor civil and criminal matters;
ii proceedings meet the basic requirements of fair trial and other relevant guarantees of the Covenant;
iii the guarantee under Article 14 (1) 'is violated if certain persons are barred from bringing suit against any other persons such as by reason of their race, colour, sex, language, religion, political or other opinion, national or social origin, property, birth or other status'; and
iv the judgements of such courts are 'validated by State courts in light of the guarantees set out in the Covenant and can be challenged by the parties concerned in a procedure meeting the requirements of Article 14 of the Covenant'.[39]

Similarly, in the context of the African normative framework for human rights, the right to equality before the courts and tribunals and to a fair trial is provided for under Article 7 of the African Charter of Human and Peoples Rights (the Charter).[40] Article 7 of the Charter is further articulated in the Principles and Guidelines on the Right to a Fair Trial and Legal Assistance in Africa (the Guidelines), which specifically enumerates the areas in which traditional courts, 'where they exist, are required to respect international standards on the right to a fair trial'.[41] Section Q of the Guidelines is multifaceted, paragraph (b) (1) – (12) is a list of the minimum requirements on the general right to equality before traditional courts, and paragraph (c) specifies requirements for the independence of courts. Paragraph (d) deals with impartiality and, finally, paragraph (e) lays down the procedural guarantees of security and tenure of employment to members of traditional courts.

Together, these legal provisions outline that the right to equality before the courts and tribunals and to a fair trial from both the international and regional legal regimes touches upon a plethora of distinct aspects. This will be addressed in greater detail in the next section of this chapter.[42]

Tensions between traditional courts and international human rights law

Based on the characteristics of traditional courts enumerated earlier, it can be deduced that there are a number of clashes with the international human rights law, although this is a contentious issue. Some scholars believe it is an ambitious task for traditional courts to subscribe to the notion of international human rights given their peculiar practice.[43] Thus, the tension generally reflects the human rights debate on the conflict between universalism and cultural relativism. In brief, universalism, as theory, takes the view that certain ethical principles are universally applicable and that, for example, every society, regardless of its culture and history, ought to have respect for human life. According to cultural relativism, on the other hand, every culture has its own ethical principles, and there is no basis for claiming that some are wrong and should change or be changed. Peart has warned that

> the danger is, however, that if customary law is to be struck down because it is in conflict with European notions of morality and ethics, there may be little left of customary law.[44]

If this holds true, then how legitimately can the African customary practices applied before traditional courts be legitimately evaluated on the basis of international human rights?

The evaluation of the African traditional practices before the traditional courts can be legally justified on the principle of *pacta sunt servanda*, according to which states must discharge the obligations assumed under treaties in good faith. Thus, Africa has become part of the global human rights movement by virtue of adopting and ratifying international human rights instruments, and African states are tacitly accepting the universality of human rights.[45] The remainder of this section will analyze the African traditional courts against a series of specific rights under section 14 of the ICCPR and Article 7 of the Charter, as further elaborated in the Guidelines and HRC General Comment No. 32 *in seriatim*.

Right to equality before the law

According to the HRC General Comment No. 32, the right to equality before the law and equal access to the court or access to administration of justice must be effectively guaranteed and no individual should be deprived of his or her rights to claim justice regardless of the type of the judicial body.[46] Similarly, Article Q (b) (1) of the Guidelines guarantees the right to equality before traditional courts for all proceedings before African traditional courts regardless of gender as a minimum requirement.

Thus, an essential element of the principle of equality is that women must have equal access to courts in order to be able to effectively vindicate their rights. A cursory glance at African traditional courts reveals that they discriminate against women in many instances. This happens in many traditions; importantly, women cannot access the courts unless represented by a male relative. In some communities, widows in mourning and menstruating women are not allowed to access traditional courts.[47] As Matavire admits, in cases where women are represented by male relatives, their opinions are mostly not represented well.[48] All things considered, the inferior status attributed to women – which they share with minors – in many African traditional courts constitutes discrimination and a violation of the right to equality before the law.

Right to equality of arms

The HRC's General Comment No. 32 recognizes the right to equality of arms as a cornerstone of the right to a fair trial.[49] Equality of arms 'means that same procedural rights are to be provided to all the parties unless distinctions are based on law and can be justified on objective and reasonable grounds, not entailing actual disadvantage or other unfairness to the defendant'.[50] On a similar note, the Guidelines state that traditional courts should guarantee 'adequate opportunity to prepare a case, present arguments and evidence and to challenge or respond to opposing arguments or evidence' by both parties to a dispute regardless of gender.[51]

Customary law, in many instances, fails to fulfil the equality of arms test when it favours some members of the community. To give an illustration, older men, particularly those who serve in the role of arbitrators as chiefs, elders, and religious priests, are likely to have an advantage over members of the community whose gender, caste, age, and marital status puts them at a disadvantage, and who are often disadvantaged in the judicial system.[52] Matavire's observations on traditional courts in Zimbabwe is that, in most cases, women are in a weaker position during proceedings to challenge men, for which reason, there is no equality of arms between men and women before traditional courts.[53]

Right to legal representation

Right to legal representation is one of the components of a fair trial.[54] Be that as it may, professional legal representation before a traditional court, for either plaintiff or defendant, is prohibited in most countries. It has been argued that it is contrary to the notion of individual rights to not be legally represented by a legal practitioner of his or her own choice.[55] Similarly, in his analysis of the controversial South African traditional courts Tobias Reinauer points out that

> not being able to have a legal representative's assistance is in court is problematic since it puts the applicant or the accused at the risk of suffering from unequal chances to decide a case for him/herself. Especially in rural areas individuals of the poorer strata of society might not well have sufficient access to and knowledge of sources of customary law and thus might have to face unfair disadvantages in court towards the better informed.[56]

The question of legal representation clearly illustrates the conflict between the principles and the actual application of human rights. The Guidelines guarantee the right to 'an entitlement to seek the assistance of and be represented by a representative of the party's choosing in all proceedings before the traditional court'.[57] It is, however, silent on the right to legal representation. It is not yet clear whether this may mean that legal representation is not a requirement. The only analysis carried out by South African Law Committee (SALC) took various factors into consideration before concluding that it was justified to exclude legal representation before traditional courts.[58]

Presumption of innocence

It is a widely held view that the interrogational procedure, whereby the chief and his councillors question a party to the proceedings in traditional courts, amounts to a presumption of guilt against the accused. In other words, African traditional courts reverse the burden of proof. This suggests that the accused person appearing before a traditional court is expected to convince the court of his or her innocence.[59] The right to be presumed innocent until proven guilty according to law is further compromised because when dealing with offences, traditional courts take into account such factors as the past conduct of the accused, or that of the accused's family.

Moreover, it has been reported that the right to silence is not respected before African traditional courts, which means that a person who is unable to clearly articulate his or her position, or who decides to maintain silence, may prejudice his or her case.[60] This is in conflict with Article 14, paragraph 2 of the ICCPR, which guarantees that everyone charged with a criminal offence shall have the right to be presumed innocent until proven guilty according to law.

Right to court records

Many African traditional courts are not courts of record; this basically means that they do not have a record of the proceedings. Many traditional courts do not have the equipment necessary to record proceedings and the situation is excerbated by the fact that, in some situations, the presiding officers are unable to read or write. A record of the proceedings is normally necessary in case of review or appeal for the higher court to be able to confirm its agreement with the decision of the lower court and ensure that proper procedures were followed. One of the principles of a fair trial specified in the Guidelines under section C (b) requires that proper systems exist for recording all proceedings before judicial bodies, for storing such information and making it accessible to the public.

Nevertheless, whether or not this is in violation of the right to a fair trial is not clear, as some scholars have held the view that records are not necessarily important for African traditional courts, since matters are heard again on appeal.[61] On the other hand, other proponents of traditional courts in Africa believe that these courts should all be made into courts of record. To that end, traditional courts must be upgraded, modernized, and equipped with the necessary personnel, as well as court buildings, offices, and court equipment.[62]

Similar cases dealt similarly

The general right to equality before courts and tribunals under Article 14 (1) of the ICCPR demands that similar cases are dealt with in similar proceedings and that any dissimilarity should be based on objective and reasonable grounds.[63] However, it is a salient feature of the African traditional courts that disputes tend to be resolved by searching for the underlying motive or for the criminal intent that instigated the wrongful act, with the objective of precluding a recurrence of the problem in the future. It has been argued that, owing to that, such cases rarely receive similar treatment.[64] In addition, there is no strict adherence to legal certainty and to due process before traditional courts, because the proceedings are mainly voluntary. At the same time, although the parties are responsible for coming up with a solution, the process is moderated by the presiding officer and other community members, who may also influence the outcome.[65]

According to the report of the Penal International Reform (PIR) on access to justice in sub-Saharan Africa, the fact that similar cases are not treated the same is 'anathema to the concept of justice which demands equality before the law based on due process, including legal certainty'.[66] Put differently, it is quite important for traditional courts to maintain uniformity for practical purposes as they deal with very similar cases.[67]

Right to appeal and review

The right to appeal the decision, to apply for a review against a criminal conviction, or to sentence is provided for under Article 14 paragraph 5 of the ICCPR and Article 7 (1) b of the Charter.[68] This right is regarded as part of a fair trial because it allows error correction. The importance of putting mechanisms for error correction in place cannot be underestimated in any legal system, owing to the inevitability of discrepancies in judgments, in fact finding, or in the application of rules.[69] For that reason, error correction can in turn serve many other functions, such as enhancing the legitimacy of the courts, creating consistency and preventing miscarriage of justice[70]

Basing his arguments on the views of a Ugandan political scientist, Mahmood Mamdani, Maru argues that 'there is a theoretical right to appeal from local courts to the formal legal system but in practice such appeals are quite rare'.[71] The author emphasizes that as such reviews are carried out by a law officer, who is a member of the executive, and not of the judiciary as required under international human rights law, it is unlikely that they are independent.[72] Likewise, Reinauer asserts that the limited knowledge people have of law sources poses a problem for the enforcement of their rights, which renders possibilities of review and appeal practically ineffective.[73]

Separation of powers

The debate about fair trial under African traditional courts has gained fresh prominence, with many arguing that, since traditional government combines legislative, executive and judicial functions, chiefs and headmen do not embody the concept of separation of powers.[74] SALC has listed factors based on a research it conducted that indicated violation of the separation of powers doctrine by traditional courts, such as the fact that traditional leaders are part of the state administrative arm for the simple reason that they implement government policies and enforce law, they are attached to the executive and, in some cases, they hold the capacity of being the 'complainant, prosecutor and the judge'.[75] At the same time, it concluded that as the judicial process of traditional courts involves administering mainly simple customary rules of law in simple disputes, a formal separation of powers between the executive and the judiciary is neither crucial nor practical at this point in time.[76]

Legal qualifications

Traditional leaders are not legally qualified and, on the face of it, that appears to be a violation of the right to be tried in a fair manner, which requires that judicial officers have training in legal studies. However, as with any other issue discussed earlier, they are two conflicting views. According to Owor, formal educational and legal qualifications are not required due to the uncomplicated participatory nature of customary law proceedings.[77] On the other hand, other proponents of African traditional courts, like Homolisa, acknowledge the need to train traditional leaders on legal principles. It is argued that traditional courts handle not only cultural and custom-related cases but also criminal and civil cases that are based on common and statutory laws. It is necessary and imperative, therefore, that the judicial officers undergo some kind of paralegal training to equip them with the requisite skills and knowledge to handle such matters.[78]

Manner of appointment

According to the HRC General Comment No. 32, the manner of appointment determines whether a court of law is independent and fair.[79] Likewise, the

Guidelines clearly specify under section A (4) (h) that the process of appointment of judicial officers should be transparent and accountable, and an independent body should be created for this purpose. The intention of the framers of the Guidelines was to make the appointment procedure for national courts replicable for traditional courts.[80] Matavire claims that traditional courts have been polarized by politicians, who at times influence the selection of traditional chiefs, as a result of which respect and legitimacy tend to be accorded to those chosen via customary means.[81]

Security of tenure

The HRC General Comment No. 32 governing the independence of the judiciary recommends not only that states adopt rules that guarantee the security of tenure of judicial officials until the mandatory retirement age has been reached, or their term of office has expired, but also that states adopt conditions that guarantee promotion, transfer, suspension and cessation of their functions, and, additionally, that the judiciary remains independent from possible political interference of the executive and the legislature.[82] Yet the majority of studies indicate that traditional leaders in many African countries do not enjoy the security of tenure accorded to judicial officers, as the minister who confers the jurisdiction in the first place may deprive them of the right to hold court.[83] Nowack observes that this constitutes a violation of the principle of independence, which requires judicial officers to serve a reasonably long term.[84] Likewise, Madhuku underscores the significance of security of tenure, arguing that if judges can easily be removed from office, there is, in reality, no independence of the judiciary.[85]

Conclusion

African traditional courts offer essential access to justice to the majority of the citizens who cannot access the mainstream courts. Despite this noble goal, tension between these courts and the international human rights norms governing the administration of justice continue to rise. Significantly, the gender imbalance before African traditional courts has the potential of corroding the efficacy and relevance of these courts. Therefore, further research is urgently needed to generate informed methods that will harmonize traditional customary law with the peremptory norms of equality, independence, and fair trial.

All things considered, it seems pertinent to remember, as warned by SALC, that African traditional courts should be treated as courts *sui generis*.[86] To that extent, the conflict between African traditional courts and the human rights law regime illustrates the dispute between universalism and cultural relativism in the application of human rights. An eminent scholar has cautioned that 'while African customary law emphasizes rights in the context of the community and kinship rights and duties of individuals to their communities, human rights norms typically enjoin state parties to treaties to respect human rights and take all appropriate measures to eliminate discrimination against women'.[87]

Above all, there is a need to strike a balance between community rights and gender rights. In this, as in other matters, international and regional instruments on human rights, such as the ICCPR and the Charter, the Guidelines, and the Human Rights Committee General Comment on the Right to a Fair Trial and Equality can be very instructive.

Notes

1 J Fremont, 'Legal Pluralism, Customary Law and Human Rights in Francophone African Countries' (2009) 40 *Victoria University of Wellington Law Review* 153 offers a succinct explanation that in many cases colonial authorities chose to impose public law while allowing for traditional private law to survive, leaving intact the fundamental sphere of social community life. In other cases, colonial authorities have squarely refused to recognize and allow for traditional rules to subsist (such as allowing marriage for children or polygamy) as against 'public order'. Moreover, colonial authorities would let traditional laws survive on the condition that they did not violate rules of 'natural justice' or 'public decency' defined by colonial authorities.
2 D Kaersvang, 'Courts in South Africa: Legal Access for the Poor' (2008) 15 *Journal of the International Institute* 4, 9.
3 See in general, DS Koyana, 'Customary Law and the Role of Customary Law Courts Today' (1997) *Consultus* 126–128.
4 JC Bekker (ed), *Seymour's Customary Law in Southern Africa* (Cape Town: Jutta 1989) 11.
5 SF Moore, Certainities Undone: Fifty Turbalent Years of Legal Anthropology 1949–1999 (2001) 7 *Journal of the Royal Anthropological Institute* 107.
6 See section 1 of the Principles and Guidelines on the Right to a fair Trial and Legal Assistance in Africa (2003) DOC/OS/(XXX) 247 of 2003, in R Murray and M Evans (eds), *Documents of the African Commission on Human and Peoples' Rights II (1999–2007)* (Hart Publishing 2007–2009) 381.
7 M Mamdani, 'Making Sense of Political Violence in Post Colonial Africa' in H Leuer and K Anyidoho (eds), *Reclaiming the Human Sciences and Humanities Through African Perspectives* 1 Sub-Saharan (Ghana Accra 2012) 181–199, 188.
8 M Owor, 'Creating an Independent Traditional Court: A Study of Jopadhola Clan Courts in Uganda' (2012) 56 *Journal of African Law* 215, 222.
9 Owor (n 8).
10 Owor (n 8).
11 M Matavire, 'Interrogating the Zimbabwean Traditional Jurisprudence and the Position of Women in Conflict Resolution: A Case of the Shona Tribes in Muzarabani District' (2012) 2 *International Journal of Humanities and Social Science* 219.
12 T Reinauer, 'Traditional Courts in South Africa as Tumbling Block on the Road Towards a Modern Constitutional State?' (Konrad-Adenauer-Stiftung, June 2012) 2 available at <www.kas.de/wf/doc/kas_31491-1522-2-30.pdf?120702103719> accessed 18 September 2013.
13 Penal Reform International, *Access to Justice in Sub Saharan Africa: The Role of Traditional and Informal Justic Systems* (Astron Printers 2000) 9.
14 Reinauer (n 12) 2.
15 Economic Commission for Africa, 'Relevance of African Institutions of Governance' (June 2007) available at <repository.uneca.org/bitstream/handle/10855/3086/bib.%2025702_1.pdf> accessed 10 October 2013.
16 The difficulty here is that there are many ethnic groups in Africa that do not have the institution of chieftaincy – the acephalous societies. The British colonizers

intervened by demanding that every community appoint a chief, but this was not in accordance with the customary laws in many communities.

17 South Africa Law Commission, 'The Harmonisation of the Common Law and Indigenous Law: Traditional Courts and the Judicial Function of Traditional Leaders' (1999) 82 *SALC* 16.

18 Matavire (n 11) 221.

19 Reinauer (n 12).

20 L Seafield, 'South Africa: The Interdependence of All Human Rights' in L Seafield and AA An-Na'im (eds), *Human Rights Under African Constitutions: Realizing the Promise for Ourselves* (University of Pennsylvania Press 2003) 295–341, 330.

21 SALC (n 17) 22.

22 Customary Law and Local Courts Act (Cap. 7:05), Sec. 16 (1) (b).

23 Ibid.

24 Resistance Committee (Judicial Powers) Statute, No. 1 of 1988.

25 Chapter 04:05 Laws of Botswana (Customary Courts) sections 11, 17.

26 Swazi Courts Act No. 80 of 1950 section 12.

27 Traditional Authorities Act, No. 17 of 1995 section 10 (3).

28 JS Israel and MK Kabesa, 'Handling Guilty Under Customary Law: Concept and Basis' available at <www.the-rule-of-law-in-africa.com/wp-content/uploads/2010/07/Handling-Guilt-Under-Customary-Law-Concept-and-Basis-Jean-Salem-Israel-Marcel-Kapya-Kabesal.pdf> accessed 15 October 2013.

29 Israel and Kabesa (n 28) 3.

30 Koyana (n 3) 127.

31 T Mennen, 'Legal Pluralism in Southern Sudan: Can the Rest of Africa Show the Way?' (2007) 3 *Africa Policy Journal* 49.

32 Mennen (n 31) 3.

33 Fremont (n 1) 150.

34 B Benson, 'The Enterprise of Law: Justice Without the State' (1990) *Pacific Research Institute* 12–15.

35 Penal Reform International Report (n 13) 26, 33.

36 GA res 2200A (XXI), 21 UN GOAR supp (no. 16) at 52: UN doc A/6316 (1996).

37 Article 14 is fourfold, para 1. The first part set out a general guarantee of equality before courts and applies regardless of the nature of proceedings before such bodies, b. entitles individuals to a fair and public hearing by an independent and impartial tribunal established by law. Para 2–5 procedural guarantees available to a person charged with a criminal offence. Para 6 compensation in cases of justice miscarriage. Para 7 prohibits double jeopardy. See Human Rights Committee, General Comment No. 32.

38 International Council on Human Rights Policy, *When Legal Worlds Overlap Human Rights, State and Non-State Law* (Geneva International Council on Human Rights Policy 2009).

39 International Council on Human Rights Policy (n 38) 29–30.

40 OAU doc CAB/LEG/67/3/Rev.5(1981), came into force 21 October 1986.

41 DOC/OS /(XXX)247 of 2003, in Murray and Evans (n 6) 381.

42 Ibid., section Q.

43 M Baderin, 'Recent Developments in the African Regional Human Rights System' (2005) 5 *Human Rights Law Review* 117, 126.

44 Quoted in Koyana (n 3) 126.

45 M Ndulo, 'African Customary Law, Customs, and Women's Rights' (2011) 18 *Indiana Journal of Global Legal Studies* 87, 90.

46 U.N. Doc. CCPR/C/GC/32 (2007) para 9.

47 Reinauer (n 12) 3.
48 Matavire (n 11).
49 U.N. Doc. CCPR/C/GC/32 (2007) para 13.
50 ICCPR Article 14 para 1 and Guidelines Q (b) (6).
51 Guidelines (n 41) Q (b) (6).
52 Penal Reform International Report (n 13) 37.
53 Matavire (n 11) 222.
54 7 (1) (c) of the African Charter, Article 14 (3 (d) of the ICCPR.
55 Article 14 para 1.
56 Reinauer (n 12) 3.
57 Guidelines (n 41) Q (b) (8).
58 See comprehensively, SALC (n 17) 36–39.
59 SALC (n 17) 4 para 222.
60 SALC (n 17) 4.
61 SALC (n 17) 15.
62 P Holomisa, 'Balancing Law and Tradition: The TCB and Its Relations to African Systems of Justice' (2011) 35 *Administration Crime Quarterly* 17–22.
63 UN HRC General Comment No. 32 para 14.
64 'Penal Reform International Report on Access to Justice in Sub-Saharan Africa' 36.
65 Penal Reform International Report (n 13) 36.
66 Penal Reform International Report (n 13) 36.
67 Cited with approval from DA Strauss, 'Must Like Cases Be Treated Alike?' (2002) 1 *Chicago Public Law and Legal Theory Working Paper No. 24* available at <www.law.uchicago.edu/files/files/24.strauss.like-cases.pdf> accessed 18 October 2013.
68 In this chapter, appeal and review are used synonymously.
69 PD Marshall, 'Comparative Analysis of the Right to Appeal' (2011) 22 *Duke Journal of Comparative and International Law* 1, 2.
70 Marshall (n 69) 3.
71 V Maru, 'The Challenges of African Legal Dualism: An Experiment in Sierra Leone' (2005) *Open Society*.
72 Maru (n 71).
73 Reinauer (n 12) 3.
74 Owor (n 8) 231.
75 SALC (n 17) 14.
76 SALC (n 17) 14.
77 Owor (n 8) 237.
78 Holomisa (n 62).
79 HRC General Comment No. 13: UN doc HRI/GEN/1/Rev.1 (1994) 14 para 3.
80 Owor (n 8) 233.
81 Matavire (n 11) 222.
82 HRC General Comment 13: UN doc HRI/GEN/1/Rev.1 (1994) 14 para 19.
83 SALC (n 17) 14.
84 M Nowack, *United Nations Covenant on Civil and Political Rights: CCPR Commentary* (Engel Publishers 2nd Edition); Koyana (n 3) 319 f para 25.
85 L Madhuku, 'Constitutional Protection of the Independence of the Judiciary: A Survey of the Position in Southern Africa' (2002) 46 *Journal of African Law* 232, 237.
86 SALC (n 17) 15 para 4.3.
87 Ndulo (n 45).

6 Protecting groups in Africa

Between international law, national law, and local customary law*

*Julia Kriesel***

Collective rights as human rights?

Since the *Universal Declaration on Human Rights* (UDHR) was adopted by the General Assembly of the United Nations in 1948, the idea of human rights has been inextricably linked to the concept of individual rights.[1] In its *Statement on Human Rights* in 1947, the American Anthropological Association argued for the incorporation of group rights within the concept of human rights, categorically stating that one was inextricable from the other. Yet the drafters of the UDHR ignored this anthropological view.[2] The inherent tension between both declarations created the never-ending dispute between universalism and cultural relativism of human rights.[3] However, subsequent human rights treaties, namely the two international covenants[4] on human rights and the two regional human rights treaties in Europe and America, adopted an individualistic concept of human rights concurrent with the UDHR.

Following World War II, however, the idea of group rights became increasingly important within public international law due to two different circumstances: First, the decolonization process led to a first-time discussion of the so-called 'third dimension rights' or 'solidarity rights'.[5] At the universal level, several declarations and conventions refer to these group rights, for instance, the rights to existence,[6] self-determination,[7] development,[8] peace,[9] and environment.[10] Second, the growing awareness of the problems of indigenous peoples and minorities forced the international community to acknowledge the need for group rights for these peoples and to regard them as subjects of international law.[11] Unfortunately, the majority of these group rights are only protected through non-binding declarations of the General Assembly of the United Nations. For that reason, the majority of group rights are not enforceable at the universal level of public international law.

Although some regional human rights treaties, such as the *European Convention for the Protection of Human Rights and Fundamental Freedoms*[12] (ECHR) and the *American Convention on Human Rights*[13] (ACHR) are enforceable, they essentially guarantee only individual rights from a positivist legal perspective. It was not before the 1990s that the Inter-American Court on Human Rights (IACtHR) began to protect vulnerable groups through an extensive interpretation of the guaranteed rights as group rights and the European Court on Human Rights began to protect groups by protecting group members.[14] Hence the explicit incorporation of group rights within the African human rights protection system in 1981 entailed a completely new perspective on human rights' concepts and treaties. In his report for the Organization of African Unity (OAU), the Secretary-General of the OAU justified the incorporation of the so-called peoples' rights within the *African Charter on Human and Peoples' Rights*[15] (ACHPR or Banjul Charter) as follows:

> Noting that, in Africa, man is part and parcel of the group, some delegations concluded that individual rights could be explained and justified only by the rights of the community. Consequently, they wished that the Draft Charter made room for the peoples' rights and adopted a more balanced approach to economic, social and cultural rights on the one hand and political and civil rights on the other.[16]

Thus, the incorporation of the peoples' rights is based on an understanding of the relationship between individual and society that is different from the European and American concept. Historically, in most African societies, the individual is primarily understood as part of a society, whereas in Western societies the society is largely understood as a counterpart to the individual.[17] The presumption that similar collective rights can be located at the national and the local level is founded upon this cultural imprint.

Adopting a public international law perspective, this chapter examines the relationship between the three relevant normative spaces – public international law, national constitutional law, and local customary law. The first part examines the positively guaranteed rights at the international and the national level. The second part identifies and analyzes the consequences of the findings from part one. Finally, the general conclusions will be presented.

Collective rights *de lege lata*: public international law and national constitutional law in Africa

Within the domain of legal theory, public international law and national law are predominantly regarded as a clash of legal orders, which has to be solved via a dualistic or a monistic approach.[18] In contrast, the history of human rights challenges the assumption of a clash or of an irreconcilable difference between the normative orders and instead presents multiple instances of interdependent interaction of public international law and constitutional law – at least when it comes to the process of lawmaking.[19] One should bear in mind that the lawmaking regional human rights treaties are 'treaties negotiated and entered into by states which oblige states parties as to their treatment of peoples, including their own nationals'.[20] As such, they are responses to experiences of structural injustices (*Antworten auf Erfahrungen strukturellen Unrechts*) and the result of a permanent learning process.[21] The first human rights treaties were adopted on a national level,[22] and later these ideas were transferred to the international level, as many of the provisions of the following UDHR reflect general principles of law.[23] Nowadays, international human rights treaties again influence constitutional orders, and a general horizontal and vertical constitutional convergence can be observed.[24] This interdependent interaction of the international and constitutional normative spaces and the previously mentioned justification of the incorporation of the peoples' rights within the Banjul Charter create the presumption of a broad reception of the concept of peoples' rights, or at least of comparable concepts of collective rights, within African national constitutions. Therefore, in a first step, two questions arise: Which collective rights are guaranteed by the Banjul Charter? And are similar rights or collective rights in general granted within African constitutions?

Group rights within the Banjul Charter

Articles 19 to 24 of the Banjul Charter, devoted exclusively to the rights of peoples (as groups), guarantee, among others, the right to equality and the right to have rights, the right to self-determination, the right to free disposal of wealth and natural resources, the right to economic, social, and cultural development and equal enjoyment of the common heritage of mankind, the right to security and peace and the right to a general satisfactory environment.[25] Compared to such other rights as civil, political, economic, social, and cultural rights, these rights that are intended exclusively for the collective reveal, on the one hand, the enormous imprint of the colonial experiences and the African anxieties about the future[26] and, on the other hand, a community-oriented approach towards human rights.[27]

Article 19 ACHPR places the right of all peoples to be equal and to have the same rights before the other peoples' rights, which is why the following articles have to be read in the context of this right. Furthermore, Article 19 sentence 2 ACHPR is designed to prevent the domination of any one group over another.[28] Very tightly connected to the right to equality is the right to existence. Compared to universal public international law, Article 20 para 1 sentence 1 ACHPR constitutes a ban not only on physical genocide but also on cultural genocide, and includes both the negative and the positive dimensions.[29] Also, the right to existence generates a logical precondition for other group rights. The right to self-determination is guaranteed in all its different facets, as it contains political, economic, and social aspects.[30] In addition, Article 20 para 2 ACHPR guarantees for all colonized or oppressed peoples the right to free themselves. Lastly, Article 20 para 3 ACHPR ascribes to all peoples the right to assistance by member states in their struggle for liberation. The right to economic self-determination is incorporated in Article 21 ACHPR, which grants the right to free disposal of wealth and natural resources. Simultaneously, Article 21 ACHPR also illustrates the negative experiences during colonial times and the everlasting exploitation of the continent by 'international monopolies'.[31]

The subsequent rights demonstrate inter alia the African anxieties about the future: Article 22 ACHPR guarantees the right to development and the equal enjoyment of the common heritage of mankind.[32] The African Commission on Human and Peoples' Rights (Commission, ACoHPR) found a way to implement the right to development, which was doubted for a long time, within its Endorois-Communication in 2009.[33] The numerous violent unrests that have taken place in Africa, and still do, explain the right to peace and security, guaranteed by Article 23 ACHPR.[34] Lastly, Article 24 ACHPR grants the right to a general satisfactory environment, emphasizing its strong ties to the rights to development and self-determination. However, this right simultaneously deviates from the right to environment in universal public international law, as Article 24 ACHPR puts the right holder – the people – and not the environment at the centre.[35]

In the years following the Banjul Charter, many concerns were raised with regard to the intended subjects, the content, and the implementation of those group rights. However, in its communications in the last 20 years, the Commission has presented a remarkable way to refute the former anxieties.[36] Although these communications are not binding, they create political pressure and can therefore be regarded as a kind of soft law. In its communications, the Commission interprets several other (individual) rights as group rights and puts them beside group rights developed exclusively for peoples. In this regard, one should mention the right to property (Article 14 ACHPR), the right to health (Article 16 ACHPR) and the right to family (Article 18 ACHPR). In the SERAC-Communication, the Commission interpreted all three rights together as encompassing the right to housing or shelter – as an individual or collective right.[37] Addressing the issue of a communal right to property, the Commission set the requirements for a collective property right for the first time in the Endorois-Communication.[38]

The noteworthy quasi-jurisprudence of the Commission presents a broad concept of collective rights, which cannot be reduced to the peoples' rights of the Articles 19 to 24 ACHPR, but also needs to be applied to traditional individual rights.

Group rights within African constitutions

Except for Morocco, all remaining 54 African states are member states of the Banjul Charter.[39] Therefore, the question arises, if and how group rights are guaranteed on the constitutional level within African states. As most of the African constitutions generally refer to the ACHPR in their preambles and guarantee in a comprehensive manner the 'traditional' human rights,[40] it would be a logical consequence to also find the peoples' rights in these constitutions. Unfortunately, this is not the case.[41] The broad idea of collective rights (a group, not an individual, is the right holder) is to some extent reflected in 14 of 55 African constitutions. The majority of these states did not adopt the comprehensive approach of peoples' rights from the Banjul Charter, and most of them only guarantee one or two specific collective rights. Cultural community rights, for example, are granted by Benin,[42] South Africa,[43] Sudan,[44] and South Sudan,[45] whereas

Burundi,[46] Cameroon,[47] and Uganda[48] grant minority rights. Even today, Ethiopia is the only state that guarantees an unconditional right to self-determination, including the right to secession.[49] The right to development, which is considered to be a genuinely African right because of its founder M'baye, is granted as an individual right in several African constitutions,[50] but only in the cases of Ethiopia[51] and Malawi[52] it is granted as a collective right. Environmental rights are guaranteed in the majority of African constitutions – however, only as individual rights.[53] Burkina Faso grants a collective right to natural resources.[54] Although Equatorial Guinea refers to the communal African tradition in the preamble of its constitution, collective rights are not explicitly granted.[55] An all-encompassing approach towards collective rights, which adopts the idea of the peoples' rights of the Banjul Charter, is only included in the constitutions of Angola (via a general understanding of rights as individual and collective rights),[56] Burundi (via the inclusion of the ACHPR as part of the constitution),[57] the Democratic Republic of Congo (via collective rights for minorities, to property, peace, and security, environment, natural resources and the enjoyment of the heritage of human mankind)[58] and Senegal (via collective rights in a quite general manner without further explanations).[59]

From the perspective of public international law, this overall low rate of adoption of the concept of collective rights is quite surprising. During the drafting process of the Banjul Charter, the vast majority of states insisted on the inclusion of collective rights. At the same time, attempts to introduce a hierarchy of individual and collective rights in favour of the latter have also been made.[60] Also, one should remember the justification for the incorporation of the peoples' rights:

> [I]n Africa, man is part and parcel of the group [that is why] individual rights could be explained and justified only by the rights of the community.[61]

Even though African societies have been characterized historically by their communal structures, the majority of African constitutions do not reflect this nature. The general mutual influence of public international law and national law on human rights and lawmaking processes cannot be confirmed, and the enormous gap between African public international law and African constitutions with regard to group rights is unexpected. Despite this situation – or perhaps exactly because of it – the consequences of this gap for the enforcement of the peoples' rights will be examined in a second step.

Collective rights in practice: negotiating normative spaces

The primary vehicles of the implementation of regional human rights treaties are the national legal systems of the member states.[62] Article 1 ACHPR states that:

> [t]he Member States of the Organisation of the African Unity, parties to the present Charter shall recognise the rights, duties and freedoms enshrined in

> the Charter and shall undertake to adopt legislative or other measures to give effect to them.

Even though the means of implementation are a matter of the domestic legal system, three new questions arise in the context of the unexpected divergence of normative spaces: How does the Commission deal with the gap between public international law and constitutional law in its communications? Which roles are ascribed to communal local customs within the communications of the ACoHPR? As the majority of the states only grant individual rights, does the Commission feel obliged to prioritize individual over group rights?

Bridging the gap between international law and domestic law

How does the gap between international law and domestic law on collective rights influence the communications of the ACoHPR? Admittedly, the number of communications involving claims of violations of peoples' rights and the Commission's decisions on the merits is not particularly high. Two of these communications are not included in this analysis since the claimed violations did not take place within the domestic sphere.[63] Considering the earlier analysis of African constitutions, it is not surprising that the majority of communications regarding group rights are cases in which – at the moment of the human rights violation – domestic law (constitutions) did not grant the respective collective right:

The Katanga claimed a right to secession, but the constitution of Zaire granted only individual rights, as a sole exception a collective right to property was guaranteed (even though in paragraph 8 of the constitution's preamble the adherence to the Banjul Charter was proclaimed).[64] Between 1986 and 1992, the 'Black'[65] Mauritanians were discriminated against, marginalized, and attacked by, inter alia, 'public forces', and claimed a violation of Articles 19 and 23 ACHPR.[66] During that period, the constitutional charter of Mauritania referred to the UDHR but did not grant any human rights.[67] The new constitution of 1991 very generally guarantees civil, political, social, and economic human rights, but no collective rights.[68] In both communications, the Commission did not comment upon the missing domestic legislation.

This changed when Sir Dawda Kairaba Jawara, the first president of The Gambia, claimed a violation of Article 20 (1) ACHPR (right to freely choose one's government) through the military coup in 1994:[69] The former Gambian constitution of 1970 was suspended during the military *interregnum* and repealed, after which the constitution of 1996 was adopted.[70] Thus, the constitutional rule was disrupted between July 1994 and January 1997.[71] The Commission found a violation of the right to self-determination and other human rights and urged the government 'to bring its laws in conformity with the provisions of the Charter'.[72] The same recommendation was given to Zambia, where – as a consequence of a constitutional amendment – 35 % of the Zambian citizens had been denied the right to stand as president.[73]

Five months later, in a landmark decision, the ACoHPR stated a duty to protect all human rights via legislation. In the SERAC case, the former federal Nigerian Military Government was directly involved in oil production, whereas the oil exploitation led to environmental degradation and health problems amongst the Ogoni.[74] Additionally, Nigerian security forces attacked, burned, and destroyed several Ogoni villages between 1993 and 1996.[75] The constitution of 1979 had guaranteed several civil and political human rights to the individual.[76] After the military coup in 1983, parts of the constitution were changed, but when a new military coup occurred in 1993, the constitution of 1979 was restored.[77] Although in 1988 the Military Government established the Federal Environmental Protection Agency, followed by the National Policy on the Environment in 1989, a right to environment was not granted. The new constitution of 1999 establishes only the non-justiciable principle to protect and improve the environment.[78] The constitution of 1999 likewise grants several civil and political individual human rights.[79] Although Nigeria ratified the ACHPR in 1983, collective rights are not provided at the constitutional level. Not only did the ACoHPR find a violation of the collective rights granted in Article 24 (environment), as well as Articles 14, 16, and 18 (housing/shelter) and Article 21 (natural resources) ACHPR,[80] it went even further and asserted the duty to respect, protect, promote, and fulfil all human rights, adding that 'the State is obliged to protect right-holders against other subjects by legislation'.[81] Of course, this does not include a duty to protection via constitutional norms, but it narrows the means of implementation of human rights to legislative measures.[82] Accordingly, a lack of the respective domestic legislation implies a violation of the duty to protect human rights. With regard to the claimed collective property rights, the Republic of Congo fulfilled its legislative obligations during the respective period of time, but the claim was not within the scope of application of the national and international norms.[83]

In the communications that followed, the ACoHPR also recommended the adjustment of national law, but without elaborating further on the contents of the duty to protect via legislation. The communication against Cameroon was brought by 14 individuals on their behalf and on behalf of the people of Southern Cameroon in which they alleged, inter alia, a violation of Articles 19, 20, 21, 22, 23, and 24 ACHPR.[84] Their primary objective was to claim the right to secession, since their constitutional proposals had been ignored by Cameroon between 1993 and 1995.[85] In its preamble, the constitution of Cameroon only grants individual rights, apart from a general reference to the protection of minorities and the rights of indigenous peoples.[86] The Commission found a violation of Article 19 ACHPR, but not of the claimed Articles 20 to 24 ACHPR.[87] Even though the ACoHPR did not find the requirements for a right to secession fulfilled, it showed the shortcomings of Cameroon with regard to the Southern English-speaking minority and her interests and urged Cameroon 'to address the grievances expressed by the Southern Cameroonians through its democratic institutions'.[88] Thus the Commission does not see the requirements for a right to secession as complied, but admits a lack of implementation of rights protected by the Banjul Charter and the need for a 'comprehensive national dialogue'.[89]

Finally, it recommends the state 'to resolve the constitutional issues'.[90] Unfortunately, the ACoHPR did not use the possibility to state exactly how the protection of minorities has to be shaped in order to be in conformity with the collective rights of the Banjul Charter. Also, in the following communication, the Commission remains very general in its recommendations.

Massive human rights violations against indigenous 'black'[91] African tribes in the Darfur region since the military coup in 1989 were addressed in the communication versus Sudan, in which the Commission found – among others – a violation of the claimed Article 22 ACHPR.[92] The formerly installed interim constitution of 1985 was suspended following the coup in 1989.[93] It took until 1998 to adopt a new constitution, which granted at least cultural community rights.[94] In its final recommendations, the Commission urged Sudan to ensure the protection of human rights, inter alia, by 'undertak[ing] major reforms of its legislative and judicial framework in order to handle cases of serious and massive human rights violations'.[95]

The Endorois-Communication is the first communication regarding group rights in which the complainants claimed a violation of the ACHPR, the constitution of Kenya and international law.[96] They claimed that Articles 8, 14, 17, 21 and 22 ACHPR had been violated because of the forced removal of the Endorois from their ancestral lands (the access to their land was denied since 1978) without proper prior consultations, adequate, and effective compensation.[97] Traditionally, international tribunals are not supposed to interpret national law as such.[98] This old proposition is challenged by the claim of a violation of the Kenyan constitution. The issue of the claim was not the guaranteed individual human rights, but the property rights coming along with the constitutional norms regarding trust land.[99] With regard to a collective right to property the Commission found

> that even though the Constitution of Kenya provides that Trust Land may be alienated and that the Trust Land Act provides comprehensive procedure for the assessment of compensation, the Endorois *property rights* have been encroached upon, in particular by the expropriation and the effective denial of ownership of their land.[100]

Furthermore, the ACoHPR asked if the removal of the Endorois satisfied both Kenyan and international law and referred to Article 115 of the former Kenyan constitution, which regulated trust land and found:[101]

> This means that the declaration of the Lake Bogoria Game Reserve by way of the 1974 notice did not affect the status of the Endorois land as Trust Land. The obligation of Baringo and Koibatek County Councils to give effect to the rights and interests of the Endorois people continued. . . . The African Commission is in agreement with the Complainants that the only way under Kenyan law in which Endorois benefit under the trust could have been dissolved is if the County Council or the President of Kenya had 'set apart' the

> land. However, the Trust Land Act required that to be legal, such setting apart of the land must be published in the Kenyan Gazette.[102]

Thus, the Commission exceeded the traditional view that national laws were merely facts not interpreted by international tribunals.[103] Instead, it interpreted the constitution on the question of collective property rights, and finally recommended Kenya to 'recognise rights of ownerships of the Endorois'.[104] Surprisingly, the Commission did not go further and did not comment on the missing national law concerning collective rights to natural resources and development.[105] Even if the new constitution of 2010 also does not guarantee collective rights, one should mention that it now contains at least an obligation for the state to protect minorities and marginalized groups.[106]

What lessons can be drawn from these findings? The primacy of individual rights on a constitutional level did not prevent the Commission from finding violations of the peoples' rights. Quite the contrary, it stressed in the SERAC case that

> collective rights, environmental rights, and economic and social rights are essential elements of human rights in Africa. The African Commission will apply any of the diverse rights contained in the African Charter. It welcomes the opportunity to make clear that there is no right in the African Charter that cannot be made effective.[107]

The Commission demands a vertical convergence between the Banjul Charter and the national law by obliging the state to protect rights holders against other subjects through legislation and the constant recommendations on national law. In summary, it can be concluded that constitutionally enshrined collective rights so far had no influence on the findings of the ACoHPR. On the other hand, given that the protection of minorities was included after the Endorois-Communication, the case of Kenya shows how communications can influence new constitutional processes.[108]

The correlation of communal local customs and public international law

Since the communal culture of African societies characterized in the Banjul Charter is not reflected in most African constitutions, one should ask the question of how communal local customs interact with public international law in consideration of the local customary law.[109] As indicated earlier, the majority of the communications from the ACoHPR concerning group rights violations do not affect specific local customs of a people but only broader human rights violations. Therefore, local customary law was often not explicitly involved. This changed during more recent communications in which local customary law played a decisive role in the application of legal terms, such as 'people' and 'property' and to solve the problem of legal representation of groups.

In a broader sense, local (communal) customs are crucial for defining who constitutes a 'people'.[110] The Banjul Charter itself provides no such definition, as the drafters wanted to avoid reservations from the states and to enable the jurisdiction to a broad interpretation.[111] Abstaining from a definition of the term 'people' in its first communications, it took until 2009 that the Commission defined it for the first time via objective and subjective criteria, which are borrowed from general public international law:

> The African Commission is thus aware that there is an emerging consensus on some objective features that a collective of individuals should manifest to be considered as 'peoples', viz: a common historical tradition, racial or ethnic identity, cultural homogeneity, linguistic unity, religious or ideological affinities, territorial connection, and a common economic life or other bonds, identities and affinities they collectively enjoy – especially rights enumerated under Articles 19 to 24 of the African Charter – or suffer collectively from the deprivation of such rights. What is clear is that all attempts to define the concept of indigenous peoples recognize the linkages between peoples, their land, and culture and that such a group expresses its desire to be identified as a people or have the consciousness that they are a people.[112]

Thus, a connective identity-creating element is of a central significance for being a 'people' in the sense of Articles 19 to 24 ACHPR.[113] In the Endorois case, the Commission had to decide whether the Endorois are a distinct group, different from the Tugen subtribe. The main criteria for the ACoHPR were the sacred relationship of the Endorois to their ancestral land and their self-identification as a people.[114] Relying on the self-identification as a distinct people,[115] the Commission transfers non-formal local customary law as a fact within the sphere of public international law. This corresponds with the traditional view, that national law (here: local customary law or rather the self-conception as a people, thus the local communal culture) must be treated as a fact from the perspective of international law.[116]

In how it understands indigenous land rights, the Commission again uses the local customary law as a fact that requires subsuming the term 'property': The complainants had contested the Endorois' concept of ownership, whereupon 'the Endorois have been accepted by all neighbouring tribes as *bona fide* owners of the land'.[117] Moreover they argued:

> that as a pastoralist community, the Endorois' concept of 'ownership' of their land has not been one of ownership by paper. The Complainants state that the Endorois community has always understood the land in question to be 'Endorois' land, belonging to the community as a whole and used by it for habitation, cattle, beekeeping, and religious and cultural practices. Other communities would, for instance, ask permission to bring their animals to the area.[118]

Within its final decision the Commission takes the non-formal local customary law of the Endorois and their neighbouring communities, according to which the Endorois are the owners of the land, as a fact for the interpretation and application of the term 'property' of Article 14 ACHPR.[119] Concerning the legal consequences of such a 'communal' right to property (within the context of indigenous populations), the Commission interprets Article 14 ACHPR in a way that to a major extent is influenced by the jurisprudence of the Inter-American Court of Human Rights[120] and the UNDRIP:[121]

> (1) traditional possession of land by indigenous peoples has the equivalent effect as that of a state granted full property title; (2) traditional possession entitles indigenous peoples to demand official recognition and registration of property title; (3) the members of indigenous peoples who have unwillingly left their traditional lands, or lost possession thereof, maintain property rights thereto, even though they lack legal title, unless the lands have been lawfully transferred to third parties in good faith; and (4) the members of indigenous peoples who have unwillingly lost possession of their lands, when those lands have been lawfully transferred to innocent third parties, are entitled to restitution thereof or to obtain other lands of equal extension and quality.[122]

Thus it appears that, first, the Commission takes the local communal conception of property as a fact and, second, public international law protects this communal traditional property in a special way.

Furthermore, the Commission had to face the problem of legal representation of a people and the right of some group members to claim the violation of peoples' rights on behalf of their group. For the first time, the Commission declared national standards inapplicable with regard to peoples' rights and thereby referred to the customary law of a local group:

> In the case of the Endorois, the African Commission is of the view that the question of whether certain members of the community may assert certain communal rights on behalf of the group is a question that *must be resolved by the Endorois themselves in accordance with their own traditional customs and norms and not by the State*. The Endorois cannot be denied a right to juridical personality just because there is a lack of individual identification with the traditions and laws of the Endorois by some members of the community.[123]

Hence, the representation problem has to be solved through the respective group and its traditional norms and customs. The Commission does not lay out any requirements that have to be fulfilled by the particular local customary law, for example, democratic or other structures through which the representation of each of the members would be guaranteed. On the one hand, one has to bear in mind that this approach of the Commission is the only one where the conception of the particular right as a group right is respected. On the other hand, it is not unlikely that one day the Commission will have to examine whether the respective members really represent their group in a communication – as this would require democratic structures and the observance of individual human rights within the particular group.

These three examples shed light on an interaction of local communal customs, non-formal local customary law, and public international law: Local communal customs serve as facts for the Commission within its communications. At the same time, public international law acknowledges the necessity of protecting these local communal structures through instruments such as the United Nations Declaration on the Rights of Indigenous Peoples (UNDRIP), the Banjul Charter or the jurisprudence of international tribunals like the IACtHR. Finally, the Commission respects local traditional norms in identifying the solution for procedural representation problems of groups, which corresponds to the character of group rights. Thus, one can observe a correlation between the normative spaces of local customary law and public international law.

Individual rights and peoples' rights: an undissolvable antagonism?

This analysis of the African constitutions has shown that the majority of these constitutions exclusively grant individual rights. With this in mind, we have to acknowledge that the Banjul Charter is one of the first human rights protection systems to deal with the protection of both concepts of rights – rights understood as individual rights and as collective rights. During the drafting process, a hierarchy between individual and peoples' rights was decided in favour of the latter, but ultimately rejected.[124] Both, the drafting history and the system of the Banjul Charter itself show that no differentiation or hierarchy between individual and group rights are allowed, as they are protected in the same way. Until now, there has been no communication as to where the Commission would have had to decide upon the question (at least in Europe most feared) of conflicts between individual and group rights. The Commission has shown in the past how conflicts between different groups and/or group rights can be resolved on a case-by-case basis. The political right to self-determination protects the people of a state and normally does not allow a right to secession, but sets high standards for an internal democratization process as a compensation for the interests of domestic peoples.[125] In terms of conflict solution concerning natural resources, the ACoHPR adopted the concepts developed by the IACtHR, whereupon compensation has to be reached via consultations, profit-sharing and a payment of appropriate damages.[126] Consultation, participation as well as prior environmental and social impact studies are also key elements of conflict solution with regard to the rights to environment and development.[127]

Still the question remains as how to solve conflicts between individual and peoples' rights. Even though the Commission did not have to decide on these conflicts in the past, a decision in that regard seems imminent. From a legal-theoretical perspective, there is a broad discourse on the general question of conflicts between individual and collective rights, which can only be summarized here.[128] In particular, it relates to conflicts resulting from harmful cultural practices, for example, female circumcision. To solve such conflicts, *Taylor* differentiates between fundamental liberties, which should never be infringed, and cultural privileges and immunities that can be restricted.[129] Others differentiate between group-internal and external conflicts. *Kymlicka*, for instance, accepts the possibility of group rights directed against group members, but refuses such rights if they would violate individual rights.[130] Approaches that respect the anthropological understanding of 'culture' reveal that there are no group-internal conflicts between individual and group rights, as no right to the preservation of a specific culture against the group members exists.[131] According to those ideas, it seems as if individual rights will always trump group rights.[132] In the case of harmful cultural practices, like female circumcision, there is hardly an argument against the primacy of the respective individual right. Though, one has to acknowledge that such a general solution of a hierarchy between both types of rights contradicts the idea of coequal human rights: A hierarchy between first, second, and third dimension rights does not exist.[133] That is why more recent approaches refer to the normality of conflicts within legal systems.[134] Recent legal history has shown that fundamental conflicts between individual rights, for example, the admissibility of abortions, can be solved without reaching a consensus on a general hierarchy between the fundamental rights of the mother and that of the unborn child. Likewise, conflicts between the individual and the state are considered normal. In general, conflicts of interest are solved via specified mechanisms, like the principle of proportionality and the maxim of non-affection of the essence of a basic right. Those general ways of balancing conflicts of interests also have to be applied in the case of conflicts between group and individual rights, for example, conflicts between a collective and an individual right to property. Even in the case of female circumcision, the application of those principles would lead to the result, that the degree of interference with the physical integrity of the individual outweighs the collective cultural interest in the practice. As a consequence, groups have to be regarded as a third actor following the individual and the state. In sum, the idea is not to decide on a general priority of individual rights or group rights, but to find a balance between the rights involved through the described ways of solving conflicts of interests – specifically when we accept the interdependence of both types of rights.[135] As the Commission has so far accepted this interdependence,[136] it will probably do the same when it has to decide on those conflicts.

Conclusion

The drafting history of the Banjul Charter, with its reference to communal structures within African societies, led to the assumption that similar collective rights can be found within domestic law. The empirical analysis of the concept of collective rights from the ACHPR and the national African constitutions has shown the opposite to be the case. Whereas a general horizontal and vertical constitutional convergence can be located, a similar general convergence concerning peoples' rights from the Banjul Charter does not exist so far. The analysis of the communications revealed that the Commission recommends (and politically demands) a vertical convergence between the ACHPR and domestic law from the member states. By developing the duty to protect via domestic legislation, it even prepared the base for a legally enforceable vertical convergence. The correlation between public international law and local customary law confirmed that national law – here communal local customs – serves as fact before international tribunals. Without local customary law as a fact it would be impossible for the Commission to assess whether the particular collective is a 'people'. The same applies traditionally to the protection of property rights, as concepts of property are always shaped in the local sphere. Therefore, it is no surprise that the Commission (like the IACtHR and the UNDRIP) adjusts the legal consequences of property rights to those (local) ensuing from collective concepts of property. Finally, the procedural issues revealed that public international law sometimes has to rely on local communal customs, as otherwise the idea of the particular right as a group right would be avoided. It is not unlikely that such cases will at last lead to a higher convergence between all three normative spaces.

In summary, a pattern of mutual influences between normative spaces can be noted: On the one hand, international law will lead (slowly but steadily) to a vertical constitutional convergence. As a consequence, one can assume a horizontal convergence of national constitutions in the future. On the other hand, local communal customs have an impact on public international law – as facts and as norms to be respected within the framework of rights conceived as group rights. Even today, the Banjul Charter is the only enforceable regional human rights treaty that positively guarantees both individual and group rights at the same time.[137] The future will show if a horizontal convergence of regional human rights treaties will emerge. At the very least, potential conflicts between individual and collective rights should not serve as an argument against increased receptivity to the concept of collective rights.

Notes

* The following results were presented at the conference in November 2013. It was not possible to take developments into account which have occurred after October 2014.

** With profound gratitude to Anne Ammermann and Gita Rajan for their critical remarks and language skills. I have previously published under my maiden name 'Schaarschmidt'.

1 Cf. only MA Jovanović, 'Are There Universal Collective Rights?' (2010) 11 *Human Rights Review* 17–45, 18; J Gledhill, 'Liberalism, Socio-Economic Rights and the Politics of Identity: From Moral Economy to Indigenous Rights' in RA Wilson (ed), *Human Rights, Culture & Context, Anthropological Perspectives* (London Pluto Press 1997) 70–110, 70 ff.; *Charter of the United Nations* (26 June 1945) available at <https://treaties.un.org/doc/publication/ctc/uncharter.pdf> accessed 29 September 2014.

2 American Anthropological Association (Executive Board), 'Statement on Human Rights' (1947) 49 *American Anthropologist* 539–543, 543: 'The problem is thus to formulate a statement of human rights that will do more than just phrase respect for the individual as an individual. It must also take into full account the individual as a member of the social group of which he is a part, whose sanctioned modes of life shape his behavior, and with whose fate his own is thus inextricably bound'.

3 An overview of this discussion is given by C Tomuschat, *Human Rights: Between Idealism and Realism* (Oxford Oxford University Press 2008) 69 ff.; RA Wilson, 'Human Rights, Culture and Context: An Introduction' in RA Wilson (ed), *Human Rights, Culture & Context, Anthropological Perspectives* (London Pluto Press 1997) 1–27, 1 ff.; cf. only M-B Dembour, *Who Believes in Human Rights? Reflections on the European Convention* (Cambridge Cambridge University Press 2006) 156; Jovanović (n 1) 17–45, 19 ff.

4 *International Covenant on Civil and Political Rights*, 16 December 1966, UNTS Vol. 999, 171; *International Covenant on Economic, Social and Cultural Rights*, 16 December 1966, UNTS Vol. 993, 3.

5 P Alston, 'Introduction' in P Alston (ed), *Peoples' Rights* (Oxford Oxford University Press 2001) 1–6, 1 ff.; Tomuschat (n 3) 48 ff.

6 *Convention on the Prevention and Punishment of the Crime of Genocide*, 9 December 1948, UNTS Vol. 78, 277.

7 *Declaration on the Granting of Independence to Colonial Countries and Peoples*, 14 December 1960, GA Res. 1514 (XV).

8 *Declaration on the Right to Development*, 4 December 1986, GA A/Res/41/128.

9 *Declaration on the Preparation of Societies for Live in Peace*, 15 December 1978, GA Res. 33/73; *Declaration on the Right of Peoples to Peace*, 12 November 1984, GA Res. 39/11.

10 *Declaration of the United Nations Conference on the Human Environment*, ILM 11 (1972) International Legal Materials 11, 1416.

11 See Article 1 para 1 UNC; Article 27 CCPR; *ILO Convention (No. 107) Concerning the Protection and Integration of Indigenous and Other Tribal and Semi-tribal Populations in Independent Countries*, 26 June 1957, UNTS Vol. 328-I-4738; *ILO Convention (No. 169) Concerning Indigenous and Tribal Peoples in Independent Countries*, 27 June 1989, UNTS Vol. 1650-I-28383; *United Nations Declaration on the Rights of Indigenous Peoples*, 13 September 2007, GA Res. 61/295.

12 *Convention for the Protection of Human Rights and Fundamental Freedoms*, 4 November 1950, UNTS Vol. 213-I-2889.

13 *American Convention on Human Rights*, 22 November 1969, UNTS Vol. 1144-I-17955.

14 A general overview of the Inter-American jurisprudence concerning indigenous peoples is given by JM Pasqualucci, 'The Evolution of International Indigenous Rights in the Inter-American Human Rights System' (2006) 6 *Human Rights Law Review* 281–322, 281 ff.; the European jurisprudence with regard to minorities is presented in J Ringelheim, *Diversité culturelle et droits de l'homme: L'émergence de la problématique des minorités dans le droit de la convention européenne des droits de l'homme* (Bruxelles Bruylant 2006) 53 ff.

15 *African Charter on Human and Peoples' Rights*, 27 June 1981, UNTS Vol. 1520-I-26363.

16 *Secretary General, Report on the Draft African Charter Presented at the 37th Ordinary Session of the OAU Council of Ministers, 15–21 June 1981*, CM/1149 (XXXVII), Annex II Rapporteur's Report, CAB/LEG/67/Draft Rapt. Rpt (III) Rev. 4 para 10, printed in C Heyns, *Human Rights Law in Africa 1997* (The Hague Kluwer Law International 1999) 95.

17 W Benedek, 'Peoples' Rights and Individuals' Duties as Special Features of the African Charter in Human and Peoples' Rights' (1985) Beiheft 12 *Verfassung und Recht in Übersee* in P Kunig, W Benedek, and CR Mahalu (eds), *Regional Protection of Human Rights by International Law: The Emerging African System* 12, 59–94, 62 ff.
18 J Crawford, *Brownlie's Principles of Public International Law* (Oxford Oxford University Press 2012) 48 ff.
19 A Peters, 'Supremacy Lost: International Law Meets Domestic Constitutional Law' (2005) 3 *Vienna Online Journal on International Constitutional Law* 170–198, 173 f.
20 Crawford (n 18) 634.
21 H Bielefeldt, *Menschenrechte in der Einwanderungsgesellschaft: Plädoyer für einen aufgeklärten Multikulturalismus* (Bielefeld Transcript 2007) 48.
22 See, for example, England 1215-Magna Carta; USA 1776 – Declaration of Independence; France 1789 – Déclaration des droits de l'homme et du citoyen.
23 Article 38 para 1 lit. c Statute International Court of Justice, Crawford n 18 2012 636; Peters (n 19) 174.
24 Peters (n 19) 173 ff.; C Meyer, 'The Reception of Human Rights Standards in Africa' (2012) 15 *Recht in Afrika* 53–68, 57.
25 A comprehensive analysis of the peoples' rights can be found in F Ouguergouz, *The African Charter on Human and Peoples' Rights: A Comprehensive Agenda for Human Dignity and Sustainable Democracy in Africa* (The Hague Kluwer 2003) 211–271; M Kamto (ed), *La Charte Africaine des Droits de L'homme et des Peuples et le Protocol y relative portant création de la Cour Africaine des Droits de l'Homme. Commentaire Article par Article* (Bruxelles Editions de l'Université de Bruxelles 2011) 444–643.
26 Ouguergouz (n 25) 212, 243 ff., 278, 308 ff., 321, 329 f., 361 ff.
27 Benedek (n 17) 62 ff.
28 This was, for example, the case in Cameroon, where the southern English-speaking part accused the northern French-speaking part to economic exclusion. The subject of the dispute was, inter alia, the relocation of important economic projects and companies from the South to the North. ACoHPR Communication 266/2003, 27 May 2009, *Kevin Mgwanga Gunme et al. / Cameroon* para 158 f.
29 C Baldwin and C Morel, 'Group Rights' in M Evans and R Murray (eds), *The African Charter on Humans and Peoples Rights: The System in Practice, 1986–2006* (Cambridge Cambridge University Press 2008) 244–288, 258; Ouguergouz (n 25) 222 f.
30 Article 20 para 1 sentences 2, 3 ACHPR.
31 See Article 21 para 5 ACHPR; Benedek (n 17) 75; UO Umozurike, *The African Charter on Human and Peoples' Rights* (The Hague Nijhoff 1997) 55; vivid ACoHPR Communication 155/96, 27 October 2001, *The Social and Economic Rights Action Center and the Center for Economic and Social Rights / Nigeria* para 56.
32 'Invented' was the right to development as a human right by K M'Baye, 'Le droit au développement comme un droit de l'homme' (1972) *V Revue des droits de l'homme* 503–534, 505 ff., see further: Benedek (n 17) 77; MA Tadeg, 'Reflections on the Right to Development: Challenges and Prospects' (2019) 10 *African Human Rights Law Journal* 325–344, 331 with further citations; Ouguergouz (n 25) 298.
33 ACoHPR Communication 276/2003, 25 November 2009, *Centre for Minority Rights Development (Kenya) and Minority Rights Group International on Behalf of Endorois Welfare Council / Kenya* para 277 ff.; see further KS Oei and J Shepherd, 'In Land We Trust: The *Endorois*' Communication and the Quest for Indigenous

Peoples' Rights in Africa' (2010) 16 *Buffalo Human Rights Review* 57–111, 57 ff.

34 Benedek (n 17) 83; OC Eze, *The African Charter on Rights and Duties and Enforcement Mechanisms* (Erkelenz Altius 2009) 187; Ouguergouz (n 25) 341.

35 Baldwin and Morel (n 29) 286; Benedek (n 17) 85; MA Mekuar, 'Article 24' in M Kamto (ed), *La Charte Africaine des Droits de L'Homme et des Peuples et le Protocol y relative portant création de la Cour Africaine des Droits de l'Homme: Commentaire Article par Article* (Bruxelles Editions de l'Université de Bruxelles 201) 626–643, 630. ACoHPR Communication 155/96, 27 October 2001, *The Social and Economic Rights Action Center and the Center for Economic and Social Rights / Nigeria* para 53.

36 J Schaarschmidt, 'Gruppenrechte als Menschenrechte: Erkenntnisse aus dem afrikanischen Völkerrecht' in Junge Wissenschaft im Öffentlichen Recht (eds), *Kollektivität: Öffentliches Recht zwischen Gruppeninteressen und Gemeinwohl, 52. Assistententagung Öffentliches Recht* (Baden-Baden Nomos 2012) 97–118, 100 ff.

37 ACoHPR Communication 155/96, 27 October 2001; *The Social and Economic Rights Action Center and the Center for Economic and Social Rights / Nigeria* para 60 ff.

38 ACoHPR Communication 276/2003, 25 November 2009; *Centre for Minority Rights Development (Kenya) and Minority Rights Group International on Behalf of Endorois Welfare Council / Kenya* para 196: '[T]he State . . . has a duty to recognise the right to property of members of the Endorois community, within the framework of a communal property system, and establish the mechanisms necessary to give domestic legal effect to such right recognised in the Charter and international law'.

39 *Ratification Table African Charter on Human and Peoples' Rights* available at <www.achpr.org/instruments/achpr/ratification> accessed 29 September 2014.

40 Meyer (n 24).

41 See the comparative analysis of African constitutions as of 2006 in C Heyns and W Kaguongo, 'Constitutional Human Rights Law in Africa: Current Developments' (2006) 22 (4) *South African Journal on Human Rights* 673–717, 673 ff. – concerning the adoption of peoples' rights 678.

42 Article 11 of the Constitution of Benin (1990) grants language and cultural rights: 'Toutes les communautés composant la Nation béninoise jouissent de la liberté d'utiliser leurs langues parlées et écrites et de développer leur propre culture tout en respectant celles des autres. L'État doit promouvoir le développement de langues nationales d'intercommunication'. *Constitution de la République du Bénin* (1990) available at <http://mjp.univ-perp.fr/constit/bj1990.htm> accessed 23 September 2014.

43 Sec 31 of the Constitution of South Africa (1997) grants community rights:

(1) Persons belonging to a cultural, religious or linguistic community may not be denied the right, with other members of that community
(a) to enjoy their culture, practise their religion and use their language; and
(b) to form, join and maintain cultural, religious and linguistic associations and other organs of civil society.
(2) The rights in subsection (1) may not be exercised in a manner inconsistent with any provision of the Bill of Rights'. *Constitution of the Republic of South Africa* (1997) available at <www.wipo.int/wipolex/en/text.jsp?file_id=315889> accessed 29 September 2014.

44 Article 47 of the Interim National Constitution of Sudan 2005 (formerly Article 27 Constitution Sudan 1998) guarantees cultural community rights: 'Ethnic and cultural communities shall have the right to freely enjoy and develop

their particular cultures; members of such communities shall have the right to practice their beliefs, use their languages, observe their religions and raise their children within the framework of their respective cultures and customs'. *Interim National Constitution of the Republic of Sudan* (2005) available at <www.wipo.int/wipolex/en/text.jsp?file_id=241714> accessed 29 September 2014.

45 Article 33 of the Transitional Constitution of South Sudan (2011) grants rights of ethnic and cultural communities: 'Ethnic and cultural communities shall have the right to freely enjoy and develop their particular cultures. Members of such communities shall have the right to practice their beliefs, use their languages, observe their religions and raise their children within the context of their respective cultures and customs in accordance with this Constitution and the law'. *Transitional Constitution of the Republic of South Sudan* (2011) available at <www.wipo.int/wipolex/en/text.jsp?file_id=250715> accessed 29 September 2014.

46 The Preamble of the Constitution of Burundi (2005) grants the protection of communities and minorities: 'La protection et l'inclusion des groupes ethniques, culturels et religieux minoritaires dans le système général de bonne gouvernance'. *Constitution de la République du Burundi* (2005) available at <http://justice.gov.bi/IMG/pdf/Constitution_de_la_Republique_du_Burundi.pdf> accessed 25 September 2014.

47 The Preamble of the Constitution of Cameroon (1972) guarantees minority rights: 'L'État assure la protection des minorités et préserve les droits des populations autochtones conformément à la loi'. *Constitution de la République du Cameroun* (1972) available at <http://mjp.univ-perp.fr/constit/cm2008.htm> accessed 25 September 2014.

48 Article 36 of the Constitution of Uganda (1995, as last amended in 2005) guarantees minority rights: 'Minorities have a right to participate in decision-making processes, and their views and interests shall be taken into account in the making of national plans and programmes'. *Constitution of the Republic of Uganda* (1995) (as last amended in 2005) available at <www.wipo.int/wipolex/en/text.jsp?file_id=170004> accessed 29 September 2014.

49 Article 39 of the Constitution of Ethiopia (1994) grants the rights of Nations, Nationalities, and Peoples:

'(1) Every Nation, Nationality and People in Ethiopia has an unconditional right to self-determination, including the right to secession.
(2) Every Nation, Nationality and People in Ethiopia has the right to speak, to write and to develop its own language; to express, to develop and to promote its culture; and to preserve its history.
(3) Every Nation, Nationality and People in Ethiopia has the right to a full measure of self-government which includes the right to establish institutions of government in the territory that it inhabits and to equitable representation in state and Federal governments.
(4) The right to self-determination, including secession, of every Nation, Nationality and People shall come into effect:
(a) When a demand for secession has been approved by a two-thirds majority of the members of the Legislative Council of the Nation, Nationality or People concerned;
(b) When the Federal Government has organized a referendum which must take place within three years from the time it received the concerned council's decision for secession;
(c) When the demand for secession is supported by majority vote in the referendum;
(d) When the Federal Government will have transferred its powers to the council of the Nation, Nationality or People who has voted to secede; and

(e) When the division of assets is effected in a manner prescribed by law.

(5) A 'Nation, Nationality or People' for the purpose of this Constitution, is a group of people who have or share large measure of a common culture or similar customs, mutual intelligibility of language, belief in a common or related identities, a common psychological make-up, and who inhabit an identifiable, predominantly contiguous territory'. *Constitution of the Federal Democratic Republic of Ethiopia* (1994) available at <www.wipo.int/wipolex/en/text.jsp?file_id=193667> accessed 25 September 2014.

50 In detail Heyns and Kaguongo (n 41) 709 f.

51 Article 43 of the Constitution of Ethiopia (1994) grants the right of development:

'(1) The Peoples of Ethiopia as a whole, and each Nation, Nationality and People in Ethiopia in particular have the right to improved living standards and to sustainable development.

(2) Nationals have the right to participate in national development and, in particular, to be consulted with respect to policies and projects affecting their community.

(3) All international agreements and relations concluded, established or conducted by the State shall protect and ensure Ethiopia's right to sustainable development.

(4) The basic aim of development activities shall be to enhance the capacity of citizens for development and to meet their basic needs'.

52 The Preamble of the Constitution of Malawi (2010) states: 'seeking to guarantee the welfare and development of all the people of Malawi'; Article 30 grants the right to development:

'1. All persons and peoples have a right to development and therefore to the enjoyment of economic, social, cultural and political development and women, children and the disabled in particular shall be given special consideration in the application of this right.

2. The State shall take all necessary measures for the realization of the right to development. Such measures shall include, amongst other things, equality of opportunity for all in their access to basic resources, education, health services, food, shelter, employment and infrastructure.

3. The State shall take measures to introduce reforms aimed at eradicating social injustices and inequalities.

4. The State has a responsibility to respect the right to development and to justify its policies in accordance with this responsibility'.*Constitution of the Republic of Malawi* (2010) available at <www.wipo.int/wipolex/en/text.jsp?file_id=317750> accessed 29 September 2014.

53 Heyns and Kaguongo (n 41) 706 ff.

54 The Preamble of the Constitution of Burkina Faso (1991) states: '[A]nimé de la volonté d'édifier un État de droit garantissant l'exercice des droits collectifs et individuels, la liberté, la dignité, la sûreté, le bien-être, le développement, l'égalité et la justice comme valeurs fondamentales d'une société pluraliste'; Article 14 grants the right to natural resources: 'Les richesses et les ressources naturelles appartiennent au peuple. Elles sont utilisées pour l'amélioration de ses conditions de vie'. *Constitution de la République du Burkina Faso* (1991) available at <http://aceproject.org/ero-en/regions/africa/BF/burkina-faso-constitution-2012/view> accessed 23 September 2014.

55 The Preamble of the Constitution of Equatorial Guinea (1991) states: 'Deseosos de mantener el auténtico espíritu tradicionalmente Africano de organización familiar y comunal adaptándolo a nuevas estructuras sociales y judiciales acordes

a la vida moderna'. *Constitución de la República de Guinea Equatorial* (1991) available at <www.wipo.int/wipolex/en/text.jsp?file_id=200133> accessed 25 Sepetember 2014.

56 Chapter II Section I Constitution of Angola (2010) grants 'Individual and Collective Rights and Freedoms'. The following rights therefore have to be understood as individual and group rights. The collective dimension of the right to property is expressly stated in Article 37 para 2: 'The state shall respect and protect the property and any other rights *in rem* of private individuals, corporate bodies and local communities, and temporary civil requisition and expropriation for public use shall only be permitted upon prompt payment of just compensation under the terms of the Constitution and the law'. *Constitution of the Republic of Angola* (2010) available at <www.wipo.int/wipolex/en/text.jsp?file_id=196467> accessed 23 September 2014.

57 Article 19 of the Constitution of Burundi (2005) guarantees: '[L]a Charte africaine des droits de l'homme et des peuples [fait] partie intégrante de la Constitution de la République du Burundi'.

58 Article 34 para 2 Constitution DR Congo (2006) grants collective property rights: 'L'État garantit le droit à la propriété individuelle ou collective, acquis conformément à la loi ou à la coutume'. Articles 50–59 are guaranteeing collective rights, inter alia:

Article 51 – minority rights: 'L'État a le devoir d'assurer et de promouvoir la coexistence pacifique et harmonieuse de tous les groupes ethniques du pays. Il assure également la protection et la promotion des groupes vulnérables et d'outes les minorités. Il veille à leur épanouissement'.

Article 52 – the right to peace and security: 'Tous les Congolais ont droit à la paix et à la sécurité, tant sur le plan national qu'international. Aucun individu ou groupe d'individus ne peut utiliser une portion du territoire national comme base de départ d'activités subversives ou terroristes contre l'État congolais ou tout autre État'.

Article 58 – environment: 'Tous les Congolais ont le droit de jouir des richesses nationales. L'État a le devoir de les redistribuer équitablement et de garantir le droit au développement'.

Article 58 – natural resources and development: 'Tous les Congolais ont le droit de jouir des richesses nationales. L'État a le devoir de les redistribuer équitablement et de garantir le droit au développement'.

Article 59 – common heritage of mankind: 'Tous les Congolais ont le droit de jouir du patrimoine commun de l'humanité. L'État a le devoir d'en faciliter la jouissance'. *Constitution de la République Démocratique du Congo* (2006) available at <www.wipo.int/edocs/lexdocs/laws/fr/cd/cd001fr.pdf> accessed 29 September 2014.

59 Article 8 Constitution of Senegal (2001) grants collective rights – even though it remains unclear which rights are understood as collective rights: 'La République du Sénégal garantit à tous les citoyens les libertés individuelles fondamentales, les droits économiques et sociaux ainsi que les droits collectifs. Ces libertés et droits sont notamment:

§ Les libertés civiles et politiques: liberté d'opinion, liberté d'expression, liberté de la presse, liberté d'association, liberté de réunion, liberté de déplacement, liberté de manifestation,

§ les libertés culturelles,

§ les libertés religieuses,

§ les libertés philosophiques,

§ les libertés syndicales,

§ la liberté d'entreprendre,
§ le droit à l'éducation,
§ le droit de savoir lire et écrire,
§ le droit de propriété,
§ le droit au travail,
§ le droit à la santé,
§ le droit à un environnement sain,
§ le droit à l'information plurielle.

Ces libertés et ces droits s'exercent dans les conditions prévues par la loi'. *Constitution de la République du Sénégal* (2001) available at <www.wipo.int/wipolex/en/text.jsp?file_id=318535> accessed 2 October 2014.

60 Regarding the drafting process of the Banjul Charter and the incorporation of group rights see HB Jallow, *The Law of the African (Banjul) Charter on Human and Peoples' Rights (1988–2006)* (Bloomington Trafford Publishing 2007) 35 ff.

61 *Secretary General, Report on the Draft African Charter Presented at the 37th Ordinary Session of the OAU Council of Ministers*, 15–21 June 1981; CM/1149 (XXXVII), Annex II Rapporteur's Report, CAB/LEG/67/Draft Rapt. Rpt (III) Rev. 4 para 10, printed in Heyns (n 16) 95.

62 Crawford (n 18) 667; RY Jennings, 'General Course on Principles of International Law' (1967) 121 *Hague Recueil des Cours* 323–606, 502.

63 Once the communication was between states, thus constitutional law excluded: ACoHPR Communication 227/99, 29 May 2003, *D. R. Congo / Burundi, Rwanda, Uganda*; another time the communication was brought by a NGO against an embargo imposed on Burundi by the respondent states: ACoHPR Communication 157/96, 29 May 2003, *Association Pour la Sauvegarde de la Paix au Burundi / Tanzania, Kenya, Uganda, Rwanda, Zaire and Zambia.*

64 ACoHRP Communication 75/92, 22 March 1995, *Katangese Peoples' Congress / Zaire* para 2 ff., see Articles 12–31 (Constitution Zaire 1990). *Constitution of Zaire* (1990) available at <www.worldstatesmen.org/Zaire1990.pdf> accessed 29 September 2014.

65 The ACoHPR used this mode of expression in its communication – even though it might be highly questionable (at least from an anthropological point of view) and is not part of the author's positions.

66 ACoHPR Communications 54/91, 61/91, 98/93, 164/97 à 196/97, 210/98, 11 May 2000, *Malawi African Association, Amnesty International, Ms. Sarr Diop, Union Interafricaine des Droits de l'Homme and RADDHO, Collectif des Veuves et Ayants-droits, Association Mauritanienne des Droits de l'Homme / Mauritania* para 1 ff., 139 ff.

67 *Charte constitutionnelle du Comité Militaire de Salut Nationale [Mauritanie]* (1985) – this is the last of five constitutional charters of the Comité Militaire du Salut National, which suspended and replaced the constitution of 1961 after the military coup in 1979, see <http://mjp.univ-perp.fr/constit/mr1985.htm> accessed 1 October 2014.

68 See the Preamble and Article 10 *Constitution de la République islamique de Mauritanie* (1991) (approved by referendum). *Constitution de la République islamique de Mauritanie* (1991) available at <http://mjp.univ-perp.fr/constit/mr1991.htm> accessed 29 September 2014.

69 ACoHPR Communications 147/95 and 149/96, 11 May 2000, *Sir Dawda K Jawara / The Gambia* para 72 f. Both constitutions are characterized by the rule of law, separation of powers, respect of fundamental rights, and guarantee regular free and fair elections of political offices, see OAS Jammeh, *The Constitutional Law of the Gambia 1965–2010* (Bloomington AuthorHouse 2011) 16 f.

70 Jammeh (n 69) 8; ACoHPR Communications 147/95 and 149/96, 11 May 2000, *Sir Dawda K Jawara / The Gambia* para 2.
71 Jammeh (n 69) 8.
72 ACoHPR Communications 147/95 and 149/96, 11 May 2000, *Sir Dawda K Jawara / The Gambia*, Finding.
73 ACoHPR Communication 211/98, 7 May 2001, *Legal Resources Foundation / Zambia* para 53; Articles 11–24 Constitution of Zambia only grant individual rights. The ACoHPR didn't find a violation of Article 19 ACHPR as 35 % of citizens do not constitute a 'people' in the sense of the Banjul Charter, see para 73. *Constitution of the Republic of Zambia* (1991) (as amended up to Act Nr. 18 of 1996) available at <www.wipo.int/wipolex/en/text.jsp?file_id=177164> accessed 29 September 2014.
74 ACoHPR Communication 155/96, 27 October 2001, *The Social and Economic Rights Action Center and the Center for Economic and Social Rights / Nigeria* para 1 ff.
75 F Coomans, 'The *Ogoni* Case before the African Commission on Human and Peoples' Rights' (2003) 52 *International and Comparative Law* 749–760, 750.
76 See Articles 30–39 Constitution of the Federal Republic of Nigeria (1979). *Constitution of the Federal Republic of Nigeria* [repealed] (1979) available at <www.constitutionnet.org/files/nig_const_79.pdf> accessed 29 September 2014.
77 Nigeria official publications, in British Library available at <www.bl.uk/reshelp/findhelpregion/africa/nigeria/acnigeria> accessed 1 October 2014.
78 In detail, O Oluduro, 'Environmental Rights: A Case Study of the 1999 Constitution of the Federal Republic of Nigeria' (2010) 4 *Malawi Law Journal* 255–268, 256 ff.
79 See Articles 33–43 Constitution of the Federal Republic of Nigeria 1999. *Constitution of the Federal Republic of Nigeria* (1999) available at <www.wipo.int/wipolex/en/text.jsp?file_id=179202> accessed 29 September 2014.
80 ACoHPR Communication 155/96, 27 October 2001, *The Social and Economic Rights Action Center and the Center for Economic and Social Rights / Nigeria* para 50 ff.
81 ACoHPR Communication 155/96, para 44, 46.
82 Also S Szurek, 'Article 1' in M Kamto (ed), *La Charte Africaine des Droits de L'homme et des Peuples et le Protocol y relative portant création de la Cour Africaine des Droits de l'Homme: Commentaire Article par Article* (Bruxelles Editions de l'Université de Bruxelles 2011) 81–117, 92 ff.
83 ACoHPR Communication 253/2002, 29 November 2006, *Antoine Bissangou / Republic of Congo* para 1, 79 ff. – he claimed a breach of Article 21 (2) ACHPR. Collective rights were guaranteed by the Articles 50–54 Constitution Republic of Congo, 15 March 1992. Article 54 stated: 'Le peuple congolais a le droit inaliénable et imprescriptible de jouir de ses richesses et ressources naturelles'. The Commission did not touch upon the constitutionally guaranteed collective rights, as it was obvious that only individual rights could have been violated in this case. Nevertheless, the fundamental act from 1997 and the constitution from 2002 only grant individual rights – the formerly granted collective rights disappeared.
84 ACoHPR Communication 266/2003, 27 May 2009, *Kevin Mgwanga Gunme et al. / Cameroon* para 19.
85 Ibid., para 182 ff.
86 Preamble Constitution of Cameroon (6/2/1972): 'L'État assure la protection des minorités et préserve les droits des populations autochtones conformément à la loi'.
87 ACoHPR Communication 266/2003, 27 May 2009, *Kevin Mgwanga Gunme et al. / Cameroon* para 195, 214.

88 Ibid., para 201.

89 Ibid., para 202. As requirements for a right to secession the Commission named earlier 'concrete evidence of violations of human rights to the point that the territorial integrity of [the state] should be called to question' and that the people claiming the right to secession 'is denied the right to participate in government as guaranteed by Article 13 (1) of the African Charter', see ACoHRP Communication 75/92, 22 May 1995, *Katangese Peoples' Congress / Zaire* para 6.

90 ACoHPR Communication 266/2003, 27 May 2009, *Kevin Mgwanga Gunme et al. / Cameroon* para 215.

91 Again, it is the ACoHPR that used the expression 'indigenous Black African tribes' in its communication – even though it is highly questionable and not expressive of the authors' positions.

92 ACoHPR Communications 279/03, 296/05, 27 May 2009, *Sudan Human Rights Organisation, Centre on Housing Rights and Evictions / Sudan* para 2 ff., 217 ff.

93 A short constitutional history (Country Profile Sudan, *The Arab Center for the Development of the Rule of Law and Integrity*) is available at <www.arabruleoflaw.org/countryprofiles/sudan.html> accessed 1 October 2014.

94 See Article 47 Constitution of the Republic of Sudan (1998). *Constitution of the Republic of Sudan* [repealed] (1998) available at <www.sudanembassy.ca/Docs/THE%20CONSTITUTION%20OF%20THE%20REPUBLIC%20OF%20THE%20SUDAN%201998.pdf> accessed 29 September 2014.

95 ACoHPR Communications 279/03, 296/05, 27 May 2009, *Sudan Human Rights Organisation, Centre on Housing Rights and Evictions / Sudan* para 228.

96 ACoHPR Communication 276/2003, 25 November 2009, *Centre for Minority Rights Development (Kenya) and Minority Rights Group International on behalf of Endorois Welfare Council / Kenya* para 2.

97 Ibid., para 2 f., 22.

98 Crawford (n 18) 53, with references to cases of the PCIJ and the ICJ.

99 Article 75 Constitution of Kenya (1969) guarantees only individual property rights and no collective rights. *Constitution of Kenya* [repealed] (1969) available at <www.kenyalaw.org/kl/fileadmin/pdfdownloads/Constitution/Constitution_of_Kenya%28Repealed%29.pdf> accessed 25 September 2014.

100 ACoHPR Communication 276/2003, 25 November 2009, *Centre for Minority Rights Development (Kenya) and Minority Rights Group International on behalf of Endorois Welfare Council / Kenya* para 199.

101 Ibid., para 219 f. See Article 115 para 2 Constitution of Kenya (1969): '(2) Each county council shall hold the Trust land vested in it for the benefit of the persons ordinarily resident on that land and shall give effect to such rights, interests or other benefits in respect of the land as may, under the African customary law for the time being in force and applicable thereto, be vested in any tribe, group, family or individual: Provided that no right, interest or other benefit under African customary law shall have effect for the purposes of this subsection so far as it is repugnant to any written law'.

102 ACoHPR Communication 276/2003, 25 November 2009, *Centre for Minority Rights Development (Kenya) and Minority Rights Group International on Behalf of Endorois Welfare Council / Kenya* para 224.

103 PCIJ 1926 Ser A No. 7, *German Interests in Polish Upper Silesia* para 52: 'From the standpoint of International Law and of the Court which is its organ, municipal laws are merely facts which express the will and constitute the activities of States, in the same manner as do legal decisions or administrative measures. The Court is certainly not called upon to interpret the Polish law as such; but there is nothing to prevent the Court's giving judgment on the question whether or not,

in applying that law, Poland is acting in conformity with its obligations towards Germany under the Geneva Convention'.

104 ACoHPR Communication 276/2003, 25 November 2009, *Centre for Minority Rights Development (Kenya) and Minority Rights Group International on behalf of Endorois Welfare Council / Kenya* Recommendations.

105 Ibid., para 252 ff., 269 ff.

106 See Article 56 Constitution of Kenya (2010): 'The State shall put in place affirmative action programmes designed to ensure that minorities and marginalised groups

(*a*) participate and are represented in governance and other spheres of life;
(*b*) are provided special opportunities in educational and economic fields;
(*c*) are provided special opportunities for access to employment;
(*d*) develop their cultural values, languages and practices; and
(*e*) have reasonable access to water, health services and infrastructure'.

Constitution of Kenya (2010) available at <www.kenyalaw.org/kl/fileadmin/pdfdownloads/Constitution_of_Kenya__2010.pdf> accessed 25 September 2014.

107 ACoHPR Communication 155/96, 10/27/2001, *The Social and Economic Rights Action Center and the Center for Economic and Social Rights / Nigeria* para 68.

108 ACoHPR Communication 276/2003, 11/25/2009, *Centre for Minority Rights Development (Kenya) and Minority Rights Group International on behalf of Endorois Welfare Council / Kenya* para 252 ff., 269 ff.

109 'Local customary law' in this context shall be understood as a legal term: a counterpart to 'public international customary law' and one form of customary law (in contrast to regulatory law). From a legal point of view the (anthropological) terms 'local law' and 'local normative orders' would be too broad as they include not only local customary law but also local law created by, for example, local parliaments.

110 Appreciating and understanding the concerns of Günther Schlee as an anthropologist regarding a definition of 'people' (taking into account the hybrid character of cultures and groups and also being aware of the 'indigenous trap' and the huge problems when anthropologists are asked to define a tribe or a people and his members), one has to admit that law, from a legal point of view, requires definitions and criteria. Without any definitions or criteria at all, law cannot provide the demanded predictability of legal decisions – or any legal certainty.

111 'Report of the Rapporteur' 4 f. quoted by Ouguergouz (n 25) 205. See also Jallow (n 60) 56. The mandate to interpret the Banjul Charter is currently assigned to the Commission (Article 45 para 3 ACHPR) and the African Court on Human and Peoples' Rights (Article 3 para 1 Protocol to the ACHPR on an Establishment of an African Court of Human and Peoples' Rights). Should the Merger-Protocol come into force, the mandate will pass to the new court, see Article 28 lit. c Statute of the African Court of Justice and Human Rights and Article 1, 2 Protocol on the Statute of the African Court of Justice and Human Rights.

112 ACoHPR Communication 276/2003, 25 November 2009, *Centre for Minority Rights Development (Kenya) and Minority Rights Group International on Behalf of Endorois Welfare Council / Kenya* para 151; see also ACoHPR Communications 279/03, 296/05, 5/27/2009, *Sudan Human Rights Organisation, Centre on Housing Rights and Evictions / Sudan* para 220 – where the Commission states that 'such criteria should only help to identify such groups or sub groups in the larger context of a States' wholesome population'.

113 See also ACoHPR Communication 211/98, 7 May 2001, *Legal Resources Foundation / Zambia* para 73.

114 ACoHPR Communication 276/2003, 25 November 2009, *Centre for Minority Rights Development (Kenya) and Minority Rights Group International on Behalf of Endorois Welfare Council / Kenya* para 156 f.

115 Ibid., para 73.

116 Crawford (n 18) 53.

117 ACoHPR Communication 276/2003, 11/25/2009, *Centre for Minority Rights Development (Kenya) and Minority Rights Group International on Behalf of Endorois Welfare Council / Kenya* para 4.

118 Ibid., para 72.

119 Ibid., para 184: 'It is thus clear that the land surrounding Lake Bogoria is the traditional land of the Endorois people. . . . The Complainants argue that apart from a confrontation with the Masai over the Lake Bogoria region three hundred years ago, the Endorois have been accepted by all neighbouring tribes, including the British Crown, as bona fide owners of their land. The Respondent State does not challenge those statements of the Complainants. The only conclusion that can be concluded is that the Endorois community has a right to property with regard to its ancestral lands, the possessions attached to it, and their animals'.

120 Concerning land rights of indigenous peoples in the Inter-American human rights system the following decisions are very important: IACtHR, Judgment of 8/31/2001, *Mayagna (Sumo) Awas Tingni Community / Nicaragua*, Series C 79 para 148 ff.; IACtHR, Judgment of 6/15/2005, *Moiwana Community / Suriname*, Series C 124 para 131 ff.; IACtHR, Judgment of 6/17/2005, *Yakye Axa Community / Paraguay*, Series C 125 para 131 ff.; IACtHR, Judgment of 3/29/2006, *Sawhoyamaxa Indigenous Community / Paraguay*, Series C 146 para 120 ff.; IACtHR, Judgment of 11/28/2007, *Saramaka People / Suriname*, Series C 172 para 89 ff.; IACtHR, Judgment of 8/24/2010, *Xákmok Kásek Indigenous Community / Paraguay*, Series C 214 para 85 ff.; IACtHR, Judgment of 6/27/2012, *Kichwa Indigenous People of Sarayuka / Ecuador*, Series C 245 para 145 ff.

121 *United Nations Declaration on the Rights of Indigenous Peoples*, 13 September 2007, GA Res. 61/295.

122 ACoHPR Communication 276/2003, 25 November 2009, *Centre for Minority Rights Development (Kenya) and Minority Rights Group International on Behalf of Endorois Welfare Council / Kenya* para 209.

123 Ibid., para 162 (emphasis added).Furthermore, the Commission stated in footnote 64 in the same Communication 'that where there is a large number of victims, it may be impractical for each individual complainant to go before domestic courts. In such situations, as in the Ogoni case, the Commission can adjudicate the rights of a people as a collective. Therefore the Endorois, as a people, are entitled to bring their claims collectively under those relevant provisions of the African Charter'.

124 Jallow (n 60) 35 ff.

125 GW Mugwanya, *Human Rights in Africa: Enhancing Human Right Through the African Regional Human Rights System* (Ardsley, NY Transnational Publishers 2003) 216; R Murray and S Wheatley, 'Groups and the African Charter on Human and Peoples' Rights' (2003) 25 *Human Rights Quarterly* 213–236, 232 ff. See ACoHRP Communication 75/92, 22 March 1995, *Katangese Peoples' Congress / Zaire* para 6; ACoHPR Communication 266/2003, 27 May 2009, *Kevin Mgwanga Gunme et al. / Cameroon* para 194, 197, 199.

126 IACtHR, Judgment of 11/28/2007, *Saramaka People / Suriname*, Series C 172 para 138 ff.; ACoHPR Communication 276/2003, 25 November 2009, *Centre for Minority Rights Development (Kenya) and Minority Rights Group International on Behalf of Endorois Welfare Council / Kenya* para 255, 261, 266 ff.

127 ACoHPR Communication 155/96, 27 October 2001, *The Social and Economic Rights Action Center and the Center for Economic and Social Rights / Nigeria* para 53; ACoHPR Communication 276/2003, 25 November 2009, *Centre for Minority Rights Development (Kenya) and Minority Rights Group International on Behalf of Endorois Welfare Council / Kenya* para 281, 283, 289.

128 In detail, MA Jovanović, *Collective Rights: A Legal Theory* (Cambridge Cambridge University Press 2012) 140 ff.

129 C Taylor, 'The Politics of Recognition' in C Taylor (ed), *Multiculturalism: Examining the Politics of Recognition* (Princeton Princeton University Press 1994) 25–73, 55 ff.

130 W Kymlicka, *Multicultural Citizenship: A Liberal Theory of Minority Rights* (Oxford Clarendon Press 1996) 36 ff.

131 D Réaume, 'Individuals, Groups, and Rights to Public Goods' (1998) 38 *University of Toronto Law Journal* 1–27, 16 f.; A Marmor, 'Do We Have a Right to Common Goods?' (2001) 14 *Canadian Journal of Law and Jurisprudence* 213–226, 223 f.

132 See *Dworkin*, who came up with the idea of rights as 'political trumps': 'Individual rights are political trumps held by individuals. Individuals have rights when, for some reason, a collective goal is not a sufficient justification for denying them what they wish, as individuals, to have or to do, or not a sufficient justification for imposing some loss or injury upon them', R Dworkin, *Taking Rights Seriously* (Cambridge, MA Harvard University Press 1977) xi.

133 Therefore, EH Riedel, 'Menschenrechte der dritten Dimension' (1989) *Europäische Grundrechte-Zeitschrift* 9–21, 11, argues, that the idea of different 'generations' of human rights is misleading and should be replaced by the idea of different 'dimensions' of human rights.

134 Jovanović (n 128) 144 ff. with further citations; G Triggs, 'The Rights of Peoples and Individual Rights: Conflict or Harmony?' in J Crawford (ed), *The Rights of Peoples* (Oxford Clarendon Press 1988) 141–158, 144.

135 Triggs (n 134) 144 ff.

136 Where the wording of the Charter does not exclusively entitle individuals or peoples as right holders, both are regarded as possible right holders. See ACoHPR Communication 155/96, 27 October 2001, *The Social and Economic Rights Action Center and the Center for Economic and Social Rights / Nigeria* and ACoHPR Communication 276/2003, 25 November 2009, *Centre for Minority Rights Development (Kenya) and Minority Rights Group International on Behalf of Endorois Welfare Council / Kenya*.

137 Within the Inter-American and the European system, collective rights are not provided by the treaties; instead, the protection of groups is realized through the jurisdiction. The *Arab Charter on Human Rights*, 22 May 2004, guarantees the right to self-determination (Article 2), development (Article 37) and environment (Article 38), English translation by MA Al-Midani and M Cabanettes in (2006) 24 *Boston University International Law Journal* 149–164, 149 ff. Even though the Charter came into force on 3 March 2008, so far, there exists no working monitoring system.

Part III

Re-negotiating normative spaces

7 Mind the gaps

Renegotiating South African legal pluralism within the post-apartheid state*

Olaf Zenker

Introduction

The first democratic elections in South Africa, held in 1994, symbolically marks the changeover from the colonial order of apartheid based on racial and ethnic segregation towards a new democratic era. This transition brought about a profound legal transformation. It began with the adoption of the Interim Constitution by Parliament in 1993 following the transitional negotiations in the early 1990s, and continued with the work of the 5-year Government of National Unity led by President Mandela between 1994 and 1999, under which the final Constitution of the Republic of South Africa was adopted in 1996. In the process, the de facto parliamentary supremacy under former apartheid was replaced by the supremacy of the Constitution with an extensive Bill of Rights, guaranteeing all citizens equality before the law. The bifurcated state – seminally characterized by Mamdani[1] as the conjuncture of a 'modern' urban system of state law and the decentralized despotism of traditional authorities ruling rural areas exclusively by means of ethnicized customary laws – was thus formally abandoned.

However, sections 30, 31, 39, 211, and 212 of the current Constitution also recognize traditional authorities as legitimate and instruct courts to 'apply customary law when that law is applicable, subject to the Constitution and any legislation that specifically deals with customary law'.[2] Although customary law in post-apartheid South Africa must therefore be consistent with the Constitution, especially with the Bill of Rights and any further statutory regulations, its formal recognition has injected a tension between individual and group rights into the new legal system, with the effect that customary law has become the subject of intense political and legal renegotiations over the past 20 years.

Statutory and judicial renegotiations of customary law in post-apartheid South Africa

Customary law in Africa and elsewhere can be defined as a constantly evolving, usually unwritten and often partly uncertain normative order observed at any given moment of time within a population, having been formed by regular social behaviour and the development of an accompanying sense of obligation.[3] In post-apartheid South Africa, the first and most important reform regarding the legal status of such customary law was achieved through its recognition in the new Constitution. Under colonialism, the Native Administration Act of 1927 had anointed the Governor General as the white 'supreme chief' of all Africans with extensive powers to recognize, change, and relocate 'tribes', to appoint and dismiss chiefs and to empower them to apply customary law in civil matters. With regard to customary law, review possibilities existed at the Native Commissioners' Courts, the Native Appeal Courts, and the Native Divorce Courts, which, in part, also applied South African common law, until the Special Courts for Blacks Abolition Act (1986) abolished the system of special courts.[4] As elsewhere in colonial British Africa, customary law was recognized under the condition of a so-called 'repugnancy clause' – as the Natal Ordinance 5 of 1849 put it in one of the earliest versions of this clause in South African law, as long as it was not 'repugnant to the general principles of humanity recognised throughout the whole civilised world'.[5] By contrast, under the new Constitution, customary law is today directly recognized as part of South African law on equal footing with the common law – subject, however, to the Constitution and any further legislation (see earlier).

While the Constitution thus provided the foundation for formally recognizing customary law in post-apartheid South Africa, further legislation specifically dealing with traditional authorities and customary law has only emerged since the early 2000s. Prior to that, several statutes relating to land rights, such as the Restitution of Land Rights Act (1994) and the Communal Property Associations Act (1996), had even explicitly strengthened individual rights at the expense of group rights administered in terms of customary law under traditional authorities. However, when Thabo Mbeki became President in 1999, his policies shifted markedly towards what he called 'African renaissance' and a re-empowerment of traditional authorities.[6]

The 1998 *White Paper on Local Government*[7] had already laid the basis for transforming local government, noting that the co-existence of traditional leadership and elected municipality councils – as the lowest of the three tiers of democratic government below the provincial and national structures – caused tensions and hence required clarification.[8] It announced a separate White Paper that would exclusively deal with traditional leadership issues. This was published in 2003 as *White Paper on Traditional Leadership and Governance*.[9] It recognized that those functions allocated by the Constitution to the sphere of a democratically elected local government could not be performed concurrently with the institution of traditional leadership. However, it also stressed that 'on matters of common interest, such as development and service delivery, co-operative relationships can be established. Also, spheres of government may allocate certain functions where this is provided for in law'.[10] These '[a]dditional roles/functions' were then characterized as including, among others, the administration and use of land, traditional systems of justice, and economic development.[11] The subsequently enacted Traditional Leadership and Governance Framework Act (2003) turned these policy recommendations into law, allowing the national or a provincial government to further specify these roles and functions for traditional authorities 'through legislative or other measures'.[12]

In the following years, various provincial legislations were enacted as required by the Traditional Leadership and Governance Framework Act, which spelled out the conditions, rights, and duties of traditional authorities within provincial boundaries. Moreover, at the national level, particularly two statutory provisions dealing with traditional authorities and customary law have led to widespread opposition and political activism: the Communal Land Rights Act (2004) and the Traditional Courts Bill (2017). The Communal Land Rights Act was intended to provide for the legal security of tenure within the so-called 'communal lands', mostly within the former 'homelands' that had been set aside under colonialism as overcrowded reserves for African people. It was strongly contested from the beginning, and ended up being successfully challenged as unconstitutional in the Constitutional Court in 2010. The surrounding controversies will be addressed in greater detail in the next section. The Traditional Courts Bill met with much opposition when it was reintroduced in Parliament in 2012 after its intermittent withdrawal. In the context of renewed substantial opposition from civil society and legal activists who feared that this new legislation would give chiefs even more judicial powers than under apartheid the Bill was again allowed to lapse in the National Council of Provinces (the second House of Parliament) just before the 2014 elections, when it became clear that the required majority of five out of the nine provinces would not support it. Critics had pointed out that this lapsed Bill would centralize customary law in the hand of chiefs, without providing for sufficient downward or upward accountability structures. As a result, for instance, lower level dispute resolution mechanisms would have been ignored, and people would have also been denied the rights to legal presentation (especially as women must be represented by males), to opt out of traditional courts and to appeal to state courts. At the same time, challenging possible chiefly (ab)use of power would have been made a criminal offence and chiefs would have been empowered to deny people land, or to sentence them, for instance, to forced labour.[13] Then, in 2017, a more progressive version of this Bill was reintroduced, accommodating some of the mentioned points of criticism. However, the revised version of this 2017 Bill that is being considered for adoption by Parliament at the time of writing (September 2018) has effectively reiterated the content of its predecessors.[14]

While traditional authorities and their local laws have thus only recently been reconstituted through contested legislation, judicial redefinitions of customary law began to be developed from early on in the new democratic era through case law (precedent), especially at the level of the Constitutional Court. Thus, in 1996, in its examination of the overall compliance of the final Constitution of 1996 with the Principles set out in the Interim Constitution of 1993, the Constitutional Court found that the new Constitution did comply with the relevant Principle for customary law 'by giving express guarantees of the continued existence of traditional leadership and the survival of an evolving customary law'.[15] According to Chuma Himonga, in this way

> the [Constitutional] Court not only underscored the adaptability and evolving nature of *living customary law*, but it also implicitly declared it to be the legitimate authoritative system of customary law under the new constitutional legal order. This statement is, in our view, a significant judicial pronouncement on the recognition of *living customary law* as part of the South African legal system.[16]

The idea of a 'living law', as opposed to 'official law' or 'state law', can be traced back to Eugen Ehrlich.[17] Ehrlich pointed out that the official state 'norms for decision' that were often 'effective only in the very rare cases of legal controversy', may be quite different from the actual living 'norms of conduct'. Diverse in their origins and not restricted to state laws, such norms of conduct de facto share in the creation of the legal order, because they 'are being recognized and followed by men [sic], in a general way at least' in everyday life.[18]

Over the past decades, this terminological distinction has gained wide currency within critical discussions of customary law in South Africa and elsewhere, especially in the wake of revisionist deconstructions of allegedly age-old 'customary law', 'traditional authorities', and 'ethnic groups' as recent colonial creations and invented traditions.[19]

'Official customary law' – also called 'lawyers' customary law' or 'state customary law'[20] – refers to the body of rules that have been recognized and applied by the courts and other state institutions since colonial times. It comprises reports of commissions of enquiry,[21] codes,[22] legislation,[23] court precedents,[24] ethnographic works,[25] and restatements[26] as state-sanctioned sources. However, in this process of state recognition, the actual 'living customary law' was often profoundly transformed for three reasons. First, it was only selectively apprehended as administrators of state law rarely had accurate or comprehensive information, especially since the choice of traditional authorities and male elders as prime sources of customary law was probably biased and transformed rules to the latter's advantage.[27] Second, such traditional law was rendered into writing (usually in English or Afrikaans) through 'codification, precedent, and restatement to impose common-law requirements of certainty and system on changeable custom'.[28] This gave rise to an ossified 'official' version that, over time, became more and more disconnected from the actual 'living law'.[29] Third, given the coercive powers of state institutions, their recognition of customary law profoundly transformed the 'living law' by clarifying, selecting and enforcing only certain customary norms out of an ambiguous broader set and by backing decisions of customary institutions hitherto dependent on, and thus more accountable to, local communities.[30]

In a number of cases, the Constitutional Court in South Africa has explicitly acknowledged the difference between 'official' and 'living laws', and emphasized that it is only the 'living customary law' that is recognized by the Constitution. In *Bhe and Others v Khayelitsha Magistrate and Others*, the Court pointed to the deficits of the anachronistic 'official version' in comparison to the 'living norms' of communities:

> The official rules of customary law are sometimes contrasted with what is referred to as 'living customary law', which is an acknowledgment of the rules that are adapted to fit in with changed circumstances. The problem with the adaptations is that they are ad hoc and not uniform. However, magistrates and the courts responsible for the administration of intestate estates continue to adhere to the rules of official customary law, with the consequent anomalies and hardships as a result of changes which have occurred in society.[31]

In another landmark case, the Constitutional Court went further and developed new principles that required the 'living customary law' to be identified and developed by courts. Throughout the 20th century, the classical test for proving the existence of custom as a source of law was to be found in *Van Breda and Others v Jacobs and Others*, according to which, in order to be recognized as law, a customary practice had to be certain, uniformly observed for a long period of time, and reasonable.[32] This test thus dovetailed with jurisprudence elsewhere in Africa and defined a 'fixed line of behaviour (*usus*)' and 'normative moment (*opinio necessitatis*)' as two requirements for a practice to constitute a rule of customary law.[33] However, in *Shilubana and Others v Nwamitwa*, the Constitutional Court noted that *Van Breda* dealt with 'custom' as an immemorial practice of unbroken antiquity. By contrast, 'customary law' was characterized as an independent and original source of law that was 'adaptive by its very nature'. 'By definition, then', the Court asserted, 'while change annihilates custom as a source of law, change is intrinsic to and can be invigorating of customary law'.[34] Against this backdrop, the Court found that a rule demanding 'absolute consistency with past practice' would be contrary to the Constitution, as this 'would result in the courts applying [official] laws which communities themselves no longer follow, and would stifle the recognition of the new [living] rules adopted by the communities in response to the changing face of South African society'.[35] A new 'three-factor test' was subsequently introduced in which 'past practice' constitutes only one factor besides the facilitation of 'the free development by communities of their own laws' as well as the need for courts to balance this imperative to facilitate emic development 'against the value of legal certainty, respect for vested rights, and the protection of constitutional rights'.[36]

As this brief overview shows, customary law in its adaptive 'living law' variant has been firmly recognized in the new Constitution, and in the constitutional jurisprudence, as a legitimate and independent source of South African law. In *Alexkor Ltd and Another v Richtersveld Community and Others*, the Constitutional Court expressed its confidence that this living customary law 'will continue to evolve within the context of its values and norms, *consistently*, with the Constitution'.[37]

The constitutional challenge of the communal land rights act (2004): a case study in the legislative and judicial remaking of customary law

The property clause of the South African Constitution protects existing property against arbitrary deprivation, securing fair and equitable compensation in the case of expropriation, while simultaneously demanding a comprehensive land reform 'in order to redress the results of past racial discrimination'.[38] It specifically provides in section 25 (6) that a person or community with insecure tenure due to past racially discriminatory laws is entitled to legally secure tenure or comparable redress, as provided for by a separate Act of Parliament. The Communal Land Rights Act of 2004, was meant to be such a statutory response to this constitutional obligation. According to its preamble, the Act is, among others, to provide for legally secure tenure by transferring 'communal land' – mostly, but not exclusively, in the areas of the former homelands – to communities and to ensure the democratic administration of communal land through bodies such as 'Land Administration Committees'.

Right from the beginning, when the Communal Land Rights Bill was first made public in 2001, it turned into an object of political debate. However, political controversy reaches even further back, as this bill had already replaced an earlier and decisively different legislative draft. According to Elizabeth Fortin,[39] the precursor of the Communal Land Rights Act – the Draft Land Rights Bill – had been first tabled in early 1999 and adopted an approach to tenure reform that confirmed, through statutory recognition, the status quo of existing de facto rights in communal areas. The Land Rights Bill thereby intended to grant people living in those areas legally recognized security of tenure, while keeping the land in state ownership. For the proponents of this 'rights-based approach', this reform model had the great political advantage of avoiding the transfer of ownership or administration of land to traditional authorities. This approach, while in accordance with the land activists' ideals of democracy and women's rights, proved controversial, however, as it challenged the traditional lobby that demanded greater powers for traditional authorities during the 1999 general elections. In line with the subsequent policy shift mentioned previously, the newly elected President Thabo Mbeki appointed a new Minister for Land and Agriculture, who promptly withdrew the Land Rights Bill and expressed her intentions to give chiefs a stronger role on matters concerning communal lands.[40]

In November 2001, when the successor legislation – the Communal Land Rights Bill – became public, it immediately aroused strong criticism. The model of reform it provided for was quite different, insofar as it entailed a transfer of ownership of the land to 'African traditional communities', albeit under the management of a 'Land Administration Committee'. This paved the way for traditional councils, where they existed, to assume this role. Given that land activists regarded traditional authorities as colonial constructs and thus inherently undemocratic, this new model was strongly criticized. These political controversies took place at the same time as debates about local government reform and the continued roles of traditional leaders.[41] As it turned out, the Traditional Leadership and Governance Framework Act that was passed in 2003, transformed, for the purposes of section 28 (4), the former 'tribal authorities' of the colonial regime into newly established 'traditional councils'. At the same time, despite strong opposition, the Communal Land Rights Bill was also approved with few amendments by Parliament in 2004.[42]

A number of rural communities had politically opposed the Communal Land Rights Bill and made written and oral submissions to the parliamentary Portfolio Committee on Land and Agriculture with the help of the Legal Resources Centre (LRC), a South African public interest law firm. During the limited involvement of the public in the legislative process, community representatives asked for the Bill to be reconsidered after a more comprehensive consultation process with the rural people affected by its provisions.[43] However, when this political activism proved ineffective and the Communal Land Rights Act was passed in Parliament, four rural communities from Kalkfontein,[44] Dixie, Mayaeyane, and Makuleke authorized the Legal Resources Centre and the private law firm Webber Wentzel Bowens to shift towards judicial activism and, in their names, jointly challenge the constitutionality of both the Communal Land Rights Act and the Traditional Leadership and Governance Framework Act.[45]

This legal team also crucially comprised activists from universities and land sector non-governmental organizations (NGOs), including Prof Ben Cousins, then director of the Programme for Land and Agrarian Studies (PLAAS) at the University of the Western Cape, and Aninka Claassens, at the time head of the Rural Women's Action Research Project (RWAR) at the Law, Race, and Gender Research Unit of the University of Cape Town. Both have been active in South African land issues for over thirty years. As Fortin points out, prior to 1999, their activism notably included their significant influence over the first model adopted in the original Land Rights Bill, with

> Cousins in his capacity as external consultant on government's Tenure Reform Core Group (TRCG) which was in existence from 1995 to 1998 and which worked on creating that model, and Claassens in her role as advisor to the minister over the same period and also as a member of the TRCG and then the LRB [Land Rights Bill] drafting team.[46]

In their extensive criticisms of the subsequent Communal Land Rights Act in a number of publications,[47] Cousins and Claassens have pointed out that this Act is highly problematic, as it reintroduces an inherently undemocratic version of 'customs' and 'traditional authorities' in the manner it was misconstrued under colonialism.[48] Vesting land ownership in vaguely defined 'communities' represented by land administration committees, which were to be replaced by traditional councils around chiefs wherever they existed – was thus seen as highly inacceptable. Furthermore, women's rights were greatly threatened under the new model. In that regard, Claassens and Ngubane have argued that, once enacted,

> the new laws would harden the terrain within which rural women struggle for change, and that whereas traditional leaders had been relatively receptive to pressure while their status was unclear, now they would revert to the arrogance and abuses of the apartheid era when they had been sure of government support . . . the Act is the expression of a pre-election deal between traditional leaders and government that reinforces versions of custom and chiefly authority that are dangerous to the interests and struggles of rural women.[49]

Critics advocated instead for vesting land rights in individuals rather than in groups, which rendered 'socially legitimate existing occupation and use, or de facto "rights"'.[50] As noted earlier, this was exactly what had been proposed in the original Land Rights Bill.[51] The subsequent court case on the constitutionality of the Communal Land Rights Act was therefore ultimately rooted in, and pre-structured by, a crucial dissent about the 'true' nature of the customary law of land tenure and the role therein of traditional authorities, giving rise to two incompatible models inscribed in the different bills.

In April 2006, the legal team of the four communities filed an application with the North Gauteng High Court in Pretoria, seeking an order to declare key sections, or all, of the Communal Land Rights Act and the Traditional Leadership and Governance Framework Act unconstitutional and invalid.[52] The 'Applicants' Heads of Argument' extensively developed the reasons supporting this application. Of particular interest for current purposes is its Chapter 1, entitled 'The nature of living customary law and customary land rights'. Here, the applicants first referred explicitly to the previously mentioned judgments by the Constitutional Court, which recognized as valid only the evolving 'living customary law' (as opposed to compromised 'official' versions) and stressed the need for studying the histories of particular communities with regard to the character and content of their specific customary land rights.[53] Subsequently, a 'fundamental characteristic of customary communal land tenure' was discussed, in particular the way in which rights, and decision-making in respect of those rights, are 'layered' or 'nested'. Drawing on the applicants' expert affidavits, notably of Professors Ben Cousins and Thandabantu Nhlapo, the applicants pointed out that complementary rights pertaining to residence, cultivating, and grazing have not been absolute in customary land law, but simultaneously and independently exercised and controlled at different levels, extending upwards from the individual to the household, the family group, the neighbourhood, the village, the ward and, finally, to the wider community or the 'tribe'. It was only within colonial misconstructions of 'official customary law', the applicants argued, that this bottom-up approach became reconceptualized in terms of delegated authority flowing downwards from a sovereign power (i.e. from the colonial state to chiefs). This undermined the strength and relative independence of systems of complementary land rights held simultaneously at different levels.[54]

Against this backdrop, the Applicants' Heads of Argument argued in Chapter 4 that the Communal Land Rights Act actually undermined rather than fostered tenure security by removing the power of a community's own democratic structures, especially its layered decision-making powers, which effectively acceded power to the disputed traditional authority structures. This was also seen as weakening land rights for unmarried women and widows, thus violating the right to gender equality as enshrined in the Bill of Rights of the Constitution.[55] In addition to this argument on the nature of 'living customary land laws', the applicants also claimed in Chapter 6 that the Act granted the minister 'unfettered discretion'[56] and further put forward two arguments regarding the alleged incorrect procedures that were followed when the Communal Land Rights Act was enacted: First, it was submitted that the Communal Land Rights Act directly affected customary law and traditional leadership (issues over which both national and provincial spheres of government may legislate) and, therefore, should have followed the longer parliamentary procedure of a section 76 Bill rather than, as was the case, being dealt with in a relatively short parliamentary process based on section 75 of the Constitution (setting out a procedure for Bills not affecting provinces); second, the applicants argued that the National Council of Provinces (NCOP) failed to fulfil its obligation to facilitate public involvement in the legislative process as required by the Constitution.[57]

The 14 respondents opposing this application included the two National Ministers of Agriculture and Land Affairs as well as of Provincial and Local Government, the Premiers of all nine provinces, the Speaker of the National Assembly, the Chairperson of the National Council of Provinces and, last but not least, the National House of Traditional Leaders. Of the multiple, extensive, and varied responses, only sections of those affidavits that specifically addressed the alleged nature of customary land tenure and traditional leadership are of interest for the current purposes.

In his 'First Respondent's Answering Affidavit', Dr Sipho MD Sibanda, Chief Director Policy and Legislation Development Unit in the Department of Land Affairs, emphasized – like the applicants – the importance of 'living indigenous land tenure systems' in contradistinction to colonial distortions of customary law, but stated that one of the major aims of the Communal Land Rights Act was precisely to address the lack of legal recognition accorded to 'living law'.[58] To some extent, Sibanda accepted that there were different social units within a community, each with decision-making powers and responsibilities regarding land rights.[59] At the same time, he claimed that all affidavits supporting the application ultimately built on Cousins' view of customary law as allegedly 'layered' – an approach, which was 'in many respects foreign to South African customary law' and ultimately incorrect.[60] Sibanda also denied the applicants' claims that traditional councils, wherever they existed, would automatically become the local land administration committees in the sense of section 21 (2) of the Communal Land Rights Act and that the Communal Land Rights Act would discriminate against women's rights. He insisted that, to the contrary, the Act actually ensured gender equality in conformity with the Constitution.[61] Finally, Sibanda stated that, despite the applicants' 'evident desire' to destroy the institution of traditional leadership,

> [e]stablished traditional authorities, now traditional councils, are part of the communal land tenure system across most of the area covered by the Act. They cannot be simply wished away as the applicants advocate because they have an ideological aversion to the institution of traditional leadership.[62]

In his 'Supporting Affidavit', Professor Jan Christoffel Bekker, who had worked under apartheid for the Department of Native Affairs between 1946 and 1970, before taking up various university positions relating to South African customary law, equally distanced himself from colonial and apartheid constructions of 'official customary law'. Arguing against Sibanda, he claimed in his discussion of 'the "true nature" of land tenure and functions of traditional land tenure' that the concept of 'layered customary institutions' was nothing new, as it was common knowledge that land belonged to community, village or family, but never to the individual.[63]

> However, the deponent [Cousins] deftly avoids the role of traditional leaders in communal land tenure. The fact is that almost without exception indigenous peoples of Africa have lived for hundreds of years . . . in units or clusters commonly referred to as tribes. . . . Almost without exception a chief ruled, and they do so to this day, as chief-in-council. . . . In this set-up the traditional leader is by no means a type of owner or trustee. European concepts and terminology are simply not suitable. In practice he is in council rather a custodian of the territory that belongs to the community concerned.[64]

According to Bekker, academics such as Cousins wished to replace the living institution of traditional leadership with 'a revamped system of communal land tenure based on local customs of layered rights to land'.[65]

In his 'Supporting Affidavit', the President of the 'Congress of Traditional Leaders of South Africa (Contralesa)', Sango Phathekile Holomisa MP, expressed a similar opinion:

> Prof Cousins and his associates were once involved in the drafting of the initial drafts of CLaRA [the Communal Land Rights Act]. They were only too happy to support those drafts for as long as they sought to undermine traditional leaders by neglecting to give recognition to the centrality of the institution in the matter of the acquisition, administration, allocation and ownership of communal lands.[66]

However, as Holomisa explained, it was inconceivable – as claimed by the applicants – that a community whose affairs were administered through customary law could not have someone who was equivalent to a traditional leader.[67] All these respondents thus insisted on the central and legitimate role of traditional authorities in the living customary law of land tenure and dismissed the applicants' rejection of powerful chiefs as colonial constructions as having been merely ideologically motivated.

While crucial to the ways in which both the legislative process and the subsequent judicial encounters unfolded, these renegotiations of customary law ended up not playing the decisive role for the ultimate outcome in the Constitutional Court. However, in the first instance, North Gauteng High Court in Pretoria actually did follow the applicants' argument in its judgment on the 30 October 2009, that the quasi-judicial rights of the minister to determine relevant 'communities' as well as the discretion of traditional councils without downward accountability mechanisms put the tenure of rural communities at risk. In light of that, the High Court declared considerable sections of the Communal Land Rights Act to be unconstitutional and invalid, while dismissing the application for declaring parts of the Traditional Leadership and Governance Framework Act as well as the entire Communal Land Rights Act as inconsistent with the Constitution. The High Court also immediately referred the case to the Constitutional Court.[68]

In its subsequent judgment on 11 May 2010, the Constitutional Court found the Communal Land Rights Act unconstitutional in its entirety due to its improper procedural enactment as a section 75 Bill (see earlier). The court additionally ordered that the procedural deficiency of the Act rendered it unnecessary to further consider whether its substantive provisions were consistent with the Constitution or whether Parliament and the National Council of Provinces (NCOP) had sufficiently facilitated public involvement in the legislative process.[69] The Communal Land Rights Act was thus struck down as unconstitutional and declared invalid. Only in 2017, a new Communal Land Tenure Bill (quite similar to the Communal Land Rights Act) was published for public comment, but nothing more has happened since then.

Mind the gaps: the contested legitimacy, historical authenticity, and justice of customary law

Although the controversy about the 'true' nature of customary law proved not decisive for the ultimate outcome in this particular case, it could have easily played an important role had the courts engaged with the substantive issues at hand, and it still might be crucial for related litigation in the future. In this sense, it may be instructive to reflect upon the underlying structures as emergent in this judicial encounter.

The first thing that comes to mind is the explicit insistence, shared by applicants and respondents alike, on a crucial distinction between the contaminated 'official' and the actual 'living' versions of customary law. All parties acknowledged that a gap existed between 'official customary law' and 'the living customary law'; each depicted their own version of customary tenure as allegedly expressing the 'living norms', while dismissing the views of opponents as misleading 'official' constructions. On the one hand, this is to be expected in the specific legal context of post-apartheid South Africa in which the law that was recently developed through constitutional jurisprudence (see earlier) explicitly declares to recognize only the 'living customary law'. It is no wonder, in other words, that all litigants attempted to claim this label to describe their own approach. On the other hand, however, such a conceptual distinction between the 'true' nature of indigenous laws and institutions versus especially 'Western' misconceptions can be traced back to the long colonial history of South Africa and elsewhere. Reports of numerous Commissions of Enquiry, attempts at codification, legislation, court precedents, restatements, and ethnographic studies since the 19th century amply demonstrate the extent to which colonial officials, settlers, and Africans (if they were asked) engaged in the eternal quest for the appropriate forms of ascertainment, the right witnesses, proper forms of documentation, and the 'true' content of customary laws and institutions.

In rejecting the earlier *Van Breda* test, based on definitions of 'custom' as 'uniformly observed for a long period of time' (see earlier), the Constitutional Court recognized the 'living law' as constantly evolving, and thus introduced an important element in the attempt to narrow the gap between living and official versions of customary law. However, new problems follow from this approach. As Janine Ubink[70] demonstrates with regard to Ghana, ascertaining 'living' customary law in contexts of social change becomes very difficult, precisely because potential future rules of customary law, currently in the making, are not yet rooted in regular social behaviour and in an accompanying sense of obligation (see the definition of customary law earlier). In other words, it seems impossible for the state to ascertain whether a local practice, which is incongruent with existing customary rules, merely constitutes a case of deviance or actually enacts the maxim for a new 'living norm', precisely because this indeterminacy could indeed be resolved in either way, but needs to be resolved from within the 'living law' itself. This makes it virtually impossible for state law to choose the 'correct' living norm.

That the gap between the official and the living customary law might thus be narrowed, but never closed completely, has been claimed for some time within socio-legal scholarship. Gordon Woodman,[71] for instance, has pointed out that the incorporation of fluid and ambiguous customary norms and institutions into rigid state structures backed by coercive power inevitably transforms the 'living law' into an 'official' version. This effectively means, however, that any attempt within state structures to not only acknowledge the existence of living customary law, but to also ascertain its formal and material characteristics immediately turns 'the living customary law' into the next version of 'official customary law'. Against this backdrop, the renegotiations of 'official' and 'living customary law' in the said court case can be seen as engaging merely a new vocabulary within an old performative game of 'representation', namely, the game to discursively position the gap between illegitimate and legitimate versions of custom in such a way as to uncover the ugly face of misconstruction behind opponents' versions of customary law, while claiming the 'true', immediate – and hence legitimate – 'representation' of such law for oneself.[72]

In this context, it is interesting to note as a second observation that despite the expressed commitment of all parties towards an evolving 'living customary law', their divergent versions of customary land tenure did not actually try to convince on the basis of new, evolving norms. It is true that the applicants at some stage also made the point that customary land tenure systems had evolved in their communities without including traditional authorities, and that the possibility of such a system was subsequently denied in principle in Holomisa's affidavit supporting the respondents (seemingly in denial of evolving living law). However, the applicants did not argue that customary land law had historically involved traditional authorities, but had now changed due to evolving law. On the contrary, the 'fundamental characteristic of customary communal land tenure' – namely its 'layered' bottom-up nature with only a limited role for traditional authorities – was presented in a tellingly ahistorical way. The same applied to the opposing claims by the respondents regarding the allegedly central role of traditional leadership 'in the matter of the acquisition, administration, allocation, and ownership of communal lands'.[73]

That opponents in a legal dispute about the 'true' nature of customary law should seek to enhance their claims to legitimate representation through an authoritative reference to 'tradition' is hardly surprising – even though, as shown earlier, the recent emphasis in South African constitutional jurisprudence on 'living law' has somewhat diminished the relative importance of 'past practice' within the new three-factor test. On the one hand, Bennett[74] observes that '[a]s a stabilising principle, tradition implies the persistence of the past, although it does not necessarily put an end to change', which does occur even if hidden behind an idiom of continuity with the past. On the other hand, it seems important to note that it is not simply the continuity of just *any* historical practice, but, rather, of an 'authentic past' that is ideally 'cast as a tradition with origins in an autonomous, pre-conquest African society'[75] and typically adds further legitimacy to allegedly customary rules.

Revisionist scholars such as Francis Snyder,[76] Sally Falk Moore,[77] and especially Martin Chanock[78] have emphasized that much, if not most, of the 'official customary law' recorded during colonialism in Africa actually constituted a new creation or 'invented tradition', forged out of contemporary interests of colonial officials and African male elites, rather than a continual practice and faithful representation of past customs. This argument has been invaluable for source-critical re-engagements with seemingly pristine customary law, as documented in various sources under colonial rule. However, it also begs a number of questions. First, as several authors have pointed out, the room for inventing anew allegedly 'old traditions' conveniently adapted to the interests of colonial powers and African elites was severely constrained by the lack of coercive colonial power on the ground. This produced a need for local legitimacy, which also required making use of pre-existing local materials, traditions, and customs. The (re)production of customary law thus typically entailed both changes *and* continuities and to that extent did not represent inventions of completely new forms.[79] Second, and building on that, while constructions of customary law – as in the example of the constitutional challenge – often one-sidedly emphasize those aspects of the past that can be represented as 'continuity', the argument of 'invented traditions' gains much of its apparent radicalism from an inverse overstatement, by one-sidedly registering only 'change'. Yet, for constructions of customary law to operate successfully in proclaimed continuity with an unchanging 'authentic past', the co-occurrence of change is not really a problem as long as people can be convinced that what 'truly' counts are those elements in continuity. Third, Chanock[80] suggests that African elites claimed certain customs as their own, not because these truly existed in the past, but because they served their interests in the present. However, this argument in itself (i.e. without additional data about the 'true' earlier customs) is not conclusive, since both aspects are logically independent, for even if one accepted this narrowly instrumentalist approach, it does not warrant the conclusion that *because* a proclaimed 'custom' served contemporary interests it *therefore* could not have existed in the past.

Last but not least, as Latour[81] demonstrates, social constructivist arguments – for instance, on 'invented traditions' – typically end up in an epistemological paradox, reserving for themselves a 'fact position' in which historical realities (e.g. custom) can be truthfully represented, while locating everyone else on a 'fairy position' from which historical realities (e.g. custom) are misconceived due to their immediate interests or similar distorting factors. In other words, such a revisionist argument does not itself escape the need to distinguish between historical 'facts' and 'misconstructions' of custom, but merely reshuffles and repositions the gap between both sides of the conceptual divide in yet another way.[82] Perhaps Paul Bohannan's old observation, made 50 years ago, still holds true today that our ignorance of African land practices 'derives less from want of "facts" than that we do not know what to do with "facts" or how to interpret them'.[83] In this sense, the renegotiations in the court proceedings of the correct place of the gap between an 'authentic' customary past and tainted histories of misconstruction can be seen as adding a temporal dimension of 'authenticity' to the performative struggle for 'legitimacy' discussed earlier.

These two dimensions concerning the present legitimacy of a 'living customary law' and its historical authenticity derived from a proclaimed continuity with a pristine past mutually stabilize and reinforce each other. Within renegotiations of customary law, a third and last dimension pertaining to questions of justice must also be added. Under colonial systems of indirect rule, the recognition of customary law to some extent also entailed the grudging acceptance of African standards of justice, for instance, on polygamy and bride wealth. As mentioned earlier, however, this was qualified by a so-called 'repugnancy clause', according to which customary law was only recognized as long as it did not violate 'the moral principles of the civilised world', 'natural justice', 'existing laws', and 'public policy'. Colonial state law pluralism thus, to some degree, opened up cultural relativist space for justice, while establishing a clear conceptual gap between 'good' (or 'good enough') customary law that was sufficiently acceptable and 'bad' customary law, which simply could not be tolerated.

With the end of apartheid, the emerging case law raised vehement objection to this 'notorious repugnancy clause', as for instance in *Mabuza v Mbatha 2003*.[84] Yet the logic that underlies the repugnancy clause, which establishes an unbridgeable gap between the acceptable 'good' and the inacceptable 'bad' customary law, was of course reintroduced into the post-apartheid legal order as well, namely by recognizing customary law as the valid law that was yet subject to the Constitution with its Bill of Rights (in close alignment with the international Human Rights regime) as well as to any further legislation. From within the modern state logic of the rule of law it is hard to imagine how any form of official recognition of customary law could be conferred without some form of justice test.[85]

This third conceptual gap also made its presence felt during the judicial encounters around the Communal Land Rights Act: as described earlier, the applicants argued that the effects of the Act violated the constitutional protection against gender discrimination by structurally weakening the land rights of unmarried women and widows, whereas the respondents – notably Sibanda representing the Minister of Agriculture and Land Affairs – not only strongly denied this, but further insisted that the Communal Land Rights Act actually contributed to gender equality as required by the Constitution. Again, the involved parties agreed on a meta-level on the high relevance of the gap between just and unjust customary laws, but differed in their respective ascriptions of these labels to the elements under dispute.

In this way, the renegotiations of customary law within the post-apartheid state – as exemplified in the constitutional challenge of the Communal Land Rights Act – can be seen as being crucially shaped by the performative feats, in a parallel tit for tat, of carefully constructing landscapes of 'custom', locating therein abyssal gaps of legitimacy, historical authenticity and justice, and skilfully navigating this shifting terrain so as to claim for oneself the moral high ground of 'good', 'legitimate', and 'authentic' living customary law.

Conclusion: infinite iterations of 'the good, the bad, and the ugly' in renegotiations of customary law

The end of apartheid raised great expectations with regard to political, legal, and economic transformations. The persistence of an entire plethora of colonial laws that enshrined racial and ethnic segregation posed a formidable challenge for the new democracy. In order to undo these structures underlying the former bifurcated state, a new constitutional system was established that guaranteed equal rights for all citizens. While this new order also acknowledged a right to culture, it was subjected, in principle, to the Bill of Rights, any relevant further legislation and a developing constitutional jurisprudence that has explicitly rejected colonial misconstructions of traditional authorities and customary law and instead celebrated the evolving, 'living' customary law.

However, putting this vision into practice has proved to be quite challenging. Various pieces of legislation have been promulgated in an attempt to harmonize diverse constitutional obligations – for instance, regarding land reform – with the constitutional recognition of traditional authorities and customary law. Several of these statutes have elicited vigorous political controversy, including the political and legal activism against the Communal Land Rights Act, on which I have focused here.

The case study of the constitutional challenge revealed familiar concerns about the 'true' nature of customary law that hark back to the colonial and postcolonial histories of various African countries, including South Africa. New questions emerged: How to establish the 'legitimate' customary law as actually practiced by the people concerned? How to identify the 'authentic' customary law, as it has been (or should have been) followed within African communities (had they been) unaffected by colonial powers? How to find 'just' customary law that was morally acceptable to all?

As I have shown, the different parties involved in the judicial encounters around Communal Land Rights Act agreed, on a meta-level, on the appropriateness of a classificatory logic that allowed, in a first step, to purify the 'handsome and presentable' from the 'ugly' customary law across gaps of present legitimacy and historical authenticity. Thus purified, the same classificatory logic allowed, in a second step, to single out the 'good' from the 'bad' customary law across a gap that separated 'justice' from its inacceptable other. Unsurprisingly, each party to the dispute applied this classificatory logic to its own advantage, claiming to represent the 'good', 'legitimate', and 'authentic' 'living' customary law, while dismissing all other versions as 'bad', 'illegitimate', and 'inauthentic'.

While it seems possible, at least in principle, to deal with each of these three gaps separately (despite all the well-known practical problems that each entails), it is evidently impossible to handle all of them in a satisfactory way at the same time: it is neither logically necessary nor empirically probable that the currently legitimate customary law should correspond to a historically 'authentic' customary law, while the mere act of state recognition, let alone any sanctioning according to external standards of justice, automatically transforms the 'living' into a distorted 'official' version of customary law. Put differently, all parties to these and comparable legislative and judicial renegotiations of customary law (including the bench) had necessarily conspired and still conspire, under the legal fiction of establishing customary law that is simultaneously good, legitimate, and authentic. As this is impossible, whatever the outcome, any result of such a judicial endeavour will be principally open to the charge of propagating precisely such a distorting 'official' version that the court case tried to overcome in the first place. This leads to potentially infinite iterations of renegotiating 'the good, the bad and the ugly' customary law within state arenas.

Ubink observes that the extensive anthropological knowledge about customary law and its functioning is most often not very useful for judges who have to apply customary law in courts.[86] This is probably the case as well for the observations made here on the renegotiations of South African customary law within post-apartheid state institutions, especially the courts. But at least such insights might generate more realistic expectations concerning the shelf life of such legislative and judicial 'solutions' and elicit less surprise and disappointment when they become contested again as yet another version of the despicable 'official' customary law.

Notes

* This chapter is based on research that was funded through an Ambizione Research Fellowship of the Swiss National Science Foundation between 2012 and 2015 (<http://p3.snf.ch/project-137094>). This version benefitted greatly from spirited debates at the conference 'Negotiating Normative Spaces: Insights from and into African Judicial Encounters', held at the Max Planck Institute for Social Anthropology in Halle/Germany (7–8 November 2013), where it was first presented, as well as from numerous discussions with colleagues thereafter. I am particularly grateful for critical comments by Kelly Askew, Hatem Elliesie, Marie-Claire Foblets, Dominik Kohlhagen, Shauna LaTosky, Maria Sapignoli, Katrin Seidel, Janine Ubink and Gordon Woodman.

1 M Mamdani, *Citizen and Subject: Contemporary Africa and the Legacy of Late Colonialism* (Princeton Princeton University Press 1996); *(Interim) Constitution of the Republic of South Africa Act* 200 (1993).

2 See *Constitution of the Republic of South Africa*, Act 108 of 1996, section 211 (3).

3 GR Woodman, 'A Survey of Customary Laws in Africa in Search of Lessons for the Future' in J Fenrich, P Galizzi, and TE Higgins (eds), *The Future of African Customary Law* (Cambridge Cambridge University Press 2011) 9–30, 10–18.

4 L Platzky and C Walker, *The Surplus People: Forced Removals in South Africa* (Johannesburg Ravan Press 1985) 88; TW Bennett, *Customary Law in South Africa* (Lansdowne Juta (2004) 41 f., 45, 51; DS Koyana, 'Traditional Courts in South Africa in the Twenty-First Century' in J Fenrich, P Galizzi, and TE Higgins (eds), *The Future of African Customary Law* (Cambridge Cambridge University Press 2011) 227–246, 246; *Special Courts for Blacks Abolition Act* 34 (1986).

5 M Chanock, *The Making of South African Legal Culture, 1902–1936: Fear, Favour, and Prejudice* (Cambridge Cambridge University Press 2001) 319; *Natal Ordinance* 5 (1849).

6 T Lodge, *Politics in South Africa: From Mandela to Mbeki* (Cape Town David Philip 2002) 86–99, 227–240; L Ntsebeza, 'Chiefs and the ANC in South Africa: The Reconstruction of Tradition?' in A Claassens and B Cousins (eds), *Land, Power & Custom: Controversies Generated by South Africa's Communal Land Rights Act* (Cape Town & Athens, OH Legal Resources Centre, Ohio University Press 2008) 238–261; *Restitution of Land Rights Act 22* (1994); *Communal Property Associations Act 28* (1996).

7 Ministry for Provincial Affairs and Constitutional Development, *White Paper on Local Government* (Pretoria Government Printers 1998).

8 Ministry for Provincial Affairs and Constitutional Development (n 7) section 4.

9 Department of Provincial and Local Government, *The White Paper on Traditional Leadership and Governance* (Pretoria Government Printers 2003).

10 Department of Provincial and Local Government (n 9) section 3.1.

11 Department of Provincial and Local Government (n 9) section 3.3.3 (c).

12 See *Traditional Leadership and Governance Framework Act* 41 (2003), section 20. At the time of writing (September 2018), the *Traditional and Khoi-San Leadership Bill* (2015), intending to include Khoi-San leaders into simultaneously revised formal traditional leadership structures and to replace the Traditional Leadership and Governance Framework Act, is being considered for adoption by the National Council of Provinces (the second House of Parliament).

13 Rural Women's Action Research Programme, 'Custom Contested – Views & Voices: Traditional Courts Bill (TCB)' (University of Cape Town 2013) available at <www.customcontested.co.za/laws-and-policies/traditional-courts-bill-tcb> accessed 3 November 2013.
14 Land & Accountability Research Centre, 'Custom Contested – Views & Voices: Latest Traditional Courts Bill Draft Flouts Constitutional Rights even More Disturbingly' (University of Cape Town 2018) available at <www.customcontested.co.za/latest-traditional-courts-bill-draft-flouts-constitutional-rights-even-more-disturbingly> accessed 19 September 2018.
15 See *Ex parte Chairperson of the Constitutional Assembly: In Re Certification of the Constitution of the Republic of South Africa* 1996 (4) SA 744 (CC) para 197.
16 C Himonga, 'The Future of Living Customary Law in African Legal Systems in the Twenty-First Century and Beyond, with Special Reference to South Africa' in J Fenrich, P Galizzi, and TE Higgins (eds), *The Future of African Customary Law* (Cambridge Cambridge University Press 2011) 31–57, 36 (emphasis added).
17 E Ehrlich, *Fundamental Principles of the Sociology of Law* (New Brunswick Transaction Publishers 2002/1913).
18 Ehrlich (n 17) 41.
19 See FG Snyder, *Capitalism and Legal Change: An African Transformation* (New York Academic Press 1981); TO Ranger, 'The Invention of Tradition in Colonial Africa' in E Hobsbawm and TO Ranger (eds), *The Invention of Tradition* (Cambridge and New York Cambridge University Press 1983) 211–262; P Fitzpatrick, 'Traditionalism and Traditional Law' (1984) 28 (1–2) *Journal of African Law* 20–27; F von Benda-Beckmann, 'Law Out of Context: A Comment on the Creation of Traditional Law' (1984) 28 (1–2) *Journal of African Law* 28–33; GR Woodman, 'Customary Law, State Courts, and the Notion of Institutionalization of Norms in Ghana and Nigeria' in A Allot and GR Woodman (eds), *People's Law and State Law: The Bellagio Papers* (Dordrecht Foris 1985) 143–163; M Chanock, *Law, Custom, and Social Order: The Colonial Experience in Malawi and Zambia* (Cambridge Cambridge University Press 1985); SF Moore, *Social Facts and Fabrications: "Customary" Law on Kilimanjaro, 1880–1980* (Cambridge Cambridge University Press 1986); AJGM Sanders, 'How Customary Is Customary Law?' (1987) 20 (3) *Comparative and International Law Journal of Southern Africa* 405–410; L Vail (ed), *The Creation of Tribalism in Southern Africa* (London Currey 1989).
20 Woodman (n 3) 24 f.; Himonga (n 16) 34.
21 For instance, by the Cape Commission on Native Laws and Customs, *Reports and Proceedings of the Cape of Good Hope Commission on Native Laws and Customs* (Cape Town Government Printers 1883).
22 For instance, *Natal Code of Native Law* 19 (1891).
23 For instance, *Native Administration Act* 38 of 1927.
24 Especially from the Native Appeal Courts, but including all judgments stating customary law.
25 For instance, HA Junod, *The Life of a South African Tribe Vol. I: Social Life* (London Palgrave Macmillan rev. and enl. Edition 1927) 418–448.
26 For instance, SM Seymour, *Native Law in South Africa* (Cape Town Juta 1953).
27 Chanock (n 19); Woodman (n 3).
28 Bennett (n 4) 141.
29 Himonga (n 16) 34 f.
30 Woodman (n 3) 22–25.
31 See *Bhe and Others v. Khayelitsha Magistrate and Others* 2005 (1) SA 580 (CC) para 87. See also *Alexkor Ltd and Another v. Richtersveld Community and Others* 2004 (5) SA 460 (CC) para 52–57.

32 See *Van Breda and Others v. Jacobs and Others* 1921 AD 330 (Van Breda) para 334.
33 J Ubink, 'The Quest for Customary Law in African State Courts' in J Fenrich, P Galizzi, and TE Higgins (eds), *The Future of African Customary Law* (Cambridge Cambridge University Press 2011) 83–102, 85, 99.
34 See *Shilubana and Others v. Nwamitwa* 2009 (2) SA 66 (CC) para 54.
35 See Ibid.
36 Ibid., para 52–57.
37 See *Alexkor Ltd and Another v. Richtersveld Community and Others* 2004 (5) SA 460 (CC) para 53 (emphasis added).
38 See *Constitution of the Republic of South Africa* Act 108 (1996) section 25 (8).
39 E Fortin, *Arenas of Contestation: Policy Processes and Land Tenure Reform in Post-Apartheid South Africa* (Unpublished PhD Thesis, University of Sussex 2008); EAD, 'Struggles with Activism: NGO Engagements with Land Tenure Reform in Post-Apartheid South Africa' (2010) 48 (3) *The Journal of Modern African Studies* 383–411.
40 Fortin (n 39) 388; *Draft Land Rights Bill* (1999) (withdrawn).
41 Fortin (n 39) 389.
42 A Claassens and D Gilfillan, 'The Kalkfontein Land Purchases: Eighty Years On and Still Struggling for Ownership' in A Claassens and B Cousins (eds), *Land, Power & Custom: Controversies Generated by South Africa's Communal Land Rights Act* (Cape Town and Athens, OH Legal Resources Centre, Ohio University Press 2008) 295–314, 303 f.
43 Claassens and Gilfillan (n 42) 304.
44 For case studies analysing the political and legal struggles of the Kalkfontein community regarding their land at local, national and transnational scales, including the constitutional challenge of the Communal Land Rights Act, see O Zenker, 'The Juridification of Political Protest and the Politicisation of Legalism in South African Land Restitution' in J Eckert, B Donahoe, C Strümpell, and ZÖ Biner (eds), *Law Against the State: Ethnographic Forays into Law's Transformations* (Cambridge Cambridge University Press 2012) 118–146 and 'Legal Pluralism, Communal Land Tenure and Multiple Livelihoods in South Africa's Countryside' *Journal of Legal Pluralism* (under review).
45 See *Tongoane and Others v. The Minister of Agriculture and Land Affairs and Others* (TPD 11678/06).
46 Fortin (n 39) 390.
47 E. g. B Cousins and A Claassens, 'Communal Land Rights, Democracy and Traditional Leaders in Post-Apartheid South Africa' in M Saruchera (ed), *Securing Land and Resource Rights in Africa: Pan-African Perspectives Cape Town* (PLAAS Western Cape University 2004) 139–154; B Cousins, 'More Than Socially Embedded: The Distinctive Character of "Communal Tenure" Regimes in South Africa and Its Implications for Land Policy' (2007) 7 (3) *Journal of Agrarian Change* 281–315; A Claassens and B Cousins (eds), *Land, Power & Custom: Controversies Generated by South Africa's Communal Land Rights Act* (Cape Town and Athens, OH Legal Resources Centre, Ohio University Press 2008); A Claassens and S Ngubane, 'Women, Land and Power: The Impact of the Communal Land Rights Act' in A Claassens and B Cousins (eds), *Land, Power & Custom: Controversies Generated by South Africa's Communal Land Rights Act* (Cape Town and Athens, OH Legal Resources Centre, Ohio University Press 2008) 154–183.
48 Cousins (n 47) 308.
49 Claassens and Ngubane (n 47) 181.
50 Cousins (n 47) 308.

51 Fortin (n 39) 390–392.
52 See 'Notice of Motion' in *Tongoane and Others* (n 45) Vol. 1, 1–7.
53 See 'Applicants' Heads of Argument' in Ibid., separate volume para 21–25.
54 See Ibid., para 65–75.
55 See Ibid., para 176–294.
56 See Ibid., para 373–399.
57 Ibid., para 8.1, 8.6.
58 See 'First Respondent's Answering Affidavit' by SMD Sibanda in *Tongoane and Others* (n 44) Vol. 2 b 952.
59 See Ibid., 945 f.
60 See Ibid., 934, 937.
61 See Ibid., 875 f., 882–888.
62 See Ibid., 941.
63 See 'Supporting Affidavit' by Jan Christoffel Bekker in *Tongoane and Others* (n 45) Vol. 2 b 1230–1233.
64 See Ibid., 1231 f.
65 See Ibid., 1235.
66 See 'Supporting Affidavit' by Sango Phathekile Holomisa in *Tongoane and Others* (n 45) Vol. 2 b 1209.
67 See Ibid., 1212 f.
68 See *Tongoane and Others v. National Minister for Agriculture and Land Affairs and Others* 2010 (8) BCLR 838 (GNP) para 62–64, 67.
69 See *Tongoane and Others v. National Minister for Agriculture and Land Affairs and Others* 2010 (8) BCLR 741 (CC) para 98–127, 133.
70 Ubink (n 33).
71 Woodman (n 3) 22–25.
72 As Bourdieu reminds us, through such acts of 'representation', both 'the represented' and 'the representative' are simultaneously created and, if successful, in such a way that this dialectical production disappears behind a seemingly natural 'correspondence' between word and world: 'The spokesperson endowed with full power to speak and act in the name of the group, and first of all to act on the group through the magic of the slogan, the password (mot d'ordre), is the substitute of the group that exists only through this surrogacy. Personifying a fictitious person, a social fiction, he raises those whom he represents from the state of separate individuals, enabling them to act and speak, through him, as one man. In exchange, he receives the right to take himself for the group, to speak and act as if he were the group made man', see P Bourdieu, 'The Social Space and the Genesis of Groups' (1985) 14 (6) *Theory and Society* 723–744, 740.
73 Holomisa's affidavit (n 66).
74 TW Bennett, 'Official' vs "Living" Customary Law: Dilemmas of Description and Recognition' in A Claassens and B Cousins (eds), *Land, Power & Custom: Controversies Generated by South Africa's Communal Land Rights Act* (Cape Town and Athens, OH Legal Resources Centre, Ohio University Press 2008) 138–153, 139.
75 Bennett (n 74)141.
76 Snyder (n 19).
77 Moore (n 19).
78 Chanock (n 19).
79 T Spears, 'Neo-Traditionalism and the Limits of Invention in British Colonial Africa' (2003) 44 (1) *The Journal of African History* 3–27; see also TO Ranger, 'The Invention of Tradition Revisited: The Case of Africa' in TO Ranger and O Vaughan (eds), *Legitimacy and the State in Twentieth-Century Africa: Essays in Honour of AHM Kirk-Greene* (Basingstoke Palgrave Macmillan 1993) 62–111; C

Hamilton, *Terrific Majesty: The Power of Shaka Zulu and the Limits of Historical Invention* (Cambridge Harvard University Press 1998).

80 M Chanock, 'Paradigms, Policies and Property: A Review of the Customary Law of Land Tenure' in K Mann and RL Roberts (eds), *Law in Colonial Africa* (Portsmouth and London Heinemann and Currey 1991) 61–84.

81 B Latour, 'Why Has Critique Run Out of Steam? From Matters of Fact to Matters of Concern' (2004) 30 (2) *Critical Inquiry* 225–248.

82 For a suggestion of how to process this epistemological, political and moral conundrum see O Zenker, 'Anthropology on Trial: Exploring the Laws of Anthropological Expertise' (2016) 12 (3) *International Journal of Law in Context* 293–311.

83 P Bohannan, 'Land', "Tenure" and Land-Tenure' in DP Biebuyck (ed), *African Agrarian Systems* (London Oxford University Press, published for the International African Institute 1963) 101–115, 101.

84 See *Mabuza v. Mbatha* 2003 (4) SA 218 (C) para 30.

85 See O Zenker and MV Hoehne, 'Processing the Paradox: When the State Has to Deal with Customary Law' in O Zenker and MV Hoehne (eds), *The State and the Paradox of Customary Law in Africa* (London Routledge 2018) 1–40.

86 Ubink (n 33) 83, 93.

8 Judicial governance in Ghana

Negotiating jurisdictional authority in the post-colonial state

Tillmann Schneider

Introduction

From conflict resolution by traditional authorities to Kadi courts in Islamic law to arbitration between international companies – conflicts are negotiated in different institutional settings. State courts are just one forum among many. The plurality of normative orders[1] thus entails different understandings of law and creates different spaces of jurisdiction.[2] Focusing on the relationship between different legal forums, the question of actors, and of how a legal forum understands and shapes its relationship to other forums, comes to the fore. In contexts of legal pluralism, those forums can best be understood as 'contact zones'[3] – arenas where not only different normative orders but also different understandings of justice encounter each other. However, despite the existence of a number of taxonomies of conflict resolution, very little attention has so far been devoted to the relationship between the different actors of the jurisdiction and the analysis of these actors as institutions within a specific socio-cultural context.[4]

The interplay between conflict-settling institutions and their users is complex, as they do not act separately, and thus independently, but are in constant interaction. Individuals can often choose between different normative orders and institutions. This possibility of forum shopping gives agency to court users, whereby courts[5] are also active players and can be described as 'shopping forums'.[6] However, the study of institutional pluralism should not be reduced to the study of competition between different forums because they do not necessarily always try to maximize influence at the cost of others. Mutual support, and even coordination between different jurisdictions can also be characteristic of legal pluralism. Still, there is a huge potential for conflicts between different logics and understandings. The relationship between state courts and other judicial actors, like traditional authorities in the post-colonial state, is a good example of the institutional side of legal pluralism. This chapter explores both aspects – conflict and cooperation – in Ghana where traditional authorities are particularly powerful and official state policy regarding their judicial function has been ambivalent to say the least.

Judicial governance in contexts of legal pluralism

Individuals seeking legal assistance and legal forums influence institutional pluralism. The ability to choose between different legal resources is usually described as 'forum shopping'.[7] In contexts of legal pluralism, individuals seeking to settle their conflicts often have the option of choosing not only between different forums but also between different normative. The term 'forum shopping' was originally used in legal scholarship on conflict of laws. While this strand of scholarship is mainly concerned with choices between different state norms and courts, the insights it generates can also inform research on other judicial actors. Particularly in legal scholarship, academic discussions often seem to describe a definite choice between alternatives, even if different forums can be approached simultaneously or successively.[8] Proceedings may start within one normative order, but they do not necessarily stay within it. This is particularly true for contexts of legal pluralism where disputes are often embedded in different normative orders that people have to navigate.

At first glance, courts seem to be rather passive players in this game. They lack the power of the initiative for they depend on the decision of individuals to bring their conflicts to them. Yet they are anything but neutral actors; they follow their own interests and agendas, interact with other judicial actors by allocating judicial authority[9] and compete for influence as potential 'shopping forums'.[10] Owing to the lack of clarity in the hierarchies between different jurisdictional actors, the behaviour of the courts takes on great significance. They also negotiate their competences and demarcate their spheres of influence against other actors.[11]

This particularly affects how decisions are understood: Court decisions, in that sense, should be seen not so much as a final answer but as part of an ongoing dialogue.[12] They can be seen as offering an interpretation to judicial actors who might not at all be involved with the concrete conflict.[13] Courts can also adopt the interpretations of other judicial actors and strengthen them. Courts disseminate information not only about their interpretation of certain norms, but also about other important factors, such as their willingness to decide, or about the costs or the duration of their procedure. They can facilitate or impede access, for example, by declaring themselves competent to decide on certain conflicts, which serves to inform the preferences of the users.[14] Thus, jurisdiction influences the 'attractiveness' and acceptance of forums. By opening up the possibility of resorting to a different court, decisions of one court can influence the procedures of other forums. This way, courts define the relationship between different jurisdictions; they create spheres of influence and autonomy and they decide which norms and interpretations should apply in a dispute. At the same time, courts mark their spheres of influence, as the case may be, by rating other jurisdictions as coequal or of lower ranking. For example, when they set aside other decisions, they generally accept another forum while claiming a higher standing for themselves. Jurisdiction, thus, entails the allocation of authority,[15] and, to that extent, this should not be understood as a neutral dialogue. Disputes and their settlements are both embedded in specific power relations, for which reason, institutional pluralism is also characterized by moments of exclusion and subordination.

These theoretical considerations suggest a number of relevant questions with regard to 'judicial governance'[16] in legal pluralist contexts. How do judicial actors relate their own jurisdiction to that of other forums? Do they try to exert direct influence on other forums? What does institutional pluralism mean in the context of the interpretation of different norms? The plurality of justice institutions shows that law is not only a means but also an object of governance. The next section will explore these questions concerning the relationship between state courts and traditional leaders in Ghana as an example of institutional pluralism in the post-colonial state.

Institutional pluralism in Ghana

As most countries in sub-Saharan Africa, Ghana is characterized by the coexistence of different cultures and different normative orders.[17] Apart from the official state law, a plurality of local normative orders, so-called customary laws, continue to govern the lives of most Ghanaians. These customary laws are acknowledged as a source of law pursuant to Article 11 (2) of the Ghanaian Constitution of 1992. In addition to the plurality of norms, the panoply of different judicial actors involved in solving disputes using different sets of norms include the state courts, the police, chiefs, elders, religious leaders, market queens, trade associations, or traditional healers, to name but a few. Some of these are officially recognized by the state, while the majority acts in an unofficial capacity. Still there is little legislative regulation, which makes the behaviour of judicial actors like the state courts all the more important.

The institutional setting

The architecture of the state court system in Ghana is formulated in the Courts Act (Act 459) of 1993. At the highest level of state jurisdiction are the 'Superior Courts of Justice', the Supreme Court in the capital city of Accra, the Court of Appeal,[18] and the High Courts in the regional capitals. This structure has remained more or less unchanged since gaining independence from British colonial rule in 1957. The state judicial system has regularly been reformed at the local level. Since the last reforms introduced in 2002, the lowest courts are the Circuit and District Courts. Due to the limited number of professionally trained lawyers, for a long time, these lower courts of justice employed lay personnel, a practice that was largely discontinued after the last reform. The magistrates sitting at the District Courts rotate regularly in order to guarantee the neutrality of the courts.

State courts and their jurisdiction are sometimes described as 'alien' institutions whose symbols, language, and ideas of justice seem strange to the majority of the population, particularly in rural areas.[19] Such descriptions sometimes rely on contrasting a small, educated urban elite with the majority of the population, which lives in rural areas and is often illiterate. This equation of spatial with social distance to state courts and the connected belief that customary law is mainly important in rural areas, while it has been replaced by state law in urban areas, is problematic, because despite the obvious differences between rural and urban populations, also with regard to access to state justice, such a dichotomized view remains a simplistic one.[20]

More recent empirical studies suggest that the distance to state courts and their law is not as big as often assumed: State courts are instead perceived as a feasible alternative with certain advantages.[21] Still a number of factors impede access to state courts (beyond the mere spatial distance, especially in rural areas, a problem that should not be underestimated when considering the scope of forum shopping). The length and the costs of the procedure become ever more important, for example, when a disappointed party seeks further legal remedies against a first judgement. Apart from material considerations, social factors also affect the choice of a particular forum. State courts are often circumvented to avoid dragging personal conflicts into a public forum,[22] while sometimes this happens because family members exert considerable pressure on individuals. Many people, furthermore, perceive the state jurisdiction as a highly corrupt system.[23] Finally, state law, with its technical language, is often hard to understand. While it is often assumed that marginalized groups would prefer the supposedly egalitarian state legal system,[24] the few empirical studies that have hitherto been conducted do not paint a clear picture of the preferences.[25] Finally, there is no research on the question of whether and to what degree the decisions of state courts are really implemented. While, theoretically, it is possible to enforce the implementation (if necessary, with the support of the police), such measures would mean an even stronger interference with the local order. For that reason, there are doubts about the possibilities of implementing a state court judgement without the support of powerful actors outside the state system.[26]

Aside from the state courts, a range of non-state institutions and actors is involved in solving conflicts. Dispute resolution presided by the traditional ruler, also known as the 'chief' is the most important,[27] as the institution of chieftaincy is deeply embedded in the cultural identity of the Ghanaian society.[28] At the same time, it is common to criticize the behaviour of individual office holders and succession conflicts that are often violent.[29] The self-perception of chiefs as the guardians of tradition is closely related to their sacral function as intermediaries between the community and its ancestors.[30] At the same time, they are influential actors in relation to the postcolonial state, for example, as vote-brokers whose support is essential to the political survival of even the highest-ranking politicians. Traditional authorities are a rather heterogeneous elite; the huge differences between ethnic communities and the different levels of hierarchy testify to that. Chieftaincy is also assigned a special status in the Constitution, whose Article 270 guarantees its existence and defines the institutional frame 'as established by customary law and usage', prohibiting any form of state influence on the occupation of traditional offices.

At the same time, Ghana is shaken by a number of long-standing, violent conflicts between different aspirants, families, and factions.[31] Individual chiefs have time and again been criticized for mismanagement, particularly on matters concerning allocation and 'selling' of community lands.[32] Some studies suggest, that traditional means of checks and balances – such as the possibility of 'destooling' a chief – to guarantee a responsible administration that is oriented towards the common good of the community, have been rendered dysfunctional these days.[33] This shows that it is important to differentiate between the approval of the abstract office and the administration by individual occupants of such an office.

The houses of chiefs – autonomy under the supervision of the Supreme Court

While interference with the personal occupation of traditional offices and disputes have been state policy ever since the establishment of the colonial state,[34] there is a growing trend of state institutions not interfering with chieftaincy matters, such as with succession conflicts or demand for greater autonomy for self-organization. Chieftaincy disputes are, for example, not adjudicated in state courts, but, rather, in the 'Houses of Chiefs'.[35] This 3-tier set of semi-state institutions where traditional authorities get together and decide on conflicts on the basis of customary law are established and funded by the state. The so-called Traditional Councils are often found at the base of the hierarchy.[36] All divisional chiefs of the area come together in these councils, which are presided by the respective 'Paramount Chief'. The Traditional Councils are only allowed to decide about traditional offices below the level of the 'Paramount Chiefs'. Each of the regions of Ghana has a Regional House of Chiefs – comprising only 'Paramount Chiefs' – that accepts appeals from Traditional Councils and serves as a first instance for conflicts between different paramount chiefs. Each of the Regional Houses elects five representatives for the National House of Chiefs in Kumasi, which serves as the highest body for appeals. The Houses of Chiefs are akin to the lower courts of justice and are treated by law as such.[37] The procedures of the Regional Houses and the National House of Chiefs are similar to those of state courts.[38] Not all members of the Houses sit court. The so-called Judicial Committees are comprised of three members of the respective House (five in the National House) and a professional lawyer.[39] Thus, in terms of the expertise of the members, there is a mix of 'traditional' and 'modern' law. Parties to a conflict can also seek legal representation and advice. Proceedings are often lengthy.[40] All members are male, a factor that is increasingly being criticized.[41] According to Article 272 (b) of the Constitution, the National House of Chiefs has the mandate to conduct research on customary law, to write down customary rules, and to develop a code of customary law that is as uniform as can be. Furthermore, the House is also responsible for evaluating 'customary practices' and suggesting strategies to eradicate harmful practices. However, all of these competences are made available in an advisory capacity, and do not entail sovereign legislative functions.[42]

As a 'modern' state, Ghana now follows a 'policy of non-interference'.[43] In particular, conflicts over succession are to a large extent withdrawn from the influence of state institutions. There is one important exception to this rule: Parties can appeal to the Supreme Court against the decisions of the National House of Chiefs. Such appeals are not unusual when it comes to important offices and chieftaincies. While the involvement of the Supreme Court is contingent on the appeal of individual parties, it still has the power to decide on the occupation of traditional offices.[44]

From the viewpoint of the judiciary, the jurisdiction of the Houses is only an expression of limited autonomy. Despite this autonomy, state courts clearly retain their position on a higher rung in the hierarchy. This becomes evident when the Supreme Court explains that

> [t]he National House of Chiefs cannot, without offence, lay any claims to the skills of the legal draftsman and pleader. The constitutional role of chiefs requires that they concentrate their talent on doing broad 'justice' within the parameters of the customary law where their true expertise lies. . . . [I]t cannot be over-emphasised that if our revered chiefs would resist the temptation of traipsing the maze of legal rules and procedures and restrict themselves to the sphere where they tower earlier everyone else, they would be providing greater service to Ghana and advancing the customary law.[45]

'Customary arbitration'

How then is the official judicial authority allocated between the state courts and the chiefs in other matters? Shortly after independence, chiefs were ousted from the state judicial system.[46] However, their jurisdiction remains important even today. Dispute resolution by traditional authorities, which must not be conflated with mediation, as the chief decides on the case and thus acts as a judge, finds general acceptance by the people.[47] One important reason for this is that such procedures are faster and less expensive than state courts and vary significantly depending on the respective communities and traditional leaders. Due to a lack of clear-cut boundaries between dispute resolution by state courts and by chiefs, there are overlaps between the functions of both. Of the few studies that have documented empirical data on the relationship between both jurisdictions in Ghana,[48] some suggest that people engage in conscious modes of forum shopping – between state and non-state jurisdictions.[49] Some claim that traditional procedures adapt certain aspects of litigation in state courts, for example, with regard to witness interrogation.[50] State norms, however, generally seem to be of minor importance in these forums.

The state recognizes the judicial function of chiefs only to a certain degree. Yet there is very little legislative regulation. The most important state legislation regulating the relationship between state and traditional institutions is the Chieftaincy Act of 2008 (Act 759).[51] The Chieftaincy Act was the first legislation that explicitly recognized 'customary arbitration'.[52] Before that, only jurisdiction in chieftaincy matters was officially sanctioned by the state. While the Alternative Dispute Resolution Act (Act 798), enacted in 2010, is supposed to regulate all forms of arbitration, including those undertaken by traditional authorities, it contains no detailed provisions about the procedure or its status with regard to the jurisdiction of state courts. Furthermore, it is not clear how well this legislation is implemented with regard to arbitration by traditional authorities.[53] Owing to limited legislative regulation, state courts therefore still have a lot of leeway.

By and large, the relationship between state courts and chiefs can be described as a cooperative one. The most important element of this cooperation is the attitude of the state courts to forum shopping. As to whether state jurisdiction is still available after the parties have sought the help of another forum has been an early concern for the state courts. In common law doctrine, the principles of *estoppel* or *res judicata* prevent a party from taking legal action if a matter has already been decided by another court.[54] On the basis of the general common law doctrine, the courts have developed a catalogue of requirements that preclude the way to their jurisdiction. The parties must voluntarily submit themselves to arbitration (and agree to accept the award before starting the procedure), and both parties must appear at the hearing. Additionally, the procedure should not violate the principles of 'fair trial' – insofar as both sides must be heard – and the award must be made public.[55] While these criteria seem to be rather concrete at the first glance, they still leave a lot of discretion to the state courts. This recognition of arbitration by the state courts has strengthened the position of chiefs, since it means that it is often not possible to resort to a state court as an alternative forum. The special status of chiefs becomes even more apparent when compared to other non-state forums, and the decisions of other actors – such as religious leaders, 'fetish priests', or female authorities – are hardly ever mentioned and not recognized by the state courts.

If such proceedings find their way into a court's decision the rejection is evident. A decision from 1992 exemplifies this.[56] The pre-trial history of the conflict, furthermore, illustrates how complex the interplay between different forums can be. The plaintiff had been accused by another member of the community to use 'juju' in order to render the local morgue unusable and to prevent a dignified funeral of a priestess. Before entering the state court system, the conflict had already been the subject of a number of settlement procedures. It was decided at a village meeting to send the accused to a ceremony at a shrine. However, upon his return, it did not accept the result of that ceremony (later described by the court as trial by ordeal). Instead the accusations were expanded and the plaintiff was now accused of also being responsible for the death of another community member. Even though the village authorities had called in a representative of the Paramount Chief, the plaintiff refused to attend that meeting. In the absence of the plaintiff, it was decided to prohibit him from having contact with the village youth. Legal proceedings were subsequently brought before the High Court in which, among others, the plaintiff claimed damages for defamation and demanded the beating of 'Gong-Gong'[57] (as a means to revoke the claim that he was a murderer). The court's remarks on the earlier ceremony at the shrine are of particular interest:

> Trial by ordeal has been known to be one of the most savage and primitive methods of trial. . . . In whatever form a trial by ordeal took, it did not have due regard to the dignity of the person accused. It is indeed a misnomer to describe what goes on at proceedings before fetish priests, witchcrafts and other forces believed to inhere in inanimate substances, as a trial. In these

> proceedings, the accused is not given an opportunity to put forward his version of the case.[58]

The remarks describe the proceedings as savage and barbaric, and generalize about all forms of dispute settlements that include metaphysical elements. The language is similar to the language that would have been used by a British colonial judge at the beginning of the 20th century. The list of deficits that the courts hold against the 'fetish priest' serves as much to deny legitimacy as to paint a positive image of the state apparatus. That the rejection of tradition is, however, only partial becomes clear when the court describes the status of the chiefs:

> The defendants are undoubtedly the chiefs of the community in which the plaintiff belongs. And as chiefs they are thus socially duty-bound to ensure peace and harmony in the area. They are the traditional rulers and leaders of the plaintiff. And they are therefore entitled to respect [and] obedience from their subjects including the plaintiff.[59]

This high regard accorded to the chiefs, however, does not mean that the courts regard them as equal partners, which is, for example, reflected in the different terminology that distinguishes the procedures: While adjudication is reserved for the activities of the state courts, the chiefs' jurisdiction is described as 'arbitration'. Furthermore, even if the state courts limit forum shopping, they still claim the competence to evaluate dispute settlements reached by chiefs, leaving no doubt as to who has the higher authority on matters of justice.

Who knows the (customary) law?

Another aspect of judicial authority is the power over the interpretation of norms. According to Article 11 paragraph 2 of the Constitution, customary law is part of the official law of Ghana. Thus, state courts are also obliged to base their decisions on customary law in certain cases. However, judges, who are often not members of the respective community and do not observe the relevant practices, lack the necessary knowledge about the local normative practices that underlie customary law. How could they possibly determine what the relevant customary laws are? During colonial times, British judges – whose lack of knowledge was even more obvious – were confronted by customary law after a conflict had already been decided in the so-called Native Courts presided by chiefs. Usually they did not doubt the content of customary norms described in those proceedings.[60] In line with the general colonial policy of indirect rule, traditional rulers thus had a special status as the trusted source of customary law. At the same time, there was also a trend to characterize customary law as 'notorious', known to the courts, which would theoretically take a number of judgments, often assumed after just one decision.[61]

Section 55 of the Courts Act contains a number of statutory provisions for ascertaining customary norms.[62] Its first paragraph states that questions of customary law are legal, not factual questions. The following paragraphs provide that a court can hold an investigation if the content of a customary norm is unclear. According to paragraph 2, courts are supposed to consider the statements of the parties, the relevant case law and the textbooks. Paragraph 3 provides that the general provisions concerning the interrogation of witnesses in courts are used accordingly in case other persons are questioned. Section 55 does not offer any details as to who is supposed to be asked. Paragraph 5 finally allows state courts to send out a written request to the respective Traditional Council or the House of Chiefs for written information. While section 55 seems to privilege the written form to a certain degree, there is no explicit hierarchy between different sources of knowledge. However, few of these provisions are binding for the courts. As to whether there is a need for an investigation in the first place, and how such an investigation is to be conducted, falls within the discretionary ambit of the courts.[63] The statute also offers no explanation as to how judges are supposed to use information, particularly on the status the result of an investigation has (e.g. the personal information of an expert), whether that is binding on a judge or not.[64]

State courts prefer written sources. Sarbah's 'Fanti Customary Laws', which was first published in 1897,[65] enjoys the highest standing among the available standard works. Besides they mainly refer to themselves and transfer – usually implicitly – the existing case law produced by state courts. Thus, in many cases – as in the following example – courts do not discuss the problem of its source:

> Customary law is now not to be proved as a fact. It is part of the established law which the courts must be presumed to know. There are precedents of decided cases by the superior courts of this country which form the basis of case law, authorities of persuasive value and force which can safely afford a useful guide in the instant case.[66]

Here, the decision to describe questions of customary law as legal questions within the statutory framework is used as an argument for assuming that state courts know the content of the respective normative orders. Consequently, the decision refers to judicial precedence. This practice should not surprise, since it is consistent with the procedural doctrines of common law. The *stare decisis* principle is often described as the main reason for the ossification of official version of customary law.[67] However, the self-reference of the Ghanaian state courts can only be understood to a certain degree in terms of this legal principle. Given the variety of different customary orders there are just not enough binding precedents within the official case law. Furthermore, the majority of the decisions referred to are those of the High Courts, and they are binding only for the lower courts, but not for other High Courts or for Courts of Appeal. These decisions are at best 'persuasive authorities', which can be used as an argument by other courts, but which are not formally binding.[68] While there certainly is a practice of self-reference, the importance of the *stare decisis* principle should not be overrated. This self-reference is problematic in two respects: First of all, it can be argued whether the norms and interpretations of older decisions can be directly transferred to more recent contexts. Customary law is said to be adaptive to changing circumstances, and the living conditions of African societies have without doubt seen major changes in the last couple of decades.[69] Secondly, the practice of the bench does not regard ethnic and local diversity within customary orders (or only to a very limited degree). The majority of the courts and educational institution can be found in southern Ghana. The classic textbooks on customary law – the work of Sarbah and Danquah, by way of example[70] – which are the most important written sources, in addition to the case law, were also created in the south. The laws and normative practices of certain communities have a strong influence for that reason.[71] Only few decisions discuss this 'ethnic' dimension explicitly.[72]

Some decisions discuss the problem of the source explicitly, particularly where no written sources (e.g. case law or textbooks) exist, and judges seek 'empirical proof' of certain customary norms. These decisions reflect the ethno-geographical character of the state jurisdiction and usually concern the north of the country. For example, with regard to the customary law of the Dagomba, an ethnic community in northern Ghana, the High Court in the city of Tamale offers the following explanation:

> Unfortunately, and I can appreciate the difficulty of counsel, no authorities of any sort were cited in support of the propositions of Dagomba customary law which were propounded with so much confidence by counsel for the parties. I did not get the northern Sarbahs and Danquahs and as I found myself entertaining grave doubts as to the nature of the Dagomba customary law . . . I decided after I had heard the submissions of counsel and after I had consulted a few books as well as documents in the National Archives at Tamale, that it was necessary to hold an inquiry.[73]

The judge explicitly discusses his own lack of knowledge about the relevant customary law. At the same time, the order of potential sources suggests that an investigation is needed because of the lack of written sources.

If judges undertake an investigation they reaffirm the special status of traditional authorities as the most important personal sources of knowledge. Particularly in the early years after gaining independence, judges called on chiefs in continuation of this colonial practice. However, the traditional office is not the only reason for their expertise:

> The occupant of a stool and the traditional elders of the stool are the repositories of the tradition and customary law of their state; it is therefore expected that they should always act in conformity with the customary law. Again, apart altogether from being an occupant of a stool, Nana Kwadade II, known in his private capacity as Mr. Ofei Awere, was, before his

> enstoolment, an outstanding legal practitioner with considerable knowledge and experience of the customary law.[74]

This reaffirms the special status of traditional authorities as 'repositories' of customary law. At the same time, the judge emphasizes the fact that the respective chief was an experienced professional lawyer, in effect arguing that not just the knowledge of tradition was relevant. The importance of juridical expertise also became clear in interviews with judges:

> Fortunately, most of the lawyers who practice here are from the north and they are conversant of the customs of the people. And as they are lawyers and officers of the court they cannot mislead the court.[75]

This division of roles and competences with regard to expertise – chiefs as experts of tradition, lawyers having professional knowledge of all forms of law – also answers the question as to whether judges are bound to certain interpretations of customary law: The chiefs can at best claim an advisory role that carries no legal authority that could potentially bind the state courts. This is explicitly stated in a number of decisions, such as the following:

> [S]ince . . . the question as to the existence or content of any rule of customary law is one of law, the court becomes the final arbiter and is not bound to follow the expert opinion if in the court's considered view, the particular custom is unreasonable, obsolete or is repugnant to principles of equity, good conscience and natural justice, or is contrary to decisions of superior courts, or not in step with modern notions.[76]

A judge of a District Court expressed a similar attitude:

> You always need to consult. As a judge you don't limit yourself. I mean you must have a very broad horizon. In case of any difficulty pertaining to the custom or the religion or the practice in an area in which you think you don't have enough knowledge you have to do research . . . You can always call traditional authorities. You can always call expert witnesses who come to court and testify. And if you think that what they are saying will be of any help you take it.[77]

While the judge articulates a clear obligation to investigate, he also refuses any duty to adhere to a certain description or interpretation, which is a clear break from the colonial practice of relying on the description of customary norms offered by chiefs.

Conclusion: contestation, cooperation, and communication

Legal pluralism – understood as the interaction between different normative orders – also involves interaction between institutions such as courts and other forums of dispute resolution interact with each other. As this chapter shows, theoretical approaches on forum shopping and governance theory can inform research on this institutional dimension of legal pluralism. Even if the relationship between these different jurisdictional actors is often characterized by conflict and competition, it cannot be reduced to just that, for judicial governance also entails cooperation and mutual support.

At least the 'official face' of legal pluralism in Ghana is significantly characterized by the jurisdiction of state courts. The discretionary powers relating to their relationship to other legal forums are particularly wide. The state courts acknowledge that the chiefs and their jurisdiction have a special standing and privilege them over other actors, but they leave no doubt that this 'partnership' is not equal. This practice of cooperating with the chiefs as privileged, yet clearly subordinated partners, strengthens their standing to a certain degree. Still it sometimes encounters resistance. For example, the National House of Chiefs sometimes recommends not appealing to the Supreme Court. That the traditional authorities do not view themselves as mere low-ranking, subordinate partners of the judiciary becomes even clearer in other areas of law, particularly when it comes to control over land. For example, the Asantehene – the traditional leader of Ghana's largest ethnic group and one of the most powerful persons in the whole country – called upon his subjects during his inauguration in 1999 to withdraw all land cases from the state courts and seek a resolution through his own arbitration efforts.[78]

Notes

1 For broad conceptual discussions of legal pluralism see, for example, Griffiths, 'Legal Pluralism' in Banakar and Travers (eds), *An Introduction to Law and Social Theory* (Oxford: Hart 2002) 289 ff.; Melissaris, *Ubiquitous Law* (Burlington: Ashgate 2009); Woodman (1998) 42 *Journal of Legal Pluralism* 21 ff.

2 Spatial metaphors have been used to describe this institutional side of legal pluralism early on, see M Galanter, 'Justice in Many Rooms: Courts, Private Ordering and Indigenous Law' (1981) 19 *Journal of Legal Pluralism* 1–47, 1 ff.

3 ML Pratt, 'Arts of the Contact Zone' (1991) *Profession* 33–40, 33.

4 See I Shahar, 'Legal Pluralism Incarnate: On Courts of Law in Colonial and Postcolonial Settings' (2012) 65 *Journal of Legal Pluralism* 133–163, 133, 135. An important exception is K von Benda-Beckmann's article on 'Forum Shopping and Shopping Forums', see K von Benda-Beckmann, 'Forum Shopping and Shopping Forums: Dispute Processing in a Minangkabau Village in West Sumatra' (1981) 19 *Journal of Legal Pluralism* 117–159, 117 ff.

5 The term 'courts' is used here in a broad sense that does not only include institutions that are organized similarly as state courts, but every form of dispute settlement that is reached by the binding decision of a third party.

6 Benda-Beckmann (n 4) 117.

7 See R Cover, 'The Uses of Jurisdictional Redundancy: Interest, Ideology, and Innovation' (1981) 22 (4) *William and Mary Law Review* 639–682, 639, 646.

8 Cover calls the possibility to seek redress at different courts simultaneously or successively as 'synchronic' and 'diachronic' redundancy, see Cover (n 7) 639, 647 f.

9 PS Berman, *Global Legal Pluralism. Global Legal Pluralism: A Jurisprudence of Law Beyond Borders* (Cambridge 2012) 27 ff.

10 Benda-Beckmann (n 4) 117.

11 This struggle for influence can be described from a neo-institutional perspective as the result of their belonging to different 'organizational fields'. These fields are characterized by different rules and values. While courts often operate within different fields at the same time, they do not always have the same influence, see Shahar (n 4) 133, 137 ff.

12 In the EU-context courts not only communicate with other courts but participate in a larger exchange with a number of actors, see, for example, the conception of courts as 'catalysts' in J Scott and S Sturm, 'Courts as Catalysts: Re-Thinking the Judicial Role in New Governance' (2006–2007) 13 *Columbia Journal of European Law* 565–594, 565, 570 ff.

13 Berman identifies this process as a phenomenon of global legal pluralism and uses – in reference to Robert Cover – the term 'jurispersuasion', see PS Berman, 'From International Law to Law and Globalization' (2005) 43 *Columbia Journal of Transnational Law* 485–556, 485, 533 ff.

14 C Whytock, 'The Evolving Forum Shopping System' (2011) 96 *Cornell Law Review* 481–534, 481, 487 ff.

15 C Whytock, 'Domestic Courts and Global Governance' (2009–2010) 84 *Tulane Law Review* 67–123, 67, 75 ff.

16 Whytock uses the term 'transnational judicial governance' to describe the decisions of domestic courts as an important element of global legal pluralism, see Whytock (n 15) 67, 71. The term governance has seen a huge dissemination in the last decades, particularly in social and political science. A whole cluster of different approaches is subsumed under the term governance theory. Their common basis is that they not only look at the institutions of the state but also include non-hierarchical, horizontal interactions between state and non-state actors, particularly with regard to the development and implementation of policies. Governance, thus, in its broadest sense, describes a certain perspective onto the phenomenon of governing that emphasizes aspects as de-centrality (or poly-centrality) and the importance of networks, see C Offe, 'Governance: An "Empty Signifier"?' (2009) 16 (4) *Constellations* 550–562, 550, 553 f.

17 While legal pluralism as an abstract phenomenon is ubiquitous in time and space, colonial subordination and its impact give legal pluralism a certain shape. This is not to suggest that there is a postcolonial legal pluralism, as colonial and post-colonial practices and policies are obviously diverse.

18 Both are based in the capital Accra. In December 2008, another Court of Appeal was inaugurated in Kumasi, the capital of the Ashanti Region, in order to decentralise the state court system.

19 U Schmid, "Legal Pluralism as a Source for Conflict in Multi-Ethnic Society. The Case of Ghana", (2001) 46 *Journal of Legal Pluralism* 1, 9.

20 See R Crook, S Affou, D Hammond, AF Vanga, and M Owusu-Yeboah, *The Law, Legal Institutions and the Protection of Land Rights in Ghana and Côte d'Ivoire: Developing a More Effective and Equitable System* (Brighton Institute of Development Studies 2007) 48 ff.

21 According to Crook et al. (n 20) 58, the main reason for choosing a state court was its authority and that is was easier to enforce a state court judgment.

22 See VS Gedzi, *Principles and Practices of Dispute Resolution in Ghana: Ewe and Akan Procedures on Females' Inheritance and Property Rights* (Düren: Shaker 2009) 140 ff., 154. In contrast, Crook et al. (n 20) 45 f. argue that family issues compose more than half of the cases in state courts they investigated.

23 There is only little empirical research on corruption within state courts in Ghana, for example, the report of the Ghana Integrity Initiative: Ayine, *Report on Judicial Corruption Monitoring Exercise* (Accra Ghana Integrity Initiative 2007), notably 14 f.

24 See Gedzi (n 22) 140 ff., who at the same time notices that in spite of this preference people often go to non-state forums due to financial constraints or social pressure.
25 See Crook et al. (n 20) 87.
26 At the same time, better implementation was deemed a clear advantage of the state legal system, see Crook et al. (n 20) 46 f.
27 On the institution of chieftaincy and its relationship to the state, see, EA Van Rouveroy van Nieuwaal, 'States and Chiefs: Are Chiefs Mere Puppets?' (1996) *Journal of Legal Pluralism* 39–78, 37 f., 39 ff. Reference to tradition as a source for legitimacy does not mean that the establishment of the colonial state did not lead to profound changes within non-state governance systems.
28 See the contributions in IK Odotei and AK Awedoba (eds), *Chieftaincy in Ghana: Culture, Governance, and Development* (Accra Sub-Saharan Publishers 2006).
29 See C Abotchie, AK Awedoba, IK Odotei et al., 'Perceptions on Chieftaincy' in IK Odotei and AK Awedoba (eds), *Chieftaincy in Ghana: Culture, Governance, and Development* (Accra Sub-Saharan Publishers 2006) 103–144, 103 ff.
30 Under British indirect colonial rule, traditional authorities also served as intermediaries between their communities and the colonial administration, see M Mamdani, 'Historicizing Power and Responses to Power: Indirect Rule and Its Reform' (1999) 66 *Social Research* 59–886, 859, 870 ff.
31 DI Ray, "Divided Sovereignty. Traditional Authority and the State in Ghana", (1996) 37–38 *Journal of Legal Pluralism* 181 ff.
32 Such conflicts over land often turn violent, see J Ubink, *In the Land of the Chiefs: Customary Law, Land Conflicts, and the Role of the State in Peri-Urban Ghana* (Leiden 2008) 146.
33 Ubink (n 32) 173 ff. Ubink explains, for example, that such proceedings for dismissal can anyway only be instigated by the respective elites.
34 See, for example, R Rathbone, *Nkrumah & the Chiefs 1951–60* (Accra Reimmer 2000).
35 See AS Anamzoya, '"Neither Fish Nor Fowl": An Analysis of Status Ambiguity of the Houses of Chiefs in Ghana' (2014) 46 *The Journal of Legal Pluralism and Unofficial Law* 218–234, 218 ff.
36 In 2007, there were 193 Traditional Councils in Ghana in all, see AS Anamzoya, Working Behind the Scenes: State Actors and Judicial Processes in the Houses of Chiefs in Ghana (KA Busia Lecture Hall 1 November 2007, University of Ghana Legon 2008) 20. However, a lot of these councils do not hold meetings, or do so only irregularly due to financial constraints.
37 Sec. 39 Courts Act.
38 See Anamzoya (n 35) 225 f.
39 Sec. 25, 28 Chieftaincy Act.
40 See DI Ray, 'Chiefs in Their Millennium Sandals: Traditional Authority in Ghana-Relevence, Challenges and Prospects' in WJ Tettey, KP Puplampu, and BJ Berman (eds), *Critical Perspectives in Politics and Socio-Economic Development in Ghana* (Leiden 2003) 254 ff.
41 For example, Lord Justice Brobbey, a senior Judge of the Supreme Court who was involved in the reform of the Chieftaincy Act demanded during the introduction of the reform that 'Queenmothers' – female traditional authorities who can be found in certain communities – should be represented in the respective Regional Houses and the National House, see <www.modernghana.com/news/185626/1/review-chieftaincy-act-on-queenmothers-justice-bro.html> accessed 29 October 2018.
42 Since 2006, the National House of Chiefs is implementing a project on the codification of customary law. No results have been published so far, see JB Akamba and IK Tufuor, 'The Future of Customary Law in Ghana' in J Fenrich, P Galizzi,

and TE Higgins (eds), *The Future of African Customary Law* (Cambridge and New York 2011) 202–224, 222 ff.

43 According to Ubink (n 32) 193 ff., one of the reasons for this policy is the growing ties between traditional and state elites.

44 This competence of the Supreme Court is sometimes criticized by traditional authorities. For example, the Asantehene asked – as a guest of honour at the Chief Justice's Forum in Kumasi in December 2007 – how he should accept an oath of allegiance and install a chief if not he or a traditional council but a state court decided that he should occupy a traditional office.

45 *Pomaa and Others v. Fosuhene* (1987–88) 1 GLR 244 (262).

46 During colonial times, chiefs presided over so called 'Native Courts'. These courts were abolished with the enactment of the Local Courts Act in 1958, which established Local Courts at the lowest level of the state court system. These courts were staffed with magistrates appointed by the Minister of the Interior, see WB Harvey, *Law and Social Change in Ghana* (Princeton 1966) 222 f.

47 Ubink (n 32) 142.

48 For example, Crook et al. (n 20) and Gedzi (n 22). Both studies highlight that their results are not necessarily representative for the whole country and that they can, therefore, not simply be generalized.

49 See, for example, Crook et al. (n 20) 46 ff.

50 Gedzi (n 22) 195.

51 The act was reformed in 2008 because the earlier version from 1971 still contained a number of provisions that allowed the government to directly influence the occupation of traditional offices. According to Article 270 of the Constitution such an influence is prohibited.

52 The legislation seems to follow the terminology used in Ghanaian case law. However, it is important to highlight a number of differences with concepts in Western law. Parties have, for example, little or no influence on who is presiding over the proceedings in customary settings, and these proceedings are often public. Other statutes recognized such procedures already before the reform of the Chieftaincy Act, such as section 21 of the Intestate Succession Law, which provides that the act is to be applied to all proceedings pending before chiefs or family heads.

53 For a detailed analysis of the provisions, see E Onyema, 'The New Ghana ADR Act 2010: A Critical Overview' (2012) 28 *Arbitration International* 101–124, 101, 114 ff.

54 In common law *estoppel* is a general term for a set of principles based on good faith. The special term is *res judicata*, however, the terminology is not always used in a uniform way, see RC Casad and KM Clermont, *Res Judicata: A Handbook on Its Theory, Doctrine, and Practice* (Durham Carolina Academic Press 2001) 3 ff.

55 The fundamental decision in Ghana is *Budu II v. Caesar and Others* [1959] GLR 410 ff.

56 *Ahevi v. Akoto IV* [1993–94] 1 GLR 512 ff.

57 Particularly in southern Ghana, this is a common ritual method for communicating certain news within a community, see JK Adjaye, 'The Technology of the Human Voice: Oral Systems of Information Dissemination and Retrieval Among the Akan of Ghana' (2008) 40 *The International Information & Library Review* 236–242, 236, 239 ff.

58 *Ahevi v. Akoto IV* [1993–94] 1 GLR 512, 530 f.

59 Ibid., 534.

60 See GR Woodman, *Customary Land Law in the Ghanaian Courts* (Accra 1996) 40.

61 Woodman (n 60) 41.

62 There has been a recent attempt to create a written version – an ascertainment – of the customary laws of Ghana, however, it is unclear how far this has advanced, see Akamba and Tufuor (n 42) 222 f.

63 Some interpret section 55 to mean that courts are obliged to investigate if a relevant customary norm is not clear, see HJAN Mensa-Bonsu, 'Of "Nuts in the Ground Not Being Groundnuts": The Current State of Customary Law in Ghana' (2002–2004) 22 *University of Ghana Law Journal* 1–24, 1, 12.
64 Mensa-Bonsu (n 63) 12 f. argues that such a binding effect is at least implied.
65 John Mensah Sarbah (1864–1910) was a lawyer and politician of the then Gold Coast. In 1887, he was admitted to the English bar. He was one of the co-founders of the Aborigines' Rights Protection Society, which organized opposition against colonial government.
66 *Amponsah and Others v. Budu* [1989–90] 2 GLR 291, 309.
67 For example, TW Bennett, *Customary Law in South Africa* (Lansdowne 2004) 5 f.; CN Himonga and W Pintens, *Family Law in Zambia* (Alphen aan den Rijn 2011) 37 f.
68 See RA Shiner, *Legal Institutions and the Sources of Law* (Dordrecht 2005) 32 ff.
69 See Himonga (n 16) 38. While this adaptability of customary law is plausible and claimed in every description of customary law, little research or conceptualization can be found with regard to the question of how this normative change actually takes place. Inspiration for such analysis could be found in discussions on the change of social norms in general, e.g. R Ellickson, 'The Evolution of Social Norms: A Perspective from the Legal Academy' in M Hechter and K-D Opp (eds), *Social Norms* (New York 2001) 35–75, 35 ff.
70 Joseph Boakye Danquah was a politician and lawyer, and one of the founding fathers of the independent state Ghana. He published *Gold Coast: Akan Laws and Customs and the Akim Abuakwa Constitution* in 1928.
71 The official practice has been criticized and termed 'Akanization' of the jurisdiction, see Kludze, *The Modern Law of Succession of Ghana* (Dordrecht Foris 1988) 154 ff. While the term rightly highlights the problem of unreflective unification, it is itself unifying in that it suggests a questionable level of homogeneity within Akan societies and their legal orders.
72 Such an instance of explicit transfer can be found in *Huago and Others v. Djangmah II and Others* [1997–98] 1 GLR 300 ff.
73 *Billa v. Salifu* [1971] 2 GLR 87, 91.
74 *Donkor v. Asare and Others* [1960] GLR 187, 188.
75 Interview with judge at the High Court, Bolgatanga (19 February 2008).
76 *Abangana v. Akologo* [1976] GLR 382, 386.
77 Interview with a judge at the District Court, Bolgatanga (21 February 2008).
78 Ubink (n 32) 153 f. According to Crook et al. (n 20) 86, only part of his subjects followed that appeal. Other titles (not specifically referred to here) are S Baer, 'Traveling Concepts: Substantive Equality on the Road' (2010–2011) 46 *Tulsa Law Review* 59–79; HP Bang (ed), *Governance as Social and Political Communication* (Manchester 2003); S Killinger, *The World Bank's Non-Political Mandate* (Köln 2003); R Keohane, A Moravcsik, A-M Slaughter, 'Legalized Dispute Resolution. Interstate and Transnational' (2000) 54 (3) *International Organization* 457–488; AKP Kludze, 'Evolution of the Different Regimes of Customary Law in Ghana Within the Framework of the Principle of Stare Decisis' in AN Allott and GR Woodman (eds), *People's Law* and *State Law: The Bellagio Papers. Conference on Folk Law in State Courts* (Dordrecht 1985) 97–104; SE Merry, 'Legal Pluralism' (1988) 22 (5) *Law & Society Review* 869–896; S Müller-Mall, *Legal Spaces: Towards a Topological Thinking of Law* (Berlin Heidelberg 2013).

9 Living customary law in South Africa

Negotiating spaces for women in traditional communities[1]

Lisa Heemann

Introduction

The Constitution of South Africa of 1996 recognizes 'customary law' as an independent source of law and obliges courts to apply it when applicable.[2] The Constitution also protects the right to culture more generally in sections 30 and 31. At the same time, it contains strong provisions on gender equality. The founding principles and, more specifically, section 9 provide for equality before law and prohibit unfair discrimination.[3] In the 1990s, many observers held that cultural rights and liberal human (women's) rights were irreconcilable.[4] However, the example of South Africa shows that solutions can be found. The development of customary law in line with constitutional values is one approach to resolve the conflict between women's rights to equality on the one hand and rights to culture on the other.

For South Africa, the new Constitution, with its comprehensive and justiciable Bill of Rights, represented a break with the past. Where human rights and democracy had been suppressed under apartheid, the new Constitution laid out the agenda for transformation.[5] Women in South African traditional communities had been excluded from access to land and political participation for a long time. That something had actually changed became evident in 2008 in a case before the Constitutional Court of South Africa. The traditional community of Valoyis claimed:

> [T]hough in the past it was not permissible by the Valoyis that a female child be heir, in terms of democracy and the new Republic of South African Constitution it is now permissible that a female child be heir since she is also equal to a male child.[6]

The Constitutional Court embraced this development. It made clear:

> Customary law is living law and will in future inevitably be interpreted, applied and, when necessary, amended or developed by the community itself or by the courts.[7]

Eugen Ehrlich was the first to use the expression 'living law' in the context of his legal sociology.[8] In South Africa, the term is today used to distinguish between the codified and the non-written version of customary laws. The discrepancy between the codified customary law and the actually practiced customary law in South Africa became apparent as early as in the 1980s.[9] The Constitutional Court later took up a classification proposed by Bennett.[10]

Accordingly, *living customary law* refers to 'the version of customary law actually observed by the people'[11] as opposed to what is known as *official customary law* in South Africa. The latter is 'the body of rules created by the state and the legal profession'[12] that encompasses a diverse and complex collection of written sources of customary laws. The idea of *living customary law* is that the norms are flexible and evolving to adapt to new social realities.

In *Shilubana*, the Court speaks of a 'development of the law' which refers to section 39 of the Constitution: The norm obliges courts to promote the Bill of Rights when interpreting or developing common as well as customary law.[13] In *Shilubana*, the Court seems to accept that both the courts and the traditional community play an active role in the transformation of customary law to conform to the Bill of Rights. I argue that the recognition and application of *living customary law* (as opposed to relying on *official customary law*) creates significant negotiation spaces for women to overcome exclusion from or barriers to access to land and politics.

The situation of women in traditional communities in South Africa is very different across regions and communities and any description of the position of women runs the risk of oversimplifying their situation. However, women in traditional communities share the experience of exclusion ranging from access to land to participation in politics (even if to different degrees). I show that the codified *official customary law* is one of the main obstacles for women in traditional communities. However, in the past 20 years, women have begun to overcome exclusion and to push for changes at the community level. In doing so, the women first made use of *living customary law* in informal negotiations with leaders and communities at local level. Eventually, at a later stage, the development of *living customary law* received support at the national level, which further enhanced women's rights (as the case of the Valoyis shows). This chapter looks in detail at the complex interactions between the community and national level and the space *living customary law* provides for women in traditional communities to overcome exclusion.

Women in traditional communities

While South African women from all backgrounds share the experience of discrimination, women in traditional communities face their own set of challenges. In South Africa, traditional communities are confined to the area of their former homelands. Under apartheid, the ten homelands in remote, rural, often infertile areas were each sub-divided into so called 'tribes' administered by so-called 'tribal authorities'. Two laws spelled out the details of the administration structures and set 'tribal' communal boundaries in the homelands: The Black Administration

Act of 1927 and the Bantu Authorities Act of 1951.[14] When the Traditional Leadership and Governance Framework Act of 2003 (TLGFA) replaced the old legislation, 'tribes' were renamed 'traditional communities'. The former 'tribal' authorities now became 'traditional authorities'.[15]

Traditional communities in South Africa still suffer from the legacy of apartheid. They are placed in remote, often infertile rural areas with little infrastructure. High unemployment and poverty meets with limited access to health and other social or legal services. About 14 million South Africans live in these areas today. Of these, the majority are women.[16] There are a number of reasons for the demographic imbalance: Under apartheid, the system of migrant labour required many men to work in the cities and leave their families behind in the rural homelands. With the end of apartheid, many men permanently stayed on in the cities to find jobs. Women often stayed behind with their children in remote rural areas, where they relied on small-scale farming. Other reasons for the demographic imbalance include the effects of HIV/AIDS. In addition, a trend in some parts not to get married at all for different reasons has led to a high number of single mothers in traditional communities.[17]

Although the situation of women may vary across the regions and from community to community, women in traditional communities are likely to share the experience of exclusion from participation and access to land. Often, women cannot take up leadership positions in the traditional governance structures and might even not be allowed to participate in community meetings and to speak up in public. They are also barred from access to land in their own right because traditional leaders refuse to allocate land for housing or farming to women. If they live or farm on land owned by their husbands or fathers they are often evicted after their death because women cannot inherit.[18]

Most of these discriminatory practices are enshrined in *official customary law*. In South Africa, *official customary law* refers to a body of rules and norms of customary laws including written sources and versions that were codified under colonial rule.[19] This body of law was officially recognized and applied by the courts under apartheid.[20] However, today this is considered a misrepresentation of customary law for a number of reasons: *First of all, one of the main characteristics of customary law in Africa is its flexibility and its adaptability to different social contexts.*[21] Writing down the rules means fixing them and reducing their meaning to one possible interpretation, seriously distorting customary law.[22] Furthermore, in South Africa the laws were mostly collected and codified by white colonial or apartheid authorities whose own interests and preconceptions influenced the process of codification.[23] In addition to that, it has been shown that the sources were mostly elder men who had an interest in pushing their version, while excluding the voices of women and younger men.[24] Finally, since the codified norms have not been revised or amended since they were first written down, the customary law has been 'frozen' meaning that more recent changes are not reflected.[25] In sum, the *official customary law* is often a misrepresentation of customary law as practiced by the traditional communities in South Africa today.[26]

Official customary law treats women as perpetual minors under the guardianship of their husbands, fathers, or brothers.[27] Since the apartheid laws (the Black Administration Act of 1927 and the Bantu Authorities Act of 1951) were built on or incorporated *official customary law*, women in the homelands had no legal status under apartheid.[28] In the late 1990s, lower courts still relied on *official customary law*, as the example of *Mthembu v Letsela* shows:

> Women generally do not inherit in customary law. When the head of the family dies his heir takes his position as head of the family and becomes owner of all the deceased's property, movable and immovable; he becomes liable for the debts of the deceased and assumes the deceased's position as guardian of the women and minor sons in the family.[29]

The reliance on *official customary law* affects women even today and effectively excludes them from participating in decision-making and from access to land.

Negotiating space to overcome exclusion

Over the past 20 years, women have begun to overcome exclusion. They have pushed for the transformation of customary law, urging decision-makers to adapt norms of customary law to the changed social realities in rural areas. Women have relied on *living customary law* as opposed to the 'ossified' *official customary law*. The process of change is linked to the current Constitution of 1996, which provided momentum and a window of opportunity as well as concrete, justiciable rights for women that are also enshrined in international human rights instruments like the Convention on the Elimination of Discrimination against Women (CEDAW).[30] Looking at the processes of change, we can discern transformations firstly at the local or community level where women slowly began to participate in informal and later even in formal decision-making structures. They also negotiated for access to land. Secondly, the changes at the local and the national levels are interconnected, as the Constitutional Court has supported the development of customary law to be in line with the Constitution in its jurisprudence since 1996. Its recognition of *living customary law* over *official customary law* has in turn boosted local developments. Through their attempts to link the local and the national levels, activist researchers have provided the scientific background and field studies to offer evidence of (more inclusive, newly developed) norms of *living customary law*.

Changes at community level

Over the past 20 years, women have successfully negotiated for access to land. They have urged decision-makers to develop the existing customary law norms on access to land to be in line with social realities and with the Constitution. Before 1994, women in traditional communities, who were treated as perpetual minors under *official customary law*, could not access and own land in their own right. They had thus even less legal rights than disenfranchized black men under the apartheid regime and were effectively barred from seeking redress in any court.

Customary tenure can be individual or communal. However, even where it is individual, it does not necessarily comprise full ownership rights as in 'Western' law. In customary law, rights to land typically included, for example, duties of the household head towards all members of the family living on and off the land. Because of that, customary tenure is often described as a complex web of duties and rights and is characterized by reciprocity. In the 20th century, scarcity of land and the (partial) introduction of a 'Western', strictly individualized concept of ownership have changed the web of duties and reciprocity in customary tenure.[31] In South Africa, as elsewhere in Africa, formal titles often went to men, which left women without access or cultivation rights.[32] In consequence, especially women have lost out in the process because they ended up losing the formal titles and, additionally, also losing the entitlements that they would have had under the customary tenure system. At the same time, the number of households headed by females who were desperate for access to land grew in the traditional communities.[33]

Since the end of apartheid, women increasingly approached traditional leaders and decision-makers in allocation committees to negotiate for access to land. They argued, citing the changed social realities and needs of their children, their birthright as community members and constitutional values.[34] Describing the negotiation, one woman in KwaZulu-Natal said: 'He says: "No, women can't have land". And I say: "No, it's not like this, things have changed; we have a constitution now"'.[35] Where traditional leaders accepted the demands and allocated land, they in turn also often explained the changes in terms of the Constitution. One man reflected, for example: 'It changed after the elections and voting that said everyone had rights'.[36] A row of studies in traditional communities shows that the customary law on land allocation has indeed developed over the past 20 years to include women.[37] The most comprehensive investigation of the *living customary law* to date was undertaken by Budlender et al., who trace the changes across different regions and communities with diverse backgrounds.[38] Although the processes of change are uneven across regions and communities, it is clear that women are increasingly accessing land in their own right.

It is important to note that de facto not all women can access land on the same terms. Research studies have shown that single mothers, especially those with sons, are more likely to be allocated land than other women.[39] Indeed, among the main obstacles in changing the rules of land allocation were fears in traditional communities that female landowners would eventually marry outsiders. In the prevailing patrilineal logic, the land would then fall to the male outsider.[40] This is why in some communities only single mothers with sons can access land. The land is given in the son's name and thus protected from takeovers by outsiders. Mothers with only daughters and unmarried women without children often remain excluded from access to land for now. The developments over the past 20 years show that customary law has not remained static, but has indeed changed in response to social needs and new realities. The reliance on this *living customary law* in local negotiation processes as well as in courts allows women to address discriminatory rules in the customary system. It is important to note, that the women who challenged those norms in traditional communities did not denounce or circumvent the customary law system as such, but decided to challenge only very specific norms only and to use the force of argument to affect changes within their communities with respect to these specific norms (like land allocation rules). They accepted customary law as applicable (and not common law, for example), but sought to change specific norms within the system.

However, negotiations might have limitations as long as the balance of power between male leaders and female bidders is not addressed. Access to land and participation in decision-making structures are thus interlinked. In other words, if women are excluded from decision-making they are also excluded from decisions and control over land. However, women who were in the past often not allowed to take up leadership positions in the customary governance structures and even banned from speaking up in community meetings have found their own ways of participating and pushing for changes.[41]

Studies show that (politically-) active women in traditional communities often started out in women-only groups.[42] These groups are socially acceptable because they address issues that are perceived as pertaining to women, such as household gardens or caring for HIV/AIDS orphans. Eventually, the women gained confidence and experience through their involvement in these groups and began to engage in other local organizations, like on water committees or in so called 'community development groups'.[43] Here they also met with men. While men and women often opted for a traditional division of labour in these committees with vocal men as leaders and quiet women as secretaries, the committee work has also been a chance for active, vocal women to prove themselves.[44] Through these processes, it became increasingly acceptable for women to participate in community decision-making. Eventually, confident and successful women were promoted to leadership positions, both within the customary and other governance structures, so that women also became headwomen.[45] As headwomen, they are customary leaders at ward level, a sub-unit of communities deciding on local disputes and informing the traditional leaders on any developments in their area.[46] It is from here that women ultimately made their way into formal customary governance structures.

Formal customary decision-making structures are governed by national and provincial laws. The TLGFA, successor to the old Bantu Authorities and Black Administration Act, provides for the existence and composition of traditional councils and the succession to traditional leadership positions. Before its promulgation in 2004, the laws excluded women from these formal customary governance structures and instead provided for the application of *official customary law*. The TLGFA changed this dramatically. It introduced a binding quota of 30% women in the traditional councils and urged for the development of customary law to be in line with the Constitution. Many traditional leaders adhered to the law and ordered vocal and active women to join the newly composed traditional councils.[47] The acceptance, experience and successes of women in the informal structures including positions as headwomen at ward level made it easier for traditional leaders to appoint women.[48] As a result, women are now often not only part of the traditional councils but actually are also accepted and active members of traditional councils. Women have used openings at lower and informal levels to become active and participate in the formal decision-making structures of their communities.[49]

The situation is, however, still different as far as women as traditional leaders are concerned. The national and provincial laws are silent on female traditional leaders. However, changes have taken place here as well. Even if a growing number of women now serve as traditional leaders, it cannot be overlooked that often they come in as regents for their young/minor sons or ill husbands.[50] In addition, the number of traditional leaders officially anointed in their own right has increased over the past years.[51] The traditional community of Valoyis became one of the most prominent examples in 2008 when they took up the question of whether a woman could be traditional leader in the Constitutional Court. Since the affirmative decisions of the Constitutional Court, women can officially adhere to traditional leadership positions.

Developments at national level

The changes at local level did not transpire in a judicial and political vacuum. Clearly, national legislation with the quota for women in traditional councils has been one of the push factors in the growing participation of women (as shown earlier). The Constitution of 1996 has been an important argument for women at the community level. Its adoption was a general signal for social change and opened a window of opportunity for marginalized groups. Moreover, women's rights received increased international attention and support in the 1990s. Importantly, the Constitutional Court offers very concrete support for the development of customary law based on an interpretation and transformation of customary law that is in line with constitutional rights, so that issues like gender equality also remain at the forefront on the turf of *customary law*: At the outset, it appeared that the courts were caught in a dilemma because the Constitution not only obliges the courts to interpret and develop common law and customary law to be in line with the Bill of Rights [section 39 (2)] but also recognizes and protects customary law in section 211 (3). In early cases, as in *Mthembu v Letsalo*, lower courts indeed concluded that discriminatory customary law norms were protected from being developed or interpreted to conform to the Constitution.

The Constitutional Court has, however, chosen a different approach: In a raft of decisions, it has indicated that it encourages the reliance on *living customary law* as opposed to the official customary law and thus supports recent local developments in the transformation of customary law described earlier.[52] In doing so, it has found a way to reconcile customary law with such constitutional rights as gender equality.

The Constitutional Court sent a first signal in its decision on the Certification of the Constitution where it already mentioned the recognition of an 'evolving' customary law.[53] In three more decisions, the Constitutional Court distinguished between the *official customary law* and *living customary law* and confirmed the constitutional recognition of *living customary law* only (as opposed to the 'ossified' *official customary law*).

The first clarification came in the Court's decision *Alexkor Ltd. v Richtersveld* in 2003. The Court discussed the nature of customary law and its recognition in the Constitution:

> [T]hroughout its history it has evolved and developed to meet the changing needs of the community. And it will continue to evolve within the context of its values and norms consistently with the constitution.[54]

The Court explained that all courts have to take the flexible nature of customary law into account: 'While in the past indigenous law was seen through the common law lens, it must now be seen as an integral part of our law'.[55]

A second landmark decision came a year later in 2004 in the *Bhe* case, where the Court dwelled on the distortion of customary law under apartheid:

> Thus customary law as administered failed to respond creatively to new kinds of economic activity by women, different forms of property and household arrangements for women and men, and changing values concerning gender roles in society. The outcome has been formalisation and fossilisation of a system, which by its nature should function in an active and dynamic manner.[56]

In the concrete case, the Court had to decide whether the customary rule of primogeniture was constitutional and whether black women could be excluded from inheriting from their deceased partners. The Constitutional Court concluded that customary law would have been different if it had been allowed space to develop under apartheid and that the rule of male primogeniture was indeed 'incompatible with the guarantee of equality under this constitutional order'.[57] Regarding the legal redress, the Court described three options: annulment of the rule by the Court, development of customary law through courts or communities, or, lastly, legal reform by parliament. In a controversial step, the Constitutional Court decided to strike down the rule because, in its eyes, none of the two other options was fast and viable enough to correct the wrong.

The most recent decision on the development of customary law is *Shilubana*. As discussed earlier, the Court had to decide whether the traditional community of Valoyis could make a woman, Ms Shilubana, its traditional leader. Ms Shilubana's cousin had challenged the decision of the royal family and the community to appoint Ms Shilubana. The Constitutional Court encouraged the Valoyi community in their endeavour to develop customary law to be in line with the Constitution. While as a result the possibility of a female traditional leader was acknowledged in public, doubts on the soundness of the legal arguments remained. The core question before the Court was how *customary law* actually develops and who may change customary rules. There are two aspects: First, can customary law suddenly change? Or can it only be changed through an extended period of practice? How will this be proven before Court? Secondly, who can develop customary law? Is it the royal family or does it need consensus of the whole community?[58] Unfortunately, the Court did not address these concerns and provided a rather hasty, unprincipled and weak reasoning with no guidance for future decisions.[59]

In sum, the three decisions by the Constitutional Court are clear in their support for the development of customary law and the recognition and application of *living customary law*. At the same time, the decisions give evidence of the difficulties in developing customary law. The Court has addressed neither the question of legal consequence for unconstitutional customary law norms nor the issue of evidence and ascertainment of customary law in a satisfactory, theoretical, principled way. In *Bhe*, the Court took a controversial decision on redress and struck down the rule because of a lack of evidence. The Court held that it was not able to ascertain another more inclusive norm in customary law. In *Shilubana*, there was ample evidence for the community's inclination to change customary law, without clarity on how new customary-law norms would have to develop to be influential before the Court. Criteria like general, long practice and acceptance have not played an important role in the decision. Legal scholars have deplored the lack of guidance for future decisions on *living customary law* in South African courts.[60] So far it is not clear as to how exactly the relevant norms are to be ascertained and proven in court. The decisions of the Constitutional Court have also not answered the question of how customary a rule has to be, how ad hoc it can be changed, and what role communities will play in undertaking these changes.

These questions are also relevant for other African countries with recognized customary law. South Africa, though, is special in many ways, for one because researchers have been very active in this field. A number of field studies in which a circle of researchers was involved have provided evidence for inclusive *living customary law* norms. The researchers have diverse academic and non-academic affiliations and are based at universities and independent research institutes or work for non-profit organizations, advocacy groups or as consultants.[61] They share a concern for land tenure reform in the former homelands in South Africa and seek to influence government policies in this regard. One of the most recent and extensive studies is by Budlender et al.,[62] who document changes in land access. Without their research, we would not know much about the developments in customary law across the different regions and communities. They have focused on the rules for access to land and how customary law has changed over the past 20 years to allow women to access land in their own right. Through the process, they have also documented the changes in the decision-making structures and the increase in the number of women in these structures.[63]

The acceptance and practice the researchers documented has been used as evidence in court. The most prominent example was the case of *Tongoane* where four traditional communities challenged the Communal Land Rights Act of 2004 in the Constitutional Court. They were supported by a group of researchers and activists who had documented their discussions and concerns for an extended period of time. Eventually, the Communal Land Rights Act of 2004 was struck down by the Constitutional Court. The involved researchers published widely on this issue even before the case was heard in court and shaped the debate.[64] Activist researchers also used the results from their field studies to inform the public more generally and lobby the government and parliament.[65] They presented their results before Parliament to contribute to debates on proposed legislation like the Communal Land Rights Bill (before its enactment 2004) and the two still pending projects the Traditional Courts Bill (since 2008) and more recently the Traditional Affairs Bill (since 2013). To date, they have successfully blocked the latter two. While they could not stop the CLAR Bill in parliament they succeeded in it being declared unconstitutional by the Constitutional Court.[66] The researchers thus serve as a link between the local communities and the developments in politics and in the Courts at the national level, in order to ensure, on the one hand, that *living customary law* receives recognition and, on the other, that spaces for developing customary law remain open.

Conclusion

Over the past 20 years, women have negotiated the space provided by *living customary law* to gain access to land in their own right. They have also succeeded in participating in decision-making structures. They used the momentum and signal of change provided by the new 1996 Constitution. This development was further encouraged as it received support from the Constitutional Court and its recognition of *living customary law* over *official customary law*. The Court in turn relied on evidence from research activists, who linked the national with the local level as they gathered and published information on changes to customary law in traditional communities.

All this makes the South African case unique. The recognition of *living customary law* has successfully opened up spaces for women to negotiate for their rights within the customary law system. The recognition of *living customary law* can create spaces for women to overcome exclusion from access to land and politics. It might also create spaces in traditional communities for the inclusion of other marginalized groups like younger men or migrants. The salience of the South African case lies in the scope and extent of activist investment in research that has successfully traced the link between the local and national level.

However, the judicial recognition of *living customary law* is only a first step. The recognition was accepted and often welcomed in public and academia.[67] While on the face of it, the reliance on the dynamically changing *living customary law* allows for an alignment of customary law and human rights, it is not clear yet how courts will ascertain these norms of the *living customary law* in practice. Following the recognition of *living customary law* in its jurisprudence, the Constitutional Court will now have to address the question of how *living customary law* will actually be developed in the communities and ascertained in the courts.[68] First, can customary law by definition suddenly change? Or can it only be changed through long practice? How will this be proven before the Court? Secondly, who can actively develop customary law? Is it the royal family or does it need consensus of the whole community? The Constitutional Court has not yet addressed these concerns. The courts will have to develop sound legal principles for credibly including *living customary law* in judicial proceedings.

Notes

1 This paper is based on a case study entitled 'Living Customary Law in South Africa: A Space for Women to Overcome Exclusion'. For this study, I interviewed women in three communities in KwaZulu-Natal in 2011 and used data from recent cases studies on the *living land law*. L Heemann, 'Living Customary Law in South Africa: A Space to Overcome Exclusion' in J Smith (ed), *Journeys from Exclusion to Inclusion: Marginalized Women's Successes in Overcoming Political Exclusion* (International Institute for Democracy and Electoral Assistance 2013).

2 Section 211(3) SA Constitution 1996; the rights to culture are set out in Sec 30, 31 SA Constitution.

3 Equality in founding provisions and section 9; see also C Albertyn and B Goldblatt, 'Equality' in S Woolman, T Roux, and M Bishop (eds), *Constitutional Law of South Africa* Vol. 3 (Juta 2007) 55.

4 For an overview of the debate in South Africa see I van Kessel and B Oomen, '"One Chief, One Vote": The Revival of Traditional Authorities in Post-apartheid South Africa' (1997) 96 *African Affairs* 561; A Rudman, *Equality Before Custom? A Study of Property Rights of Previously Disadvantaged Women Under Land Reform and Communal Tenure in Post-Apartheid South Africa* (University of Gothenburg 2009); C Albertyn, 'The Stubborn Persistence of Patriarchy? Gender Equality and Cultural Diversity in South Africa' (2009) 2 *Constitutional Court Review* 165; On the African and international debate: S Moller Okin et al., *Is Multiculturalism Bad for Women?* (Princeton University Press 1999); CN Musembi, 'Are Local Norms and Practices Fences or Pathways? The Example of Women's Property Rights' in AA An-Na'im (ed), *Cultural Transformation and Human Rights in Africa* (Zed 2002); F Banda, *Women, Law and Human Rights in Africa* (2005); J Bond, *Voices of African Women: Women's Rights in Ghana, Uganda, and Tanzania* (Carolina Academic Press 2005); R Holtmaat and J Naber, *Women's Human Rights and Culture: From Deadlock to Dialogue* (Intersentia 2011).

5 N Mandela, 'Foreword' in P Andrews and S Ellmann (eds), *The Post-Apartheid Constitutions Perspectives on South Africa's Basic Law* (Witwatersrand University Press 2001) vii.

6 *Shilubana and Others v. Nwamitwa* [2008] (2) SA 66 (CC) para 4.

7 Ibid., para 81.

8 See E Ehrlich, *Grundlegung der Soziologie des Rechts* (Duncker & Humblot 1913) 126; M Rehbinder, *Die Begründung der Rechtssoziologie durch Eugen Ehrlich* (Duncker und Humblot 1986).

9 AJGM Sanders, 'How Customary Is Customary Law?' (1987) 20 *Comparative and International Law Journal of Southern Africa* 405.

10 *Bhe and Others v. Magistrate Khayelitsha and Others* [2004] (1) SA 580 (CC) para 87.

11 TW Bennett, '"Official" vs "Living" Customary Law: Dilemmas of Description and Recognition' in A Claassens and B Cousins (eds), *Land, Power & Custom Controversies Generated by South Africa's Communal Land Rights Act* (UTC Press 2008) 138.

12 Bennett (n 11).

13 Section 39 (2) SA Constitution: 'When interpreting any legislation, and when developing the common law or customary law, every court, tribunal or forum must promote the spirit, purport and objects of the Bill of Rights'.

14 For a critical account, see M Jara, 'Traditional Councils Perpetuate Apartheid Tribal Schema' (2011) 510 *De Rebus*; P Sithole and T Mbele, *Fifteen Year Review on Traditional Leadership* (2008). See <www.customcontested.org.za> for maps showing how the zones of the former homelands and today's traditional communities match; *Native Administration Act* 38 (1927).

15 See section 28 (3) and (4) TLGFA on the transitional arrangements: (3) 'Any "tribe" that, immediately before the commencement of this Act, had been established and was still recognised as such, is deemed to be a traditional community contemplated in section 2 (. . .)'

> (4) 'tribal authority that, immediately before the commencement of this Act, had been established and was still recognised as such, is deemed to be a traditional council contemplated in section 3 and must perform the functions referred to in section 4;'
>
> On the recognition of traditional communities generally section 2 (1) TLGFA: 'A community may be recognised as a traditional community if it – (a) is subject to a system of traditional leadership in terms of that community's; (b) observes a system of customary law'.

16 D Budlender et al., *Women, Land and Customary Law* (CASE 2011) 9.

17 A Claassens and S Ngubane, 'Women, Land and Power: The Impact of the Communal Land Rights Act' in A Claassens and B Cousins (eds), *Land, Power & Custom Controversies Generated by South Africa's Communal Land Rights Act* (UTC Press 2008) 177.

18 Claassens and Ngubane (n 17).

19 Bennett (n 11) 138.

20 Section 1 (1) of Law of Evidence Amendment Act of 1988.

21 GR Woodman, 'A Survey of Customary Laws in Africa in Search of Lessons for the Future' in J Fenrich, P Galizzi, and TE Higgins (eds), *The Future of African Customary Law* (Cambridge University Press 2011) 89.

22 Bennett (n 11) 139.

23 Bennett (n 11).

24 JM Ubink, 'The Quest for Customary Law in African State Courts' in J Fenrich, P Galizzi, and TE Higgins (eds), *The Future of African Customary Law* (Cambridge University Press 2011).

25 Ubink (n 24).

26 *Bhe and Others v. Magistrate Khayelitsha and Others* [2004] (1) SA 580 (CC) para 90.

27 Section 11 (3) (b) of the Black Administration Act of 1927 (before its repeal).

28 *Bhe and Others v. Magistrate Khayelitsha and Others* [2004] (1) SA 580 (CC) para 90; see also South African Law Reform Commission, *The Repeal of the Black Administration Act 38 of 1927* (South African Law Reform Commission ed, South African Law Reform Commission 2004).

29 *Mthembu v. Letsela and Another* [2000] (3) SA 867 (SCA) para 8.

30 For the link between international and local developments, see SE Merry, *Human Rights and Gender Violence: Translating International Law into Local Justice* (University of Chicago Press 2006).

31 See B Cousins, 'Contextualising the Controversies: Dilemmas of Communal Tenure Reform in Post-Apartheid South Africa' in A Claassens and B Cousins (eds), *Land, Power & Custom Controversies Generated by South Africa's Communal Land Rights A* (UTC Press 2008); HWO Okoth-Ogendo, 'The Nature of Land Rights

under Indigenous Law' in A Claassens and B Cousins (eds), *Land, Power & Custom Controversies Generated by South Africa's Communal Land Rights Act* (UTC Press 2008) 99.

32 A Claassens and S Mnisi, 'Rural Women Redefining Land Rights in the Context of Living Customary Law' (2009) 25 *South African Journal on Human Rights* 491; On titling processes in Africa more generally, see A Whitehead and D Tsikata, 'Policy Discourses on Women's Land Rights in Sub-Saharan Africa: The Implications of the Re-turn to the Customary' (2003) 3 *Journal of Agrarian Change* 67, 72.

33 Claassens and Mnisi (n 32) 501; an example of negotiations in one community is given by A Claassens and D Gilfillan, 'The Kalkfontein Land Purchases: Eighty Years on and Still Struggling for Ownership' in A Claassens and B Cousins (eds), *Land, Power & Custom Controversies Generated by South Africa's Communal Land Rights Act* (UTC Press 2008).

34 Claassens and Ngubane (n 17).

35 Author's interview with Patience Nosipho Phiri, Paralegal at Sakhanya Advice Office.

36 Budlender et al. (n 16) 129.

37 Budlender et al. (n 16); other examples are A Claassens, *"It Is Not Easy to Challenge a Chief": Lessons from Rakgwadi* (Programme for Land and Agrarian Studies Research Report, 9, Belville: Univ. of the Western Cape 2001); Claassens and Mnisi (n 32); B Cousins, *Imithetho yomhlaba yaseMsinga: The Living Law of Land in Msinga, KwaZulu-Natal* (2011); C Cross and D Hornby, *Opportunities and Obstacles to Women's Land Access in South Africa* (Promoting Women's Access to Land Programme 2002); S Mnisi, *Reconciling Living Customary Law and Democratic Decentralisation to Ensure Women's Land Rights Security* (2009); Rudman (n 4); critical: E Fortin, 'Struggles with Activism: NGO Engagements with Land Tenure Reform in Post-Apartheid South Africa' (2010) 48 *Journal of Modern African Studies* 383.

38 See Budlender et al. (n 16).

39 Budlender et al. (n 16).

40 Claassens (n 33) 307.

41 JM Williams, *Chieftaincy, the State, and Democracy Political Legitimacy in Post-apartheid South Africa* (Indiana University Press 2010) 119; Claassens and Gilfillan (n 33).

42 D Hemson, '"Women Are Weak When They Are Amongst Men": Women's Participation in Rural Water Committees in South Africa' (2002) 52 *Agenda* 24.

43 The officially recognized customary governance structures, like traditional councils, are not the only structures at local level: Other bodies include informal groups concerned with 'development' (i.e. access to water, electricity or funds for agricultural development) that became very popular in the 1990s. Some of them, e.g. the water committees have been formalized und used by the Ministry of Water to organize the communities locally. See Williams (n 41) 177.

44 Hemson (n 42).

45 AM Lang, *Traditionale Herrschaft in Südafrika: Anpassungsstrategien und Aushandlungen in einem demokratischen Staat* (Lit 2004) 177.

46 For more information on the ward system in South Africa, see Williams (n 41) 130.

47 Cousins (n 37).

48 Lang (n 45) 197; L Heemann, *Living Customary Law in South Africa: A Space for Women to Overcome Exclusion* (IDEA 2013) 145.

49 For more examples, see Williams (n 41) 119.

50 William and Goodenough provide anecdotal evidence of a rising number. Most of the female traditional leaders are regents, meaning that they hold the position only until the rightful traditional leader attains full age, recovers from sickness, or

a new male traditional leader is appointed. The number of officially recognized female traditional leaders in their own right is still low. C Goodenough, 'Living Customary Law in South Africa: A Space to Overcome Exclusion' in J Smith (ed), *Journeys from Exclusion to Inclusion: Marginalized Women's Successes in Overcoming Political Exclusion* (International Institute for Democracy and Electoral Assistance 2013).

51 There is no countrywide data available. For KwaZulu-Natal, the increase is reported to have been from 2 in 1995 to 11 in 2001, see C Goodenough, *Traditional Leaders – A KwaZulu-Natal Study: 1999 to 2001* (2002) 89.

52 For a good overview, see Rudman (n 4).

53 Before the Constitution could enter into force, the Constitutional Court had to certify that the final Constitution complied with the binding constitutional principles that had guided the whole constitutional negotiation process: *Certification of the Constitution of the Republic of South Africa 1996* [1996] (4) SA 744 (CC) para 197.

54 *Alexkor Ltd. v Richtersveld Community and Others* [2003] (5) SA 460 (CC) para 53.

55 Ibid., para 51.

56 *Bhe and Others v. Magistrate Khayelitsha and Others* [2004] (1) SA 580 (CC) para 90.

57 Ibid., para 91.

58 JC Bekker and CC Boonzaaier, 'Succession of Women to Traditional Leadership: Is the Judgment in Shilubana v. Nwamitwa Based on Sound Legal Principles?' (2008) 41 *Comparative and International Law Journal of Southern Africa* 449.

59 TW Bennett, 'Re-Introducing African Customary Law to the South African Legal System' (2009) 57 *American Journal of Comparative Law* 1.

60 C Himonga and C Bosch, 'The Application of Customary Law Under the Constitution of South Africa: Problem Solved or Just Beginning' (2000) 17 *South African Journal of Law* 306; C Himonga, 'The Future of Living Customary Law in African Legal Systems in the Twenty-First Century and Beyond, with Special Reference to South Africa' in J Fenrich, P Galizzi, and TE Higgins (eds), *The Future of African Customary Law* (Cambridge University Press 2011); D Cornell, 'The Significance of the Living Customary Law for an Understanding of Law: Does Custom Allow for a Woman to Be Hosi?' (2009) 2 *Constitutional Court Review* 395; Bekker and Boonzaaier (n 58); Bennett (n 59); TW Bennett, 'Re-Invention of Customary Law: South African Courts as Constitutional Law-Makers' (2009) 12 *Recht in Afrika* 1.

61 Fortin (n 37) 383.

62 Budlender et al. (n 16).

63 Budlender et al. (n 16).

64 *Tongoane and Others v. The National Minister for Agriculture and Land Affairs and Others* [2010] (6) SA 214 (CC); see the volume of Claassens and Cousins (n 11).

65 A Claassens, *Community Views on the Communal Land Rights Bill* (Research Report 2003).

66 *Tongoane and Others v. The National Minister for Agriculture and Land Affairs and Others* [2010] (6) SA 214 (CC).

67 P de Vos, 'Victory for Woman in Developing Customary Law' (2008) available at <http://constitutionallyspeaking.co.za/victory-for-woman-in-developing-customary-law> accessed 9 January 2011.

68 Bennett (n 59); Himonga (n 60).

Part IV

Adapting normative spaces

10 The legal laboratory in Rwanda

Experimentalization and adaptation

Stefanie Bognitz

Introduction

In times of interdependencies and global mobility, public awareness and transnationally spread networks of people, their actions, and responsibilities, the controversy over how normative orders are (re-)configured and what modes of governance should be employed is constantly being negotiated. The convergence of global flows of laws, modes of governance, techno-science and their translation into and from different contexts has come to produce new meanings along with transformation of orders and disorders. Such a translation does not seem to leave the international and domestic practice of lawmaking itself unaffected. Indeed, the making of new meanings as a result of translation can itself be said to be a product of an expectation of generating different legal institutions and normative orders.

As evidence from Rwanda shows, the dialectics of confirmation and critique are constitutive for any institutional or organizational arrangement of normative orders. Based on that, clearly, it entails *contestations* of knowledge or 'best practices' that are already immanent in institutions and organizations. Besides relying on a set of rules, legal institutions need to accommodate reflexivity and critique in order to remain actualized in societies with histories of violence and genocide. In light of the fact that knowledge and critique are contested, anticipated normative orders can be shaped by what I call experimentalization of law. Indeed, this is a fragile and temporary endeavour with which the lawmaker in post-genocide Rwanda approaches the fabric of society. How this experimentalization plays out in the public realm of everyday legal actions, and actions of those implicated in dispute and the legal sphere, is equally part of the testing arrangement. The legal laboratory[1] can sustain itself only if this public exposure allows the means of testing to be put into action.

With adaptations of legal aspects, the existing body of laws expands and pushes into new realms. Experimenting with the law relies on a number of variables such as measurements, numerical representations and statistical forms of evidence. I understand experimentalization as a purposeful action of subjecting empirically relevant observations, real-world scenarios, or everyday lived experiences to processes of experimentation. The phenomenon of experimentalization of law involves the necessary process of generating new insights and results that can be introduced into lawmaking in contexts in which actors are confronted with the challenge of living together in precariously poised peace arrangements. Against this backdrop, lawmakers in Rwanda began to turn to precolonial norms on disputing and agreement in an effort to seek resolution to the challenges of dealing with the ravages of the 1994 genocide.

This chapter traces experiments with certain assemblages of law in the ongoing effort to (re-)create normative orders on the basis of empirical data I collected in Rwanda in 2012/13 with respect to legal reform at the Rwandan Ministry of Justice in the capital city of Kigali, as well as in the respective fields of the application of legal experimentalization in the Southern Province of Rwanda. Again, the notion of translation, characterized by processes of contestation, revision, displacement, and transformation, moves centre stage in my discussions on the practice of experimenting with the law of emerging states or with legal transplants in post-transitional justice contexts. Through creative adaptations, tinkering, and rearrangement of already existing normative orders, such as blending in elements from precolonial legal history with technological and administrative innovations, not only is state-law reshaped but also new itineraries are set up to accelerate the legitimacy of laws and the justification of certain modes of governance.

Experience and experiment in the Rwandan legal laboratory[2]

For more than a decade, the Rwandan state has been experimenting with legal institutional designs. Some of these experiments were radically innovative, while others were crafted explicitly on the basis of customary legal formats. Consequently, recreations of hybrid judicial norms alongside administrative reforms characterize continuous forms of experimentations and adaptations in the Rwandan legal laboratory where the phenomenon and practice of mediation continues to play a significant role.

The notion of experimentalization analytically grasps the adaptation of mediation. In the oscillation between the old and the new, chains of associations are drawn from 'precolonial' times or the era of 'customary practice' and adapted to fit the present context and need, with the purpose of innovatively responding to the prevailing needs and concerns. This represents the Archimedean point of repetition and difference.[3]

Mediation in Rwanda, as a form of public social experiment, is situated in a normative order, as stipulated by highest-ranking juridical forms of inscription – the Constitution and organic law. It is nevertheless carried out and most meaningful in socio-legal arenas where proximity between the litigation in question, litigants, mediators, and the public is the closest. The basic idea of any experimental arrangement is to test a variety of ideas, variables, innovations or re-configurations against the backdrop of a certain context. Knorr-Cetina's view on configurations of experiments could be substantially opened up to embrace any social or, in our case, legal arena shaped by the making of law. '[T]hrough the technology they employ, experiments embody and respond to reconfigurations of natural and social orders'.[4]

Yet, to put it differently, the experimental arrangement of mediation establishes a causal link between the highest levels of government with the lowest levels of governance. The form of mediation is passed down the decentralized administrative-judicial arrangement; yet, if it is to be meaningful and effectively functional at all, it must be imbued with local content. The meaning and practice of mediation is displaced with the introduction of a law governing it. Compare that to a local mediator's take on mediation on establishing the links between local practice, law, and governance:

> The main difference between mediation of our time and the past is that we have laws. Mediation of today is based on and governed by law, however, mediation as such is not a law. But, we, the mediators can be punished on the basis of law if we don't perform our duties.[5]

Therefore not just mediation but also a transnational circulating model of dispute management within a local arena offers the opportunity to pursue a stake. It is displaced since the force of law places the institution of mediation within the realm of state and law officialdom, and the reason why it is inscribed with legitimacy is because of public participation and reliance on plaintiff and claimant citizens, or volunteer mediators. Even if the mediation assemblage is constituted by law, the fact that mediators engage ordinary people makes it functional, for instance, in the very act of submitting disputes for mediation in anticipation of a better resolution.

The form and content of mediation merge in the public of the mediation forum in negotiations over the repetition and difference of form on which the content ultimately depends. Bruno Latour pushes the boundaries of the experiment further into the lifeworld, but understands the violence that accompanies this translation. Latour describes a possible situation of public experiment as follows:

> No experiment can be studied by being just in the laboratory, in the literature or in the agonistic field. It is a story to be sure and studiable as such, but a story *tied* to a situation where new actants are undergoing terrible trials plotted by an ingenious stage manager; and then, the stage manager is undergoing terrible trials at the hands of his colleagues who try out what *ties* there are between the first story and the second situation. An experiment is a text about a non-textual situation tested by others to decide whether or not it is a text. If the final trial was successful then it *was not just a text*, there is indeed a real situation *behind* it, and both the actor and its authors are endowed with a common new competence.[6]

The making of facts through laboratory experiments and the making of law share a dependency on inscription devices. The power of (scientific) facts and the force of law cannot be brought to life, to disseminate and circulate, without relying on the written word and the processes and procedures of inscription.[7] The adaptation of the institutional form of mediation legally stipulates mandatory or so-called obligatory mediation for civil (<US $4,500)[8] and criminal (petty) cases below a certain value. This limits access to courts for cases and litigants to refer or restrict them to having access to mediation.[9] Community-level justice,[10] justice of proximity,[11] local justice, popular justice, reconciliatory justice, traditional justice[12] or even informal justice are among the attempts to classify mediation in light of Rwanda's investment in customary legal forms.[13] However, the focus of the mediation assemblage is not the achievement of some form of justice in the first place but the provision of basic and equal access in its broadest sense to the judiciary.

Mediation is deeply rooted in Rwandan history and customary legal culture. The practice of mediation (***kunga, ubuhuza***), which has been trans*form*ed into a common *form* as a circulating dispute resolution model, is almost virtually known to every Rwandan, and therefore recognized as something inherently familiar to all Rwandans. Moreover, people can relate to it easily since it was once commonly performed on the hills and its practice became widespread after the family elder or the chief responded to the call to participate. Indeed, the practice of mediation on the hills is intrinsic to local legal history and practices, unlike the Courts and the institutionalized bureaucratic procedures, which still evoke a sense of alienation among Rwandans. Citizens in the Rwandan post-colony have turned to scrutinize institutions enforced by colonial powers, while elites resorted to means that advanced their own political ambitions.[14] Mediation remains a long-established form of internal conflict resolution, of conciliation between antagonists and a means of re-establishing social order in the community.

The transformations that have transpired as a result of the introduction of mediation can be noted in courts of first instance, primary courts, which are no longer situated at the lower end of the Rwandan justice system. Mediation committees of first and second instance are now the entry points to the judiciary. The establishment of mediation as a dispute resolution mechanism is foreseen by the Constitution and adopted in the jurisdiction of the country.[15] First run in 2004 as a legal experiment, mediation committees are an established institutional form, at work since 2006, when it was characterized as an 'innovation'. By 2012, it was viewed as a 'service' to citizens. This type of service-orientation is salient, especially compared to such institutions as courts in everyday life worlds, which are frequently complained about by litigants.

Not only is the legal form subject to experimentation, but also the way it is lexically and semantically expressed. The neologism 'mediation committee'/*Komité y'Abunzi* is a compound noun, borrowed from the French word *comité*, and a nominalized form of the verb ***kunga*** meaning either 'to rejoin a broken bone' or 'to bring something or someone together'. The emphasis here is on conciliation through a process of mediation that entails creating a common ground on which to proceed. The noun 'mediators'/*Abunzi* is in use only since the enactment of the law on mediation. Blending local language with law, the Rwandan lawmakers creatively shaped the process of the institutionalization of mediation and its capacity to be adapted by legal linguistic innovation. Yet there is more to the adaptation of terminology on the authority of mediation, in that the borrowing of terms from the courtroom, like 'summons', 'plaintiff', 'defendant', 'witness' or 'evidence', contributes to situating mediation as a state institution in the realm of officialdom.

Nevertheless, it must be borne in mind – beyond state power and influence – that social or, as in this case, long-term experimentalization of law would be meaningless without public participation and without engendering a certain degree of flexibility to render the form (of the experiment) open to interpretation, refashioning or remodelling altogether. This is to ensure that law cumulatively results from social participation rather than being imposed on society by external agents and is also perceived as such. It is in this sense that law can be seen as being made by society and being in the hands of society. In short, there are at least two sides to every experiment: the idea and the intentionality of its designers. In Rwanda, not only lawmakers or the state, but also the participants for whom it is intended and on whom the whole endeavour depends are involved in the design of the mediation. A mediator describes this aspect of the experiment and emphasizes its duality, residing in the aspect of culture and of lawmaking.

> I see that it was not the idea of the people themselves, it was the government which thought about it and they found that how they created Gacaca and they found that in order for a problem to be solved faster, there is a need to establish mediation which is based on the experience of Gacaca courts where the cases were solved in a fair way and they suggested for the judicial system to establish Mediation Committees because even mediation existed before in Rwanda. . . . For Rwandan culture it is not a new thing, but in law it is new. It helps in the resolution of disputes of proximity and it is done so fast. It was also in the context of decreasing high numbers of cases going to courts.[16]

For better understanding the popular purchase of mediation in Rwanda's local communities, it is important to recall the powers of association that are engrained in the success of this circulating model.[17] For the case of mediation in Rwanda, the newness that is introduced can only be sustained by reference to the old, and it is a capriciously balanced arrangement that oscillates between continuities and ruptures. This arrangement reconciles past experiences and future expectations. The adaptability of mediation as a form is probably only possible because of such oscillations. The deep rupture of shattered social bonds among neighbours and relatives during and after the genocide reaches far into contemporary resentments, mistrust, and inhumanity or mutual alienation among Rwandans – such ruptures nourish new and lasting continuities. But, nevertheless, it is also the continuities that tend to reach far back into Rwandan legal culture, driven by expectations that new values and norms may supersede previous animosities and violence that could again give rise to the risk of genocide.[18]

Experimentalization can be viewed from yet another angle, which is the possibility, and probably the necessity, of a bargaining process in mediation committees. The 'making' of a dispute is part of a bargaining process, envisaged as an experimental arrangement enabled by the mediation assemblage. At the beginning of each bargaining process during the mediation session, two central questions are sought to be resolved: What is at the heart of the dispute? What is its subject matter? By distinguishing matters of fact from matters of concern during the bargaining process, based on explicit and implicit variables, the contours of the dispute are defined in a way that enables it to be seen beyond the context of the initial dispute. Once a dispute enters a legal process, the issue is narrowed down to define what is to be decided or what is at stake. A relationship is established between the whole and the parts, i.e. the relevant facts must be distinguished from those deemed irrelevant so that the resultant parts of the dispute will have been carefully selected. The selection itself, the trajectory of which demands a move from the whole to the parts (and never the other way around), is determined by the legal process. A dispute I followed during a mediation process, in which two parties were in disaccord over the inheritance of a house, exemplifies this relationship. The mediators had to address ownership and property relations as well as kinship affiliations, and they had to consider previous court cases to decide on the facts on which the inheritance dispute was grounded. While the parties in dispute tried to convey the fairness of the inheritance and their families' dependency on having a house to live in, the mediators established the parts as follows: The house, built on the land of a diocese, served the purpose of a cooperative to store and sell their produce. One of the parties happened to be organized as a cooperative, but without ownership rights to the house. Both house and land were therefore assigned to the diocese but not to the parties to the dispute. By moving into the fabric of property relations as well as relations between persons – from the whole to the parts – the mediators established that the dispute was without any legal basis.[19]

The object of the dispute – what is at the heart of the dispute – or the matter of contempt is arrived at through a bargaining process. This presupposes that the object of the dispute is carved out throughout the process until it is transformed into a legal matter that correlates with legal rules in all its parts, and that includes communication and misunderstandings between disputants, third parties, and the public or the audience. Two issues are at the centre: how a dispute is shaped in the bargaining process, i.e. its dimensions and the similarities or discrepancies between the represented and actual dispute.[20]

Juridification

> 'The law' thus accumulates, but it never passes; at any instant, it represents a totality. It is by definition complete, yet its completeness does not preclude change. It is a human achievement, yet, by its reversible and lateral excursions, and by its collective voice, it is not identifiably the product of any particular individual or group.[21]

In reference to Greenhouse's notions of adaptability and timeliness that are fundamental to law as a commonly achieved public good, I would like to put more emphasis on the inherent process that drives law to meet such ends through the process of juridification.[22] Again, it is important to briefly reiterate interrelated layers in the proliferation, expansion, and differentiation of law emerging just in time[23] from juridification, which has many faces. 'Norms constitutive for a political order can be established and adapted according to the competences of the legal system'.[24] The regulating capacity of practices by law increases, conflict and dispute resolutions are increasingly undertaken using the existing law, the legal apparatus gains significant power through juridification to the extent that it may become a self-sustaining and self-enabling system. Juridification can be understood as a process of legal framing within which individuals think of themselves and relate to others as legal subjects.[25] Habermas generally defines juridification as a tendency towards an increase of formal law that brings together two processes: First, the expansion of law in the sense that it legally regulates social matters that have before only been informally ordered, and second, the increasing density of law which covers the specialization of legal statements, i.e. nuanced details of law that have been deduced from more abstract global facts that are perceived to be legally relevant.[26]

Once the mythical foundations of law are deconstructed and the making of law can be viewed as a space of public-popular participation towards the achievement of justice, it is worthwhile to follow the actors in their practices of acceptability and confirmation of legal institutions. Participant's perceptions of new legal institutions are determined by circulating knowledge about them. As Barbara Oomen understands the Rwandan nomosphere in the transitional justice paradigm, an increase in knowledge about and the experience with such existing and accessible institutions will thus have an impact on the legitimacy and effectiveness of new institutional designs in the justice sector or the legal laboratory.[27] This marks a noteworthy turn towards the legitimization of lawmaking and relevant legal processes. As the processes transpire in the public sphere, they are seen, recognized, known and understood to a certain extent via institutions symbolizing and incorporating 'the law'. It is in these institutions 'of law' that knowledge and the public converge and (re)emerge at the same time. Popular legal knowledge and public legitimization co-produce each other in legal institutions.

Administering the judiciary

> The debate on the plurality of legal orders needs to be put in the context of the state and interstate system. The 'state has to be brought back in' but at this time it is brought back into a 'place' which it has not occupied before. In the current condition, the centrality of the state as an organizing principle lies in the extent to which the state itself knows how to decentre itself, as in community-driven policies for instance. What follows from this is that the boundaries between what is considered as state and non-state become increasingly blurred.[28]

One of the results of decentralization is that the organization of the judiciary mirrors that of the administration, and vice versa, at both the local and national levels.[29] An example of this is the selection and election procedure of members on mediation committees and the legal stipulation that is adapted from the law on national elections procedure. Moreover, this mirroring of the organizational and institutional forms influences the functionality of both systems and establishes mutual surveillance, punishment, and performance measuring mechanisms. The promise of access to justice implied in administrative and judicial forms holds the possibility of an independent and fair justice apparatus under the governance of rational legal authority based on the re-enactments of the officialdom.

Experiments in mediation are an integral part of the Rwandan judiciary. They are carried out on the premise of voluntary participation of mediators. As they are elected for a voluntary mandate of five years, many of the mediators wait not so much for the end of their mandate as for a point in time when disputes would no longer exist and they would be able to once and for all lay to rest their voluntary office as mediators in the Rwandan officialdom and become private individuals, without the burden of having to dedicate a weekday to mediation. Bearing individual responsibility implied taking on a certain risk, especially for someone younger, less experienced and new to the local community, for a variety of reasons such as population movements and resettlements or villagization programmes (*imidugudu*). It is not common to get involved in the affairs of others, let alone offer opinions or render decisions about family matters publicly. This can only be done when volunteers and mediators act in an official capacity, bringing to bear upon their interventions all the relevant symbols, signifiers and markers.[30] The more experienced mediators, who, for instance, could be experienced lay judges (*inyangamugayo*) in Gacaca courts, performed their official duties more pragmatically, methodically, and efficiently with a firm conviction about the appropriate course of action or decision. However, it is their age, class, status in the community and gender that substantially bolsters their confidence.

Two aspects of dispute resolution via community mediation need to be addressed. Power dynamics and control/regulation are at the heart of the convergence of the judiciary and the administration. Critical studies on community justice, especially in the context of the US, would ideally trace the element of expanding and intensifying state control through local/community justice forums.[31] In light of that, the state is thus rendered present in contexts that represent 'informal settings', i.e. outside the formal state structures. For Pavlich, the phenomenon of a state-imposed control network in community justice settings is a regulatory arena governed by centralized structures.[32] However, independent and community-based assemblages enable locally embedded demands for justice in the very same realms where this idea of justice has been violated, other than moving the case to the courtroom. In this regard, the setting for dispute emergence (conflict, crime, violence) is identical to that for dispute resolution (actors, location). Abel reformulates critical studies on community justice institutions, arguing 'if the primary business of informal institutions is social control',[33] we would need to enquire whether 'they expand or reduce state control'.[34] I intend to show how a certain form of state-regulated governance of claims and disputes is managed at the intersection of local administration and judicial apparatus, as a result of which the arrangement of the facts of the dispute and their contextual and broader interpretation in the public arena, as distinctive from a mere problem or claim in the private sphere, is realized by assigning two distinctive dimensions to the dispute. First, its formal identification in the realm of administration, where it is inscribed with the symbolic value of state bureaucracy; and second, its legal identity in the realm of justice or the judicial apparatus for which the symbolic value of the bureaucratic form is a precondition. The bureaucratic form translated the problem into a circumscribed legal case with the capacity to travel easily back and forth between administration and judiciary.

Emerging forms of justice

What is more to experimenting with elements of restorative justice is a convolution of elementary forms of a range of justice repertoires. The question that comes up is whether restorative justice approaches should be integral to any or so called conventional legal processes – in a supplementary or *substitutional* way. Experimenting with restorative justice approaches could introduce innovative legal means to hybrid legal processes, reform, juridification, which may be adapted over time or discarded if found inadequate.[35] This would add yet another dimension to law as well as to that which Greenhouse acknowledges as being beyond the completeness of law at all times, albeit through change and adaptation.

> 'The law' thus accumulates, but it never passes; at any instant, it represents a totality. It is by definition complete, yet its completeness does not preclude change. It is a human achievement, yet, by its reversible and lateral excursions, and by its collective voice, it is not identifiably the product of any particular individual or group.[36]

What is significant to law and legal processes that make up law in post-conflict states as the earlier insights in Rwandan developments and changes in the legal arena have shown is moreover the ability of law to be flexible enough to be accommodating to new or challenging circumstances, and to be shaped by social change in states and normative orders of transition.

> [C]ommunity justice is yet another element of fragmented justice, whose calculations and practices embrace particular (neo-liberal) political rationalities and techniques under postmodern conditions. [D]evoid of the faith in universal principles, singular rationalities and indeed innately rational subjects, the calculations of justice become ordered around markedly different practices and idioms [e.g. community mediation].[37]

Given the complex interplay of the administration and the judiciary, new forms of justice and justification emerge along the intersections outlined earlier. These forms of justice refer to processes that contribute not only to a sense of justice underlying the resolution of a dispute, but also to the perception of fairness and equality on the path to the final agreement or decision respectively in the lowest rungs of the Rwandan judiciary, namely the mediation assemblage. Emerging forms of justice, regardless of the essential perception of justice, are imperative for the acceptance and participation of the public, the local community, in the implementation of a justice assemblage of proximity. It is functional only by way of popular participation in both aspects of it – administration and judiciary. It is against this backdrop that ***procedural justice*** demonstrates how individuals perceive fairness with respect to the inherent rules and procedures that regulate decision-making processes and result in legal agreements. Justice is measured according to the application of the rules, i.e. the degree to which there is compliance with the rules.[38] Moreover, procedural justice could be amplified by establishing the right to voice disagreement and demand change for the public, thereby strengthening the aspect of popular participation, which is of substantial value for the mediation assemblage, insofar as mediation is upheld through service provided by voluntary mediators.[39]

Yet another emerging form of justice that can be identified pertains to the litigation or dispute that is enabled through the mediation forum. Since property-, succession-, and inheritance-related disputes make up a large chunk of cases mediated in respective committees, it is important to settle such cases inclusively for all the concerned parties to the dispute, and thereby prevent future disputes. For that, the aspect of ***distributive justice*** has to be taken into account by the mediators based in ideas about equal distribution and shares of the local community. For that reason, distributive justice can often be traced in disputes relating to resource allocation, for which different criteria can be applied for fair and just distribution. Such criteria have to be negotiated and allocated throughout the process of mediation. This often involves integrating witness accounts and knowledge from within the community dealing with a dispute over land or property. Equality, proportionality, and need are significant variables in the achievement of distributive justice.[40] In summary, distributive justice and ***prospectivity*** of mediation are intrinsically related.

A third form of justice relating to the experimental side of the judiciary in a phase of post-transitional justice[41] is ***restorative justice***. While there are different approaches to it, I restrict myself here to one purpose. In reference to restorative justice mechanisms, Braithwaite discusses responsive regulation,[42] which follows a certain identified need for legal regulation and adaptation, however, under the premise of inclusion of local actors in a conceptual phase. 'The basic idea of responsive regulation is that governments should be responsive to the conduct of those they seek to regulate in deciding whether a more or less interventionist response is needed'.[43] Responsive regulation and adaptation in the Rwandan context has been exercised in the Gacaca courts for instance.[44] But the experience of Gacaca has thus triggered subsequent experimental forms of responsive regulation and legal codification (juridification) of mediation and mediation committees. I argue that only the conceptual character, as Braithwaite argues, of responsive regulation in restorative justice enables the recognition and articulation of the two earlier-mentioned emerging forms of justice. Taken together, these three aspects of justice can be read as a unique constitutive element in the adaptation of mediation in the Rwandan (popular) justice system.

The popular justice system can be conceptualized in two ways. Firstly, it is popular to the extent that it requires and promotes the participation of the public and, secondly, the justice system builds on the inclusion of a representative sample of society to secure the functioning of a popular justice apparatus.

Decentralization

> *Kwegereza ubuyobozi n'ubushobozi abaturage* – to give the power back to the people (the Kinyarwanda expression for decentralisation initiatives)
> Throughout Rwanda, citizens meet to agree on key development priorities for their village – a new road or classroom, a bridge or a well. We have found that empowering local leaders, while demanding accountability, is an effective catalyst for development. As well as helping ensure development meets the needs of the population, it builds capacity at a local level and gives citizens a meaningful stake in their future.
>
> Paul Kagame, President of the Republic of Rwanda, 2013

Across a number of states, good governance and legitimacy are measured on the basis of the proximity of the modes of governance to local conditions as well as the transparency and accountability of the central government as to its citizens.[45] '[O]ne of the main ideas behind the introduction of decentralization was that by bringing the government closer to the people, local resources for development would be mobilised more easily'.[46] Here Bierschenk refers to a reconsideration of local needs and assets, which Kagame also refers to earlier, primarily through the lens of development. Development, in different respects, is seen to be achieved more effectively through the recognition of a certain expertise and capability of the local population. The needs and problems of localities can best be identified by the local communities themselves. This re-orientation to the local can be theorized through the concept of *subsidiarity*, a principle according to which any authority positioned at the centre should ideally accommodate a subsidiary function in performing only those tasks that cannot be tackled at a more local level. Put differently, the local government has the mandate to perform tasks according to its capacities and abilities before passing them on to the next level in the upper rungs of government hierarchy. Issues or tasks of lesser importance should be delegated from top to bottom by the central governmental authority, which no longer needs to be concerned with tasks that could more easily and perhaps more effectively be taken on or solved by the lower levels of government. It is notably the principle of subsidiarity that produces creative forums as enabling devices, most prominently the locally embedded institution of mediation committees that, by popular participation, tackle problems and settle disputes in the same localities where they have come into being, as already alluded to earlier. Furthermore, the responsibility for certain claims and disputes is redirected from courts of first instance to mediation committees. Decentralized rungs and local levels of governance, authority, and judiciary are installed, however, at the same time, state presence increases by moving away from a centralized mode of regulation to a decentralized structure, whereby central state organs are mirrored at the lowest levels of local government.

Decentralization is stipulated in Article 167 of the Constitution[47] on decentralized authorities:

> Public administration shall be decentralised in accordance with the provisions of the law. Decentralised entities shall fall under the Ministry in charge of local government.
>
> The law determines decentralized local administrative entities with legal status and administrative and financial autonomy. Such entities are the basic foundation of community development.
>
> Local administrative entities with legal status shall be entitled to become members of national and international organisations which promote development through decentralisation.
>
> A law determines the organisation, the functioning and the collaboration between these organs and various other organs which have a role in the administration and development of the country. A law shall also determine the manner in which the Government transfers powers, property and other resources to decentralised entities.

The National Decentralization Policy divides the process along the following lines:

> Decentralization will be implemented according to three modes of deconcentration, delegation and devolution. Services, resources, functions, power, authority and responsibility, under deconcentration, will be executed by central government public servants located in local governments but hierarchically responsible directly to central government; under delegation, will be delegated to local governments and the requisite resources transferred to them for effective provision of these delegated services; under devolution, will be transferred to local governments which will be created by law as legal entities with powers to sue and to be sued.[48]

Subsidiarity is a normative principle of justice concerned with organizing responsibilities[49] of people and institutions.[50] The combination of justice and subsidiarity in Rwanda has been the underlying idea of the local courts of genocide (Gacaca). Even though Gacaca is a genuine model of justice and truth-finding process introduced and imposed by the state for different categories of genocide-related crimes, it passes on considerable decision-making powers to actors who are positioned outside the central state power structures. In so doing, a recognizable significance emerged for the local embeddedness of a justice process, which was adapted by the government.[51] By applying the principle of subsidiarity in the realm of justice, 'it demands a certain justification for the transfer of responsibilities to higher entities'.[52] What is more, the government, in investing in local justice models and structures, removed itself *ex ante* from any undue influence over the process and granted citizens the right to address local concerns in a local sphere by adopting local means of truth-telling that legitimized the legal process at local levels.[53] In this respect, Daly also argues that the sheer number of Gacaca courts across Rwanda thus rendered the process free of government influence, since the participatory nature was supported by the high number of present and active citizens as necessary condition for the truth- and evidence-finding legal framing of the Gacaca courts.[54]

> The principle of subsidiarity in its classic form explicates the conditions for its application very clearly: it is only applicable if smaller and larger social institutions and entities relate to each other like parts to a whole. Interpreted in this way, the principle of subsidiarity presupposes a hierarchical order and is concerned mainly with the internal arrangements of competencies in this order.[55]

Gosepath asserts the recognition of the principle in modern theories on society such as systems theory.[56] However, he identifies a void with regard to empirically informed theorizations of the concept.

> It would be interesting to investigate in more detail this peculiar and rather new evolution of the term and find out its underlying political reasons. My hypothesis is that the rise to the forefront of the principle of subsidiarity can be seen as a reaction to signs of a crisis.[57]

In the Rwandan context, the justification for the introduction of the principles of subsidiarity in administration and the justice system is rooted in the origins of genocide, as explained by centralized power and the post-genocide crisis. It further alleges that national unity and reconciliation can only be achieved through decentralization. This has been accompanied by aspirations of forging an integrated local community sensitized by their responsibility for bringing about justice as a way of preventing genocidal mass violence.[58]

Conclusion

Decentralized mediation is a lens through which the judicial and administrative structures in the Rwandan context must be analyzed. Although decentralization brings with it new bureaucratic and institutional forms, it effectively puts dispute management in the hands of those who share the same context, ensuring that agreements are reached at lowest institutional capacities possible at almost no cost. In the mediation process that the Rwandan lawmakers have designed, dispute management is decentred, disputes are re-localized, and removed from the oversight of a higher legal or state authority. However, bearing in mind that the alternative to mediation, commonly known as local customary practice, has been blended into law under the order and auspices of the state, it transforms mediation into a central codified dispute resolution process of the state designed to decentralize such disputes that are deemed not suitable or desirable for central state oversight.

Notes

1 This expression is also used by B Oomen, 'Justice Mechanisms and the Question of Legitimacy: The Example of Rwanda's Multi-Layered Justice Mechanisms' in K Ambos, J Large, and M Wierda (eds), *Building a Future on Peace and Justice: Studies on Transitional Justice, Peace and Development* (Berlin and Heidelberg Springer 2009) 175–202, 180.
2 Inspired by B Latour, 'The Force and the Reason of Experiment' in HE LeGrand (ed), *Experimental Inquiries: Historical, Philosophical and Social Studies of Experimentation in Science* (Dordrecht Kluwer 1990) 49–80, 56.
3 G Deleuze, *Repetition and Difference* (New York Columbia University Press 1968/1994).
4 K Knorr-Cetina, *Epistemic Cultures: How the Sciences Make Knowledge* (Cambridge Harvard University Press 1999) 32.
5 *Liberata* (1 November 2012).
6 Latour (n 2) 61 f. (emphasis in the original).
7 See also Latour (n 2) 63; B Latour, *The Making of Law: An Ethnography of the Conseil d'État* (Cambridge Polity Press 2012).
8 1 ha land to be purchased for $1700, see M Lankhorst and M Veldman, *Enhancing Legal Empowerment Through Engagement with Customary Justice Systems* (International Development Law Organization 2011).
9 See also Lankhorst and Veldman (n 8) 25.
10 Lankhorst and Veldman (n 8).
11 KC Doughty, *Contesting Community: Legalized Reconciliation Efforts in the Aftermath of Genocide in Rwanda* Publicly accessible Penn Dissertations Paper (2011) 333 available at <http://repository.upenn.edu/edissertations/333> accessed 25 October 2018.
12 M Mutisi, 'Community-Driven Conflict Resolution: The Abunzi Mediators in Rwanda' in S Maruta (ed), *Sustainable Peace and Development at Community Level: Beneficiaries Are Actors Too* (Harare Southern Institute of Peace-Building and Development 2012) 138–159.
13 Abel provides a substantial critique on the contradictions of informal justice, especially on the increase of state control over private dispute resolution and the ambiguities between public and private matters, or fluid boundaries and intricate transgressions therein. See RL Abel, 'The Contradictions of Informal Justice' in RL Abel (ed), *The Politics of Informal Justice* (New York Academic Press 1982) 267–320. On the role of state interference in informal justice arrangements, see also B De Sousa Santos, 'Law and Community: The Changing Nature of State Power in Late Capitalism' in RL Abel (ed), *The Politics of Informal Justice: The American Experience* (New York Academic Press 1982) 249–266.
14 See A Mbembe, 'On Private Indirect Government' in A Mbembe (ed), *On the Postcolony* (Berkeley University of California Press) 66–101.
15 Rwandan Constitution, section 4: The Mediators Article 159 (Amendment n°2 of 08 12 2005) There is hereby established a 'Mediation Committee' responsible for mediating between parties to certain disputes involving matters determined by law prior to the filing of a case with the court of first instance. The Mediation

Committee shall comprise of persons of integrity and acknowledged for their mediating skills. An organic law shall determine the organization, the territorial jurisdiction, the competence and the functioning of Mediation Committee. It shall also determine the number that the mediation committee and the organ that elects it must be comprised of.

16 Mediator Olive, Nyamugali Cell, Gasaka Sector, Nyamagabe District, Southern Province of Rwanda, 20 November 2012.

17 See B Latour, 'The Powers of Association' in J Law (ed), *Power, Action and Belief: A New Sociology of Knowledge?* (London Routledge 1986) 264–280.

18 In Kinyarwanda, the language of all Rwandans, past and future tense is denoted using one and the same word. The word 'ejo' refers to 'tomorrow' and 'yesterday', so that the tense – what is past and what will happen in the future – is marked as past/future actions in the verb, but not in the time indicator, commonly placed at the beginning of a sentence. It is possible to infer from this small word that past and present carry the same value or significance.

19 Mediation Committee, Nyamugali Cell, Gasaka Sector, Nyamagabe District, Southern Province of Rwanda, 19 November 2012.

20 B de Sousa Santos, *Toward a New Legal Common Sense: Law, Globalization and Emancipation* (London Butterworths LexisNexis 2002) 104.

21 CJ Greenhouse, 'Just in Time: Temporality and the Cultural Legitimation of Law' (1989) 98 (8) *The Yale Law Journal* 1631–1651, 1640.

22 The aspect of time, however, should not be forgotten at this point. Western thought produces the certainty of a linear conception of time, which proceeds from past to present, perceived in the state of the here and now. For more on the notion of the present, see Greenhouse (n 21) 1642. The question remains as to whether we could not some kind of linkages between the 'old' and the 'new' in law itself or constant attempts to remake and/or modify the work of law? In Deleuze's *Repetition and Difference*, time represents a reference point in that repetition occurs within the different levels of time. Only the present can be conceptualized as time, since it is the only instance in which past and future are experienced or imagined – there is no time but the present time in which past and future are inscribed, see Deleuze (n 3) 70 ff.

23 Greenhouse (n 21).

24 LC Blichner and A Molander, 'Mapping Juridification' (2008) 14 (1) *European Law Journal* 36–54, 36.

25 Blichner and Molander (n 24) 36 f.

26 J Habermas, *Lifeworld and System: A Critique of Functionalist Reason* (Boston Beacon Press 1989) 357.

27 Oomen (n 1) 180.

28 De Sousa Santos (n 18) 94.

29 Consider, for instance, power imbalances and differences between elected and appointed authorities, as in B Ingelaere, 'The Ruler's Drum and the People's Shout: Accountability and Representation on Rwanda's Hills' in S Straus and L Waldorf (eds), *Remaking Rwanda: State Building and Human Rights After Mass Violence* (Madison University of Wisconsin Press 2011) 67–78.

30 Cf. De Sousa Santos (n 18) 117 f.

31 S Cohen, 'The Critical Discourse on "Social Control": Notes on the Concept as a Hammer' (1989) 17 *International Journal of the Sociology of Law* 347–357.

32 GC Pavlich, *Justice Fragmented: Mediating Community Disputes Under Postmodern Conditions* (London and New York Routledge 1996) 78 f.

33 Abel (n 13) 5.

34 Abel (n 13) 6, also cited in Pavlich (n 32) 78 f.

35 C Menkel-Meadow, 'Restorative Justice: What Is It and Does It Work?' (2007) 3 *Annual Review of Law and Social Science* 10.1–10.27, 10.1.

36 Greenhouse (n 21) 1640.
37 Pavlich (n 32) 87 f.
38 DE Peachey, 'What People Want from Mediation' in K Kressel and DG Pruitt (eds), *Mediation Research: The Process and Effectiveness of Third Party Intervention* (San Francisco Jossey-Bass Publishers 1989) 300–321, 301.
39 See Article 3, Organic Law 'On Mediation' (2010) in Organic Law N° 02/2010/OL of 9 June 2010 on organization, jurisdiction, competence and functioning of the mediation committee, O.G. n°24 Bis of 14 June 2010.
40 Peachey (n 38) 301 f.
41 See also chapter 1, section After Transitional Justice.
42 J Braithwaite, *Restorative Justice and Responsive Regulation* (New York Oxford University Press 2002) 29.
43 Braithwaite (n 42) 29.
44 NA Jones, *The Courts of Genocide: Politics and the Rule of Law in Rwanda and Arusha* (Abingdon and New York Routledge 2010) 72 f.
45 See also F von Benda-Beckmann and K von Benda-Beckmann, *Recreating the Nagari: Decentralisation in West Sumatra. Working Papers* (Halle, Saale Max Planck Institute for Social Anthropology 2001).
46 T Bierschenk, 'The Local Appropriation of Democracy: An Analysis of the Municipal Elections in Parakou, Republic of Benin, 2002–03' (2006) 44 (4) *The Journal of Modern African Studies* 543–571, 565.
47 Constitution of the Republic of Rwanda, Amendment n°2 (8 December 2005).
48 Republic of Rwanda, 'National Decentralization Policy' (Kigali Rwanda Ministry of Local Government and Social Affairs 2001) 7; Republic of Rwanda, 'Constitution of the Republic of Rwanda' (Kigali Rwanda 2005); see also Republic of Rwanda, 'Rwanda Decentralization Strategic Framework: Towards a Sector-wide Approach for Decentralization Implementation' (Kigali Rwanda Ministry of Local Government, Community Development and Social Affairs 2007) 7, 18.
49 S Gosepath, 'The Principle of Subsidiarity' in A Follesdal and T Pogge (eds), *Real World Justice: Grounds, Principles, Human Rights and Social Institutions* (Dordrecht Springer 2005) 157–170, 158.
50 Gosepath (n 49) 161.
51 K Daly, 'Restorative Justice: The Real Story' (2002) 4 (1) *Punishment & Society* 55–79, 377; Jones (n 44) 73.
52 Gosepath (n 49) 162.
53 Jones (n 44) 73.
54 Daly (n 51) 377.
55 Gosepath (n 49) 165.
56 Gosepath (n 49) 159.
57 Gosepath (n 49) 160.
58 RoR (n 48) 8.

11 Negotiated outcomes in low-resourced courts

Tanzania's land courts system

Kelly Askew

Introduction[1]

In the 1990s, countries across Africa embarked on major land reform programmes to facilitate land markets, promote individualization of land tenure and fast-track land titling, and to increase foreign investment in land – all in the name of alleviating poverty and promoting economic development. Under pressure from external actors, Tanzania followed suit, however, it began by first appointing a presidential commission under the leadership of a legal scholar, Professor Issa Shivji, to collect opinions on land matters from across the socio-economic spectrum of mainland Tanzania. The commission's 1992 report[2] was intended to inform the new 1995 National Land Policy (though many of its primary recommendations were rejected). The 1995 National Land Policy in turn laid the foundation for the 1999 *Land Act No. 4* and 1999 *Village Land Act No. 5*. Soon thereafter, the *Land Disputes Courts Act No. 2* of 2002 was passed by Parliament, establishing a new set of special courts to adjudicate land disputes at nested administrative levels, e.g. village, ward, and district, superseded by the Land Division of the High Court and finally the Court of Appeal. With land reform measures occurring across the continent, the introduction of an expanded system of land dispute courts may have been a necessary corollary, for as Lund and Boone have noted in a recent essay, '[c]ontestation over land and resources often involves struggles not only over land *per se*, but also over the legitimate authority to define and settle land issues'.[3]

Land disputes in Tanzania are on the rise and feature weekly, if not daily, in national and international media.[4] Calls from the activist and civil society sectors have grown ever louder for Tanzania to protect its land from foreign land grabbers and from regional, land-poor neighbours. Indeed, current tensions flaring within the Member States of the East African Community can be viewed in large part against the backdrop of Tanzania's resistance to open up its land market to non-Tanzanians.

The dispute that has perhaps garnered the most attention in the international press is the on-going crisis in Loliondo, an area within Ngorongoro District. In 1958, when the British coerced the Maasai to move out of the Serengeti Plain to create what is now the Serengeti National Park, they signed an agreement with the Maasai, promising them land in Ngorongoro 'in perpetuity'. The government of Tanzania, however, clearly does not feel bound to an agreement that stems from the colonial era and that it was not party to, for in July 2009 it started evicting the Maasai from a 4,000 km^2 area encompassing 25 villages in Loliondo. The government had by then granted the land as a hunting concession to a firm based in the United Arab Emirates for the private use of Arab royals. Tagged 'Loliondogate' in the press, the land had been reassigned despite the existence of official surveys of and registered land certificates for villages in the disputed area. As the case remains mired in the court system, it continues to be the subject of an international petition campaign on AVAAZ (www.avaaz.org) that has put considerable pressure on the Tanzanian government and triggered a barrage of angry Twitter and text messages from around the globe directed at Tanzanian members of parliament. A second related case wending its way through the courts also concerns Maasai evictions – again in Loliondo division – from land claimed by the American tour operator Thomson Safaris. Violent conflicts involving shootings have been reported between Thomson guards, the local Maasai, and the police over Thomson's efforts to establish the Enashiva Nature Reserve, which would prohibit movement by the Maasai through a longstanding corridor to seasonal pasture and watering holes. In outright contradiction to its actions on the ground, the Thomson Safaris website claims it to be 'socially responsible in the communities and environments where we operate, treading lightly on the land and giving back to the people who welcome us so graciously'.[5]

These are only some of the most sensational cases playing out in the Tanzanian judiciary and the court of international public opinion.[6] Most conflicts do not concern Arab royals or American tour operators, but instead pit Tanzanians against fellow Tanzanian clansmen and neighbours, or parents against their children, husbands against their wives, and wealthy elites against the poor. Many conflicts, and typically the most violent ones, do, however, mirror the previous pattern of claims lodged against land used and owned by pastoralists.

In its efforts to address the situation, the government passed the *Land Disputes Courts Act No. 2* of 2002, in particular, to establish a new mechanism to deal with land disputes. It had been named but not described in Part XIII of the *Land Act No. 4*, entitled 'Dispute Settlement: Establishment of Land Courts'. The purpose was 'to ensure that land disputes are adjudicated in a just and expeditious way by an independent institution'.[7] The new courts for land disputes would replace the formerly active Ward Tribunals, Customary Land Tribunals, Customary Land Appeals Tribunals, Regional Housing Tribunals, and Housing Appeals Tribunals, which were viewed as inadequate for the task of confronting the rise in land-related disputes, and which created 'an extensive overlapping of jurisdiction and conflicting decisions'.[8]

Yet ten years after implementing the new land courts described next, disputes have continued to rise, which put Prof Anna Tibaijuka, the Minister of Lands, Housing, and Human Settlements Development, on the defensive[9] and raised concerns that these special courts are exacerbating, rather than mitigating, the problem of unrelenting increase in land conflicts. In August 2014, while swearing in a new batch of twenty High Court Justices, Tanzania's Chief Justice Othman

Chande affirmed that land-related lawsuits now constituted the majority of cases filed in the court system. '"The land court has only six judges while we receive 850 land cases annually", he said, adding that due to the scarcity of judges there were around 1,500 pending land cases' at that time.[10]

The first half of this chapter examines the special courts known as 'land tribunals' that were established by the *Land Disputes Courts Act No. 2.* It describes their functions, key characteristics, and operating procedures. The second half of the chapter is devoted to three land disputes that were heard at different levels of the new system: one observed at the Ward Tribunal level, one at the District Tribunal level, and one at the High Court level. I aim to first describe the decade-old new system, which has received scant scholarly attention, and then provide an ethnographic analysis of how these tribunals operate, how disputes come to be heard in these settings, how officials perform their responsibilities, how disputants respond to the proceedings, and then also to identify embedded power relations, as well as the attendant constraints, successes, and challenges.

Manyara Region, where two of the three cases presented here were observed (at the ward- and district-levels), constitutes part of the former 'Maasai District' established under British colonial rule. It has a high proportion of indigenous Maasai pastoralists as well as large and growing populations of farmers from other ethnic groups who migrated to flee land shortages in their own areas and decreasing soil fertility due to overpopulation and lack of affordable inputs. The third case reviewed here (at the High Court level) was observed in Mbeya Region, a region famous for coffee and tea plantations with significant populations of Maasai, Sukuma and other pastoralists. While not viewed as indigenous to that area, the Maasai had established communities in the region by the 1940s and are thus not considered recent migrants.

In all three cases, the disputes occurred between non-Maasai farmers and Maasai pastoralists. Taken together, they exemplify the alarming trend throughout Tanzania of rising contestation over pastoralist lands. For under the 1999 Land Acts, land defined as 'unoccupied' is subject to state appropriation. By this criterion, rangelands used by pastoralists for rotational grazing are legally vulnerable since 'occupation' is not 'evident' in the same way as agriculturalist occupation – with rows of neatly planted maize, beans, or coffee. Pastoralist herds move across land designated for pasture and leave few visible traces, aside from their droppings, enticing covetous neighbours, would-be investors, wealthy elites, conservationists, or government institutions to lay claim to it. As Kennedy Gastorn has noted, 'occupancy of the land became narrowly defined as tilling whereas pasturage and fallow were not seen as occupancy'.[11] Pastoralist lands are thus the locus of intense conflict, increasingly being reallocated to other uses by a central government avidly seeking foreign investment opportunities and expansion of the conservation areas that annually draw so many wealthy tourists. Long-standing prejudice against pastoralists, viewed by government leaders and other loud voices in society and in the press as uneducated traditionalists obstructing national progress and development, also contribute to the alarming trend of encroachment on and widespread appropriation of pastoralist lands.

Village Land Councils (*Baraza za Ardhi za Vijiji*)

The 2002 *Land Disputes Courts Act* sought to relieve the pressure that land conflicts were placing on an already strained judiciary by creating a separate track for adjudicating land disputes. It established a system of special courts called 'land tribunals', composed of nested levels in the administrative hierarchy depending on the size and/or market value of the land in dispute, listed next from the lowest to highest level:

1 The Village Land Council (*Baraza la Ardhi la Kijiji*)
2 The Ward Tribunal (*Baraza la Kata*)
3 The District Land and Housing Tribunal (*Baraza la Ardhi na Nyumba la Wilaya*)
4 The High Court (Land Division) (*Mahakama Kuu, Kitengo cha Ardhi*)
5 The Court of Appeals of Tanzania (*Mahakama ya Rufaa*)

Each level affords the option of appealing a negative ruling at the next level in the hierarchy, with the exception of the Court of Appeal, whose rulings are final. According to the 2002 Act, each of the 12,000+ villages in the country must establish a Village Land Council: 'The Village Land Council shall consist of seven members of whom three shall be women, and each member shall be nominated by the village council and approved by the Village Assembly' (section 5.1; the Village Assembly is the body composed of all voting members of the village). Even though villages are only empowered to grant land allocations in parcels no larger than 50 acres, the Village Land Council has unlimited pecuniary jurisdiction over village land. Advocates are not allowed to argue cases at this level.

The Village Land Council's primary function is 'to mediate between and assist parties to arrive at a mutually acceptable settlement of the disputes on any matter concerning land within its area of jurisdiction' (section 7c). Ideally, this is where the resolution of land disputes would begin: at the most local level where those adjudicating would be best positioned to evaluate the claims of the disputants, which is also a key recommendation of the Presidential Inquiry into Land Matter (known as the Shivji Commission). However, in some cases, it is the very fact of being assessed by one's neighbours that leads some aggrieved parties to seek redress in the first instance at the next level up: the Ward Tribunal (*Baraza la Kata*). And because the Village Land Council primarily serves a mediatory function and lacks power of enforcement, some people view it as a waste of time. Gastorn points out that the Village Land Council is also legislatively enabled to serve as a 'court of law', which invests two functions in the same body. He asks,

> if parties to a dispute decide to obtain the mediation services of the village land council, they can, for whatever reason proceed to institute the same case in the land court defined to include the village land council. Would the very Village Land Council change its capacity as a mediator and constitute itself as a court of law to handle the matter?[12]

Ward Tribunals (*Baraza za Kata*)

A 'Ward' in Tanzanian governance is an administrative unit that encompasses typically four to six villages. Unlike the Village Land Council, which is a sub-unit reporting to the Village Council (village government composed of 25 elected officials), the Ward Tribunal is not limited to addressing land issues. Instead, land disputes are included within its broader mandate to resolve disputes occurring within its jurisdiction. Each Ward Tribunal 'shall consist of not less than four, nor more than eight, members of whom three shall be women' (section 11). When the tribunal receives application to hear a dispute, the tribunal Chairman (*mwenyekiti*) selects three other tribunal members (*wajumbe wa baraza*), one of whom must be female, to constitute a quorum of four. Like the Village Land Council, the Ward Tribunal's primary function is mediatory and 'to secure peace and harmony' (13.1), but it lacks the powers of enforcement. It holds pecuniary jurisdiction over disputed land valued up to and not exceeding, Tanzanian Shilling (Tsh) 3,000,000 (~US $1350). Thus upon receipt of an application, the tribunal secretary is to ask the claimant: 'If the land in question were to be sold today, what price would it command?' That then determines whether or not the case should be heard there or referred directly to the district level. Unlike at the village level, there are no limits on the size of the holding, since the determining factor is property value, and property values vary considerably. Thus 20 acres of land in a maize-growing area, for instance, would likely fall within the jurisdiction of the Ward Tribunal, whereas 20 acres of irrigated rice fields would likely not, since irrigated plots carry higher market value.

Although specified as also serving the role of mediation, the Ward Tribunal is nevertheless granted more power than a village land council and specifically can

1. order the recovery of possession of land;
2. order the specific performance of any contract;
3. make orders in the nature of an injunction both mandatory and prohibitive;
4. award any amount claimed;
5. award compensation;
6. order the payment of any costs and expenses incurred by a successful party or his witnesses; or
7. make any other order, which the justice of the case may require (section 16.1).

Yet, because it lacks power of enforcement, its rulings require the assent and compliance of the parties involved to be effective. Although lacking powers of enforcement itself, Ward Tribunal decisions may be enforced by the next level in the system: the District Land and Housing Tribunal (*Baraza la Ardhi na Nyumba la Wilaya*). An additional point is that – as at the Village Land Council – no disputant at the Ward Tribunal may be represented by an advocate: disputants either represent themselves or obtain permission of the Tribunal to be represented by a relative or household member. Should the tribunal's ruling be found unacceptable to a disputant, s/he has the right of appeal at the District Land and Housing Tribunal.

District Land and Housing Tribunals (*Baraza za Ardhi na Nyumba za Wilaya*)

Disputes over property in land valued over three million shillings and up to forty or fifty million shillings in movable and immovable property respectively (typically concerning 50–100 acres of rural land, depending on location) are referred to the District Land and Housing Tribunal. The district tribunal consists of a legally trained Chairman, appointed by the Minister of Lands and sworn in by the Regional Commissioner and up to seven appointed assessors (*wajumbe wa baraza*), at least three of whom must be women. A tribunal hearing is duly constituted when held by the Chairman and two assessors, who hold three-year terms and are eligible for re-appointment. Both assessors are required to give their opinion before the Chairman can issue a judgment, although the Chairman is not bound to accede to the assessors' opinions. At the district level, the party to the dispute is allowed to self-represent or to be represented by an advocate, a relative or a household member. As both Massay[13] and Olengurumwa[14] have pointed out, the fact that the tribunal officials are appointed by politicians violates the rule of impartiality and puts into doubt the independence of the tribunal.

The functions and powers of the district tribunal exceed those of the Ward Tribunal, as is signalled by the increased expertise found at this level of the system in both the Chairman (who must be a trained in law) and presence of advocates. Three types of cases are brought before the District Tribunal:

1 *Applications* for new cases of dispute,
2 *Appeals* from the Ward Tribunal level,
3 *Miscellaneous*, which covers the following:

   a) *Enforcement of orders from the ward*;
   b) *revision of Ward Tribunal decisions*, perhaps because the ward level made its decision without having quorum;
   c) *enforcement of the district tribunal's orders*, which have to be executed by the District Tribunal itself, because there are no 'court brokers' here, unlike at urban centres, which means that the office of the District Commissioner is responsible for the enforcement. Examples of enforcement include issuing orders of eviction, orders to destroy illegal dwellings, or to collect property/assets from the losing party to a suit to be auctioned off as restitution.

The procedures for hearing a case at this level entail:

1 filing of application by the claimant;
2 issuing summons to the respondent;
3 submission of written statement of defense by respondent;
4 hearing of the case by Chairman and two assessors;
5 delivering of the judgment;
6 issuing of the decree.

These procedures can take place over an extended period of time and each requires the disputants (or their representative) to travel to the tribunal for the relevant paperwork. Exorbitant fees, increased as of August 2012, are assessed for each procedure as outlined in the chart for Table 11.1:[15]

Table 11.1 Fees for District Land and Housing Tribunal. Reprinted with permission from GE Massay (2013) 'Adjudication of land cases in Tanzania: A bird eye overview of the District Land and Housing Tribunal', *Open University Law Journal* 4(2): 170–171.

No	*Item*	*Old fees in Tsh.*	*New fees in Tsh.*
1	On obtaining application form	500	4,000
2	On filing an application, where the subject matter does not exceed ten million	5,000	40,000
3	On filing an application, where the subject matter exceeds ten million	15,000	120,000
4	On filling written statement of defense	2,500	20,000
5	On filling chamber application	5,000	40,000
6	On filling an affidavit	1,500	12,000
7	On filling annexure(s) to the pleadings, each document	500	4,000
8	On filling memorandum of appeals arising from the Ward Tribunal	2,000	16,000
9	On filing petition to the Land Division of the High Court	As may be applicable to the High Court (Land Division)	As may be applicable to the High Court (Land Division)
10	On filing reply to the petition of appeal	As may be applicable to the High Court (Land Division)	As may be applicable to the High Court (Land Division)
11	For a copy of proceedings for each typed page	500	4,000
12	For copy of judgment or ruling	2,000	16,000
13	For copy of decree or drawn order	500	4,000
14	For service of application, written statement of defense, chamber application or affidavit within a city or Municipality, the process server shall be paid	3,000	24,000
15	For service of application, written statement of defense, chamber application or affidavit in any other areas other than the city or municipality, the process server shall be paid	2,000	16,000
16	On issuing witness summons or notice	500	4,000
17	On filling bill of costs	5,000	40,000
18	On filling application for execution	2,000	16,000
19	On filing or obtaining any other document which is not specified in the schedule	5,00	4,000

Given that in rural Tanzania the average per capita daily income is around US $0.66,[16] it is evident from these fees that the average rural villager in Tanzania is unlikely to be able to afford to file a claim, no matter how legitimate the grounds.

Moreover, although the *Land Act No. 4* directed the Minister of Lands to establish a District Land and Housing Tribunal 'in every district, region or zone',[17] as of February 2019 – nearly 15 years after the Act's implementation – only 53 out of 165 districts in mainland Tanzania have a functioning district tribunal due to insufficient personnel and inadequate budgetary support.[18] This means that in some regions, such as Lindi Region (which encompasses 18,000 km^2), there is only one district tribunal, while in Manyara Region (which encompasses 51,000 km^2), there are only two: Babati (with jurisdiction over Babati, Hanang, and Mbulu districts) and Simanjiro (with jurisdiction over Kiteto and Simanjiro districts). This creates great hardship for many involved in land disputes, since the journey to the district tribunal normally takes two days, but much longer during the rainy season, which affects food, lodging, as well as transportation costs and arrangements. Mr Mussa Mahelele Sukumba, Chairman of the Simanjiro District Land and Housing Tribunal, admitted that this creates another imbalance in access to justice:

> It is typically only those with means who make the trip to Orkesumet (Simanjiro). The poor typically cannot afford to do so and if they cannot come to make or defend their case, they automatically lose even though I know very well there are two sides to every story. I can only judge a case on the basis of evidence presented, and if the only evidence presented comes from one side, that's all I have to go on. In the absence of opposing evidence, the one who made the trip wins.[19]

A final key distinction from the Ward Tribunal concerns the language of the district tribunal. While hearings and evidence may be argued and submitted in Kiswahili, the language for recording, making final submissions and for issuance of rulings is English. As Massay points out: 'Without the service of translators or an advocate, the party will effectively be unable to plead his case because he can't engage with it and follow what is going on'.[20]

High Court (Land Division) (*Mahakama Kuu, Kitengo cha Ardhi*)

Disputes concerning movable and immovable property valued above forty (~US $17,400) and fifty million shillings (~US $21,750) respectively fall under the jurisdiction of the Land Division of the High Court. Whereas Land Divisions were established only at the High Court registries of Dar es Salaam and Arusha, it was recently mandated, due to the backlog and consequent delays in disposal of cases, that all High Court registries in Tanzania establish a Land Division and entertain land cases. Beyond holding jurisdiction over appeals from the district tribunal, the High Court (Land Division) also adjudicates all proceedings concerning property held by the Tanzania Investment Centre, all proceedings involving Public Corporations (parastatals), and any other proceedings related to land for which jurisdiction is not limited to any particular court or tribunal. Appeals are heard by a single judge and two assessors. Parties may appear before the High Court (Land Division) in person or be represented by an advocate or other representative, but it is not typical for parties to self-represent at this stage. As with the ward and district tribunals, which are required to take into consideration the customary law practices of the wards/ districts/regions where they operate, the High Court is bound to make a determination on the application of customary law. Finally, the High Court (Land Division) holds supervisory power over the District Land and Housing Tribunal.

Court of Appeals (*Mahakama ya Rufaa*)

An aggrieved disputant has the right to appeal the decision of the High Court to the highest court in the land, the Court of Appeals, on points of law and not the facts, where it will be heard by three judges. As a general rule, only advocates with more than five years of practicing experience can appear before the Court of Appeals. There is no route for appealing a decision issued by the Court of Appeals, but the aggrieved may apply for revision of the same decision in the same court before the bench of five or seven judges.

Although presented as nested authorities and indeed appealable up the hierarchical levels of courts, from Village Land Councils through to the Court of Appeals, a significant flaw in the new system is that the land tribunals do not follow a single line of supervisory oversight. On the contrary, the tribunals report to three different authorities in the central government: (1) the President's Office, (2) the Ministry of Lands, Housing, and Human Settlements Development, and (3) the judiciary. This would seem to create unnecessary bureaucratic impasses and confusion in basic procedures, such as with the archiving of documents in cases that move across administrative domains. Village Land Councils and Ward Tribunals are answerable, and pay any collected fines, to the District Executive Director, who represents the President's Office Regional Administration and Local Government (PO-RALG). The District Land and Housing Tribunals and the Land Division of the High Court, however, both report to the Minister for Lands, Housing, and Human Settlements Development (which appoints the District Tribunal chairs), and yet High Court judges, whether in the Land Division or otherwise, are drawn from the judiciary. Finally the Court of Appeals is grounded solely in the judiciary.

However, Gastorn points out that 'the law requires each of the above land courts to be independent in discharging their stipulated mandates, although they are administratively accountable to their establishing authorities. The government authorities cannot legally dictate the outcome of any disputes presented to these tribunals'.[21]

It is one thing to establish a system in theory, in law, and on paper, but another altogether to see it in action. The following three cases seek to bring to life how these new institutions are enacted on the ground, engaging with people whose lives and livelihoods are at stake when facing threats to their claims to land. We turn first to a case that was heard in June 2012 at the Ward Tribunal level in Lengatei, Kiteto District, Manyara Region.

Case #1: Lengatei Ward Tribunal case concerning Mafisa villagers (Kilindi District) caught illegally clearing within a Lesoit village (Kiteto District) forest reserve (2012)

Lengatei Ward in Kiteto District is located on the easternmost edge of the district and abuts the border with the neighbouring district of Kilindi. In the past years, the border was hotly contested, but agreed upon through mediation and is marked with concrete 'beacons', set apart by distances spanning several kilometres. In other words, the border is not obvious to the naked eye. Lengatei Ward consists of four villages: Lengatei (composed primarily of ethnic Nguu farmers), Lesoit (composed primarily of Parakuyo Maasai pastoralists), Olkitikiti (composed primarily of Kisongo Maasai pastoralists) and Engang'uengare (again composed primarily of Kisongo Maasai pastoralists). All four villages had contributed portions of their village lands to the creation of a community-managed forest spanning nine villages, called Suledo Forest. It falls to the villages to monitor and patrol their sections of the forest to prevent illegal logging and clearing for cultivation.

Mr Samwel Tetea, Chairman of the Lengatei Ward Tribunal (LWT), is a Parakuyo Maasai resident of Lesoit, whereas the secretary, Mr Juma Mgoma, a Nguu resident of Lengatei, is a farmer serving a second five-year term as secretary (a salaried position under the district government), whereas Mr Tetea, like the other tribunal representatives (*wajumbe*), is serving a three-year unpaid term. In keeping with legal requirements, not taking into consideration the position of the secretary, the tribunal is composed of eight representatives, including the chairman, called *wajumbe* (four of whom must be women) drawn from the four villages. They indicated that on average they heard 2–3 land dispute cases per month, and only sent 1–2 cases per year up to the Simanjiro Land and Housing Tribunal for review, enforcement or appeal.

On the morning of Saturday, 30 June 2012, Lesoit's village patrol apprehended four men who were clearing bush in Suledo forest to prepare the land for cultivation. The 'invaders' (*wavamizi*) claimed they had been hired by a wealthy farmer from Mafisa and were only carrying out orders. They were taken into custody, marched to the Lengatei village lock-up, and calls went out to both Lesoit and Mafisa village leaders, as well as to the chairman and secretary of the LWT to hear the case. The tribunal, composed of Chairman Tetea, Secretary Mgoma, and three *wajumbe* (including two villagers from Lesoit), convened that afternoon with the quorum of a minimum of four tribunal members being met. In addition, the proceedings were attended by the village chairmen of both villages, as well as the Village Executive Officer (VEO) of Mafisa. (The VEO of Lesoit was unavailable.) A few interested villagers and I also attended.[22]

> Once everyone was settled and the tribunal officials took their positions at a head table facing the rows of chairs where the rest of us sat, Chairman Tetea officially opened the proceedings. He granted the Mafisa Chairman the right to speak first. He began with a complaint. The Mafisa Chairman argued that proper procedure had been violated with the summary arrest of the men and insisted that instead a formal letter should have been written to him so he could have been allowed the chance to resolve the situation first.

Secretary Mgoma replied that, no, what needed to be determined first was whether the men had the right to clear that area in another village. The situation was not internal to Mafisa village but was alleged to have occurred in the village of Lesoit, within the Suledo forest where cultivation is prohibited due to being a forest reserve.

The Mafisa VEO spoke next. He argued that what was necessary was a site visit by the tribunal to determine whether or not the village boundaries had been breached. 'Were these men within the Suledo forest or were they clearing land on the Mafisa side of the border?' He went on some length, speaking to the value of two neighbouring village governments coming together to solve a shared problem and the need to determine where real fault lies. 'The law must be respected and if the border was breached then we will ensure that no further farming activities continue at that site'.

The Lesoit Chairman spoke next. He admitted that he had not visited the site where the men had been caught and agreed it was necessary. But he argued that this problem of invading and illegally clearing within the Suledo forest kept occurring despite 'Ujirani Mwema' ('Good Neighbourliness') negotiations between the villages. 'The difficulty lies in the different land use patterns on each side of the border: farming on the Kilindi District [Mafisa village] side and forest conservation on the Lesoit side, which is something that benefits everyone not just the people of Lesoit. Moreover, a site visit will be difficult since it will have to involve district land officers from both Kiteto and Kilindi districts'. To this, everyone agreed.

Chairman Tetea next decided that the respective parties (including the named wealthy farmer who had hired the men) should all be informed by letter to appear again before the tribunal the following Monday (two days hence).

Mafisa Chairman: 'We have told our villagers many times not to simply start clearing without first submitting a request to the village government because this country is ruled by laws and by peace'.[23]

A debate then ensued as to whether or not to phone the wealthy farmer, Salimu M., right then and there. It was decided to do so, and the Mafisa Chairman stepped outside the building to speak with Mawete. The Lesoit Chairman followed him out (presumably to listen to the conversation). Salimu M. was told to come now and pay bond to release the remandees. While this was happening, another man in the room spoke up and offered to pay the prisoners' bond on the condition that Salimu M. would indeed appear at the Monday hearing.

When the Mafisa Chairman re-entered the room, his tone had changed. 'How is it that there can be any fault if people are clearing in an area long known to be a farming area'?

The volunteer guarantor repeated that he was willing to cover the bond for their release but that if any of them failed to appear, it should be Mawete who would have to pay the no-show penalty, not him.

Chairman Tetea now spoke, addressing the remandees: 'You clearers-of-bush [wafyekaji]: no lies. You should know you cannot clear land without a permit. You as Tanzanians know the law. When you enter a different village, you should seek out the leaders of that village. Worse things could have happened to you – you could have been killed'. He set their bail at Tsh 200,000/- per prisoner.

Mafisa VEO: 'Everyone needs a permit today. You can't say you are still following customary ways of clearing wherever you want'. He then turned to the remandees and told them he had work for them if they wanted it.

At that point, the hearing was adjourned and Secretary Mgoma set about writing the necessary letters: a summons letter to Salimu Mawete; a letter of bond for three of the remandees; and a letter of bond for the fourth, who was guaranteed by someone else. I copied them in my notebook and present the first two letters here, translated into English.

Ward Tribunal
Lengatei
30/6/2012

Re: Summons to the Ward Land Tribunal, Lengatei

Receive this summons to appear before the Ward Tribunal.

You must appear on 2/7/2012 at 9 a.m. in the morning.
You must come to answer the complaint against you.
If you fail to appear, you will face serious consequences.

Tribunal Secretary's Signature

Signature of Witness

Figure 11.2a Summons letter

These people invaded the forest reserve to start establishing farm plots.

Certificate of Bond 30/6/2012

I, Julla K., give surety for the release of the following persons identified by name below for their case being heard here in the Lengatei Ward Tribunal.

This case will be heard by the tribunal on 2/07/2012.

If they fail to appear, I will pay the sum of Sh. 200,000/= for each person, a total of Sh. 600,000/= (six hundred thousand shillings).

The persons are:

1. *name*
2. *name*
3. *name*

Figure 11.2b Letter of bond

Case #2: Simanjiro District Land and Housing Tribunal, Land Case Application No. 6 of 2011, Rashidi Omari Kiboma vs. Mkoa Kaipai and Ndatuya Tang'idi[24]

One day in January 2011, Lesoit's village patrol caught another trespassing farmer. Rashidi Kiboma, from the neighbouring village of Lengatei, had driven his tractor to a grassy area near the centre of the village and started ploughing illegally. It was land that had been set aside by village decree as pasture for young goats and calves. The village patrol ordered that he stop, and when he refused, they called Lesoit Chairman Mkoa Kaipai and Lesoit VEO Ndatuya Tang'idi. A well-to-do farmer who looked down on his Maasai neighbours, Kiboma refused all demands to cease and depart, so they summoned the police from the nearest town. Only under threat of arrest did Kiboma finally stop, but not before he was charged with trespassing and misconduct.

Lesoit has a population of around 2,000 residents, 99% of whom are Parakuyo Maasai. The village was founded in 1992 after Lengatei split in two, with its Parakuyo residents joining the village of Lesoit, taking half the village's land with them. Lengatei retained the predominantly ethnic Nguu farmers (95%) with a small minority Maasai population (5%). Lingering resentments remain two decades later since Lengatei's population has grown to more than twice that of Lesoit, generating a shortage of land.[25]

Back in 1997, Lesoit had ratified its Village Land Use Plan (a requirement of the *Village Land Act No. 5*) in its Village Assembly meeting, which, much like a zoning ordinance, designated specific areas for residences, for pasture, for the protected natural spring, and for the community-managed forest. Thus the village authorities were well within their rights to file a criminal case against Kiboma for trespassing. They won this case and he was subjected to a 90-day probation period. In turn, he filed a civil lawsuit at the Simanjiro District Land and Housing Tribunal (Kiteto District did not have its own land tribunal), suing Chairman Kaipai and VEO Tang'idi for preventing him from farming land that he claimed was his. Kiboma's wealth (signalled by his tractor) enabled him to hire a paralegal (locally called a 'bush lawyer') to represent him. Lesoit's leaders had to represent themselves throughout the nine-month-long proceedings, though they received periodic advice from the Kiteto District Council's lawyer. The case required them to make multiple trips to Simanjiro to file documents, submit evidence, and attend the hearing and return for the judgment.

I attended the hearing, which took place on 11 May 2011 at the Simanjiro District Land and Housing Tribunal in Orkesumet, Simanjiro. Mr Kiboma, who did not attend the hearing, was represented by his son and a friend (to serve as witnesses) and Mr Nyoki, the paralegal.[26] The Lesoit delegation included Chairman Kaipai, VEO Tang'idi and one witness. Mr Nyoki tried hard to dominate the proceedings, employing tactics he must have seen employed on TV. They included frequent interruptions and objections, and misquoting his opponents' arguments to advance his position. He argued that Kiboma owned the disputed land under customary law from 1986, preceding the emergence of Lesoit, that he had been continuously farming there, and that he did not recognize the existence of Lesoit nor its purported leaders nor their claim to authority over the land.

The case was resolved easily enough following a site visit in August 2011 by the tribunal chairman and two assessors to the contested pasture, a barren grassland where the lack of any signs of cultivation exposed Kiboma as a fraud and unsuccessful land grabber. All expenses for the tribunal's visit had to be borne by the disputants, including travel and accommodation costs, per diem allowances for all three tribunal officials, plus a payment to the driver, equalling Tsh 70,000/- (~US $50 at the time) for each party. Facing almost certain defeat, the paralegal employed one last tactic to try and win Kiboma's case. Mr Nyoki wrote his summary argument in English, a significant departure from the rest of the proceedings, which had taken place entirely in Kiswahili, and in it he continued to insist that the disputed land was an established farm. Quoting from the *Constitution*, the *Land Acquisition Act* of 1967, the *Local Government (Local Authorities) Act* of 1982, and the *Village Land Act No. 5* of 1999, Cap 114, he argued:

> Therefore plaintiff owing to the evidence he has adduced before this Honourable court, it is quiet [sic] obvious and clear that he acquired ownership of his suit land Tenure system which is most cases the system applicable in rural areas . . . as far as the village land Act no 5 cap 114 R.E. 2002 IS CONCERNED. An individual who has been in existence in a particular locality for 12 years or more becomes a true and lawful owner of the respective locality.
>
> [. . .]
>
> Applicant doesn't accept the falsely tendered before you [sic] Honor the said Lesoit village Registration Certificate, for the reason that the whole area is within Lengatei Village.
>
> [. . .]
>
> Your Honour: having so submitted, let us now deliberate on the issue as to whether the plaintiff deserve compensation as far as this matter is concerned. . . . Applicant has suffered irreparable losses to the extent that he did not cultivate in his farm last season amounting to loss of an average Tsh 6,000,000/=[27] not forgetting that Applicant is entering in great expenses in running this case by way of Transport, food, accommodation, etc.
>
> Honorable chairman of the Tribunal I finally and humbly beg to rest my submission, by emphasizing that the defense side has completely failed to prove their defense.
>
> Applicant finally surrender his fate unto the might [sic] wisdom of your honorable Tribunal.[28]

The tendering of the applicant's final submission in English now required that the Lesoit respondents also had to submit their summary argument in English, and they were able to get assistance from the Kiteto District Council attorney in drafting it. They reiterated that Lesoit was an officially recognized village, an administrative unit belonging to Lengatei Ward, with its own government-funded primary school and health clinic staffed by government-paid employees. They stated that as such, Kaipai as the elected village leader, and Tang'idi as the district-appointed VEO, had the authority to stop illegal trespassers from entering and cultivating village land. They then pointed out the holes in Kiboma's case:

> Honorable chairman, the respondents still find the application has no merit as the evidence testified by prosecution side is different from the case filed. In his application, the applicant said the Suitland is at Lesoit village and respondents are residents of Lesoit village. At the hearing the applicant and his witnesses said the Suitland is at Lengatei Village. This is a great contradiction the Tribunal cannot remain silent on it. Here the applicant seem [sic] not to be aware of where the Suitland is.
>
> Honorable chairman, at the hearing, the applicant raised a new matter that Lesoit is not a Village but is part of Lengatei Village. This Tribunal has no ground to play his new game and it was brought out of right time. The respondents tendered village Registration Certificate and a map showing its land use plan. Lesoit become a village since 1992 from Lengatei village. Lengatei kept silent since then watching Lesoit proceeding in all manner as all other villages usual act. Neither Lengatei Leaders nor its people can challenge the existence of Lesoit at this juncture, before this tribunal as well as in this case.[29]

In his ruling, Simanjiro District Tribunal Chairman Mr Mahelele stated his reasons for denying Kiboma's application for both the land and damages:

> From the above evidence I see no base for the applicant to sue the respondents in this manner. . . . After all I do not see any interest respondents have in their personal capacity to object the applicant from using a suit land. So . . . I consider that if the respondents evicted the applicant from suit land they did so as Village leaders.
>
> The respondents testified the suit land to be within a grazing land. When we visited a Suitland we found it was surrounded by a forest/uncultivated land. . . . In my view I cannot allow the applicant go back [sic] to a Suitland for it will bring a dispute between him as a farmer and pastoralists. So status quo of the Suitland be maintained.[30]

Chairman Mahelele's judgment did, however, allow the respondents to claim costs against Kiboma, and for all the two-day long trips from and to Simanjiro, as well as the costs of the tribunal delegation's site visit, which were significantly high. And yet Lesoit's leaders chose not to claim them. They told me 'it was not worth the time, trouble and expense to try to do so, and that Kiboma would likely refuse to pay . . . We're just happy we secured our land', said Chairman Kaipai.[31]

Case #3: High Court of Tanzania at Mbeya, Misc. Land Application No. 17 of 2008: Judith Atilio Ngajiro et al. vs. Matabele Mwadunguru and Tera Kurubai

In 1973, the Usangu Farmers' Co-operative Society from Mbeya united with the Mbeya Development Co-operative to establish a cattle ranch called USAMBECO encompassing 12,700 hectares of land in Mbarali District. At that time, the Parakuyo Maasai pastoralists were already living on the land. They were ordered to vacate the land, but refused and took their complaint all the way to the President's office. USAMBECO fenced the land with rocks, built its office, started ranching practices and in 1976 received a Certificate of Occupancy for the land for a 99-year period. In 1977, USAMBECO started to evict the pastoralists with police involvement, yet when the people refused to be evicted, the Parakuyo community decided to form its own village and build a school. They requested permission to do so on the land adjoining the USAMBECO ranch, and dated the establishment of their village called Matebete to 1977. I was told that theirs was the first village in Mbarali District of Mbeya Region to have a Maasai chairman.

Soon afterwards, however, the ranch went into default on its loans to the Cooperative Rural Development Bank (CRDB). The CRDB initiated foreclosure proceedings and publicized its intent to auction off the property. The Parakuyo of Matebete village organized themselves and raised the necessary funds through cattle sales to bid on the property; they won the bid in 1978. It was joined to their village land, and now consists of a total village area of ~14,440 hectares, of which 12,700 hectares are a part of the former USAMBECO property. Thus the village is an odd composite of village land (1,740 ha) plus land under statutory title deed thus technically 'general land' but in the name of Matebete Madunguru, a registered group composed of village pastoralists. They officially registered their village in 1982.

Neighbouring farming villagers, however, have always contested the acquisition of the ranch by Matebete Madunguru. Once the pastoralists obtained possession, angry farmers streamed in from outside, destroyed all the buildings on the premises, looted the machinery, and destroyed the cattle dip (a very valuable resource for the pastoralists), and some settled on the land in defiance. Time passed and relations with the neighbours were somewhat normalized, resulting in the current village demographics of 75% / 25% pastoralist to farmer ratio. Other farmers, however, looked with envy on the pastoralist lands and kept encroaching. Time and again the village authorities tried to evict the squatters but have been largely unsuccessful.

In 2008, a case was filed against the Matebete Madunguru group and the Matebete village chairman Tera Kurubai, in the High Court of Mbeya.[32] It is a representative suit in the name of four individuals representing 214 others who argued that they were being unlawfully evicted by Matebete village authorities from the 12,700 ha that constituted the former USAMBECO ranch within Matebete village, which they claimed to have lived on for more than 20 years. Although filed in 2008, the case languished in the High Court docket for years due to a shortage of judges in the Mbeya High Court. Finally, the government decided to deal with some of the backlog by sending a number of cases to Dar es Salaam for *in absentia* adjudication. Attorney Mbise, the lawyer representing the Matebete respondents, had, in his pleadings in January 2009, raised preliminary objections on four counts, arguing that the case be dismissed without going to a full hearing:

1 The application was based on false affidavits.
2 The intended suit is hopelessly out of time.
3 The list of names of people said to have authorised the Applicants to sue on their behalf does not bear the signature of the persons concerned.
4 The intended Plaint was not annexed.[33]

Victor Mkumbe, the lawyer for the applicants who filed his rejoinder with the High Court in February 2009, argued that the counter affidavit filed by Attorney Mbise did not dispute the key argument of the case, namely that the 214 people were living on the 127,000 hectares of land, for which reason the case should proceed. He went on to claim:

> That, as of now, it is the 214 persons who are in physical occupation of the disputed land for over 20 years. The respondents are nowhere near the disputed land. It is, therefore, in the best interests of justice, as well as in the interests of the respondents themselves, that this matter be determined in court. Otherwise, the 214 persons have every legal right to continue occupying the disputed land.[34]

This was a rather outrageous statement, since the land is not only fully integrated within the village, but constitutes the vast bulk of a village officially recognized on all government registers as 'Matebete Village', with a government-funded primary school, a government-recognized Village Chairman and Village Executive Officer, and over a thousand residents recognized as Matebete villagers on the national census.

On 20 September 2012, the ruling from the Dar es Salaam High Court judge was read aloud at the Mbeya High Court. The Matebete village leadership had told me that their case was finally to be heard at the court; they had not realized that this was not to be a hearing but just the reading of an initial judgment about the future of the suit. I attended the proceedings that day in the company of the former Matebete Chairman (and named respondent in the suit) Tera Kurubai, and the Matebete VEO Raphael Daimon. Their lawyer, who was not able to be present, sent an aide to represent his office.

The four of us waited outside the small room where the decisions were to be read out (all of us, with perhaps the exception of the aide, still thinking it was to be an actual hearing). At some point, I was called aside and in response to an earlier request I had made, taken to the room where the advocates prepared themselves for the hearings and allowed to sit at an empty desk to quickly read through the documents of the case (since the Matebete leadership did not have copies themselves). At last, it was announced that the morning's proceedings were to begin. With all the other advocates, applicants and respondents whose cases were to be addressed that morning, I rejoined my group and we pushed our way into the small room where a court clerk would read the decisions from Dar.

The first case concerned a conflict between the Rungwe District Commissioner and a village in his district. It was dismissed for lack of a prior approval necessary to file a representative suit (presumably on the part of the aggrieved village). The judgment was read first in English and then paraphrased in Kiswahili so that all could understand. Because it had been dismissed on a technicality, the Registrar told the applicants that they had the right to re-submit their suit later.

The second case concerned a conflict over clan land that had been redeemed from debt by an individual. The clan elders had argued that as longstanding clan land, it should be returned to the clan because clan rules posit that land cannot be held by an individual. But the clan member who had paid to redeem the land argued it was now his to own privately. The judge, so read the clerk, ruled in favour of the individual as owner and cited two other cases as precedent. The judgment was again read out aloud, first in English and then paraphrased in Kiswahili for the benefit of the three clan elders in attendance, who had just lost their case. The clerk ended by reminding them that, if dissatisfied with the ruling, they had the right to take their case to the Court of Appeals.

The third case concerned an appeal from the Ward Tribunal level where the judge found irregularities in the Ward Tribunal's handling of the case back in May of 2008. The case was allowed to continue.

Finally, the Matebete case was called. Former chairman Kurubai and VEO Daimon stood up and moved to stand before the clerk to receive their judgment. The clerk read aloud in English the ruling from Judge Latifa Mansoor, dated 29 June 2012, which responded to the complaints of Advocate Mbise as follows:

1 **Re: false affidavits**–The truth or falsehood of submitted affidavits could only be verified through examination and cross-examination, and that therefore this was not cause to dismiss the suit as a preliminary objection.
2 **Re: suit being out of time** – 'I think that this objection is prematurely raised, as the suit is yet to be filed, and the contents of the suit are yet to be known to the court. . . . I therefore dismiss this second point of objection'.
3 **Re: lack of sufficient signatures** – Enough, if not all, of the signatures were obtained to enable the suit to proceed and, secondly, that it is permissible to have others sign on their behalf to minimize costs.

4 **Re: improper filing** – The technicality of this objection may be correct in detail but the application was sufficiently sound overall to permit the case to proceed.

The ruling was read in English. Unlike all the previous cases, the clerk did not paraphrase the ruling in Kiswahili because the parties were represented by advocates.[35] The Matebete delegation was quickly dismissed, and the next case was called up. As we filed out of the courtroom, it became clear that my colleagues from Matebete thought they had won the day and had the case dismissed. They had not understood the proceedings, since it was only read aloud in English. Their lawyer was not present and his aide had either not understood the outcome or had demurred to convey the bad news to them. So it fell to me to have to tell them that the case was going to continue and that they would have to return and continue the fight to save their land.

While bias is difficult to ascertain, and granting Judge Mansoor the benefit of the doubt that people ought to be allowed to argue their positions in a court of law, It beggars belief that a suit filed in 2008 claiming the majority of land in a village officially registered by the government in 1982 – a full 26 years earlier! – would not be considered somewhat 'out of time'. The 214 applicants were essentially trying to reduce Matebete village to the subvillage it had been prior to obtaining the USAMBECO parcel, claiming ownership rights to a full 88% of the village's land. That these 214 individuals were known to represent four of the seven villages that border Matebete speaks volumes to the difficulties Matebete has had obtaining recognition and legitimacy from its neighbours.

Nevertheless, on 4 February 2014, Mbeya High Court Judge Hon JCM Mwambegele dismissed the case due to errors, contradictions, and inaccuracies in the evidence presented by the applicants. Specifically, the judge was not convinced of their claim to represent 214 others in a representative suit. According to their application, a key meeting had taken place in 2008, at which 214 aggrieved persons decided to press forward with the lawsuit against Matebete and selected three among them to represent the group collectively. Judge Mwambegele concluded:

> [T]he so called list of 214 participants indicated in item 1 above has caused me some anxiety. Firstly, the list does not bear 214 names as claimed. . . . Secondly, the signatures signed against some of the names leave a lot to be desired. Most of the names appear to have been authored by one and the same person. . . . Some names have a similar signature thereby suggesting that one person signed for them. Thirdly, to clinch it all, the documents are dated 04.12.2007. . . . While the meeting was convened on 20.07.2008 the names and signatures were obtained on 04.12.2007 in public rallies conducted at difference venues. In the circumstances, this court doubts the genuineness of the minutes and their accompanying names of persons intended to be represented.

> In the absence of definite and certain terms that the 214 persons intended to be represented in the intended representative suit, this court will be exposing them to painful consequences of litigation to which they perhaps did not consent. This ailment alone disposes the application. I therefore will not go into the discussion of other issue [sic] raised during the hearing of the application, for doing so will be but an academic endeavour on which I do not want to indulge at this moment.[36]

Matebete villagers' claim to the majority of their land has, for the time being, been secured. Yet that victory is tempered by the facts that the case took six years, consuming their time and labour and millions of shillings on legal fees, transportation expenses, court fees and more.

Analysis and conclusions

These three cases are highly revealing on multiple counts. They constitute three success stories for Maasai pastoralists, yet taken as a set, one sees how the powers of pastoralists to manoeuvre and negotiate within these special courts wanes the further up the land courts system they go. At the Ward level, the proceedings were the fairest of all. All relevant parties were in attendance: the accused, the accusers, village authorities from both villages, and a duly constituted tribunal. Costs were minimal, entailing a few phone calls and transportation to the Lengatei village office – a short distance for all involved. And the tribunal included pastoralists in positions of authority (the Chairman, as well as two *wajumbe*) alongside farmers. It was democratic, civil, and followed all the legal requirements on issues, ranging from composition of the tribunal to the dispensing of court summons and posting of bond for all the accused. As Eckert and colleagues have recently argued in an analysis of the reciprocal effects of laws on society and of society on law: '[I]n the use of law, law transforms those who use it, their understanding of the world, of their conflicts and their normative orientations – in other words, their political subjectivities'.[37] It would appear that Tanzania's land tenure reform has encouraged the development of legislation-respecting political subjectivities in the rural village settings presented here, where both farmers and pastoralists were successfully interpellated by the state. In following up the case afterwards, I was told that the tribunal's site visit established that the clearing work had indeed taken place on the Lesoit side of the village border, and thus a hefty fine was assessed against the farmer Mawete. He paid, and I learned that the site has remained unviolated ever since.

In the District-level case, the tribunal was composed of a non-pastoralist chairman and two assessors, one of whom was Maasai. The Chairman told me in an interview that it was important to him to have at least one assessor who could instruct him on the customs of the Maasai, who are the majority population in the two districts, Simanjiro and Kiteto, then in his jurisdiction.[38] Although the Maasai are not represented on the tribunal in proportion to their demographics in this jurisdiction, where they constitute the majority, this did not negatively affect the outcome, owing to the Chairman's apparent concern for equity and his public deference to his companion assessors, both of whom agreed with his opinion in favour of the Lesoit villagers and against the false claim of ownership by the neighbouring farmer. It was remarkable to me how impassive the three tribunal officials were during the hearing of the Lesoit case. Mr Nyoki's over-the-top performance incited no response from them at all beyond calm stares. That, in turn, had a calming effect on the Lesoit delegation, which at a couple of points in the proceedings seemed at risk of rising to Nyoki's bait and allowing their tempers to flare, with attendant slips of the tongue (likely Nyoki's aim). The tribunal officials had likely witnessed his antics many a time before, for he had built himself a rather large client base and was no stranger to the District tribunal (even though I was told he had a very poor record of actually winning his cases). The Lesoit leaders secured a just outcome, enabled by a tribunal that performed its inculcated political roles to perfection, learning in the process how to perform their assigned roles as well. But the ordeal proved very expensive and required multiple rounds of fundraising from the villagers to defend and secure their rights to their village land.

In the High Court case, we see the same dynamic of farmers invading Maasai lands repeating itself – now magnified several times over – on the part of the purported 214 applicants suing Matebete village. In their suit, they parrot the same falsified claim of long-term (20 years) occupation that Rashidi Kiboma had employed in his suit against Lesoit's village leaders. This emerges as the key strategy that farmers are employing nation-wide against pastoralists in their stream of suits: the claim of what is legally referred to as 'Adverse Possession' in which ownership rights to land can be claimed by a party that can prove to have occupied it peacefully and uninterruptedly for at least 12 years. Maasai and other East African pastoralist communities are indigenous peoples committed to pursuing their distinctive way of life and they are suffering widespread marginalization and outright economic and political persecution as a result.[39] They thus often tend to be poorer and less educated than their farming neighbours, and more often than not find themselves in the role of respondent in legal disputes over land, rather than initiating the suits themselves – despite the fact that it is usually the case of someone else encroaching on ***their*** land. (The Ward Tribunal case is the only one of the three presented where legal action was initiated by pastoralists.) The strategy of claiming rights of adverse possession is being employed by many to call pastoralists' rights to land into question. This sums up both the Lesoit and Matebete cases, with the costs of defending the land increasing exponentially the higher up the court ladder one goes. Askew, Maganga, and Odgaard[40] indeed argue that Tanzanian courts are being used as a technique for dispossessing poorer opponents (often but not always pastoralists) of their land, by 'out-lawyering' and outlasting financially the valid landowners in the lengthy and expensive process of litigation.

Also evident in both the district and High Court cases is the attack on the legitimacy of Maasai-majority villages, in Matebete just as in Lesoit. Nationwide, from politicians' speeches to newspaper editorials, a repeated rhetoric can be heard that pastoralists are nomads who therefore cannot lay permanent claim to land. This can be interpreted as, at base, an assault on pastoralism itself. For while paying lip service to the idea of pastoralists as being full-fledged citizens of the state of Tanzania entitled to all the privileges of citizenship including the right to land and a livelihood, the resounding call is for pastoralists to give up pastoralism and become settled farmers like everyone else. Or better yet, to leave altogether.

In summary, the land courts system in Tanzania works in some senses and fails in others. The desire to bring justice to the people by offering venues for the resolution of land conflicts at the village and ward level is indeed enabling some communities the opportunity to find peaceful and just solutions to their conflicts. Good governance can prevail, and the laws of the state performed to perfection. The higher up in the hierarchy of the courts, the scales of justice tip alarmingly in the direction of those with means: the ones who can pay the high fees associated with bringing a suit to court and to hire expert representation and witnesses. Going to the District Tribunal, let alone the High Court, means having to spend meagre resources on transportation, advocates, filing fees, and more filing fees, overnight accommodation for themselves and for witnesses, and more. In one sense, the cases of Lesoit and Matebete presented here are the more hopeful ones. They involve the rights to land for all the people in the villages, so that ~1,000 people in Matebete and ~2,000 people in Lesoit can facilitate fund-raising collections allowing a more equitable distribution of the burden of these expenses, and, thus, not to unduly affect any one individual. But if it were the case of an individual fighting to retain or to reclaim their rights to land, a rural villager, whose profile resembles that of the average villager in Tanzania making well under the international poverty line of $1.90 a day, would find justice immeasurably beyond reach. The District Tribunal and High Court, let alone the Court of Appeals, are in theory good options for a country beleaguered with ever-increasing conflicts over land, but in practice fall a great deal short of their mission as stated on the Tanzania Judiciary's website: 'To carry out the administration of Justice to the General Public in dealing with disposal of land cases effectively and efficiently'.[41]

Notes

1 My sincere thanks to Rie Odgaard, Kennedy Gastorn, Katrin Seidel, and Hatem Elliesie for their helpful comments during the writing of this paper, and to Katrin Seidel for organizing the November 2013 workshop, entitled *Negotiating Normative Spaces: Insights from and into African Judicial Encounters* at the Max Planck Institute for Social Anthropology, where an early draft of this paper was presented. Collaboration in the *Transformations in Poverty and Property Rights* research project (2008 – present) with Rie Odgaard, Faustin Maganga, and Howard Stein also greatly informed this paper; and one of the three case studies included herein was previously published in K Askew, F Maganga, and R Odgaard, 'Of Land and Legitimacy: A Tale of Two Lawsuits' (2013) 83 (1) *Africa* 120–141. My sincere thanks go to them, to our talented research assistants, and to the National Science Foundation and Royal Danish Embassy of Tanzania that funded our work. Any and all errors in fact or interpretation, however, remain solely with me.

2 United Republic of Tanzania, *Report of the Presidential Commission of Inquiry into Land Matters 1: Land Policy and Land Tenure Structure* (Government Printers 1994); I Shivji, *Not Yet Democracy: Reforming Land Tenure in Tanzania* (IIED 1998); D Tsikata, 'Securing Women's Interests within Land Tenure Reforms: Recent Debates in Tanzania' (2003) 3 (1–2) *Journal of Agrarian Change* 149–183; A Rwegasira, *Land as a Human Right: A History of Land Law and Practice in Tanzania* (Mkuki na Nyota 2012) 88–92.

3 C Lund and C Boone, 'Introduction: Land Politics in Africa – Constituting Authority Over Territory, Property and Persons' (2013) 83 (1) *Africa* 1–13, 2.

4 'Minister of Lands Lukuvi Takes Seven Hours To Hear 400 Land Disputes' (19 December 2018) *Mwananchi*; 'Each Land Dispute Has Its Own Court' (19 October 2018) *Mwananchi*; 'Land Disputes Hinder Industrial Drive' (13 October 2018) *The Citizen*; 'Darkness Falls as Minister of Lands Lukuvi Confronts Land Disputes' (24 September 2018) *Mwananchi*; 'President Magufuli Says Land Disputes Should Be Tackled Jointly' (11 September 2018) *The Citizen*; 'Water Woes, Land Disputes Dominate President JPM's Tour' (6 September 2018) *The Citizen*; 'Conflicts Between Farmers and Pastoralists Result in Killings' (25 August 2018) *Nipashe*; 'Prime Minister Promises End to Land Disputes in Tabora Region' (21 August 2018) *Nipashe*; 'Minister Issues Order on Land Disputes Resolution' (17 August 2018) *The Citizen*; 'When Will Land Disputes Be Addressed?' (8 August 2018) *The Guardian*; 'MPs Highlight Problem of Land Conflicts, Government Agrees' (31 May 2018) *The Guardian*; 'Ministry is Determined to Resolve Land Problems' (30 May 2018) *Mwananchi*; 'Efforts Needed to End Land Conflicts' (6 March 2018) *The Guardian*; 'Strengthen Methods to Resolve Land Disputes' (31 January 2018) *The Citizen*; 'People with Land Disputes Flock to Regional Commissioner Makonda's Office' (30 January 2018) *The Citizen*; 'Prime Minister Majaliwa Regrets the Increase in Land Conflicts' (20 January 2018) *Mtanzania*.

5 A. Renton, '"Tourism is a curse to us",' *The Guardian* (5 September 2009) https://www.theguardian.com/world/2009/sep/06/masai-tribesman-tanzania-tourism

6 Another example is the ongoing controversy concerning Iowa-based AgriSol Energy's procurement of over 800,000 hectares of Tanzanian land for purposes of corn and soybean production. The case has received the investigative attention of Dan Rather, not least because if unchecked, the scheme will displace over 160,000 refugees from Burundi. See *Dan Rather Reports* (27 September 2011 and 21 February 2012); also 'Investor Admits Mistakes' (21 July 2012).

7 GE Massay, 'Adjudication of Land Cases in Tanzania: A Bird Eye Overview of the District Land and Housing Tribunal' (July 2013) 1 available at <http://lets-talk-land-tanzania.com/s/down-load/reports/Ad-judication%20of%20-land%20cases%20in%20-Tanzania.pdf> accessed 1 November 2013. DW Mangure, 'Effectiveness of Ward Tribunals in Dispensing Justice as Land Courts in Tanzania: Case of Arusha City' (2017) 6 (5) *International Journal of Science and Research (IJSR)* 2045–2050.

8 K Gastorn, 'The Dynamics of Change and Continuity in Land Dispute Mechanisms in Mainland Tanzania: The Jurisdictional Debate' in Jörn Bernreuther (ed), *Festschrift für Ulrich Spellenberg zum 70. Geburtstag* (München Sellier European Law Publishers 2010) 571–585, 571.

9 'State Defends Land Tribunal Relevance' (8 February 2013) *Daily News*; 'The Land Tribunals Will Never Be Abandoned' (30 July 2011) *Nipashe*.

10 A Ryeyemamu, 'Land Cases Takes the Lead with 850 Filed Annually' (16 August 2014) *The Guardian* available at <www.ippmedia.com/frontend/index.php?l=71086> accessed 18 August 2014.

11 K Gastorn, *The Impact of Tanzania's New Land Laws on the Customary Land Rights of Pastoralists: A Case Study of the Simanjiro and Bariadi Districts* (Münster

LIT 2008) 25, quoted in O Olengurumwa, '1990s Tanzania's Land Laws Reform and Its Impact on the Pastoral Land Tenure' Paper presented during Pastoral Week, Arusha (14–16 February 2010) 2 available at <www.tnrf.org/files/E-INFO_LHRC_New_Land_Laws_Paper_Pastoral_Week_2010.pdf> accessed 1 November 2013.
12 Gastorn (n 8) 574.
13 Massay (n 7) 5.
14 Olengurumwa (n 11) 11.
15 Massay (n 7) 3 f.
16 This amount is calculated from data gathered by the 'Transformations in Property Rights and Poverty in Tanzania' research project (2008 – present) encompassing 2027 rural households spanning eight districts in Tanzania. See H Stein, K Askew, F Maganga, and R Odgaard, 'Formalization of Land Rights and Class Differentiation in Rural Tanzania' Paper presented at the 61st African Studies Association annual meeting, Atlanta, GA, 1 December 2018.
17 Stein et al. (n 16) 12.
18 Massay (n 7); C. Tomitho (2012) 'Concept note on the state of land use conflicts in Tanzania: The status of the land disputes organs in dispute settlement'. Available from author: tmtomitho@yahoo.com. In February 2013, the Minister for Lands, Prof Anna Tibaijuka, announced her intent to request in her budget to Parliament resources to create tribunals in every district ('State Defends Land Tribunal Relevance'). However, as of May 2014, the number of established tribunals had increased to 49, but the number of actually functional tribunals was by government admission 42, see AK Tibaijuka, 'Hotuba ya Waziri wa Ardhi, Nyumba na Maendeleo ya Makazi, Mheshimiwa Prof Anna Kajumulo Tibaijuka (MB), Akiwasilisha Bungeni Makadirio ya Mapato na Matumizi ya Wizara ya Ardhi, Nyumba na Maendeleo ya Makazi kwa Mwaka wa Fedha 2014/2015' ['Speech of the Minister of Lands, Housing and Human Settlements Developments to Parliament for the Budget Year 2014/2015'] (delivered 29 May 2014) available at <www.parliament.go.tz/docs/05ce0-hotuba_ardhi.pdf> accessed 10 October 2015; also G Kitabu, 'Land, Housing Tribunals Yet to Prove Their Worth' (7 January 2014) *The Guardian* available at <www.ippmedia.com/frontend/index.php?l=63487> accessed 7 January 2014.
19 Interview with author, Orkesumet, Simanjiro (10 May 2011).
20 Massay (n 7) 4 f.
21 Kennedy Gastorn, correspondence with author (15 December 2014).
22 The identified paragraphs are taken directly from my field notes.
23 [*N*]*chi hii inaongozwa na sheria na amani.*
24 For a more detailed analysis of this case, see Askew, Maganga, and Odgaard (n 1). Reference is also made to it in the 2013 film *The Chairman and the Lions* (Documentary Educational Resources, 46 min., dir. Peter Biella).
25 Interview with Lengatei Ward Tribunal chairman S Tetea and secretary J Mgoma, Lengatei (28 June 2012).
26 A pseudonym.
27 Roughly $4,285 at the time.
28 In the District Land and Housing Tribunal for Simanjiro, at: *Simanjiro, Land Application Case No. 6 of 2011*: Rashidi Omari Kiboma (Applicant) vs. Mkoa Kaipai/Ndatoya Tang'idi (Respondents), Final Submission (19 August 2011) 2 f.
29 In the District Land and Housing Tribunal for Simanjiro, at: *Simanjiro, Land Application Case No. 6 of 2011*: Rashidi Omari Kiboma (Applicant) vs. Mkoa Kaipai/Ndatuya Tang'id (Respondents), Respondents Joint Final Submission (5 September 2011) 4.

30 In the District Land and Housing Tribunal for Simanjiro, at: *Simanjiro, Land Application Case No. 6 of 2011*: Rashidi Omari Kiboma (Applicant) vs. Mkoa Kaipai/Ndatuya Tang'idi (Respondents), Judgment (8 November 2011) 6.
31 Interview with author (April 2012).
32 Misc. Application No. 17 of 2008.
33 MT Mbise (Advocate for Respondents), 'In the High Court of Mbeya (Land Division), *Misc. Land Application No. 17 of 2008, Notice of Preliminary Objections*' (2009) 1.
34 V Mkumbe (Advocate for Applicants), 'In the High Court of Mbeya (Land Division): *Misc. Land Application No. 17 of 2008, Reply to Counter Affidavit*' (2009) 2.
35 My thanks to Kennedy Gastorn for explaining this to me.
36 *Miscellaneous Land Application No. 17 of 2008*, Judith Atilio Ngajiro, Juma Mwalisu, and Hosana Andrea Mhalia v. Matebele [sic] Mwadunguru and Tera Kurubai Ruling: The High Court of Tanzania (Land Division) at Mbeya (4th, 10th February 2014) 7–9.
37 J Eckert, B Donahoe, C Strümpell, and ZÖ Biner (eds), *Law Against the State: Ethnographic Forays into Law's Transformations* (Cambridge Cambridge University Press 2012) 1.
38 Interview with author (10 May 2011), Orkesumet, Simanjiro. Kiteto District has since opened its own district tribunal.
39 See N Ndaskoi, *Pastoralism on the Horns of a Dilemma: A Report of Consultancy Commissioned by the PINGOs-Forum* (Arusha Pastoralist Indigenous Non Governmental Forum 2009) for a distressing account of the unlawful evictions, human rights violations, and extrajudicial killings and attacks suffered by pastoralist communities in Tanzania since 2006.
40 Askew, Maganga, and Odgaard (n 1).
41 United Republic of Tanzania, 'Land Court' available at <www.judiciary.go.tz/index.php?option=com_content&view=article&id=48:land-court&catid=14:the-judiciary&Itemid=71> accessed 12 May 2019.

12 Land grabbing in Ethiopia

Questioning FDI and big government projects

Daniel Behailu Gebreamanuel

Introduction

The term 'land-grab' generally refers to large-scale, cross-border land deals or transactions that are carried out by transnational corporations, or initiated by foreign governments.[1] But it increasingly also covers large land grabs that represent government expropriations for huge government-led projects, city expansion, and infrastructure development as well as large land grabs by powerful local investors. Embedded in the definition of 'land grab' are key criteria, which include land deals, large size of the land (large-scale land acquisition), international contracts, government expropriations, and involvement of corporations and governments. Accordingly, land acquisitions or deals are often concluded via lease or sale or outright expropriation. In the case of Ethiopia, land acquisition takes the form of lease concessions, often ranging between 30–50 years[2] for investors and simple expropriation by government enterprises for huge projects, but other countries have often also resorted to purchase of large tracts of land. Hence, land grabbing is fast becoming a concern that affects not only the residents of the area where the land grab is taking place but also the world at large.

There is also the general outcry among those affected by the havoc caused by large-scale land acquisitions, expropriations or land grabbing[3] in the sub-Saharan African countries and a few countries around the world by investors and big governments. Debates on the impact of the investment have been largely polarized. At the core of the debates and objections to this large-scale land acquisition is that, in the majority of the cases, the land so acquired is being used for city expansions, infrastructure development, and the production of biofuel,[4] crops for export, cash crops like sugarcane in contrast to crops meant for local food demand. Moreover, the ensuing evictions of native communities, farmers and/or peri-urban areas settlers, robbing them of their only means of livelihood, and the possible environmental damages caused as a result of large-scale land investment are some salient objections to the ongoing land grab. On the other hand, some see the foreign direct investment (FDI) by investors and the host government as a catalyst for economic development, means of technology transfer, boost in food security, and as a source of employment. Nevertheless the question arises as to what drives these kinds of land deals? Why is land-grab the buzzword? The answer might lie in the drivers – the push and pull factors – of land grabbing.

Large scale land acquisitions: push and pull factors

Several push and pull factors underlie large-scale land acquisitions, especially for FDI. These include food security concerns, particularly in investor countries, which are a key driver of government-backed investment. Food supply problems and uncertainties are created by constraints in agricultural production due to limited availability of water and arable land by bottlenecks in storage and distribution and by the expansion of biofuel production, an important competing land and crop use.[5] In many ways, the global economy constitutes another important underlying driver of land change related to land grab, because economic conditions influence the pressure on land. The international financial crisis and the collapse of housing and stock markets worldwide in 2008, for example, created a vacuum for investment. This led to an increasing interest in new investment opportunities on the part of the financial sector, large international investors and banks.[6] The foreign direct investment on land has become the buzz of the day following the world food crisis of 2008:

> Since 2008, rising financial investments in land have contributed to more than 200 million hectares of land being taken from small farmers, fisher folk, and other rural communities, robbing them of their means of survival. Land grabbing also frequently involves violent evictions and human rights violations. Institutional investors are expected to increase by 500 % their agricultural investment portfolios by 2017.[7]

Another intimate link between the economic conditions and land demands is related to food habits. It is well documented that a general increase in wealth tends to increase the preferences for animal-based diets.[8] Other drivers also encourage land investment overseas. These include an overall increase in world population, climate change, weaker land governances and land rights in the recipient countries of investment. A sharp increase in urbanization and changing diets has also pushed up global food demand. For that reason

> [t]he current land grab is partly a result of a combination of globalisation, the liberalisation of land markets and the worldwide boom in FDI. In a globalising world, local development is increasingly played out in a matrix of links that enable connections to be made between people and places on a world scale.[9]

Another key influencing factor is the type of government. For instance, Ethiopia calls itself a developmental state that requires the government to be in the driver's seat of development efforts. Large-scale land is expropriated for developmental purposes. Primary evidence can be found in the South Omo-Kuraz Sugar Projects, which are spread over 175,000 hectares of land and cities expanding to peri-urban lands like Addis Ababa, which grew threefold in the last twenty years alone. The Government of Ethiopia is not only facilitating land grabs by investors but it is also the main actor. In Ethiopia, land is expropriated at ease with nominal compensation schemes, and it is always enforced at the expense of the local people whose livelihood depends on the land being grabbed or expropriated. Since development occurs at the expense of the people, no discourse on development can eschew the question of sources and destinations of the investment: Where is the investment (especially FDI) coming from and towards what ends is it being used?

These investments, in particular FDI, are often made in sub-Saharan African countries and a few other countries around the world, where large chunks of unused or underutilized land are thought to be available. The investment is largely driven and backed by the governments of the respective investing bodies, mainly from oil-rich Middle Eastern countries with meagre arable land (e.g. Saudi Arabia and Qatar), populous nations needing to feed large populations and provide energy (e.g. India, China, South Korea), and the rich Western nations (The Netherlands and other countries with giant multinational companies motivated by profit-making). The host countries include Ethiopia, Sudan, Tanzania, Madagascar, and Cameroon in the sub-Saharan African context, and certain countries in Latin America and Southeast Asia. Moreover, foreign loan and diaspora remittances are being used by '*developmental states*' towards huge government-driven projects that require large tracts of land.

Land grabbing, or large-scale land-related FDI, shows a clear pattern. The first pattern is that the massive concentration of the large-scale land investment is concentrated in countries with weaker land governance and corrupt institutions. The global financial network has admitted that large-scale land deals involving foreign investors are often being made in countries notorious for weak land governance and corrupt institutions.

A second major pattern is the massive concentration of foreign acquisitions in sub-Saharan Africa. Of the publicly reported deals, 948 land acquisitions totalling 134 million hectares are located in Africa, of which 34 million hectares have been cross-referenced. This compares with 43 million hectares reported for Asia (of which 29 million hectares have been cross-referenced) and 19 million hectares in Latin America (of which 6 million hectares have been cross-referenced). The remainder (5.4 million hectares reported and 1.6 million hectares cross-referenced) is located in other regions, particularly Eastern Europe and Oceania.[10] The host countries of these large-scale land deals are often third-world countries striving for investment of any nature coming their way.

The third pattern or salient feature of the investment concerns the property regime of the host countries. Often, the host counties sanction state ownership of land, or have weak or unrecognized customary land rights.[11] The rights of landholders or land users are not as sufficiently protected when acquisition of land in extractive and/or big-government states is easy. Where big government and corrupt institutions facilitate easy acquisition of land, essentially by robbing it from the locals, the ultimate beneficiaries are the investors and co-grabbers of the land (often the government) in host countries. In the case of Ethiopia, the government has a land-bank scheme for accumulating land for potential investors.

The other feature of the investment is on the particular use of the land so acquired for the investment. The use is largely directed at the production of biofuel as compared to food production.

> Cross-referenced data from the Land Matrix show biofuel production accounts for 40% of land acquired. In comparison, food crops account for 25% of cross-referenced deals, followed by 3% for livestock production, and 5% for other non-food crops. Farming broadly understood accounts for 73% of cross-referenced acquisitions. The remaining 27% of land acquired is for forestry and carbon sequestration, mineral extraction, industry, and tourism.[12]

The last salient feature of the land grab is that it is happening in countries where the government has unfettered access to land, or owns land under the policy of public ownership, or the land tenure is weaker there. Besides, these big governments also have ambitious developmental schemes. For instance, the Ethiopian government can easily expropriate large tracts of land for government development projects with nominal compensation, or no compensation at all where the land belongs to a pastoral community.

Large-scale land acquisitions in Ethiopia

Framing the debates

Large-scale land deals are the buzz of the day in Ethiopia, too. Fertile land located at the lowlands often crisscrossed by giant rivers is either earmarked for investors or expropriated for government projects. It appears that global financial institutions are also interested in extending capital to the investors and the government for these purposes. The Government has come up with a legal framework that enables it to expropriate land from the locals and deposit it into its 'land bank'. The Agricultural Investment Land Administration Agency was recently established to facilitate that, but has had to put its operation on hold owing to popular unrest targeting such investments.[13] Governments of many other countries similarly directly engage in or facilitate land grabbing.

> In our analysis of various country cases of land grabbing, we realize that national states are engaged in systematic policy and administrative initiatives aimed at capturing so-called 'marginal lands' for large-scale investments.[14]

The Government of Ethiopia[15] has claimed that it has deposited over 3.3 million hectares of land into its land bank and in majority of cases the land was sourced from inaccessible and unused lowlands of the nation where water is available for irrigation. The government argues as well that utilizing these otherwise inaccessible and hitherto unused fertile lands in the lowlands of the nation is the right approach for boosting foreign earnings and even ensuring food security[16] of the nation. According to Desalegn Ramato, the government is of the opinion that

> [t]he commercialization of land and the shift to large-scale agriculture is being presented by the Ethiopia government and international bodies such as the World Bank as an essential measure for agricultural modernization and the improvement of productive efficiency which is said to lead to increased food production and economic growth.[17]

On the other hand, there are those who argue against the practice of land-grabbing and the ensuing investment claims and in favour of the use of land by (semi-)pastoralist communities who wander from place to place and use expansive land, which the state often claims as 'unused' land. Thus, even if large tracts of land seem unoccupied at a particular point in time, this may not necessarily be the case at a different point in time, especially during a season when land is suitable for use.[18] Moreover, land banking also has the effect of evicting settled communities to pave the way for such investments, thereby endangering their livelihood. 'A greater proportion of foreign investors produce export crops, and the floriculture and biofuel sectors in particular are foreign dominated'.[19]

The large-scale land deal has also been criticized for often negotiating lease contracts in violation of human rights laws, unleashing great conflict potential, and for the magnitude of environmental destruction that ensues from such investments. According to the Human Rights Watch report on Gambella, one of the regional states of Ethiopia where such investments primarily take place makes the following claim:

> The Ethiopia government has not recognized traditional systems of land tenure in *Gambella*, continuing to call the land 'unused' or 'underutilized'. This is despite there being a strong basis in the constitution for the recognition of customary rights. Article 40 (5) of the constitution states: 'Ethiopian pastoralists have the right to free land for grazing and cultivation as well as the right not to be displaced from their own lands. The implementation shall be specified by law'.[20]

The Human Rights Watch report and Article 40 (5) of the Federal Democratic Republic of Ethiopia (FDRE) Constitution that calls for the recognition of the rights of the pastoralists have made the position of the Ethiopian government less tenable and declared it to be in violation of the supreme law of the land. Moreover, the fact that the federal government handles and oversees the lease contracts on large-scale land deals has also raised issues of constitutional rule. The FDRE Constitution gives the land administration right to the regional governments.[21] The regional government is better equipped to understand the plight of the pastoralists than the federal Ministry of Agriculture (MoA), which is far removed from the land and the affected population. MoA has been authorized by the 29/2001 proclamation of the Council of the People's Representative to administer any large-scale land deal for land holdings exceeding five-thousand hectares. Thus, as stipulated in the FDRE Constitution, no regional state is allowed to conduct land deals with any investor, whether local or foreign, if the land size meant for investment is more than the indicated expanse. The reasons stated by the federal government for granting itself such powers range from the inefficiency, incompetence, and rampant corruption in the regional states to the fact that investors prefer to deal with a single authority that is responsible for the investment for the entirety of the country. Especially in this regard, the foreign investors complained that different regions had different investment standards and their calls to create uniform rules for the entire country had not been taken seriously.

In effect, the arguments for and against the large-scale land investments are formulated by different stakeholders. Government, investors, and occasionally, international organization justify it as being key to economic development. Those who argue against such investments paint a stark picture of the consequences of the current extent of investment in Ethiopia, and cite as their reasons the need for environmental protection, customary land rights protection, and greater compliance with human rights laws.

However, both positions focus only on one aspect: Development is meaningless if it is not sustainable, but at the same time not investing in development is far worse than poverty, since poverty is a far more powerful weapon that destroys nature than large-scale land investments, and such destruction is perpetuated owing to a series of human rights infringements. As far as possible, the debate must centre on alleviating poverty and promoting sustainable development; a compromise must be found when formulating the idea of sustainable development and by putting more emphasis on alleviating poverty.

Land governance: confirming big power of the government

In Ethiopia, the legal regime and the overarching policy governing land and natural resources are defined and delineated in the Constitution of the FDRE. In the process of drafting the current constitution, the Constitutional Inquiry Commission[22] called for an extensive debate on the land issues. The debate focused on two positions, one advocating private ownership of land and the other state ownership.[23] The transitional government by then only claimed that the land issues had to be resolved by the forthcoming constitution. Ending the deadlock in August 1995, the Constitution became effective after Article 40 was incorporated. According to Article 40 (3) of the FDRE Constitution:

> The right to ownership of rural land and urban land, as well as all natural resources, is exclusively vested in the state and the people of Ethiopia. Land is a common property of the Nation, Nationalities and Peoples of Ethiopia and shall not be subject to sale or to other means of transfer.

The FDRE Constitution delineates the functions of the federal government and the states as they relate to land-governance issues.[24] Accordingly, the federal government enacts framework laws while the regional governments administer land as per the framework laws enacted at the federal level. The regional governments can enact their own laws within the scope granted to them in the Federal Framework Land Law.

The first framework legislation enacted to implement the constitution was the Federal Rural Land Administration Proclamation No. 89/1997; however, the proclamation was repealed and replaced by the Rural Land Administration and Land Use Proclamation No. 456/2005 (hereinafter referred to as Proclamation No. 456/2005). Hence, the first framework legislation was repealed shortly thereafter and had little impact. On the other hand, the first comprehensive framework legislation to be enacted by the federal government is Proclamation No. 456/2005. It confirms in its preamble the overarching constitutional principle that land belongs to the state and the people of Ethiopia. Besides, land is not to be sold, mortgaged, or transferred in any other form other than as stipulated by law or within the limitation of the law. There must be free access to land for subsistence farming. It should be noted that the preamble refers to the notion of sustainable development. The second paragraph of the preamble reads as follows:

> [W]hereas, it has become necessary to sustainably conserve and develop natural resources and pass over to the coming generation through the development and implementation of sustainable rural land use and planning based on the different agro-ecological zones of the country.

Thus, the notion of sustainable development, as stipulated in in the Federal Framework Land Law, calls for an investigation into the current trend of land grab and its major impact on the land use patterns, on the local people, on food security both at the national and local level, and on the environment. The law must take into consideration how land grabs impact in the long term. It is also important to investigate the notion of sustainable development in terms of large-scale land investment *vis-à-vis* water usage, sustainable livelihood, and protection of biodiversity.

Access to land: paving the way for unscrupulous land acquisitions

As there are many types of land in rural Ethiopia, landholders identify the category of the land they hold; land-holding categories that help to generate a comprehensive picture of the types of land available in the rural areas are fundamental to resolving the question of access to rural land. The access referred to in here concerns both the Ethiopian farming community and the investors (local and foreign). The different land types are discussed next.

Private holding

A private holding is defined as the holding of a peasant or farmer, a semi-pastoralist or a pastoralist or any other body entitled to use rural land under law, the minimum size of which is specified and to which usufruct rights are extended, including the renting and inheriting rights under law.[25] Private holding must not be confused with free holding or private property, for in the Ethiopian legal system, private holding is simply a holding right with the right of the land use indefinitely extended to the holder. According to the land policy, which affords land for free,[26] the national average size of private holdings is less than one hectare. This has led to land fragmentation, soil erosion, and forest denudation as the number of peasants surge and climate change compounds the problem. Hence, private holdings could be subject to land grab and that is exactly what happened, for instance, with farmlands around major cities, but particularly those close to Addis Ababa, which were expropriated and given over mainly to European flower companies.

Communal holdings

The second type of holding defined under Proclamation No. 456/2005 is a communal land. It is a rural land granted by the government to local residents for common grazing, forestry, and other social services.[27] Thus, the land is under the custody of the community bestowed by the government for common use. The community can use the communal holdings for animal grazing, growing perennials, and perhaps even for the purpose of organizing social functions on it. A communal land by definition allows access of use to every residing member of the community, although in practice this is a recognized member of the community. However, such land is less secure than the private holding, as the government can decide to distribute it to private users at any time.[28] Moreover, such land is also subject to large-scale land acquisition; in fact, the government prefers giving up such land for investment, as it is 'less hassle' compared to private holdings, where the issue of compensation is fraught.

State holding

Another category of rural land is defined by the law as:

> Land demarcated and those lands to be demarcated in the future as federal or regional holding; and include forest lands, wildlife protected area, state farms, mining lands, lakes, rivers and other lands.[29]

The definition is not only too broad but it also raises some issues: if a certain piece of land is neither a private holding nor communal, it automatically falls under the domain of the state holding because of the legal phrase 'and other land', and hence is by definition included within the domain of state land. Moreover, one could ask about the rights of the locals. To be specific, can the locals exercise fishing rights as they can exercise grazing rights on communal land? One possible explanation can be offered along state-controlled use, in that these lands are simply controlled by the state and use rights are continuously regulated without making it private holding or communal holding or, in some cases, the resources on these lands are exploited by the state itself. The facts suggest that especially as far as lakes and forestlands are concerned there is open access, and open access means that the use entails no environmental or resources oversight.

On the other hand, state holdings include practically all land that is not currently registered as communal holding or customary land, especially pastoral lands. It is this land segment that is now primarily the investment target of the government, albeit largely at the expense of the pastoral community that roams around vast expanses of land for their livelihood. The FDRE Constitution, however, affirms the right of the pastoralists to not be evicted from their land.[30] For the right to be respected, the land must have been registered, mapped, and certified in the name of a given pastoral community. It seems there is no consistent legal framework to do so, since the law focuses on the highland agrarian society and leaves out the pastoral community as far as land registration and certification are concerned. This has put the pastoral land under the definitional operation of government land, thereby making it easy target for large-scale land investment.

Lease holding

Both urban and rural land can be accessed via lease. As per the lease proclamation,[31] urban land is accessed via leasing, whereas rural land is only for investors.[32] Rural land can be leased out to investors, be that domestic investors or foreign investors, and, additionally, investors can also be afforded the right to mortgage the land,[33] a right not available to other rural land users. Thus, leasing is the approved mode of large-scale land acquisition in Ethiopia. Lease right is mortgaged and transferred both in urban setting and (only to investors) in rural land setting. Expropriated private holdings, or community or government lands, are transferred to investors via leasing. Often, the lease rights extend to more than 50 years, within a period when full transfer and mortgaging rights are also granted.

Land selection criteria for 'investment'

At the federal level, land for investment is selected based on soil suitability, water availability, and the lack of human settlement. The land selection process begins with regional governments that carry out the socio-economic assessments on candidate lands. Based on these assessments, the federal and regional governments evaluate the appropriateness of the land for large-scale investment. The appropriateness of the land is gauged based on the availability of human settlement, depending on the extent of human settlement; where human settlement is scattered, land becomes eligible for investment. Moreover, the soil suitability and water availability are crucial factors for deciding if the land can be made eligible for the federal land bank awaiting investment. Thus, the land meant for investment is often located in lowlands with sparse population settlement, where water is available and the soil is suitable. According to a UN report:

> The land which has been most in demand is that which is close to water resources and can therefore be irrigated at a relatively low cost in terms of

> infrastructure, and land which is closest to markets and from which produce can be easily exported.[34]

The processes for investing in land in Ethiopia are constantly evolving. Investments involve different government actors. The FDRE Constitution provides regional governments with the mandate for rural land administration. Consequently, these regional governments have negotiated the bulk of land investments, and continue to do so even today. However, in January 2009, the process was changed with Proclamation No. 29/2001, now corroborated by the Council of Ministers Regulation No. 283/2013, which established an agency. The Agricultural Investment Support Directorate (AISD) was upgraded to Agricultural Investment Land Administration Agency in 2013 and is part of the Federal Ministry of Agriculture and Rural Development (MoARD), which is responsible for identifying potential land for agriculture, for receiving land from all regions and for transferring it to investors. It also monitors the activities of the investors and provides them with both technical and administrative support. Hence the mission of the AISD is as follows: to identify and delineate potential agricultural investment areas, to transfer agricultural investment lands to investors by evaluating their capacity based on the relevant agricultural investors, to create a conducive and attractive environment for investors to invest in agricultural sector, and to provide them with the necessary technical and administrative support.

The Oakland Institute has affirmed the following:

> While AISD is now responsible for all foreign agricultural land investments over 5,000 ha, all investments under 5,000 ha are still the mandate of the regional governments. Whether at the federal level or the regional level, there are three components to the land investment process: (1) the investment certificate; (2) the land use agreement; and (3) land acquisition.[35]

While defending the need to establish the AISD, then Prime Minister Meles Zenawi said:

> We saw large-scale interest, we as a federal government felt that we had to take another step to make sure there are no mishaps. We have to make sure that [investors] interact with one entity, that there is a process that is transparent . . . and which is with eyes wide open.[36]

At first, it was the regional government that handled the land deal all together; however, many mishaps, and corruptions were reported. After repeated complaints from the investors and the local community, the federal government felt compelled to take the matter into its own hands, and a law was proclaimed that confers upon it the authority to do so. Accordingly, there is a federal organ (AISD) for administering the land contract and acquisition process in close collaboration with the regional government where the land in question is located.

However, since 2015, there has been massive popular unrest in Ethiopia that largely targeted investments on expropriated land that had led to the eviction of the locals and which forced Prime Minster Hailemariam Desalegn to resign in March 2018. Having understood the impact, the Government of Ethiopia indefinitely suspended the policy of giving out large-scale land for investments as a result of popular unrest (2015–2018), which culminated in major political reform. Besides, the government is taking measures to return land that is fenced but not developed back to the locals.

Nature and negotiations of the lease contract

'The investors that have so far come forward are a mix of states and private agro-industrial complexes'.[37] The investors take land via lease concessions. At the beginning, the lease agreement was drawn between the investors and the regional states, but, later on, the federal government took over to introduce modifications to contracts that had already been concluded as well as to realize some degree of uniformity. However, land is often leased out at throwaway prices. The terms and conditions of a contract are usually designed to be quite favourable to the investors. The control mechanisms are weak and the conditions of the contract do not, or hardly, address the human rights and environmental concerns, nor do they address the interests of the country at large. A lease contract must have been negotiated on strong terms to ensure the expected benefits such as investment in the development of infrastructures, technology transfer, and boosting productivity. Moreover, negotiations must involve the affected groups, and community level participation should be the guiding principle. However, what is happening on the ground is something completely different.

Global Witness, together with the Oakland Institute and the International Land Coalition, asserted in a joint publication that it is essential that land leases or purchases are fully transparent and that the revenues are used for the benefit of the local population. It would appear that, in some cases, land is leased at very low prices, or sold below the market price, or even given away against vague promises of employment creation or transfer of technology. While states have a right to engage in economic affairs, it is a corollary under the *Declaration on the Right to Development* that they should formulate appropriate national development policies that aim to constantly improve the well-being of the entire population and of all individuals by promoting their active, voluntary and important participation in land development and in the fair distribution of the benefits resulting therefrom.[38]

Decision-making on land-related allocations and investments is frequently done in secrecy, without the knowledge, or without securing the consent, of the affected communities. They are consequently unable to hold governments or business enterprises to account for the negative impacts they suffer. Such a lack of mechanisms or the political will to ensure transparent, accountable, and equitable decision-making and allocation of concessions undermines governance and the democratic process.[39]

The practice of negotiating the terms and conditions of the contract has been a point of acute criticism in Ethiopia, especially by the way it was handled by the regional states. This has forced the federal government to take up the matter and engage in the negotiation process. However, the federal government has also entered into skewed contracts that often give priority to the interests of the investing body and undermine the interests of the local population, environmental concerns, and, above all, effectively usurp the jurisdiction of the regional governments.

> To substantiate the matter let us examine terms and condition of a typical land lease contract signed in Ethiopia. The lease contract between an Indian company and MoA would give us a vivid picture and insight as to the nature of a typical lease contracts signed in Ethiopia: The contract was signed between MoA and *karuturi* Agro-products plc. (Cancelling prior contract signed between the company and the regional government) in 25th October 2010. As revised after the federal government negotiated a deal with all regional government to administer any lease contract where the land size is more than five thousand hectare. The lease contract is signed for fifty years at 20 birr rent (approximately one US dollar) per hectare per annum. The lease contract is signed for hundred thousand hectare of land with the condition that another two hundred thousand hectare of land will be added as the company develops the presently agreed upon land within two years of the execution of the contract.[40]

The lessee has the right to use the land for palm, cereal, and pulses production, and develop the necessary infrastructure. The company also has the right to use river water and underground water for irrigation purposes. Whereas the contractual obligation of the lessee includes the vague term and condition about caring for the land and natural resources situated in and around the leased land, the obligation relates to conserving plantations that have not been cleared for the development of the land, thereby licensing the company to clear forests and preserve nature on leased land. The obligations also include submitting an Environmental Impact Assessment (EIA) report within three months of the implementation of the contract. The contract is to be implemented within a month of its signing. Thus, the lessee is expected to take the land within one month of signing of the contract, and correspondingly the government is under obligation to clear the land of any encumbrances, including forcing people to relocate, if need be, within a month. The lessee is expected to develop the land for the indicated purpose within two years and transfer rights can be exercised only after developing 75% of the leased land. Of course, unauthorized use of the land is not possible, yet the realities on the ground have been different.[41]

The lessor, on the other hand, has the right to monitor the discharging of the obligations as per the contract (by the lessee) in a manner that does not hamper the activity of the lessee. Thus, care is taken to not disrupt the operations of the company while monitoring and to evaluate the progress and activities of the company, although it is not clear as to what exactly constitutes 'disruption of operations'. Moreover, the lessor is under obligation to give special investment incentives, for instance, to allow duty-free import of machineries.

On the other hand, the lessor also has the right to terminate the contract upon giving six months advance notice on the grounds of failure to develop the land. The major grounds to terminate the contract are failure to develop the land, failure to discharge yearly fees, and damage to natural resources. Yet the lease contract can be renewed under the same terms and conditions of the contract and the laws applicable to dispute settlement are Ethiopian laws. However, four years after the contract was signed, the land has not been fully developed, and even in 2017, the government had not taken it back. Nonetheless, recently the government cancelled the contract owing to complications in the company's situation. But this land grab has rendered the situation of those who have lost their land to the investors precarious.

Thus, if one examines the terms and condition of the contract being signed in Ethiopia, it would be easy to conclude that the terms and condition are very lax and meant to favour the investors at the expense of protecting human rights, the environment and, at times, even the national interests. The idea of developing the land is certainly tantalizing; however, it has to be done in a manner that ensures and protects the causes of human rights and the environment. More often than not, the investors are engaged in a practice detrimental to the interests of the locals and the environment. The rent is nominal, but the farther away the land is from the capital city and modern infrastructure, the lower the rent. Besides, the contracts make no mention of the local people, such as the issues of compensation or benefits in terms of employment, and so on. EIA report is neither taken seriously nor conducted well, and the local peoples' participation in the decision-making is negligible. Above all, control mechanisms to ensure that commitments to technology transfer, infrastructure development, and employment creation are fulfilled are not included in the terms and conditions of the contract.

On the other hand, a researcher has summarized the investment privileges enjoyed by the foreign investors in Ethiopia as follows: The investment legislation is very generous to foreign investors. The capital requirements of foreign businesses wishing to invest in the country ranges from zero (for those exporting 75% or more of their output) to US $25,000 (for those in joint-venture with domestic investors) and US $100,000 (for foreign investors). Investors have the right to fully repatriate, in foreign currency, all profits and dividends, principal and interest payments on external loans, proceeds from technology transfers and from asset sales in the event of liquidation of the investment, and proceeds from the transfer of shares or ownership to a domestic investor. Expatriate employees may remit their salaries and other payments accruing from their employment in foreign currency. Investors, foreign or domestic, are guaranteed protection from expropriation or nationalization, but, as required, not from actions taken in public interest. In the event of this happening, full compensation is payable at the prevailing market value. Foreign investors may repatriate compensation paid in foreign currency.[42] However, land contracts do not protect the interests of the locals, nor do they serve the cause of sustainable development.

Land contracts must be structured so as to maximize the contribution of the investment to sustainable development. This includes devising incentive schemes to promote inclusive business models, and giving legal teeth to commitments on investment levels, job creation, infrastructure development, public revenues, environmental protection, safeguards in land takings, and other aspects.[43] Furthermore, without transparency, accountability, and open debate, decision-making over land continues to be swayed by vested interests at the expense of rural land users.[44]

Human rights concerns

Pastoralists/natives or local individuals/local communities living on or adjacent to the land offered to the investors (or expropriated for mega-government projects) are often told to move to new settlements that are put together by the government. This resettlement agenda has also created havoc among affected communities. The large tracts of land offered to investors at mega scale are often utilized for biofuel production and this impedes human food and crop production, impacting the right to food. The indigenous people also claim that the natural settlement of their habitat is the source of their cultural heritage, medicine and, at times, even source of food. Thus, all land deals must respect such human rights notions.

Ethiopia is signatory to the International Bill of Rights, and the provisions enshrined in this Bill of Rights, directly or indirectly, protect the peasants, the indigenous community, and the environment when dealing with large scale land leases. Accordingly, as a signatory to these international human rights instruments, Ethiopia must see to it that the edicts of the instruments are observed and citizens are also protected. Some of the rights threatened by the large-scale land deals include the right to food, the right to adequate standard of living, the right to shelter, the right to culture, the right of indigenous people, the right to work, and the right to a clean and safe environment.

The nature of the obligation of state parties to the International Convention on Economic, Social and Cultural Rights (ICESCR), which incorporates all the rights threatened by land grabbing has been articulated under Article 2 of the Convention. The principal obligation, for instance, is to take gradual steps towards the full realization of the right to adequate food. This imposes an obligation to move as expeditiously as possible towards that goal. Every state in Ethiopia is obliged to ensure that everyone under its jurisdiction has access to the minimum essential food, which is sufficient, nutritionally adequate, and safe.

According to the ICESCR, the obligations of the state are threefold: to respect, protect, and fulfil, for instance, the human right to food.

> The State is obliged to refrain from infringing on the ability of individuals and groups to feed themselves where such an ability exists (respect), and to

> prevent others in particular private actors such as firms from encroaching on that ability (protect). Finally, the State is called upon to actively strengthen the ability of individuals to feed themselves (fulfil).[45]

As far as land grabbing is concerned, the situation in Ethiopia reveals that the government is shying away from its obligations to respect and protect human rights directly adopted from the ICESCR and incorporated into Ethiopian Constitution. Local communities have resultantly been driven out of their land and forced to settle somewhere else, so that the land, as claimed by the government, can be put to 'more productive use'. Thus, resettlement is at the core of the investment agenda as well. People are moved from their land thereby compromising their ability to feed themselves, this is tantamount to encroaching upon their right. Moreover, their ability to work on their land and feed themselves has been compromised immensely. The government was also supposed to protect them from the investing companies that threaten and destroy their way of life and their community habitat. Forced resettlement destroys the right to culture and cultural rights as well. At the core of the matter are people who have no connection to the new habitat allotted to them and are prohibited from making a living on their natural community land. Their way of life is also greatly affected.

The human right to food would be violated if people depending on land for their livelihoods, including pastoralists, were cut off from access to land, without suitable alternatives; if local incomes were insufficient to compensate for the price effects resulting from the shift towards the production of food for exports, or if the revenues of local smallholders were to fall, following the arrival of cheaply priced food on domestic markets, produced on the more competitive large-scale plantations developed by the investors. In concluding agreements on large-scale land acquisitions or leases, states should take into account the rights of current land users in the areas where the investment is made, as well as the rights of farm workers. They should also be guided by the need to secure the rights of the local population, for instance, the right to self-determination and the right to development.[46] At the same time, it is essential for the host countries to be sensitive to the culture of the community where the investment is being made. It is always advisable to ensure that participatory decision remains the guiding principle in decisions to lease land to foreign or local investors.

In one case, an Indian investor was asked by elders of a local community to not cut trees believed to be home to ancestral spirits, because it represented protection from the scorching sun and the torrential rain. The arrogant response of Indian site manager was: 'We will bring you umbrellas from India, if need be'. This case illustrates how insensitive and offending the reactions of foreign investors are to local culture and local sentiments.

Environmental concerns

> If it is unacceptable for Ethiopians to go to India, China or Saudi Arabia and clear their land without consulting the people, it is unacceptable here. We are

> human too and we care about the future of our children like everyone else . . . my message to the foreign investors is, listen to the owners of the land.[47]

This assertion is the plight of a local who is worried about the damage caused to the environment by the foreign investors. Investors are allowed to clear forests and destroy habitats of precious wildlife. Some have even engaged in producing and selling charcoals instead of developing the land as per the lease contract. Rivers have been redirected from their natural course, thereby compromising the livelihood of the communities who depend on the water. The biodiversity of the area, hitherto unaffected, has been simply cleared off to plant *jantropha*, flower, cotton, palms, and pulses. Environmental impact assessments are rarely addressed in land contracts. Some of the investors were accused of felling trees and destroying wildlife reserve areas. Some engage in activities contrary to the terms and condition of the contract, others still use chemicals prohibited by the world community, thereby affecting ground water and the local people who depend on it for their life.

An independent researcher in an interview informed the author that toxic chemicals from huge plantations fields, open mining pits, and flower farming are left untreated. Such chemicals are sometimes discharged into open rivers or will find their way in to pollute the tributaries and major local rivers essential for the survival of the local population, all of which has already caused serious public health problems. Heavy metals like lead and copper, as well as toxic chemicals, are being discharged directly into rivers used by the locals for drinking. Evidence shows that the Ethiopian state lacks the capacity and the political will to enforce national regulation or international conventions on the protection of the environment. Research confirms that deforestation, because of extensive agricultural land clearing, mining, and flower farms, has exacerbated the problem of soil erosion.

Wildlife has also suffered and has out-migrated, or risks extinction, as large agricultural machines find their way in to clear forests with the help of enormous agricultural investments. Indigenous trees are lost, biodiversity is compromised, and, in general, the environmental peril is of untold magnitude. Large-scale land acquisitions need to be environmentally sensitive and managed in a sustainable manner. As the facts stand now, environmental impact assessment is rarely undertaken in Ethiopia and the investors have been given free rein to make maximum profit at all costs.

Conflict factor

The current large-scale land deal is full of controversies. There is no consensus on the manner of the land deal and the effects thereto. It has been argued that the ill effects by far exceed the positive effects. Without a doubt, the groups most affected by the land deal resent the entire process, and some of the landholders and the pastoralists affected by the large-scale deals report bitter experiences.

Settlements made in the aftermath of such land grabbing deals have reportedly been disastrous.

At the core of the problem, Merera Gudina (PhD), a scholar and a leading opposition party leader in Ethiopia, revealed his unease in an interview:

> Neither the pastoralist nor the landholders are willing to vacate the land under investment. Moreover, they are not made part and parcel of the deal, there is no public participation in the whole processes. The people are simply bullied into believing the propaganda of the government and often empty promises of alternative livelihood.

According to him, even if there is alternative livelihood or if compensations are paid, the peasants are not happy about it; for them, land cannot be reduced to its economic value. The people have spiritual link to the land as well.

Many promises made to the communities that have been relocated have been in vain. They include the government's promises concerning new places of settlement, new schools for their children, health facilities, electricity, and other infrastructures, alternative land and employment opportunities, as well as temporary food rationing. However, at the new settlement, the promises often turn out to be empty or the facilities are utterly inadequate. Furthermore, in cases where individuals receive compensation, which could serve as temporary justification for the government, the money is not well managed. People are not trained to use the money and invest it into long-term ventures. Thus, the one-time compensation is lavishly spent and gives rise to resentment, which potentially results in violence and conflict.

Opposition party leaders and scholars in the field have raised complaints concerning the stated promises of large-scale land deals. The benefits include technology transfer, development, new sources of employment and boosts to export earnings, all of which do not measure up to the promised standards. This issue is a source of conflict and divides the nation.

In an in-depth interview with the aforementioned scholar, who is an outspoken opponent, it was revealed that:

> The large-scale land deal is a form of new colonisation, a new scramble for Africa. In Ethiopia the motto 'land to the tiller' has been replaced by the government motto of 'land to the investors'; large fertile tracts of land are given at throwaway prices, tax holidays has been granted to the investors, machines are imported duty free, forests are cleared at mega scale, wildlife's are destroyed, and above all humans are made to suffer.

Judging by the history of the nation, all conflicts of major scale have their roots in land-related resentments. This scramble could be a time-ticking bomb waiting to go off anytime. 'Conflict entrepreneurs use land disputes to manipulate the emotional, cultural, and symbolic dimensions of land for personal political or material gain, fomenting civil strife as in the cases of Rwanda and Burundi'.[48]

Corruption in Ethiopia is rampant and widespread, especially with regard to land and land-related deals, be that land in the urban areas or large-scale land investments. This phenomenon has also exacerbated resentment and conflict between the people and the government personnel. The scholar interviewed added that:

> You cannot silence the people all the time, soldiers are protecting the investors for now but it is difficult to suppress all the people all the time. One moment could be the explosion. It could also be source of future conflict between the federal government and regions; the federal government is the major player side-lining the regions against their constitutional right to administer land.

Therefore, resettlement of communities, as communities are displaced from their land for large-scale land investment, is wreaking havoc and spreading resentment. Instances of resistance at the community level, especially at the Gambella Regional State, are well documented. International non-governmental organizations, such as Human Rights Watch and media reports, suggest that the picture painted by the government is not accurate and that has given rise to many human rights violations and environmental disasters. Where compensations are paid, it is arbitrary and meagre. Once money from the compensation is used up, proud farmers and pastoralists become beggars. As they need land, replacement land is often given as compensation. In some instances, however, it does not match the quality of the previous land, and the land is often located at quite a distance. All these factors, coupled with the constitutional issues of the regional governments and massive corruptions happening in this regard, could be a definitive source of major conflict, calling for a timely intervention with proper land policy guide. The last three years (2015–18) have witnessed a series of popular unrest primarily around land grab issues. It brought about government change and the new government is seriously embarking on reform on all fronts. One of the most expected reforms would be on governance.

Conclusion and recommendation

Large-scale acquisitions are the buzz of the day, but ever more so in Ethiopia, and the issue continues to be polarizing. The problem of land grab has come at a high cost to peasants, the fishing and local communities alike; it violates human rights and destroys the environment as well. On the other hand, it is often depicted as being key to 'development', to technology transfer, and to achieving a boost in productivity of an otherwise idle land in the Ethiopian lowlands in particular. These polarized positions need to be navigated to reach a compromise.

Many million hectares of land are being given away and, in Ethiopia, the government has put almost 3.3 million hectares of land into a land bank for investment purposes, especially to garner foreign direct investment (FDI). This land is often found in the sparsely populated lowlands of the nation where pastoralists often live. In the highlands, especially surrounding the capital city and big cities, flower companies have taken over substantial tracts of land for floral productions. Investment is encouraged and supported by the government as a shortcut to the agro-industry development.

However, many problems are cropping up. They range from the way land is identified for investment, the manner of negotiation and lease contracts, to evictions, human rights violations, empty promises of compensations, and environmental destructions. It is also undeniable that the investment and the mega government projects might bring about substantial changes in food production and security, expediting development if handled and negotiated well within the framework of sustainable development and with the involvement of the local community.

Notes

1 A Zoomers, 'Globalization and the Foreignization of Space: Seven Processes Driving the Current Global Land Grab' (2011) 37 (2) *Journal of Peasant Studies* 429.

2 *Federal Democratic Republic of Ethiopia Rural Land Administration and Land Use Proclamation* No. 456 (2005), Article 8 (4): Note that the time span for the lease is indicated from contracts signed to date.

3 It has been argued by some that the phrase 'land grab' undermines the legal aspect of the agreement as the land acquisition takes place with the full consent of the government of the host country or is expropriated by itself. On the other hand, some argue that the term is appropriate given the plight of the locals who ultimately suffer from the loss of their land under the undemocratic regime or because the land deal did not involve free and informed consent. However, I use the phrase land grab and large-scale land acquisitions interchangeably.

4 According to the *2010 Poverty Report* of International Fund for Agricultural Development, 'Biofuels debates are underpinned by particular competing discourses either in favor of its promotion or calling for its suspension. Mainstream discourses underpinning biofuels are the win-win discourses and the populist discourses. At the global level, the major actor subscribing to the win-win discourses are International Fund for Agricultural Development (IFAD) which see biofuels as pro-poor as well as a means to achieve energy security for rural communities in developing countries'.

5 L Cotula, S Vermeulen, R Leonard, and J Keeley, *Land Grab or Development Opportunity? Agricultural Investment and International Land Deals in Africa* (FAO IIED and IFAD 2009) 4.

6 C Friis and A Reenberg, 'Land Grab in Africa: Emerging Land System Drivers in a Teleconnected World' (2010) 1 *GLP Report* 4.

7 Sourced from *Global Financial Network Website News* available at <www.equities.com/news> accessed 12 December 2012.

8 Friis and Reenberg (n 6) 5.

9 Zoomers (n 1) 430.

10 S Sassen, *Land Grabs Today: Feeding the Disassembling of National Territory* (Columbia University, published online 15 February 2013) 30.

11 LA Wily, 'Briefs on Reviewing the Fate of Customary Tenure in Africa' (2012) 5th Anniversary 1 *Rights and Resources*, Wily defined customary land tenure as such: 'Tenure means landholding. Customary land tenure refers to the systems that most rural African communities operate to express and order ownership,

possession, and access, and to regulate use and transfer. Unlike introduced landholding regimes, the norms of customary tenure derive from and are sustained by the community itself rather than the state or state law (statutory land tenure)'.

12 Sassen (n 10) 30.

13 Refer in General, *Council of Ministers Regulation* No. 283 (2013) and *Proclamation* No. 29 (2001).

14 SM Borras, JC Franco, and C Wang, *The Challenge of Global Governance of Land Grabbing: Changing International Agricultural Context and Competing Political Views and Strategies, Globalizations* (Routledge 2014) 1, 167.

15 See, generally, D Rahmato, *Land to Investors: Large-Scale Land Transfers in Ethiopia* (Addis Ababa Forum for Social Studies 2011) 1. He argues that 'the new five-year Growth and Transformation Plan (GTP), which is to run from 2011 to 2015, and which was launched in the last quarter of 2010, envisages agriculture to grow at the rate of 14.9% annually, and expects to double farm output by the year 2015. The plan predicts that the country will meet all the MDG targets in 2015, and by 2028, Ethiopia will become what it calls a "middle income" country. One of the strategies for rapid agricultural growth is to be private investment in large-scale farms for which the government will provide support and encouragement. The land expected to be transferred to large-scale investors in the Plan period (not including land already allotted) is expected to increase from 0.5 million hectares in 2011, to 2.8 million in 2013 and 3.3 million in 2015'.

16 The major vision of Ministry of Agriculture is to ensure the benefit of the country and the people through endeavors of developmental investors who are capable of producing competitive agricultural exportable produces in the global market.

17 Rahmato (n 15) 4.

18 In Ethiopia, seasons are defined as rainy or dry season, hence during the dry season, the pastoral community moves to wet areas in search of pasture and water.

19 T Lavers, 'Land Grab' as Development Strategy? The Political Economy of Agricultural Investment in Ethiopia' (2012) 39 (1) *The Journal of Peasant Studies* 116.

20 '"Waiting Here for Death" Forced Displacement and "Villagization" in Ethiopia's Gambella Region' (January 2012) *Human Rights Watch Report* 73.

21 *Constitution of the Federal Democratic Republic of Ethiopia* (1995), Article 52 (6).

22 The commission was established during the transitional period (1991–1994) to draft and approve the Constitution.

23 Refer for the details of the debate that took place Minutes of the Constitutional Inquiry Commission (Vol. 4).

24 See generally, *Constitution of the Federal Democratic Republic of Ethiopia* (1995), Articles 51–52.

25 The cumulative reading of *Federal Democratic Republic of Ethiopia Rural Land Administration and Land Use Proclamation* (n 2), Articles 2 (4) and 2 (11) provides, '"holding right" means the right of any peasant farmer or semi-pastoralist and pastoralists hall have to use rural land for purpose of agriculture and natural resource development, lease and bequeath to his, family or other lawful heirs, and includes the right to acquire property produced on his land thereon by his labor or capital and to sale, exchange, and bequeath same, and "minimum private holding" means rural land in the holding of peasants, Semi-Pastoralists and Pastoralists, and other bodies who are entitled by law to use rural land'.

26 *Federal Democratic Republic of Ethiopia Rural Land Administration and Land Use Proclamation No. 456* (2005) Article 5 (1).

27 Ibid., Article 2 (12).

28 See the regional land proclamations, especially *Amhara and Oromia Land Proclamation* (the *Amhara National Regional State Land Administration and Use Proclamation No. 133* (2006) and *Oromia National Regional State Rural Land Use and Administration Proclamation No. 130* (2007).

29 *Federal Democratic Republic of Ethiopia Rural Land Administration and Land Use Proclamation* (n 2) Article 2 (13).

30 *Constitution of the Federal Democratic Republic of Ethiopia* (1995), Article 40 (5).

31 See, in general, the FDRE *Re-Enactment of Urban Lands Lease Holding Proclamation* No. 272 (2002).

32 *Federal Democratic Republic of Ethiopia Rural Land Administration and Land Use Proclamation* No. 456 (2005), Article 5 (4) (a).

33 See, in general, *Federal Democratic Republic of Ethiopia Rural Land Administration and Land Use Proclamation* No. 456 (2005), *Investment Proclamation* No. 769 (2012) and *Regional Land Laws*; the cumulative reading of which gives a vivid picture that the investors' land rights is much more protected and transferable.

34 O de Schutter, *Report of the Special Rapporteur on the Right to Food, Addendum, Large-Scale Land Acquisitions and Leases: A Set of Minimum Principles and Measures to Address the Human Rights Challenge* (United Nations General Assembly 28 December 2009) 5.

35 The Oakland Institute, *Land Investment Deals in Africa Country Report: Ethiopia* (OI USA 2011) 28.

36 The Oakland Institute (n 35).

37 F Makki and C Geisler, 'Development by Dispossession: Land Grabbing as New Enclosures in Contemporary Ethiopia' Paper presented at the International Conference on Global Land Grabbing (6–8 April 2011) available at <www.iss.nl/fileadmin/ASSETS/iss/Documents/Conference_papers/LDPI/29_Fouad_Makki_and_Charles_Geisler.pdf>.

38 Schutter (n 34) 14 f.

39 Global Witness/Oakland Institute/International Land Coalition, 'Dealing with Disclosure: Improving Transparency in Decision making over Large Scale Land Acquisition, Allocation and Investment' (2012) *Report* 5.

40 At first, the company was given 300 000 hectares of land by *Gambella* regional government, yet the phenomena met with a lot of resistance, which forced the federal government to take over the matter and negotiate a new deal, which reduced the size of the land to 100,000 hectares. The rest of the land will be handed over once the contractual size is developed within two years. To date (three years from the signing of the contract), the company has not developed even 5 % of the land it has taken, nor has the government taken back the land as per the contractual rights.

41 It was the biggest scandal of 2012 that the company was engaged in felling trees for charcoal production rather than for developing the land for the stated purpose. The two years' time given for the development of the land has not been observed either.

42 D Rahmato, *Land to Investors: Large-Scale Land Transfers in Ethiopia* (Addis Ababa Forum for Social Studies 2011) 9.

43 Cotula et al. (n 5) 107.

44 S Umbadda, 'Agricultural Investment through Land Grabbing in Sudan' in J Gertel, R Rottenburg, and S Calkins (eds), *Disrupting Territories: Land, Commodification & Conflict in Sudan* (Suffolk Woodbridge 2014) 45.

45 Schutter (n 34) 3.

46 Schutter (n 34).

47 F Koprucu, 'Ethiopian Land Grab' (July 2011) *ICE Case Studies* Number 246 (comment by *An Anuak Man from the Gambella Regional State of South-western Ethiopia)* available <www1.american.edu/ted/ice/ethiopia-land-swap.htm#r4> accessed 20 December 12. Note: It is also the official policy of China to convert

its crop land to forest land while buying and leasing forest lands in Africa and converting it to crop land.

48 RT Abdulai, 'Land Registration and Poverty Reduction, in Ghana' in R Home (ed), *Local Case Studies in African Land Law* (Pretoria University Law Press 2011) 159; ME Margulis, *Special Issue: Land Grabbing and Global Governance* (Abingdon Routledge).

13 Whither courts? Forest protection in Kenya

Case of Mau Forest[1]

Hannah W Wanderi

Introduction

Kenya's forests are as important for the country's economic development and its ecosystem services as they are for the preservation of its social and cultural values. Forests play a key role in conserving biological diversity, regulating water supplies, and sequestering carbon dioxide. Forests are also a major wildlife habitat.[2] Forest depletion has led to environmental degradation, not least owing to excessive carbon dioxide in the atmosphere, changes in the water cycle, an increase in soil erosion, and a decrease in biodiversity. The removal of trees causes higher rates of erosion, increasing risks of landslides, which in turn presents a direct threat to many living close to deforested areas. As forests get destroyed, so does the habitat of millions of animals. It is estimated that 80% of the world's known biodiversity lives in the forests, and the destruction of these forests is accelerating extinctions at an alarming rate.[3]

In East Africa, adverse impact on climate change has been observed in the form of a rise in sea levels, submergence of some small islands in the Indian Ocean, for example, Maziwe and Fungu la Nyani, and intrusion of sea water into fresh water wells along the coast of Tanzania, beach erosion in Mombasa, Kenya, and rampant floods and droughts across the same region.[4] Further, the melting of glaciers has caused flooding and, resultantly, also an increase in vector-borne diseases, such as malaria, as well as more frequent and prolonged droughts. It has led to a decline in water supply and crop yields, which has exacerbated the problem of food insecurity.[5] The environment in Kenya faces significant challenges from increasing levels of poverty. Human activities such as unsustainable exploitation of natural resources, deforestation for further agricultural activities, and human settlement are the greatest contributors to environmental degradation.[6] Environmental degradation impacts the socio-economic status and livelihoods of people, increasing vulnerability to environmental challenges.[7]

Kenya continues to suffer from the problems associated with forest degradation. Table 13.1 shows the state of Kenyan forests from 2005 to 2010:[8]

It was observed that the general decline of forestland up until 2003 was directly due to the degazettement of forestland: the decline thereafter was occasioned by the destruction of trust land forests to open up those areas, especially the Mau

Table 13.1 Kenya forests from 2005 to 2010

Forest Resources Assessment-2010	*Area (1000 hectares)*			
	1990	*2000*	*2005*	*2010*
Forest	3,708	3,582	3,522	3,467
Other woodland areas	29,092	28,829	28,710	28,650
Other land	24,114	24,503	24,682	24,797
Land with tree cover	9,420	10,020	10,320	10,385
Inland water bodies	1,123	1,123	1,123	1,123
Total	58,037	58,027	58,027	58,027

ecosystem, for agriculture.[9] Such degazettement was strategic in that it allowed politicians to limit restrictions on the use of the forestland and, where possible, even remove legal protection for such forests to further private interests. This is akin to the practice of 'PADDD' (Protected Area Downgrading, Downsizing and Degazettement),[10] which refers to 'legal changes that ease restrictions on the use of a protected area, shrink a protected area's boundaries or eliminate legal protections entirely'.[11]

Inland water bodies, including lakes and water reservoirs, have remained almost constant, as no major dam was constructed during the period. Thus, there is a need to conserve the water catchment areas for present and future use.[12] Encroachment of people has been identified as a problem in Mount Kenya Forest, Mau Forest, and Aberdares Forest, and is one of the major causes of climate change and also has affected crop production in Kenya.[13]

Mau Forest continues to suffer depletion on a wider scale.[14] The allocation of forestland for settlements was the most important cause of forest loss in Mau.[15] The conversion occurred through forest excisions and, in particular, the settlements sanctioned in 2001 and further encroachments affected 136,469 hectares of forestland.[16] The impact of deforestation has never been fully assessed.[17] No environmental impact assessment was carried out prior to the forest excisions, although such requirements are stipulated in the Environmental Management Coordination Act.[18]

Nonetheless, some of the known direct effects on the water resources notably in the years after the excision in 2001 are manifold.[19] The Mara River level gets very low in the dry season, threatening the river-dependent wildlife in the Maasai Mara and the Serengeti ecosystems.[20] In the areas surrounding the Mau Complex, 40 streams were reported to have dried up within a span of ten years, and the effects are being felt even today.[21] In 2015, low discharge levels were noted in the Amala and Nyangores tributaries, which flow into the Mara River.[22] The quality had also declined due to the deforestation activities and poor land use along the riparian land.[23]

No one has successfully challenged the illegal excisions and settlements in court despite the existence of law enforcement mechanisms that provide for criminal sanctions. Sanctions are being imposed on minor perpetrators who are arrested possessing forest produce without permits. Some members of the Ogiek community have challenged their eviction from the land within the Mau Forest and the allocation of the same land to other persons. The court has at times come to the rescue of the Ogiek by declaring their rights as a minority group and directing the responsible agencies to allocate them alternative land.[24] The backlog of court cases has encouraged further invasion and forest encroachment due to delays in rendering a final determination of the cases in question. The Ogiek community also filed a case with the Africa Commission of Human and Peoples' Rights which handed over the case to the Africa Court of Human and Peoples' Rights.[25] The case concerned the 2009 evictions that resulted in allegations of violations of various rights under the African Charter of Human and Peoples Rights.[26] The rights include: the right to development,[27] rights to culture and religion,[28] and right to education.[29],[30] The court held that the government of Kenya was in violation of these rights and needed to take measures to remediate the loss suffered.[31] A task-force was set up to advise on how the remedial measures would be implemented.

The legal framework for forest protection in Kenya

Kenya has passed an array of environmental legislation on forest protection, among them: the Forest Conservation and Management Act,[32] Environmental Management and Coordination Act (EMCA),[33] Wildlife Conservation and Management Act,[34] Land Act,[35] and others.[36] Some of the policies applicable to the conservation and management of forests include: the Forest Policy,[37] Land Policy,[38] Environment Policy,[39] National Climate Change Response Strategy and Action Plans,[40] which inform the legal approach on forest management and protection.

The Forest Management and Conservation Act provides for the establishment, development, and sustainable management, including conservation and rational utilization, of forest resources for the socioeconomic development of the country. The Act establishes Kenya Forest Service as the main body vested with the mandate to enforce law on the ground.

The Environmental Management and Coordination Act (EMCA) provides for the establishment of an appropriate legal and institutional framework for the management of the environment and matters connected therewith. The National Environmental Management Authority (NEMA), established under EMCA,[41] plays a supervisory role on sectoral agencies, such as the Kenya Forest Service (KFS), which enforces the law on forest protection.

There has been a paradigm shift on environmental conservation and management due to the wider protection given by the 2010 Constitution of Kenya. The right to a clean and healthy environment is protected under Article 42 of the Constitution of Kenya, 2010. Article 42 provides that,

> every person has the right to a clean and healthy environment, which includes the right to have the environment protected for the benefit of present and

> future generations through legislative and other measures, particularly those contemplated in Article 69 and to have obligations relating to the environment fulfilled under Article 70.

Article 69 contains the guiding principles that should be adhered to with respect to the management of the environment and natural resources. The principles include sustainable exploitation, utilization, management, and conservation of the environment and natural resources, equitable sharing of the accrued benefits; achieving and maintaining a tree cover of at least 10% of the land area of Kenya; protecting and enhancing intellectual property, and indigenous knowledge pertaining to biodiversity and the genetic resources of the communities; encouraging public participation in the management, protection, and conservation of the environment; protecting genetic resources and biological diversity; establishing systems of environmental impact assessment, environmental audit and monitoring of the environment; eliminating processes and activities that are likely to endanger the environment; and utilization of environment and natural resources for the benefit of the people of Kenya.

Article 70 gives the full force of the enforcement of environmental rights. It allows one to vindicate their right to a clean and healthy environment in Court. The Court awards remedies as it deems appropriate. Such remedies include injunctions to either compel or prohibit an action in the interests of the environment. The Court may also order compensation for victims whose right to a clean and healthy environment is infringed.[42] To enable easier vindication of environmental rights, a claimant does not have to prove causation, which means that an applicant does not have to demonstrate that any person has incurred loss or suffered injury.[43] Enforcement provisions in the Constitution, which allow for any person to vindicate an environmental right, have also strengthened public interest litigation[44] Therefore anybody can challenge any activity in Court that is detrimental to forest conservation.

Genesis of the Mau Forest problem

The Mau Forest Complex has been depleted by irregular and unplanned settlements, by controlled and illegal forest extraction, and by land conversion to agricultural production. A series of forest excisions, spanning 107,707 hectares, had purportedly been carried out for the settlement of the landless; this meant that approximately 25% of the Mau Complex Area had been converted to settlements and farmlands over the past 15 years.[45]

The problems affecting Mau date back to the 1940s, when the colonial government declared the 'need' to settle the Ogiek.[46] The need to implement the settlement plans was spurred by the interests of the colonialists in commercializing forest timber, and the Ogiek community represented a hindrance to their intended activities. The Ogiek is a community of approximately 10,000 to 20,000 people scattered in various parts of East Africa.[47] They were known for hunting wild game and gathering fruits and honey.[48] Although most of their ancestral names are similar to those of the Maasai, they strongly disassociate themselves from the Maasai and Kalenjin communities.[49] A good number keep livestock, while others practice peasant farming mainly dealing with beekeeping and farming. Some are good herbalists, while others are skilled in iron-making and pottery.[50] The word 'Ogiek' literally means 'caretaker of all animals and plants'.

According to the government, the Ogiek had changed their lifestyle such that they could no longer conserve and protect their forestlands and natural resources.[51] Based on that assessment, when the government started evicting the Ogiek, the forest was left bare. In the 1970s, other communities took advantage of the situation and invaded the forest for settlement.[52]

In 1992, the Kenya Indigenous Forest Conservation (KIFCON) Project submitted a proposal to the government with plans for the settlement of the Ogiek outside the forest reserves or on the fringes of the forests, where they could be permitted to continue with traditional forest activities that were compatible with the sustainable management of the forest. In 2001, the government excised the forest for the purpose of resettling the Ogiek. Unfortunately, the larger part of the excised land was irregularly adjudicated, and the beneficiaries were those who were then affiliated with the government, leaving the problem of resettling the Ogiek unresolved.[53]

Kibwana rightfully observed that the government, only too late, began to appreciate the ills of environmental mismanagement.[54] The Mau Forest Taskforce was formed to deal with the problem of invasion of the Mau forest.

Taskforce on Mau Forest conservation

Realizing the imminent danger of irreversible environmental damage, the Prime Minister's office established a taskforce for Mau Forest conservation on 22 July 2008. The taskforce investigated the causes of forest degradation and came up with recommendations for preventing degradation and facilitating the restoration of the forest.[55] They found that the beneficiaries of the 2001 excisions, which included companies, politicians, and government officials, were non-deserving, as the land had been earmarked for settling the Ogiek and the victims of the 1990 land clashes.[56]

It was recommended that the forestland that had been irregularly allocated be repossessed, which entailed cancellation of subject title deeds and repossession of unoccupied parcels of land. According to the Ndung'u report,[57] which provided details concerning which land had been illegally grabbed, executive orders were to be issued for the 'gazettement' of the Maasai Mau Trustland Forest and the repossession of Mau forestland. The taskforce further recommended the removal of encroachers, provision of financial resources for the protection and conservation of Mau Forest Complex to ensure boundary marking, resettlement, law enforcement, and management as key areas of priority.[58]

Several rounds of evictions have been carried out since 2009 on expansive swathes of encroached forestland. Some of the evictions were carried out without a resettlement scheme.[59] As a result, some of the Mau Forest evictees have resettled back on a 148,800-hectare portion of the forest while others have not yet been resettled. The government continually issues eviction warnings to those who keep returning to the forest. This creates a cycle of evictions, as weak legal framework and enforcement mechanisms do not prevent evicted squatters from returning to forest areas.[60]

The Committee also found that encroachment of the remaining part of the Mau Forest continued despite government efforts to settle the Ogiek and the landless. There were also large-scale farms on land that formally forms a part of the Mau Forest. The areas that had been settled by the Ogiek, such as Nessuit, Mariashoni, and Tinet, exhibited more tree cover than other areas of resettlement and a number of rivers had also dried up.[61]

With regard to encroachment, the taskforce highlighted the problem in the Sururu Extension settlement scheme, in particular with respect to the Sururu Enderet forest block measuring 5,394.58 hectares, which 16 invaders from Nandi district invaded on 26 December 2003, claiming they possessed valid titles. Upon arrest, the invaders filed a suit claiming ownership of land that has never been settled to date. The delay in the resolution of the case has already given rise to 500 more invaders,[62] and those numbers will continue to rise and cause further destruction of the forest areas. It was the opinion of the taskforce that it was of paramount importance that the Courts understood the problems surrounding Mau to be able to play a key role in diffusing these problems rather than exacerbating them.

Role of the judiciary in forest protection

The judiciary plays a crucial role in enforcing the law on conservation and management of forests. Environmental principles are effectuated through its judicial pronouncements to ensure that the problem of environmental harm is solved. As the bearer of people's mandate, the judiciary is the primary and ultimate arbiter when the operations of several public bodies run into conflict, and it is also the dominant interpreter, not only of the totality of the Constitution, but also of all other applicable laws in the land.[63]

According to Wamukoya, many factors must be taken into consideration during environmental proceedings in order to arrive at a just decision regarding an environmental crime. They include assessment of not only the direct and immediate as well as the indirect and long-term environmental and socio-economic impact, but also of the degree of harm or risk to human health and of human fatality, the negative impact on biodiversity and the potential and actual risks of the environmental crimes resulting from negligence or accident.[64] Other factors to be assessed include the characteristics of the pollutant, the state of mind of the offender, the relationship with the regulatory authority and the attitude of the latter to regulation, licensing (whether there was a breach of regulations, whether the party had a license, or had fraudulent papers), economic gain for the accused (profit, evasion, cost saving), offence pattern (repeat offender, isolated incident), abatement, and reparation (restoration and compensation), and factors in mitigation.[65] Often, these factors are not considered by the prosecution or the bench in the adjudication of the cases. The magistracy courts[66] handle offences recognized under the Forest Management and Conservation Act. For injunctions and declaratory orders, the High Courts are mandated to handle such applications and issue such orders. The judiciary plays a key role in providing an interpretation of the environmental rights before issuing orders.

The interpretation of environmental rights

Courts are the interpreters and guardians of the Constitution and the values contained therein.[67] The Constitution provides the direction the Courts should take in interpreting the application of human rights embedded in the Constitution, including the right to a clean and healthy environment and the right to life, which are the most relevant in this case.

The Constitution provides that the purpose of recognizing and protecting human rights and fundamental freedoms is to preserve the dignity of individuals and communities and to promote social justice and the realization of the potential of all human beings. The Court is expected to adopt the interpretation that most favours the enforcement of a right or fundamental freedom.[68] Furthermore, the court is required to promote the values that underlie an open and democratic society based on human dignity, equality, equity, and freedom and promote the spirit, intention, and objectives of the Bill of Rights.[69]

As Justice PN Bhagwati of India has emphasized, the judiciary is assigned the most important task of safeguarding and protecting the constitutional rights of the individual.[70] The judiciary in Kenya stands between the citizen and the state as a bulwark against executive excesses and misuse or abuse of power or against transgression of the constitutional or legal limitations by the executive as well as the legislative bodies.[71] This would include misuse of the forests, which are regarded as natural resources to be used for the benefit of the citizenry.[72]

The High Court is vested with jurisdiction to hear and determine applications for redress of a denial, violation or infringement of, or threat to, a right or fundamental freedom in the Bill of Rights. The subordinate courts will also be vested with jurisdiction to hear and determine applications for redress of a denial, for violation or infringement of, or threat to, a right or fundamental freedom in the Bill of Rights upon enacting an enabling legislation.[73] Upon hearing such a matter, a court may grant appropriate relief.[74]

In Article 162 (2) (b) of the Constitution, the Environment and Land Court was established to hear environmental related matters.[75] The court's jurisdiction involves hearing matters relating to environmental planning and protection, climate issues, land use planning, title, tenure, boundaries, rates, rents, valuations, mining, minerals, and other natural resources; compulsory acquisition of land; land administration and management; public, private and community land and contracts, choses in action or other instruments granting any enforceable interests in land; and any other disputes relating to environment and land.[76]

The Court is also expected to deal with applications for redress of a denial, violation or infringement of, or threat to, rights or fundamental freedom relating to a clean and healthy environment under Articles 42, 69, and 70 of the Constitution. Further, the Court shall exercise appellate jurisdiction over the decisions of subordinate courts or local tribunals in respect of matters falling within the jurisdiction of the Court.

In making the decisions, Courts are encouraged to interpret the Constitution using the purposive approach, to ensure that the intended purpose of the provisions is achieved. Lord Wilberforce, in delivering the opinion of the Privy Council in the case of *Minister of Home affairs v Fisher*[77] concerning the interpretation the Bill of Rights in the Constitution of Bermuda, proposed the approach of a wide interpretation as opposed to restrictive interpretation. Courts in Kenya are encouraged to not resort to technicalities. The Constitution provides that justice must be administered without undue regard to procedural technicalities,[78] and hence creativity is encouraged for the purpose of developing jurisprudence for environment protection. Article 259 (1) empowers the Courts are empowered to make an original contribution to the shape of the laws in force.[79]

Kenya has evolved democratically, and its citizens are now empowered to put their government to the task of fulfilling its duties to the citizens. The country has emerged from a past replete with executive excesses and misuse or abuse of power or transgression of constitutional or legal limits by the executive as well as the legislature. The forests were destroyed with impunity. The land in the forests was allocated illegally to reward political loyalists.[80] The situation has not changed much as institutions and government officers continue stealing both public and private land.

In this era of new constitutional dispensation, there is a need for vibrant interpretation of the provisions of the Bill of Rights so as to give full effect to the right to a clean and healthy environment.

The position of the judiciary in Kenya

The judiciary has been seen to play a proactive role in environmental governance. The Courts have been incorporating environmental principles within their jurisprudence, interpreting, and remedying anomalies in contemporary environmental laws and in articulating citizens' rights to a clean and healthy environment.[81] Besides adjudicating cases, the Court plays an educative role in the articulation and development of jurisprudence in the enforcement of environmental law. The impact of the Courts with regard to how to manage and conserve such resources is immense.[82]

In *Waweru v Republic*,[83] the Court affirmed its role to protect the environment from wide-scale degradation. The Court, in quoting Klaus'[84] address to the Global judges forum in 2005, noted that the judiciary was a crucial partner in promoting environmental governance, upholding the rule of law, and in ensuring a fair balance between environmental, social, and developmental considerations through its judgments and declarations.[85] The Court further held that in case of land resources, forests, wetlands, and water ways, the government and its agencies are under a public trust to manage them in a way that maintains a proper balance between the economic benefits of development with the need for a clean environment.[86]

In their efforts to protect the Mau Forest, the Courts have increasingly sought to have the Ogiek members settled elsewhere, away from the forest they previously occupied and were evicted from, as in *Peter Kibiegon Rono & 25 Others v National Land Commission*[87] and *Joseph Letuya & 21 Others v Attorney General and Five Others.*[88]

However, there has been an increased realization on the poor state of environment destruction occasioned by the destruction of forests. The government has been repossessing land that was formerly forestland, and the Courts have been grappling with numerous land cases arising from government efforts to repossess land previously considered forestland. The conflict between the right to own property[89] and the government's right to regulate land use,[90] as enshrined in the Constitution, has occasioned forest degradation due to delays in solving the cases. Kibwana has argued that this was because none of the multiple environment instruments dealt with the problem of environment degradation[91] and noted that the judiciary was yet to become an activist judiciary. In his opinion,

> [t]he remedial action against the offenders is slow or even non-existent. The executive in part has not prioritized environmental issues which course of action could act as a spur to the judiciary.[92]

In their decisions on interim applications, the Courts have at times upheld the public good in favour of individual rights to own property. The Courts have also been keen on enhancing the role of public bodies, such as the Kenya Forest Service, as caretakers of forests in the service of public good. Kenya has been bedevilled by the problem of land grabbing of public land and the forests have fallen prey to corrupt government officials and politicians.

In *Barnabas Kiptarus and Others v Director of Forests, Head of Mau Conservancy*,[93] the applicants were denied leave to commence judicial proceedings against the respondents, to bar them from gazetting Likia Extension as forestland. The land was being repossessed by the government as it had been illegally allocated to various persons. The land had been declared part of the Mau Forest. The respondents had already started planting trees and the applicants, who had titles to the subject land, contended that their rights had been breached under Article 40 of the Constitution, since they had not been given alternative land.

The judge agreed with the submissions of the respondents that Article 66 of the Constitution of Kenya 2010 bestowed on the government the mandate to regulate land use in the interest of public health, public order or land use planning notwithstanding the provision of Article 40, which protected the individual rights to property. However, according to Article 40 (3(b)), a party cannot be deprived of any interest or right in land, unless the exercise results in acquisition for a public purpose, or in done in public interest, but which has to be carried out in accordance with the Constitution or the relevant legislation, which provides for prompt payment. The Court noted that the land belonging to the applicants had been compulsorily acquired, and, therefore, they had to access courts to seek compensation.[94] The Court upheld the submissions of respondents, whose reason for acquiring the land was for forest conservation, essentially for public good.

In *John Peter Kamau Ruhangi v the Attorney General*,[95] the plaintiff sued the defendant, namely the government, for trespassing on the suit property. The defendant had stopped the plaintiff from developing his land because it was allegedly a state forest. The suit property had been listed in the Ndung'u report as having been illegally acquired.[96] The judge noted that where the applicant had a title that resulted from alienation of public land by the Commissioner of Lands, it was incumbent upon the Court, which had the responsibility to protect public land, to examine the title and the process of its acquisition to ensure that the law had been complied with all the way. The Court noted that the examination was necessary in order to prevent 'what is now commonly known as grabbing of property'.[97] The Court declined to give an injunction and found that the balance of convenience tilted in favour of maintaining the status quo.

The Court in *Rodgers Muema Nzioka v Tiomin Kenya Ltd*[98] asserted that in evaluating the test of balance of convenience in the award of injunctions there was a need to revise the traditional test in matters involving environmental protection. It was noted that since environmental degradation affected the public, the balance of convenience test should be applied with a view to considering the convenience of the public as opposed to the convenience of the person involved in the suit. This would go a long way towards giving protection to the endangered forests. In the earlier cases, the Courts can be lauded for playing a pivotal role in protecting forests from falling casualty to individual or private interests.

Most cases involving the right of ownership to land from the Mau Forest are pending. No case has yet been conclusively decided in a manner that could serve as a precedent for dealing with the right of ownership arising from controversial allocations of forestland.[99] This is an indication that the Courts have not been bold enough to take decisive action in public interest towards forest protection.

In *Joseph Rotich Kipkones v Jackson Kimatian Kumare & Others*,[100] the land under dispute formed part of the Mau Forest. The defendants who belonged to the Ogiek community challenged the plaintiff's right of ownership. The land had been transferred to the plaintiff after the Court had stopped further allocation of the land within the larger Mau Forest pending determination of the case of *Joseph Kimaiyo Towett & 21 Others v Attorney General* which would solve most of the Mau Forest conflicts.[101] The case that is pending is a replica of most cases that were filed in court when the government started repossessing the former Mau forestland.

Kimaiyo's case is about the determination of the rights of the members of the Ogiek community as it relates to the larger Mau Forest including the parcel that forms the subject matter of the case. This case has been of interest and has been pending since 1997. Kimaiyo, one of the officials of the Ogiek Welfare Council had this to say about the nature of the case:

> Indeed, a legal system which provides extensive and simplified procedures for converting public land to private ownership, or which gives a reckless access to public national resources, with little or no regard for ecological and sustainable social development impacts, is a national enemy of the people. We must be free from ecological ignorance. A just system which does not uphold efforts to protect the environment for sustainable development is a danger to the enjoyment of human rights.[102]

Clearly, the Court has been accused of dragging its feet in the adjudication of cases involving forestland that was illegally acquired. This has contributed to continued degradation of forests and has delayed conservation efforts in the rehabilitation of Mau Forest.

In most cases, Courts issue injunctions in an attempt to stop the government from repossessing the illegally acquired land pending determination of cases. Most parties sit on the orders when cases are not prosecuted to their full completion. One case that was highlighted by one of the main newspapers involves Kenya Forest Service and the Jockey Club and concerns the alienation of a part of Ngong' forest, as the defendants had started development works in violation of the conditions given to them. The defendants are riding on *ex parte* orders given to stop the plaintiff from interfering with defendants' activities.[103] The courts ought to assist in case management so as to facilitate faster conclusion of cases. This would help in safeguarding the public land by ensuring that justice is not delayed. The Courts need to rise to the occasion and defend the Constitution and the citizenry by choosing to safeguard the natural resources and the environment.

The taskforce on Mau Forest recommended that the illegally allocated land be repossessed and efforts be initiated to restore the forest to its lost glory. The challenge is that there is no legal backing through legislation or guiding decisions of the Court on how to deal with land allocations that were previously considered a part of the Mau forestland.

We shall see how Courts in other jurisdictions have had to be active in protecting the environment and even issuing orders against the government.

A comparative study of judicial contribution in other countries

There are many legal aspects Kenyan courts can learn or adopt from other countries. The courts in Kenya need to be more proactive in the adoption of international law and principles.

International law is considered the supreme law by the international tribunals and in the domain of international relations. As a matter of principle, the state must not be able to override international law by invoking the national law.[104]

The Kenyan Constitution provides that any treaty ratified by Kenya shall form part of the law and the general rules of international law shall also form part of the Kenyan law.[105] Therefore the environmental norms arising from the international law are justiciable, especially once the international law is incorporated into the Constitution and has been ratified where applicable.

The adoption of such principles is yet to be actively seen in the Kenyan decisions of the Environment and Land Court Division. The decisions are heavily guided by what is presented in the pleadings and the input of the lawyers.

Courts have also taken judicial notice of studies done by international organizations as evidence of environmental damage. In *Pedro Flores y Otros v Corporation del Cobre*[106] a Chilean court referred to a finding of a United Nations Environmental Programme (UNEP) study to the effect that the coastline in question was one of the most seriously polluted in the Pacific Ocean.

The Courts also need to be active in developing the jurisprudence surrounding the environmental law principles. Most cases have been decided on procedural technicalities, as discussed earlier, leaving the underlying issues involving environmental protection unsolved. In other cases, development is given more credence. And yet much more is lost when environmental protection is treated as a lesser concern. All is not lost. With the creation of the Environment and Land Division environmental concerns are now being taken into consideration.

In *Antonio Oposa et al. v The Honorable Secretary Fulgencio Factoran & Another*,[107] 45 children instituted a representative suit through their guardians on behalf of future generations. The action was brought against the government for granting timber licences beyond the sustainable capacity of the forest. The Supreme Court of Philippines held that the agreements were contrary to the principle of sustainable development as recognized in the constitutional provision guaranteeing a balanced and healthy environment. Intergenerational equity in light of sustainable development is one of the principles that helped in making a decision in favour of the applicants. This principle is yet to be championed in and by the Kenyan courts with regard to forest protection.

The courts should also work on the enforceability of environmental rights. Other rights that strengthen the environmental rights include the right to information and public participation. Various international, constitutional, and statutory provisions contain these rights that are continuously being invoked for environmental protection. The requirement for an environmental impact assessment (EIA)[108] demonstrates this right to information, for they must be made available for public scrutiny. The EIAs provide information for decision-making, thus promoting environmentally sound and sustainable development.[109] The Courts, as the custodians of the law, would go a long way in ensuring that such rights to information and public participation (exercised through the conduct of an EIA) contribute to forest protection. In *Joseph Leboo & 2 Others v Director of Kenya Forest Service and another*,[110] it was apparent that an EIA had not been conducted for the harvesting of the forest trees. The applicants claimed that the community was not involved in the granting of licences for harvesting of trees. A decision was made in their favour.

National Environment Management Authority has taken KFS several times to court for failure to carry out EIAs while issuing licences for harvesting timber.[111] It has been emphasized that public participation ought not to be a mere formality; instead, opinions should be sought with the express purpose and understanding that the views of the people will be incorporated into the final decision.[112]

The Courts need to have a common approach for balancing land use regulation and property rights when making decisions. Many cases involving the Mau Forest remain in court due to claims of private individuals and companies that the land that was formerly a part of the Mau forestland was regularly allocated to them. Land use regulation often conflicts with laws regulating the property rights, which the Constitution safeguards. One right cannot be invoked in disregard of another.

In the case of *Donato Furio Giodano v Ministry of Environment and Renewable Natural Resources*,[113] a Venezuelan Supreme Court held that property rights were not of an absolute character and that the Ministry of Environment could order demolition without compensation of works that threatened to damage the environment.

There is need for the Kenyan judiciary to give decisions in favour of environmental conservation, as opposed to continued protection of individual property rights at the expense of the environment. Clearly, courts in other jurisdictions have recognized that individual rights are no longer sacrosanct and have ruled in favour of public good.

The Courts also need to be innovative in the enforcement and award of remedies. The Court awards remedies where required by law, and invokes inherent powers where the remedy is not provided by law. The rule of law in environmental law demands that the violators do not benefit when they cause pollution or engage in other misdeeds.[114] The Court may halt an unconstitutional conduct and direct that specific remedial actions are undertaken, past wrongs are redressed, and/or a complex prolonged regime of performance is provided for.[115]

The Indian judiciary has been very creative in combining reliefs, so as to ensure environmental restoration. In *Vellore Citizens Welfare Forum v Union of India*,[116] the court issued several orders to the tanneries that were causing pollution and fined each tanner, to the extent that the fines were used to form an environmental protection fund to restore the environment and compensate the victims of the pollution. They also set up common effluent treatment plants or individual pollution control devices, failing which the tanneries would be closed, and systems were put in to monitor compliance with the Supreme Court orders and a special bench, called the 'the green bench' was appointed to monitor compliance with the orders.[117]

In Kenya sanctions against violations with respect to the forest are provided for under the Forest Act. In the award of fines, the Courts are mostly seen to be guided by the Act and no other issues are taken into consideration. However, economic gains should be taken into consideration in a court decision on the sanction to give. The fines should include the supposed income to be gained from trading with forest products. This is overlooked in most cases in Kenya where the courts only impose the fine provided by law despite the economic gains acquired by the violators.

Injunctions are other important remedies to secure compliance with the law and require affirmative remediation of harmful environmental conditions. Mandamus orders have been used as a way to direct governmental agencies to comply with obligations violated. In *Prakashmani Sharma & Others v HMG & Others,*[118] the Court issued a series of mandamus orders to various government agencies to ensure protection of the environment as well as of religious and cultural sites of importance. This is a remedy that can be used by the Kenyan courts to ensure that the government fulfils its responsibility of protecting the forests.

Damages offer another category of remedy and are used by the international courts to compensate in full for the losses and expenses arising from environmental harm.[119] Valuation is important for assessing damages because most environmental components have no market value but have numerous uses that contribute to the economic value of a resource, such as a forest. This factor must be taken into account by Kenya's courts in assessing the appropriate amount of damages for violations.

The monitoring of compliance with judgments, while present in other jurisdictions, is lacking in Kenya. This is important for securing enforcement of judicial pronouncements on environmental protection. Courts in India and Pakistan have appointed oversight commissions to monitor compliance and to report back on measures or adjustments that may be required. In serious cases, an environmental source can even be put in receivership.[120] In *General Secretary, West Pakistan Salt Mines Labour Union (CBA) Hkewra v Director, Industrial and Mineral Development, Punjab, Lahore,*[121] the mining company was directed to shift its operations. A commission of four persons was appointed to oversee compliance by inspecting, recording evidence, examining witnesses, and reporting back to the Court. The Court retained the jurisdiction to halt the company operations and can punish for noncompliance. In *M/s Aziz Timber Corp & Others v State of Jammu & Kashmir,*[122] the Court issued a show cause order when the state was found to have permitted logging in violation of a Supreme Court order. In Kenya, once a decision is given, the Court becomes *functus officio.* No compliance mechanisms have been put in place by the Courts to ensure the compliance of court orders.

The courts in other countries have taken a central role in protecting the forests. In *Amirebica Quarry Works v State of Gujarat & Others,*[123] the Court upheld the state's decision to disallow the renewal of a mining lease, which occasioned using a forest area for non-forest purposes. The issue concerned finding a balance between the need to exploit natural resources lying within forest areas, the preservation of ecological balance and the curbing of environmental degradation. The Court stated that its primary duty was to the community and thus to preventing further deforestation.

Uganda, one of the neighbouring states of Kenya, has been more proactive in environmental protection. In *Siraji Waiswa v Kakira Sugar Work Ltd*,[124] the Court stopped the continued deforestation to allow agriculture by issuing a six-month injunction while the main suit was pending, or until the government provided a lasting solution to stop further destruction of the forest. In *Joseph Rotich Kipkones*,[125] the Court stalled in declaring rights over forestland that had been converted to private land. The Court had to await an outcome for *Joseph Kimaiyo Towett*,[126] as the case would have resolved issues of ownership concerning Mau Forest. There is a need for the Courts to start taking bolder decisions in favour of environmental protection.

Conclusion

Justice Ojwang's suggested approach to adjudicating cases on environmental protection is exemplary, as the Kenyan Courts cannot afford to be bystanders in such important cases. It was noted that environmental issues are rarely raised in pleadings before Court, so that the Court is constrained from pronouncing itself on such matters. According to him,

> Whenever the court has an opportunity to declare the law on environmental question the shape of that law should be conservatory of the environment and natural resources and the court should apply this principle to determine where possible such rights or duties as may appear to be more linked to economic, social, cultural or political situations. The court sometimes is denied an opportunity to apply such principles of construction. The court is not expected to depart from the lines of pleadings before it. A party therefore could forego an opportunity to engage the court on environmental principles, leaving no occasion for a decision other than a technical one based on the limitations of the civil procedure.[127]

He argues that courts should give guidance by inviting the parties to address the broader constitutional context of the claim[128] This is one avenue to which courts resort, in order to protect the environment. The Constitution lifts the veil on completely abiding by the procedural requirements in hearing matters. As a matter of practice, it is not possible to engage in issues that have not been raised in the pleadings. By doing so, the courts would enhance their role in safeguarding fundamental human rights.

In comparison, courts in other jurisdictions have come out strongly in favour of protecting the environment for public benefit. Safeguarding the forests requires strengthening all agencies involved in law enforcement that would aid in the conservation and management of forests in Kenya. By safeguarding the country's natural resources, by taking decisive actions where other agencies fail to protect such resources, the Court would be defending the rights of its citizens in its capacity as one arm of the government.

Notes

1 This is a paper extracted from the author's dissertation namely: HW Wanderi, *Enforcement of Law on Conservation and Management of Forests* (Dissertation, University of Dar es Salaam Tanzania 2013).

2 See more at L Gichuki <http://eawildlife.org/the-news/eawlsnews/334-a-ray-of-hope-for-forests-in-kenya#sthash.HdVufyCX.dpuf> accessed 20 September 2013.

3 'Resource Depletion' available at <www.wikipedia.org> accessed 1 November 2012.

4 Available at <www.eac.org> accessed 1 November 2012 quoting *Intergovernmental Panel on Climatic Change* (2007).

5 Available at <www.eac.org> accessed 1 November 2012 quoting *Intergovernmental Panel on Climatic Change* (2007).

6 *NEMA State of Environment Report* (2006–2007).

7 R Kibugi, 'Development and Balancing of Interests in Kenya' in M Faure et al. (eds), *The Balancing of Interests in Environmental Law in Africa* (Pretoria University Law Press 2011) 194.

8 'Global Assessment Report on Forest Resources' in Kenya <www.fao.org/docrep/013/a/543E/a154.pdf> accessed 31 October 2014.

9 Global Assessment Report (n 8).

10 Conservation International, 'How Well Protected Are the Protected Areas? Tracking Legal Changes to Protected Lands and Waters' available at <www.con-servation.org/pro-jects/Pages/PADDD-Protected-Area-Downgrading-Down-sizing-Degazettement.aspx> accessed 20 November 2018.

11 Conservation International (n 10).

12 <http://greentreesforruralforest.com/kenyaforestconservation.htm> accessed 2 February 2013.

13 Ibid.

14 Mau forest supports the ecosystem that is the home of the famous wildebeests of the Maasai Mara Game Reserve and Serengeti National Reserve.

15 'Frequently Asked Questions About Mau Forests Complex, A Compilation Prepared by the Interim Coordinating Secretariat Office of the Prime Minister' (Version 1–2 November 2009).

16 Ibid.

17 Ibid.

18 S 58, Act No. 8 of 1999, Laws of Kenya.

19 See (n 16).

20 Ibid.

21 Ibid.

22 Ibid.

23 Emma Meurs, 'Water Is Life: The Current Status of the Mara River' (IHE Delft 2015) <www.un-ihe.org/stories/water-life-current-status-mara-river-kenya> accessed 20 November 2018; see also S Domasa, 'Could the Mara River Disappear?' (13 March 2018) *The Niles.*

24 See Joseph Letuya & Others v. the Attorney General & others ELC Civil suit number 821 of 2012 available at <http://kenyalaw.org/caselaw/cases/view/95729> accessed 20 November 2018.

25 African Commission on Human and Peoples Rights v. Republic of Kenya, Application No. 6 of 2012 available at <http://en.african-court.org/images/Cases/Judgment/Application%20006-2012%20-%20African%20Commission%20on%20Human%20and%20Peoples%E2%80%99%20Rights%20v.%20the%20Republic%20of%20Kenya.pdf> accessed 27 February 2019.

26 The Charter was adopted in Nairobi 27 June 1981 and entered into force 21 October 1986.

27 Africa Charter on Human and Peoples' Rights, Article 22(2).
28 Ibid., Article 17 (2) and 8 respectively.
29 Ibid., Article 17 (1).
30 Ibid., Article 22.
31 Judgment was made on 26 May 2017.
32 Act Number 34 of 2016.
33 Act Number 8 of 1999; See also Environmental Management and Coordination (Amendment) Act, No. 5 of 2015.
34 Ch 376, Laws of Kenya.
35 Act Number 6 of 2012, Laws of Kenya.
36 Other Acts include Agriculture Act Ch 318 Laws of Kenya, Penal Code, Ch 63, Laws of Kenya.
37 Sessional Paper 1 of 2007.
38 Kenya Sessional Paper 3 of 2009 available at <www.lands.go.ke> accessed 1 November 2012.
39 Dated 6 July 2012 available at <www.environment.go.ke> accessed 1 November 2012.
40 It relates to 2013–2017 available at <www.kccap.info> accessed 1 November 2012.
41 Section 7, EMCA.
42 Article 70 (1–2).
43 Article 70 (3).
44 See Article 70 (2–3).
45 H Musaki, *Mau Environmental Conflict and the Human Security of the Evictees* (Masters in International Development Studies Thesis, University of Nairobi 2010).
46 J Kimaiyo, *Ogiek Land Cases and Historical Injustices 1902–2004* Vol. 1 (Nakuru Ogiek Welfare Council 2004) 8 f.
47 Kimaiyo (n 46).
48 Kimaiyo (n 46).
49 Kimaiyo (n 46).
50 Kimaiyo (n 46).
51 Kimaiyo (n 46).
52 Kimaiyo (n 46).
53 Kimaiyo (n 46).
54 K Kibwana (ed), 'Land Tenure, Spontaneous Settlement and Environment Management in Kenya' in Smokin Wanjala (ed), *Essay on Land Law: The Reform Debate in Kenya*, Faculty of Law, University of Nairobi (2000) 107.
55 Kibwana (n 54).
56 These were fights between various communities in the Rift Valley that happened before the 1992 elections.
57 Ministry of Lands, Commission of Inquiry into Illegal/Irregular Allocation of Public Land commonly known as Ndung'u Report Vol. II p 674 No. 38 K4.
58 Office of the Prime Minister, Report of the Government's Taskforce on the Conservation of Mau Forest Complex (Nairobi Kenya March 2009) 10–16.
59 Musaki (n 45) 56.
60 'Government Threatens to Evict Mau Forest Squatters: . . . Asked to Leave' (Friday 22 March 2013) *Kenyan Daily Post* <www.kenyan-post.com/2013/03/government-threatens-to-evict-mau.html> accessed 1 April 2013.
61 Prime Minister's Report (n 58) 13.
62 Prime Minister's Report (n 58) 14.
63 J Ojwang, *Ascendant Judiciary in East Africa* (Strathmore University Press 2013) 26.
64 G Wamukoya, 'Enhancing Regional Enforcement Against Environmental Crimes' in W Kipkore (ed), *Partnership for Enhancing Regional Enforcement of Laws Against Environmental Crimes: ISS Conference Report 30–31 July 2008* (Uganda Entebbe 2008) 26.

65 Wamukoya (n 64).
66 The Courts referred to as subordinate courts are constituted under Article 169 (1) of the Constitution.
67 P Kabudi, *Human Rights Jurisprudence in East Africa: A Comparative Study of Fundamental Rights and Freedoms of the Individual in Tanzania, Kenya, and Uganda: Contribution of Courts to the Development of Law* (Baden-Baden and Berlin 1995) 20, quoting MP and SN Jain, *Principles of Administrative Law* (Bombay Tripathi Private 1979) 59.
68 Article 20 (3), Constitution of Kenya.
69 Article 20 (4), Constitution of Kenya.
70 Kabudi (n 67), quoting A Chand, *Politics of Human Rights and Civil Rights* (Delhi UDH Publishers 1985) 17.
71 Kabudi (n 67), quoting PN Bhagwati, 'Pressures and Obstacles to the Independence of the Judges and Lawyers' (1989) 23 *(CIJL) Bulletin*.
72 This is in accordance to Article 69 (1) (a), Constitution of Kenya.
73 Ibid., Article 23 (2).
74 Ibid., Article 23 (3). These reliefs include: declaration of rights; an injunction; a conservatory order; a declaration of invalidity of any law that denies, violates, infringes, or threatens a right or fundamental freedom in the Bill of Rights and is not justified in an open and a democratic society; an order for compensation; and an order of judicial review.
75 The Environment and Land Court was established through the Environment and Land Court Act, Act No. 19 of 2011.
76 Environmental and Land Court Act, s 13.
77 [1979] 3 All ER 21.
78 Article 159 2 (d), Constitution of Kenya.
79 Ojwang (n 63) 28.
80 In 2001, 167,000 hectares of land was excised from Mau forest by the incumbent government as a way of rewarding the political cronies.
81 Kabudi (n 67), PK Mbote, 'Kenya' in L Kotze et al. (eds), *The Role of the Judiciary in Environmental Governance* (Kluwer Law International Netherlands 2009) 505, 687 respectively.
82 Mbote (n 81) 506.
83 High Court Nairobi, Misc Civil App No. 118 of 2004.
84 A former UN Environment Programmes Executive Director.
85 Kabudi (n 67) 688.
86 Kabudi (n 67) 692.
87 Petition 43 of 2016, [2017] eKLR.
88 ELC Civil Suit no. 821 of 2012 (S) e[2014].
89 Article 40, Constitution of Kenya.
90 Article 66, Constitution of Kenya.
91 Kibwana (n 54) 125.
92 Kibwana (n 54). 130.
93 High Court, Nakuru Misc Civil Application No. 60 of 2011.
94 Ch 296, Laws of Kenya.
95 High Court at Nairobi (E&L) Case Number 141 of 2010, e (KLR).
96 Ministry of Lands, Commission of Inquiry into Illegal/Irregular Allocation of Public Land Commonly known as Ndung'u Report Vol. II 674 No. 38 K4.
97 Ibid.
98 2006 1 KLR (E & L) 423.
99 This was after research on cases involving Mau forest. One judicial officers in Nakuru region affirmed that there was no case emanating from Mau that had been conclusively completed.
100 High Court Civil Case Number 116 of 2012 (pending).

101 Nairobi HCCA 635 of 1997 (pending).
102 Kimaiyo (n 46).
103 T Mosoba, 'Environment Stakeholders Opposed to Development on Government Land: Jockey Club in Land Sale Tussle' (*Sunday Nation* Nairobi, 7 April 2013) 10.
104 Vienna Convention on the Law of the Treaties (adopted 22 May 1969, entered into force 27 January 1980) 1155 U.N.T.S. 331 Article 27.
105 Article 2 (5, 6), Constitution of Kenya 2010.
106 *Conse de Appeleciones* (23 June) 1988 Rol 12.753.FS641 Supreme Court Chile, cited in D Shelton, *Judicial Handbook on Environmental Law* (UNEP Earth Print 2005) 14.
107 (1994) 33 ILM 173 cited in K Ebeku, 'Judicial Contributions to Sustainable Development' (2003) 15 (3) *Environment, Law & Management* 171.
108 An environmental impact assessment refers to a procedure that identifies, predicts, and evaluates the environmental effects of proposed actions and projects. It aims at preventing, mitigating, and offsetting significant adverse effects of proposed developments.
109 <www.eclatconsult.com/FAQ.html> accessed 20 February 2013.
110 [2013] e KLR, Environmental and Land Court in Eldoret, Case No. 273 of 2013.
111 Most cases are settled out of court because they are viewed as conflicts between government agencies. It is not clear whether KFS is made to follow the procedures provided under the law.
112 K Kakuru, 'Environmental Law: A Tool in the Peaceful Resolution of Conflict' in W Kipkore (ed), *Partnership for Enhancing Regional Enforcement of Laws Against Environmental Crimes* (Entebbe Uganda, ISS Conference Report 30–31 July 2008) 23.
113 *Supreme Court of Justice*, Venezuela (25 November 1999); Shelton (n 106) 41.
114 Shelton (n 106) 53.
115 Shelton (n 106).
116 AIR 1996 SCC 2715, UNEP Compendium Summaries Judgments Environment Related Cases 147.
117 Shelton (n 106) 53.
118 Shelton (n 106), Writ no. 3017 (1995) SC Nepal 54.
119 Ibid., 55.
120 Ibid., 62.
121 1994 SCMR 2061, ibid., 62.
122 Ibid.
123 Ibid., 106. AIR 1987 SC 1073.
124 Ibid., 106. High Court of Uganda Jinja No. 69 of 2001.
125 See (n 101).
126 See (n 102).
127 Ojwang (n 63) 92.
128 Ojwang (n 63).

Epilogue

Beyond a linear model of law in space and time

Anne Griffiths

The diverse contributions to *Normative Spaces and Legal Dynamics in Africa* demonstrate the power of law in all its instantiations as 'a key category of contemporary world-making'.[1] For its significance is evident from its wide-ranging remit in managing plural legal systems, in dealing with human rights abuses, in promoting sustainable economic development and in regulating security of tenure. It is critical to the distribution of, access to, and control over resources such as land, particularly in the light of population density as well as handling the growing market in land and its commoditization, including informal land transactions and their effects. Law's power is widely acknowledged, but what is novel about the treatment of it in this volume is its analytical location within the framing of normative spaces. This is important, especially in the context of post-colonial states in Africa, because it departs from a singular vision of law that claimed universality in its application although this was based on a particular model derived from nation-states in Europe in the 19th and 20th centuries. By locating the many dimensions of law in space, the authors situate law within a broader social compass, exploring its relationship with other bodies, challenging Western notions of what constitutes a legal domain, while still acknowledging the power of this model in framing legal discourse around the 'rule of law' that is applied in many parts of the world today.

In doing so, the authors extend the notion of what constitutes a legal domain beyond rule-based formulations to incorporate views of 'law as process'. These derive from a heterogeneous range of actors, including international and non-governmental organizations, corporations, foreign states, government officials, traditional authorities, legal experts, individuals and groups, all of whose perspectives have an impact on how law is constructed, perceived, and transformed across a number of fields and at a number of levels. Such fields include approaches to transitional justice and genocide (Hoehne and Sánchez, Bens, van Lier, Bognitz), the role of courts and the judiciary (Yusuf, Maguchu, Zenker, Schneider, Heemann, Askew, Wanderi) and the dynamics of governance (Kriesel, Gebreamanuel). Many of the chapters engage with a number of these fields simultaneously along with their political underpinnings. They highlight differing normative ideas about law derived from the plurality of contexts in which they come into being and the ways in which they intersect with one another, whether in local, national, regional or transnational arenas. They demonstrate how these aspects of law with their greater degree of interconnectedness do not produce homogeneous outcomes in their application, but result in the making of highly diverse, uneven, and unequal sets of relationships.

Engaging with law beyond the state

In documenting these multi-sited actors and arenas, the authors reveal the particularities or specificities that arise through these interrelations between people, places, and events that challenge abstract models of state law and national sovereignty and transnational law associated with globalization. For in these processes of circulation what is 'local' and what is 'global' becomes open to question, since these categories acquire more flexible dimensions that cannot simply be set apart from, or juxtaposed against, one another, but come to be seen as sets of relations that connect and reconnect, or rupture, in a variety of ways in a number of different places. These transformational processes have varying effects on the way in which resources, including law, are apportioned through differing social networks. What is clear is that they are not simply the product of local conditions but are also caused in part by wider processes of political, economic and social disbursement.

These observations become evident through the adoption of a spatial approach to law. This is one that rejects the territorial and jurisdictional boundaries associated with the nation-state that provide the foundation for *a* certain form of law's legitimacy and authority that claims to be universal. It is one that goes beyond the remit of the nation-state. Its wider perspective is vital to an understanding of how law operates. This is because neither the fate of transnational law nor its impact on local legal constellations can be understood without attending to the interactions connecting actors at all levels in their multi-sited arenas of negotiation. It also requires a recognition of the power relations engaged in these interactions.

Space and global governance

This is necessary, for as Cottrell and Trubek observe, in today's world, more far-reaching forms of governance are at work that form part of 'global space'. This term refers to 'an evolving regulatory environment created by globalization and the increasing role international norms play in domestic settings'.[2] It is one that acknowledges transnational forms of law and ordering derived from diverse sources.[3] This conception of space is one that challenges the construction of discrete and bounded domains where there is a demarcation between a state's external and internal dimensions. It is one that, as Walker observes,

> involves the blurring of the general (internal-external) divide between the exercise of internal state sovereignty and external state sovereignty, with states increasingly pooling their capacity in international organizations,

> which in turn undermines the (internal-internal) sense of their uniformity and mutually exclusively divided internal sovereignty.[4]

Thus sovereignty affects not just how external relations shape the way in which states operate but also has an impact on a state's internal dynamics, moving beyond boundaries in the creation of new sets of relations and forms of law.

The multiplicities of space

In spatializing law through the concept of normative spaces, its multiple dimensions become apparent, for space not only embraces a grounded, physical and territorial space, but also represents the more intangible universe of social relations that, according to Massey,[5] represent 'different sets of linkages, both local and to the wider world'.[6] Given that law forms part of this social universe, it cannot be treated as separate from space but must be viewed as 'conjoined and co-constituted'.[7] In the processes that this entails, it is clear that space is not neutral or passive, that it cannot be divorced from the realms of ideology or politics.[8] For space embodies a number of dimensions that reflect internal and external orientations that carry with them diverging claims to legitimacy and political and economic authority. It embraces what Lefebvre[9] refers to as 'spatial practice'; that highlights lived-in space, and 'representations of space' that reflect state-centred conceptions and ordering of space, as well as 'representational spaces' that reflect the ways in which space is perceived from citizens' perspectives. All these aspects of space in their differing combinations feature in the chapters in this book.

What is clear from these chapters is the extent to which law 'serves to produce space yet in turn is shaped by the socio-spatial context'.[10] For in engaging with the complexity and uncertainty of social life 'legal agents – whether judges, legal theorists, administrative officers or ordinary people – represent and evaluate space in various ways'.[11] In documenting what this entails it is necessary to understand how the legal representation of space is viewed, 'as constituted by – and in turn – constitutive of – complex, normatively charged and often competing visions of social and political life under law'.[12] The authors aptly demonstrate the many ways in which this takes place in locations across the African continent, underpinning the extent to which legal spaces are embedded in broader social and political claims.

As this volume shows, exploring the differential and yet overlapping dimensions that are at work in governments', institutions', communities', or individual households' relationships with space and law involves questions of scale and projection. These cover a wide horizon, ranging along a continuum from more micromanaged and circumscribed parameters to a more macro and wide-ranging set of features. They involve a dialectical relationship that varies according to the nexus of relations that apply. This is one shaped by the ways in which families, communities, cities, states, regional, and global factors come together and impact upon legal negotiations in specific contexts.

The importance of analysing law from this perspective is that it acknowledges a plurality of spaces co-existing *at the same time*. It does not privilege one space over and above the others at any moment in time but allows for a plurality of spaces that exist simultaneously, that may overlap or conflict with one another in ways that create differential access for action. In these encounters in which plural legal orders may be invoked, more than one interpretation of law may apply. Thus legal pluralism provides a critical resource in constituting and legitimating power that is highly sought after in local, national and transnational arenas. It is central to creating, producing and enforcing concepts such as justice, authority, rights and formulating notions of legality. Thus it has a direct bearing 'on the way power is deployed and social life structured'.[13] Giving priority to some legal orders over others creates dilemmas and opportunities for contestation to which the chapters in this volume are a testament. The chapters highlight the ways in which actors seek to reinvent or revitalize the legal landscape by restructuring the legal spaces to which they have access. In adopting this approach, they demonstrate the complex constellation of relations that law embodies which creates fluid and shifting domains for action. This underlines the multifaceted nature of law and the legal spaces it inhabits.

Spatializing law in Africa

Such an understanding of space is highly significant for dealing with law on the African continent. This is because of the way in which colonial powers imposed their legal regimes on colonial subjects. For law, as Chanock observes, was 'the cutting edge of colonialism'[14] that promoted a particular vision of social order and property rights in its attempts to control and govern its colonial subjects. This superimposition reflected an ideological quest for power through the inscription of law on territory. This was achieved through a colonial model of law that created separate legal regimes, which distinguished between, and were applicable to, the colonizers and the colonized. This approach, embodying separate and parallel systems of law,[15] was one in which one type of law applied to the colonizers while another applied to the colonized assigned to 'tribal areas' by their colonial overlords.[16] As a result, colonialism 'created and maintained boundaries through dualistic or pluralistic legal structures, boundaries in physical space defined and managed by laws and regulations'.[17] Not only were these areas of law clearly demarcated but they also existed in a hierarchical relationship. Thus although traditional or customary law was recognized by the colonial state, especially in relation to domestic and personal relations, it was subject to the repugnancy clause that applied in many African jurisdictions. This clause provided for its recognition only in so far as customary law was not contrary to morality, humanity or natural justice. This issue was conclusively determined by courts of higher authority within the colonial system, such as the High Court. A number of the chapters illustrate the problems this has caused for post-colonial legal systems and the relationship of customary law with other forms of law. They particularly stress the difficulties this has created in assessing its relationship with human rights and the constitutional frameworks within which it is embodied. In South Africa, for example, this has given rise to the Constitutional Court upholding a notion of *living* customary law that is flexible and constantly evolving, one that works from the ground up, as opposed to recognizing codified *official* or *state* customary law upheld by state courts associated with the apartheid era, that operate from the top down.

The temporal dimensions of space: past, present, and future

These competing visions of customary law are based on constructions of social space. On the one hand, reflecting an understanding of the role of 'significant historical events, of transactions that are involved in various vindications'[18] of customary law. On the other, upholding a vision of 'a timeless past, a reservoir of "how things have always been done" in a constant flow of time'.[19] These differing interpretations, however, share the fact that they are based on a form of temporal logic. For the former lays claim to legal space through the perception of time as an evolving linear past, while the latter perceives of time in terms of an enduring traditional past. Both perceptions have been employed by social actors in their strategies for invoking legal claims. Thus space has temporal dimensions and cannot be divorced from time, for 'space without time is as improbable as time without space'.[20] This is because human behaviour 'is located in and constructed in space'[21] that is linked through time to human experience. As such, it involves a plurality of spheres that, as Fabian[22] demonstrates, give rise to a number of different interpretations of time at different moments in history.

The colonial or Western model of law is one based on a linear understanding of time. This dimension embraces a model of time that is evolutionary in nature, in that it is seen to be constantly moving forward. Its linear form is one that engages 'with its continual juxtaposition of equivalent intervals'.[23] In this process what is key is the power of selection that such a model embodies. For this model is one that upholds a 'single principle of selection'[24] that denies any legitimacy to any other form of temporality or law. This is because its hierarchical nature rejects any plurality of views that may be simultaneously in existence. Instead it endorses one particular approach to law that acts to the exclusion of all others. As a result this model lays claim to a universality, a form of timelessness that Greenhouse refers to as an 'all-time perspective'.[25] This temporal construction of law gives rise to what Fitzpatrick[26] has termed 'the mythology of modern law' that through its presentation of self lays claim to neutrality that renders it 'capable of balancing competing interests and engaging in value-free discourse'.[27] It represents a juridical or weak form of legal pluralism that characterizes a lawyer's view of law, operating within a highly regulated, hierarchical legal framework. For this reason, scholars such as Evans-Pritchard,[28] Bohannan,[29] and Roberts[30] declined to talk about 'law' when documenting how societies outside Europe regulate themselves. For this model of law involves a particular reconstruction of history that presents a picture of continuity over time that is unbroken and that proclaims itself to be unchallengeable. The chapters in this volume reveal the complex aftermath of this model of law, as it exists today in postcolonial African states, and the dilemmas that it presents in dealing with contemporary questions of governance in a postnational landscape.

Yet, aspects of this ethnocentric model of law, that was the product of a particular historical convergence, have come to have global outreach in its deployment in countries across the world. Its impact and approach to normative ordering are still readily apparent at an international or transnational level. This is especially the case when dealing with the implementation of human rights and the International Covenant on Civil and Political Rights and the International Covenant on Economic, Social and Cultural Rights, both of which have been adopted by the General Assembly of the United Nations and form part of the International Bill of Human Rights. As Walker observes, the 'UN framework possesses and exercises a depth and scope of normative authority unprecedented in any self-styled planetary legal regime'.[31] It is integral to the UN and international agencies' promotion of the Millennium Development Goals (MDGs), now Sustainable Development Goals (SDGs), officially known as Transforming Our World: The 2030 Agenda for Sustainable Development.[32] These include, among others, the eradication of poverty (SDG 1); achieving food security (SDG 2); achieving gender equality (SDG 5); and promoting sustained, inclusive, and sustainable economic growth (SDG 8).

Beyond a linear model of law in time and space

The power of the global invested in the UN and other international agencies carries enormous normative authority in promoting these goals. This is despite the fact that their frameworks for progress are predicated on a singular world vision. Their assessments of progress and the way in which policies are formulated and implemented treats space in a very particular manner; for example, in their rankings of countries as being *developed* or *undeveloped* on the basis of techniques that measure GDP and other factors such as the Human Development Index. Yet, as Massey[33] observes, where space 'represents that dimension of the world in which we live', it is one 'within which distinct trajectories coexist'.[34] This perspective, however, is negated by ranking countries in the way that these international agencies do. By classifying a country as *developing*, the country is no longer viewed as being on par with *developed* countries, and thus, even though it exists simultaneously in space, in terms of time it is 'a country which is following our path to becoming a developed country like us'. In employing this form of categorization, 'we are denying the simultaneity, the multiplicity of space . . . and turning all these differences into a single historical trajectory'.[35]

This negative aspect of governance is based on a trajectory that derives from a linear notion of time. It is built on the concept of progressively ongoing intervals underpinning a single, evolutionary narrative operating as *the* only authentic, authoritative, and legitimate perspective to the exclusion of all others. It also represents that aspect of the global and globalization that is premised on moral superiority or hegemonic discourse that relies 'on exclusion as much as inclusion'.[36] This perspective results in 'turning space into time, turning geography into history. . . [and] is a way of denying the possibility of something different' and of opening up 'politics to the possibility of alternatives'.[37] Where, however, the power of time that operates in this way is challenged, by confronting claims to a historical authenticity that is based on an assumed natural order of things and where one reconstruction of the past (or construction of the present) may be displaced, then there is the possibility of creating a disjunction, so that what Lund[38] has called 'the inevitability of history' may become 'unsettled'. This disruptive juncture is necessary because, as Santos[39] observes, 'The linear time presiding over the Western logic of development – based on a linear conception of development, according to which different pasts converge in a single future' must be contested by acknowledging 'a pluralistic conception of time based on the idea that there are alternative development paths and that therefore different pasts underlie different presents and may lead to different futures'. The contributors to this volume have taken a step in this direction by highlighting the complexities of spatial configurations of law that are at work in Africa today and it is to be hoped that other scholars will continue this trend.

Notes

1 M Goodale, *Anthropology and Law: A Critical Introduction* (New York University Press 2017) 17.
2 MP Cottrell and DM Trubek, 'Law as Problem Solving: Standards, Networks, Experimentation and Deliberation in Global Space' (2012) 21 *Transnational Law and Contemporary Problems* 359–393, 362.
3 See F von Benda-Beckmann, K von Benda-Beckmann, and A Griffiths (eds), *The Power of Law in a Transnational World: Anthropological Enquiries* (Berghahn 2009a), *Spatializing Law: An Anthropological Geography of Law in Society* (Ashgate 2009b) and A Hellum, SS Ali, and A Griffiths (eds), *From Transnational Relations to Transnational Laws: Northern European Laws at the Crossroads* (Ashgate 2011).
4 N Walker, *Intimations on Global Law* (Cambridge University Press 2014) 13.
5 D Massey, 'A Dialogue Between Doreen Massey and Nigel Warburton' (1 February 2010) *Social Science Bites* available at <www.socialsciencespace.com/2010/02/podcastdoreen-massey-on-space> accessed 11 November 2016.
6 D Massey, 'A Global Sense of Place' (1994) *Space, Place and Gender* 146–156, 156.
7 I Braverman, N Blomley, D Delaney, and AS Kadar, 'Introduction: Expanding the Spaces of Law' in I Braverman, N Blomley, D Delaney, and AS Kadar (eds), *The Expanding Spaces of Law: A Timely Legal Geography* (Stanford University Press 2014) 1–29, 2.
8 H Lefebvre, *The Production of Space* (Blackwell 1991).
9 Lefebvre (n 8) 33.
10 N Blomley, *Law, Space and the Geographies of Power* (Guilford 1994) 51.
11 Blomley (n 10) xi.
12 Blomley (n 10) xi.
13 Blomley (n 10) xiii.
14 M Chanock, *Law, Custom and Social Order: The Colonial Experience in Malawi and Zambia* (Cambridge University Press 1985) 4.

15 See MB Hooker, *Legal Pluralism: An Introduction to Colonial and Neo-Colonial Laws* (Oxford University Press 1975).
16 Although they were never really separate in practice, see A Griffiths, *In the Shadow of Marriage: Gender and Justice in an African Community* (University of Chicago Press 1997).
17 R Home, 'The Colonial Legacy in Land Rights in Southern Africa' in B Chiagra (ed), *African Development Community Land Issues: Towards a New Sustainable Land Relations Policy* (Routledge 2012) 8–26, 9.
18 C Lund, 'The Past and Space: On Arguments in African land Control' (2013) 83 (10) *Africa* 14–35, 14.
19 Lund (n 18) 14.
20 M Crang and N Thrift (eds), *Thinking Space* (Routledge 2000) 3.
21 SM Low and D Lawrence-Zúñiga (eds), *The Anthropology of Space and Place: Locating Culture* (Blackwell 2003) 1.
22 J Fabian, *Time and the Other: How Anthropology Makes Its Object* (Univeristy of Columbia Press 1983).
23 C Greenhouse, 'Just in Time: Temporality and the Cultural Legitimation of Law' (1998) 98 (8) *Yale Law Journal* 1631–1651, 1637.
24 Greenhouse (n 23) 1636.
25 Greenhouse (n 23) 1650.
26 P Fitzpatrick, *The Mythology of Modern Law* (Routledge 1992).
27 Greenhouse (n 23) 1642.
28 Sir E Evans-Prichard, *The Nuer: A Description of the Modes of Livelihood and Political Institutions of a Nilotic People* (Oxford University Press 1940) 162.
29 P Bohannan, *Justice and Judgment Among the Tiv* (Oxford University Press 1957).
30 SA Roberts, *Order and Dispute: An Introduction to Legal Anthropology* (Penguin 1979).
31 Walker (n 4) 60.
32 See <www.un.org/sustainabledevelopment'development-agenda> accessed 3 May 2017.
33 Massey (n 5).
34 Massey (n 5).
35 Massey (n 5).
36 D Fassin, 'That Obscure Object of Global Health' in MC Inhorn and EA Wentzell (eds), *Medical Anthropology at the Intersections: Histories, Activisms and Futures* (Duke University Press 2012) 95–115, 99.
37 Massey (n 5).
38 Lund (n 18) 30.
39 B de Sousa Santos, 'Beyond Neoliberal Governance: The World Social Forum as Subaltern Cosmopolitan Politics and Legality' in B de Sousa Santos and CA Rodriguez-Garavito (eds), *Law and Globalization from Below: Towards a Cosmopolitan Legality* (Cambridge University Press 2005) 29–63, 31.

Glossary of acronyms

A.C.	Appeal Cases
AC	Action Congress [Nigeria]
ACHPR	African Charter on Human and Peoples' Rights (Banjul Charter)
ACHR	American Convention on Human Rights
ACoHPR	African Commission on Human and Peoples' Rights
AISD	Agricultural Investment Support Directorate
Art.	Article
Banjul Charter	African Charter on Human and Peoples' Rights
BBC	British Broadcasting Corporation
CCP	Comparative Constitutions
CCPR	International Covenant on Civil and Political Rights
CDA	Constitution-Drafting Assembly/الهيئة التأسيسية لصياغة الدستور الليبي (*Al-Hai'at at-Ta'sīsīyat li-Ṣiyāġat ad-Dustūr al-Lībī*)
CEDAW	Convention on the Elimination of Discrimination against Women
CESCR	International Covenant on Economic, Social, and Cultural Rights
cf.	confer
CJA	Centre for Justice and Accountability [USA]
CJN	Chief Justice of Nigeria
CKGR	Central Kalahari Game Reserve [Botswana]
CLaRA	Communal Land Rights Act [South Africa]
CNB	Court Nationale Bashingantahe
CNDD-FDD	Conseil national pour la défense de la démocratie–Forces pour la défense de la démocratie
CNN	Cable News Network
Commission	African Commission on Human and Peoples' Rights
CRDB	Cooperative Rural Development Bank
CUZ	Communal Use Zone
DFID	Department for International Development
DNA	Deoxyribonucleic acid
ECHR	European Convention for the Protection of Human Rights and Fundamental Freedoms
Ed(s) / ed(s)	Editor(s) / edited

EFCC	Economic and Financial Crimes Commission
EIA	Environmental Impact Assessment
EPAF	Equipo Peruano de Antropología Forense [Peru]
et al.	*et alii/et aliae/et alia*
etc.	*et cetera*
et seqq.	*et sequens/et sequentia*
EU	European Union
f.	*folio*[and the following (page, paragraph)]
FAO	Food and Agriculture Organization
FDI	Foreign Direct Investment
FDRE	Federal Democratic Republic of Ethiopia
ff.	and the following (pages, paragraphs)
fn	footnote(s)
FPK	Report to the First People of the Kalahari [Botswana]
GA	General Assembly [United Nations]
GIS	geographic information system
GNA	Government of National Accord
GNC	General National Congress/المؤتمر الوطني العام (*al-Muʾtamar al-Waṭanī al-ʿĀmm*)
GTP	Growth and Transformation Plan
HoR	House of Representatives/مجلس النواب (*Mağlis an-Nūwāb*)
HRC	Human Rights Committee
IACtHR	Inter-American Court of Human Rights
Ibid. / ibid.	*ibidem*
ICC	International Criminal Court/*Cour pénale internationale*
ICCPR	International Convention on Civil and Political Rights
ICESCR	International Convention on Economic, Social, and Cultural Rights
ICRC	International Committee of the Red Cross/*Comité international de la Croix-Rouge*
ICSS	Interim Constitution of Southern Sudan
Id. / id.	*idem*
IDEA	Institute for Democracy and Electoral Assistance
IFAD	International Fund for Agriculture and Development
IIED	International Institute for Environment and Development
IK	indigenous knowledge
ILM	International Legal Materials
ILO	International Labour Organization
INEC	Independent National Electoral Commission [Nigeria]
IRIN	Integrated Regional Information Networks
ISS	Institute for Security Studies
KFS	Kenya Forest Service
KLR	Kenya Law Report
LPA	Libyan Political Agreement
MJSC	Monthly Judgments of the Supreme Court [Nigeria]
MDG	Millennium Development Goal
MoA	Ministry of Agriculture

MoARD	Ministry of Agriculture and Rural Development
NCOP	National Council of Provinces [South Africa]
NEMA	National Environmental and Management Act
NGO	Non-governmental organization
NILR	Nigeria Internet Law Report
NJC	National Judicial Council
No./No	Number, numéro
NTC	National Transitional Council / المجلس الوطني الانتقالي (*al-Mağlis al-Waṭanī al-Intiqālī*)
NWLR	Nigeria Weekly Law Report
OAU	Organization of African Unity
Para. / para.	Paragraph/paragraph
PCA	President of the Court of Appeal
PCIJ	Permanent Court of International Justice
PDP	People's Democratic Party [Nigeria]
PIR	Penal International Reform
PLAAS	Programme for Land and Agrarian Studies [South Africa]
Res.	Resolution
RoL	Rule of Law
RWAR	Rural Women's Action Research Project [South Africa]
S.C.	Supreme Court Reports [Nigeria]
SA	Constitution of the Republic of South Africa of 1996
SALC	South African Law Committee
SFB	Sonderforschungsbereich
SC	Supreme Court
SERAC	Social and Economic Rights Action
SNM	Somali National Movement/*Dhaq dhaqaaqa wadaniga soomaliyeed*
TIA	Tribunal of Inquiries Act
TLGFA	Traditional Leadership and Governance Framework Act of 2003
UDHR	Universal Declaration on Human Rights
UK	United Kingdom
UN	United Nations
UNC	United Nations Charter
UNDP	United Nations Development Programme
UNDRIP	United Nations Declaration on the Rights of Indigenous Peoples
UNEP	United Nations Environmental Programme
UNSMIL	United Nations Support Mission in Libya
UNTS	United Nations Treaty Series
US/USA	United States of America
v	*von*, *versus*
Vol	Volume
WCIC	War Crimes Investigation Commission/*Xafiiska Badhi-taanka Xasuuqa*
WLR	Weekly Law Reports [UK]
WRN	Weekly Reports of Nigeria

Index